Favorite Recipes ® *of America*

DESSERTS

including party beverages

FAVORITE RECIPES PRESS,
Louisville, Kentucky

Contents

© Favorite Recipes Press, 1968
Post Office Box 18324
Louisville, Kentucky
Library of Congress Catalog Card No. 68-25331

Introduction

Homemade dessert—magic words. There is nothing that America enjoys more. Ummm!! You can almost smell them baking. The line-up seems endless. Cakes, pies, meringues, ice creams, tortes, and souffles . . . These are only a few of the mouth-watering desserts that are included in this collection.

Take your choice—you'll find desserts of every description in this unusual collection of FAVORITE RECIPES OF AMERICA. You'll find recipes that are a snap to prepare, while others are more complicated and require more patience. Some are definitely not for weight watchers, while others are a blessing for the calorie conscious. You'll find recipes for desserts just like Grandmother used to make. Others have been simplified for the busy homemaker of today. The special section containing recipes for party beverages is an added attraction.

These recipes were selected from my files of more than 100,000 favorite recipes to represent the desserts that Americans like best. Many outstanding recipes are from winners of Blue Ribbon at fairs, officers' wives, and home economics teachers. With well won reputations as experts and excellent cooks, they share with you their special favorites.

The acknowledged queen of cookery in the heartland of the United States is the winner of the Blue Ribbons at the county fair. She may be young or she may have snowy white hair, but one thing is certain—she is a proven good cook. Her recipes are sought after as rare treasures.

Travel enlightens. In her travels the military wife acquires many unique recipes. Now she shares them. Such remarkable recipes make it understandable why she is noted for her good cooking and gracious entertaining.

For experience, know-how, and practicality the home economics teacher heads the list. Her recipes not only reveal imagination but they contain many short cuts for the busy homemaker.

Every recipe has been home tested by an American homemaker just like you. Each recipe was personally endorsed by the homemaker whose name appears under the recipe. You'll find that these recipes come from every section of the country and can be used for family meals or special occasions when you entertain.

Once you have tried a few of these desserts you'll know why they are FAVORITE RECIPES OF AMERICA. They will become your favorites, too.

When preparing your menu, remember the dessert . . . it's the last impression that lingers on.

Mary Anne Richards
Staff Home Economist
Favorite Recipes Press

A La Mode	Served with or garnished with a topping of ice cream.
Au Lait	A beverage made and served with milk.
Bake	To cook by dry heat in an oven.
Bavarian	Dessert pudding made with a gelatin-cream base.
Beat	To whip with a spoon, hand beater or electric mixer in order to combine food or incorporate air as in beating egg whites and whipping cream
Bisque	A rich frozen dessert of cream, macaroons and nuts.
Blend	To mix ingredients until thoroughly combined.
Bombe	A frozen dessert of two or more mixtures such as ice cream or sherbet packed into a melon-shaped mold.
Candy	To cook fruit and fruit peel in heavy syrup until transparent and plump.
Caramelize	To heat dry sugar or food containing sugar until light brown and caramel flavored.
Charlotte	A dessert made by lining a dish with strips of cake, lady fingers or bread and filling it with fruits, whipped cream, custard or other filling.
Coat-The-Spoon	To cook until a mixture adheres to the stirring spoon in a thin layer.
Cream	To work or beat shortening until light and fluffy. Sugar and/or flour and eggs may be creamed into the shortening.
Cut	To combine shortening with flour and other dry ingredients by chopping it into the mixture with two knives or spatulas.

AND PROCESSES

Dissolve	To melt or liquefy.
Dredge	To coat with flour or finely ground ingredient.
Eclair	A small custard or whipped cream-filled, finger-shaped pastry.
Fold	To combine ingredients by blending with a spoon or wire whisk, using an up-and-over motion.
Glaze	To coat with a thin sugar syrup that has been cooked to the crack stage; or to cover with a thin icing.
Ice	A sweet frozen dessert of fruit juice, water and sugar.
Knead	To manipulate with a pressing motion plus folding and stretching.
Macaroons	Small cakes made from egg whites, sugar and ground almonds or almond paste.
Mousse	This dessert is frozen without stirring. It is made from a sweetened, flavored whipped cream and may or may not contain fruit.
Scald	To heat liquid to a temperature just below the boiling point. A thin skim forming over milk indicates sufficient heating.
Sherbet	A fruit juice, sugar, egg whites, milk or water mixture which is frozen.
Sift	To shake dry ingredients through a sieve or sifter.
Simmer	To cook in liquid that is just below the boiling point.
Whip	To incorporate air into a mixture by beating rapidly by hand or with an electric mixer.

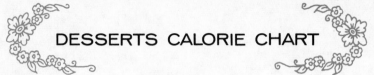
Apple betty	½ cup	175
Cakes:		
Angel cake	2-inch sector (1/12 of 8-inch round cake)	110
Butter cakes:		
Plain, without icing	1 piece, 3 by 2 by 1½ inches	180
	1 cupcake, 2¾ inches in diameter	130
Plain, with icing	2-inch sector (1/16 of 10-inch round layer cake)	320
	1 cupcake, 2¾ inches in diameter	160
Chocolate, with fudge icing	2-inch sector (1/16 of 10-inch round layer cake)	420
Fruitcake, dark	1 piece, 2 by 2 inches by ½ inch	105
Gingerbread	1 piece, 2 by 2 inches by ½ inch	180
Pound cake	1 slice, 2¾ by 3 inches by ⅝ inch	130
Sponge cake	2-inch sector (1/12 or 8-inch round cake)	115
Candy:		
Caramels	1 ounce (3 medium caramels)	120
Chocolate creams	1 ounce (2 to 3 pieces, 35 to a pound)	110
Chocolate, milk, sweetened	1 ounce bar	145
Chocolate, milk, sweetened with almonds	1 ounce bar	150
Chocolate mints	1 ounce (1 to 2 mints, 20 to a pound)	110
Fudge, milk chocolate, plain	1 ounce (1 piece, 1 to 1½ inches square)	115
Gumdrops	1 ounce (about 2½ large or 20 small)	95
Hard candy	1 ounce (3 to 4 candy balls, ¾ inch in diameter)	110
Jellybeans	1 ounce (10 beans)	65
Marshmallows	1 ounce (3 to 4 marshmallows, 60 to a lb.)	90
Peanut brittle	1 ounce (1½ pieces, 2½ by 1¼ inches by ⅜ inch)	125
Cookies, plain and assorted	1 cookie, 3 inches in diameter	110
Cornstarch pudding	½ cup	140
Custard, baked	½ cup	140
Figbars, small	1 figbar	55
Fruit ice	½ cup	75
Gelatin dessert, plain, ready-to-serve	½ cup	80
Ice cream, plain	1 container (3½ fluid ounces)	130
Ice milk	½ cup (4 fluid ounces)	140
Pies:		
Apple	4-inch sector (1/7 of 9-inch pie)	330
Cherry	4-inch sector (1/7 of 9-inch pie)	340
Custard	4-inch sector (1/7 of 9-inch pie)	265
Lemon meringue	4-inch sector (1/7 of 9-inch pie)	300
Mince	4-inch sector (1/7 of 9-inch pie)	340
Pumpkin	4-inch sector (1/7 of 9-inch pie)	265
Prune whip	½ cup	100
Rennet dessert pudding, ready-to-serve	½ cup	125
Sherbet	½ cup	120

BAKING CHART

DESSERT BREADS	TEMPERATURE	TIME IN MIN.
Muffins	375-425	15-25
Nut Bread	350	40-60
Coffeecake	350-375	25-40
Sweet Rolls (yeast)	375-400	10-25
CAKES		
Cakes with shortening		
Cupcakes	375	20
Layers	350-375	20-35
Squares, oblongs, upside		
down cakes	350	25-40
Loaf cake	300-350	45-80
Angel (tube)	375	30-40
Chiffon (tube)	325	55
then	350	10-15
Sponge (tube)	325	55-60
Fruit cake	275	2½-3½ hr.
COOKIES		
Drop	350-400	8-15
Rolled	350-375	5-12
Refrigerator	350-400	8-15
Filled	350-375	8-12
Bars	325-375	10-35

CANDY	TEMPERATURE OF SYRUP
Thread	230-234
Soft ball	234-238
Medium ball	238-244
Firm ball	244-248
Hard ball	248-254
Very hard ball	254-265
Light Crack	265-285
Hard Crack	290-300

ABBREVIATIONS USED IN THIS BOOK

Teaspoon . . . . tsp.
Tablespoon . . . . tbsp.
Cup . . . . c.
Ounce . . . . oz.
Pound . . . . lb.
Dozen . . . . doz.

Large . . . . lge.
Package . . . . pkg.
Small . . . . sm.
Pint . . . . pt.
Quart . . . . qt.
Gallon . . . . gal.

EQUIVALENTS

3 tsp. = 1 tbsp.
2 tbsp. = ⅛ c.
4 tbsp. = ¼ c.
8 tbsp. = ½ c.
16 tbsp. = 1 c.
5 tbsp. + 1 tsp. = 1/3 c.
12 tbsp. = ¾ c.
4 oz. = ½ c.
8 oz. = 1 c.
16 oz. = 1 lb.
1 oz. = 2 tbsp. fat or liquid
2 c. fat = 1 lb.

2 c. = 1 pt.
2 c. sugar = 1 lb.
⅝ c. = ½ c. + 2 tbsp.
7/8 c. = ¾ c. + 2 tbsp.
1 lb. butter = 2 c. or 4 sticks
2 pt. = 1 qt.
1 qt. = 4 c.
A few grains = Less than ⅛ tsp.
Pinch = As much as can be taken between tip of finger and thumb.
Speck = Less than ⅛ tsp.

SUBSTITUTIONS

1 tablespoon cornstarch (for thickening) = 2 tablespoons flour (approximately)

1 cup sifted all-purpose flour = 1 cup plus 2 tablespoons sifted cake flour.

1 square chocolate (ounce) = 3 or 4 tablespoons cocoa plus ½ tablespoon fat.

1 teaspoon baking powder = ¼ teaspoon baking soda plus ½ teaspoon cream of tartar.

1 cup bottled milk = ½ cup evaporated milk plus ½ c. water.

1 cup sour milk = 1 cup sweet milk into which 1 tablespoon vinegar or lemon juice has been stirred; or 1 cup buttermilk.

1 cup sweet milk = 1 cup sour milk or buttermilk plus ½ teaspoon baking soda.

1 cup cream, sour, heavy = 1/3 cup butter and 2/3 cup milk in any sour-milk recipe.

1 cup cream, sour, thin = 3 tablespoons butter and ¾ cup milk in sour-milk recipe.

1 cup molasses = 1 cup honey.

Beverages

Cafe Brulot Diable

¾ c. cognac
6 tsp. sugar
6 whole cloves
1 1-in. cinnamon stick
Rind of ½ lemon
Rind of ½ orange
1 ½ c. strong, hot coffee

Combine all ingredients except coffee in the blazer of a chafing dish. Set blazer over flame and heat, stirring constantly, until cognac is heated through. Light cognac, stirring while it burns. After a minute or two, slowly pour in coffee while stirring. When flame subsides, ladle into heated demitasses, being careful not to serve spices or rinds. Yield: 4-5 servings.

Mrs. Chas. Buck, Las Vegas, Nev.

 ## Cafe Cappuccino

½ c. evaporated milk
2 tbsp. powdered sugar
¼ tsp. vanilla
¼ tsp. cinnamon
6 c. hot expresso coffee
Grated chocolate (opt.)

Chill milk until half frozen. Add powdered sugar, vanilla and cinnamon; beat until thick and fluffy. Fill cups 1/3 full with hot coffee. Top with grated chocolate. Hot percolator coffee may be used. Yield: 6 servings.

Mrs. T. E. O'Donovan, Fort Story, Va.

Coffee Deluxe

8-12 c. extra strong hot coffee
½ pt. heavy cream, whipped
Sugar
Rum or brandy extract
Ground nutmeg or cinnamon
8 brandied cherries (opt.)
8 cinnamon sticks

(Continued on next page)

To attractive mugs of steaming hot, stronger than morning coffee add a generous serving of chilled whipped cream which has been sweetened and flavored with extract. Sprinkle with nutmeg. Garnish with a brandied, stemmed cherry. Place a cinnamon stick in as "muddler." Serve hot. Yield: 8-12 servings.

Mrs. James A. Shannon, Pres. Officers' Wives' Club, Lakehurst, N. J.

 ### Gold Coast Coffee

> *1 c. instant cocoa mix*
> *⅓ c. instant coffee*
> *4 c. boiling water*
> *Whipped cream*

In glass coffee maker mix all ingredients except whipped cream. Add a dash of whipped cream on top. Yield: 4 servings.

Mrs. James Zadra, Kalispell, Mont.

 ### Irish Coffee

> *Strong hot coffee*
> *Irish whiskey*
> *Sugar*
> *Heavy cream*

It doesn't make any difference what you serve this delight in—cup, mug or anything handy; but a long-stemmed glass goblet looks best. Before pouring the hot coffee, remember the old trick of putting a spoon in the glass to keep the heat from cracking it. Pour into each goblet enough coffee to reach about ½ inch from the top. Dissolve teaspoon sugar in each glass. Pour in shot of whiskey in each glass and top with heavy cream, poured over the back of a spoon so it floats. Don't stir coffee; drink through the cream.

Mrs. H. E. Horton, Officers' Wives' Club, Guam, Mariannas Islands

 ### Luck Of The Irish

> *1 oz. or jigger Irish whiskey*
> *1 tsp. sugar or to taste*
> *Strong hot coffee*
> *Whipped cream*

(Continued on next page)

Pour jigger Irish whiskey into each 7-ounce stemmed glass. Add sugar. Fill glass to within ½ inch of brim with black coffee; stir well. Top with whipped cream. Do not stir after adding cream. The flavor is obtained by sipping hot beverage through cool cream. NOTE: Irish coffee is after dinner coffee, dessert and liqueur all in one. Yield: 1 serving.

Mrs. Norval K. Heath, Syracuse, N. Y.

  Cranberry Eggnog

> *6 eggs, beaten*
> *1 pt. heavy cream, whipped*
> *¾ c. sugar*
> *2 pt. cranberry juice*

Combine eggs and whipped cream; fold in sugar. Combine with cranberry juice; serve. Yield: 12 servings.

Mrs. Clarence H. Kemp, Oakland, Calif.

  Eggnog Supreme

> *12 eggs, separated*
> *1 ½ c. sugar*
> *1 qt. apple brandy or whiskey*
> *2 qt. milk*
> *1 pt. light cream*
> *1 pt. heavy cream*
> *Nutmeg*

Blend egg yolks with sugar. Add brandy. Add milk and light cream. Beat egg whites to a soft peak. Whip heavy cream until fluffy. Fold egg whites and whipped cream into yolk mixture. Chill. Serve sprinkled with nutmeg. Yield: 40 servings.

Mrs. C. W. Hassler, Chicago, Ill.

  Honey Eggnog

> *4 eggs, well beaten*
> *½ c. honey*
> *1 qt. chilled milk*
> *4 tsp. vanilla extract*
> *Nutmeg*

(Continued on next page)

Beat together eggs and honey. Beat in milk and vanilla. Pour eggnog into glasses. Sprinkle each serving with nutmeg. Yield: 6 servings.

Mildred Warren, Calhan, Colo.

 ## Eggnog

> 32 eggs, separated
> 1 lb. confectioners' sugar
> 1 qt. coffee cream
> 1 qt. heavy cream, whipped
> 2 qt. whole milk
> 4 c. brandy
> 2 c. rum

Place egg yolks in large mixing bowl. With electric mixer, beat yolks until light. Gradually add confectioners' sugar. Transfer mixture to 6 quart container. Beating constantly, add coffee cream, whipped cream and milk. Refrigerate until serving time. If desired, whip a few egg whites until stiff; fold into nog just prior to serving. For each 3 quarts nog, add 2 cups brandy and 1 cup rum. Place in punch bowl and sprinkle with nutmeg. Yield: 50-60 servings.

Mrs. G. E. Nancarrow, Officers' Wives' Club, Suffolk, England

 ## Party Eggnog

> 5 eggs, well beaten
> 1 46-oz. can orange, pineapple or apple juice
> ½ lb. honey

Beat eggs well; blend with juice and honey. Chill well before serving. Yield: 15-20 servings.

Mrs. Judy Bronnenberg, Perry, Iowa, Favorite Recipes Food Fair

 ## Southern Perfect Eggnog

> 6 eggs, separated
> ¾ c. sugar
> 2 c. heavy cream
> 2 c. milk
> 2 c. brandy or 90 to 100 proof rye whiskey
> 1 oz. Jamaica rum
> Grated nutmeg

(Continued on next page)

Beat egg yolks with ½ cup sugar until thick and lemon colored. Beat egg whites very stiff, adding ¼ cup sugar while beating. Fold egg whites into beaten yolks. Stir in cream and milk. Add brandy; stir thoroughly. Serve very cold with grated nutmeg on each serving. Yield: 5 pints eggnog or 30-35 servings.

Mrs. Gerald M. Johnson, Officers' Wives' Club, Norfolk, Va.

 ## Gourmet Hot Chocolate

> 4 *squares unsweetened chocolate*
> 1 *c. sugar*
> ½ *c. water*
> 2 *tsp. instant coffee*
> ¼ *tsp. cinnamon*
> ⅛ *tsp. salt*
> ½ *c. heavy cream*
> *Hot milk*

Combine chocolate, sugar, water, instant coffee, cinnamon and salt in a heavy saucepan. Bring to a boil; simmer gently for 3 to 4 minutes, stirring constantly. Cool. Whip cream and fold into cold chocolate mixture. To serve, place about 2 tablespoons chocolate mixture in each cup; fill with hot milk. Blend. Yield: 16 servings.

Mrs. H. T. Ritchie, Ewing, Va.

 ## Hot Cocoa

> 1 ½ *c. cocoa*
> 2 *c. sugar*
> ½ *tsp. salt*
> 2 *tsp. vanilla*
> 1 *pt. warm water*
> 1 *qt. boiling water*
> 8 *qt. milk*
> 50 *marshmallows*

Combine cocoa, sugar, salt and vanilla with warm water. Add to boiling water; cook about 5 minutes. Add to milk and heat; do not boil. Serve hot with marshmallow floating on each cup of cocoa. Yield: 50 servings.

Mrs. Harold Rushton, Salt Lake, Utah

French Chocolate

¾ c. semisweet chocolate pieces
½ c. light corn syrup
⅓ c. water
1 tsp. vanilla
1 pt. whipping cream
2 qt. milk

Blend chocolate pieces with syrup and water over low heat until chocolate is melted. Add vanilla; pour into a jar and refrigerate until cool. In a large mixing bowl, beat cream at medium speed while gradually adding chocolate syrup. Continue beating until mixture mounds when dropped from spoon. Turn into serving bowl; refrigerate. Just before serving, scald milk; pour into heated coffee pot or carafe. Fill serving cups half full of chocolate-whipped cream mixture. Fill with hot milk; blend. Yield: 16-18 servings.

Mrs. Lorraine R. Fiedler, Home Economics Teacher, Carleton, Mich.

 ## Mexican Chocolate

¼ lb. sweet chocolate
1 c. hot water
5 ½ c. milk
½ c. cream
1 tbsp. cinnamon
⅛ tsp. nutmeg
1 tsp. vanilla
8 cinnamon sticks, 2½ in. long

Combine chocolate and hot water in top of double boiler; melt over hot water. Stir. In 3-quart saucepan, combine milk, cream, cinnamon and nutmeg; beat with rotary beater or wire whisk until well combined. Over medium heat, heat milk mixture until bubbles form around edge of pan; stir occasionally. Remove from heat. Stir in melted chocolate and vanilla; beat with rotary beater until foamy. Serve with cinnamon stick in each cup. Yield: 6 servings.

Mrs. Jack O'Neill, Home Economics Teacher, Belmont, Wis.

Apple Blossom Punch

1 10-oz. can apple juice
2 qt. ginger ale
1 bottle light rum
Juice of 12 limes
3 oz. grenadine

(Continued on next page)

15

Stir apple juice and ginger ale into punch bowl. Add large block of ice or ice cubes; stir. Add rum, lime juice and grenadine. Stir well; decorate with apples, pineapple rings and cherries. Yield: 12-15 servings.

Mrs. John R. Murphy, Home Economics Teacher, Point Loma, Calif.

 ## Budget Fruit Punch

> *1 pkg. cherry powdered drink mix*
> *Sugar*
> *2 qt. water*
> *1 No. 3 can Hawaiian Punch*
> *1 No. 3 can pineapple juice*
> *1 qt. ginger ale, chilled*

Mix powdered drink mix by directions on the envelope with sugar and water. Add juices; chill. Add ginger ale just before serving. This is a red punch. If a yellow punch is desired, use the Tropical Punch and lemon drink mix. If desired, the powdered drink mix may be omitted for a richer but more expensive punch. Yield: 35-40 servings.

Mrs. R. P. Hughes, Jr., Treas., Walter Reed Army Med. Cen., Washington, D.C.

 ## Chaplain's Punch

> *3 qt. unsweetened pineapple juice*
> *4 qt. dry ginger ale*
> *2 qt. champagne*
> *Juice of 8 lemons*
> *Juice of 4 oranges*
> *Juice of 3 limes*
> *Mint leaves, crushed*
> *2 c. sugar*
> *1 pt. strawberries*

Mix pineapple juice, ginger ale and champagne; let stand. Add remaining ingredients and a block or cubes of ice. Yield: 60-70 servings.

Mrs. R. P. Swofford, Jr., Pres. Officers' Wives' Club, Montgomery, Ala.

 ## Apple-Cranberry Punch

> *1 1-lb. can jellied cranberry sauce*
> *2 c. water*
> *2 c. apple cider*

(Continued on next page)

1 stick cinnamon
4 whole cloves
1 c. fresh orange juice

Crush cranberry sauce in can with fork; put in saucepan and gradually beat in water with egg beater. Add cider, cinnamon and cloves. Simmer 5 minutes; add orange juice and serve hot. Keeps well and may be reheated.

Marlene Blom, Columbus, Mont.

 ## Cranberry Punch

½ c. brown sugar
1 c. water
½ tsp. cinnamon
¼ tsp. nutmeg
¼ tsp. ground cloves
½ tsp. allspice
2 cans jellied cranberry sauce
3 c. water
1 qt. pineapple juice
1 tbsp. fresh lemon juice
2 tbsp. butter
Stick cinnamon

Bring first 6 ingredients to boil. Melt cranberry sauce in water; add to syrup. Add pineapple and lemon juice; sprinkle in butter. Serve hot with stick cinnamon. Yield: 15 cups.

Mrs. Ralph Turner, Rochester, N. Y.

 ## Hot Buttered Cranberry Punch

¾ c. brown sugar
4 c. water
¼ tsp. salt
¼ tsp. nutmeg
½ tsp. cinnamon
½ tsp. allspice
¾ tsp. cloves
2 1-lb. cans jellied cranberry sauce
4 c. unsweetened pineapple juice
Soft butter

Combine sugar, 1 cup water, salt and spices and bring to boiling point. Mash cranberry sauce; add remaining water and beat until smooth. Add pineapple

(Continued on next page)

juice; add to spiced syrup and simmer 5 minutes. Serve hot with about ⅛ teaspoon butter in each cup. Yield: 2 ½ quarts.

Mrs. Audrey Curts, St. Marys, Ohio

 ### Pink Elephant Punch

> 2 qt. cranberry juice cocktail
> 1 pt. pineapple juice
> 1 qt. ginger ale
> 1 fifth vodka

Combine all ingredients. Add ice just before serving. Yield: 48 servings.

Mrs. G. L. Mager, Officers' Wives' Club, Suffolk, England

Spiced Cranberry Punch

> ¾ tsp. cloves
> ½ tsp. allspice
> ¼ tsp. ginger
> ½ tsp. cinnamon
> ¼ tsp. nutmeg
> 1 c. sugar
> ¼ tsp. salt
> Water
> 3 c. cranberry juice
> 1 6-oz. can lemonade concentrate
> 4 c. apple juice

Mix spices, sugar, salt and 1 cup water in small pan. Bring to rolling boil. Mix with juices and 1 quart water. Heat and serve. Yield: 30 servings.

Betty Heflin, Additon, Ill.

Easy Raspberry Punch

    1 3-oz. pkg. raspberry gelatin Jell-O
    1 pkg. raspberry Kool-Aid
    1 6-oz. can frozen lemonade
    1 c. sugar
    3 qt. water
    Ice

In gallon container, mix Jell-O according to directions; add Kool-Aid, then frozen lemonade. Stir in sugar. Add water and ice to fill container. Yield: 4 quarts.

Mrs. Leonard Anderson, Malta, Mont.

 ### Frosty Fruit Punch

    2 46-oz. cans unsweetened pineapple juice
    2 ⅔ c. orange juice
    1 ⅓ c. lemon juice
  ⅔ c. lime juice
    2 c. sugar
    2 1-qt. bottles ginger ale, chilled
    2 1-qt. bottles plain carbonated water, chilled

Combine fruit juices and sugar; chill thoroughly. Pour over large cake of ice in punch bowl. Pour ginger ale and carbonated water slowly down side of bowl. For trim, float twists of sliced orange and sprigs of fresh mint on block of ice. Yield: 9 quarts.

Mrs. Melvin W. Mosher, Brockport, N. Y., Favorite Recipes Food Fair

Fruit Smash

    2 c. hot water
    2 3-oz. pkg. strawberry, cherry or raspberry gelatin
    6 c. cold water
    1 ½ c. lime or lemon juice
    1 No. 2 can pineapple juice
    5 c. orange juice
  ½ to 1 c. sugar
    5 to 6 fully ripe bananas
    1 qt. chilled ginger ale

Add hot water to gelatin in large mixing bowl; stir until dissolved. Add cold water and fruit juices; stir in sugar. Chill. Just before serving, whip bananas

(Continued on next page)

until smooth and creamy; beat into mixture. Add ginger ale. Garnish with fluted slices of bananas, pineapple, lime, lemon or orange. Yield: 1 gallon.

Mrs. Ralph Higginbotham, Jackson, Miss.

 ### Gala Champagne Punch

>   3 c. sugar
>   2 ½ c. water
>   2 lge. cans pineapple juice
>   5 lge. cans orange juice
>   2 sm. cans lemon juice
>   1 qt. ginger ale
>   2 pt. frozen crushed strawberries
>   1 to 2 trays ice cubes

Combine sugar and water to make syrup; pour in juices. About 1 hour before serving, pour over ginger ale, crushed strawberries and ice cubes; mix well. Yield: 50 servings.

Mrs. Betty Campbell, Morris Plains, N. J.

Islander's Punch

>   1 46-oz. can pineapple juice
>   1 46-oz. can Tropical Fruit Punch
>   3 7-oz. bottles lemon-lime carbonated beverage
>   ½ c. grenadine syrup
>   ¼ c. lemon juice
>   1 No. 2 can pineapple chunks
>   Maraschino cherries

Chill all ingredients for several hours before serving. Combine all liquid ingredients in a punch bowl; stir. Add ice cubes and garnish with pineapple chunks and maraschino cherries.

Mrs. Eugene A. Taylor, Pres. Officers' Wives' Club, Corvallis, Oreg.

 ### Low-Calorie Party Punch

>   1 pkg. presweetened orange Kool-Aid
>   1 46-oz. can unsweetened pineapple juice, chilled
>   4 cans dietetic ginger ale, chilled
>   Sliced orange
>   Sliced lime

(Continued on next page)

Prepare Kool-Aid by package directions; pour all ingredients except fruit slices over cracked ice in a punch bowl. Float orange and lime slices on top. Yield: 4 quarts punch.

Mrs. Duane Sterling, Warrensburg, Mo.

 ## Holiday Punch

   1 c. sugar
   1 2-in. piece cinnamon stick
   5 whole cloves
   5 whole allspice
   2 c. water
   2 6-oz. cans frozen lemonade
   2 6-oz. cans frozen limeade
   2 lge. bottles quinine water
   2 lge. bottles carbonated water

Combine sugar, cinnamon, cloves, allspice and water in a small saucepan; heat to boiling and simmer 5 minutes. Strain into a medium bowl; cool. When ready to mix punch, pour spiced water into a punch bowl; stir in frozen lemonade, limeade, quinine and carbonated waters. Float block of ice made in fancy mold on top. Surround bowl with clusters of green grapes, if desired. Garnish with rings of alternating lemon and lime slices. Punch will be a cool green color. Yield: 50 punch cup servings.

Roseanna Bouch, Seward, Penn.

 ## Orange Batida

  16 c. orange juice
   8 ripe bananas, sliced up
  46 diced maraschino cherries
   3 c. crushed ice

Place ingredients in blender or electric mixer; blend until contents are smooth. Yield: 20 servings.

Mrs. Frank Reed, Thompsonville, Mich.

 ## Mock Tom Collins

  1 ½ c. sugar
  Rind and juice of 2 lemons
  1 tsp. lemon extract

(Continued on next page)

2 c. milk
Tom Collins mix

Combine ingredients, except Tom Collins mix. Beat in blender or mixer. Chill until ready to serve. To serve, combine one shot of above mixture; fill glass with Tom Collins mix. Decorate with red cherry.

Mrs. Ronald Gall, Sheboygan Falls, Wis.

 ## Party Fruit Cup Punch

9 10-oz. pkg. frozen strawberries, sliced and partly thawed
¾ c. currant jelly
¾ c. lime juice
6 c. finely crushed ice
6 c. water
1 lge. lime, sliced thin

Combine 3 packages strawberries, ¼ cup currant jelly and ¼ cup lime juice in electric blender; cover. Beat until smooth; pour into large punch bowl. Repeat process twice with remaining berries, jelly and lime juice. Stir in ice and water until well blended. Float lime slices on top; serve in punch cups or dainty glasses. Yield: 25 servings.

Mrs. Mary Beth Tustison, Detroit, Mich.

 ## Peachy Champagne Punch

1 pkg. frozen peaches
1 bottle peach brandy
4 bottles champagne
4 qt. club soda
Ice cubes
Maraschino cherries, chopped

Place frozen peaches in large punch bowl. Pour in remaining ingredients; mix and serve. Yield: 50 servings.

Mrs. Ernest D. Ficco, Norfolk, Va.

 ## Berlin Peach Punch

2 No. 2½ cans sliced peaches
1 lb. granulated sugar
1 c. brandy

(Continued on next page)

1 bottle white dry wine
1 magnum champagne

Combine peaches, sugar and brandy in deep chinaware bowl. Mix without crushing peaches. Let stand in refrigerator at least 24 hours. Just before serving, add wine and champagne. Stir until blended. Add only enough ice cubes to keep chilled. Peach blossoms or orchids can be added as a decorative measure to float on top of punch. Yield: 12 servings.

Mrs. M. J. Cathcart, Officers' Wives' Club, Midway Island

Peppermint Delight

5 32-oz. bottles ginger ale, chilled
1 sm. jar maraschino cherries
1 sm. can mandarin orange sections
1 46-oz. can pineapple juice, chilled
1 12-oz. can frozen orange juice, thawed
1 tsp. peppermint extract

Pour 3 bottles ginger ale into 4 ice cube trays; place 1 maraschino cherry into each cube in 2 trays and 1 orange section into each cube in 2 trays. Freeze. When ready to serve pour pineapple juice into punch bowl and combine with thawed orange juice; add peppermint extract and slowly pour in remaining ginger ale. Add 1 tray of cherry ice cubes and 1 tray of orange ice cubes; place 1 ice cube in each cup when serving. Yield: 25-30 servings.

Donna H. Suyes, Oklahoma City, Okla., Favorite Recipes Food Fair

Rhubarb Punch

2 c. ½-in. slices rhubarb
1 c. sugar
½ c. water
½ c. unsweetened pineapple juice
¼ c. lemon juice
Few drops red food coloring
2 c. ginger ale

Combine rhubarb, sugar and water; cook till rhubarb is tender. Strain; add fruit juices. Tint with coloring; chill. Add ginger ale last minute; serve over crushed ice or ice cubes. Yield: 8 servings.

Mrs. Raymond Evenson, Parshall, N. D.

Pineapple-Apricot Shrub

1 8½-oz. can crushed pineapple
1 tbsp. lemon juice
1 c. apricot nectar
2 c. cracked ice

Combine all ingredients in glass container of blender. Cover and blend until smooth, about 30 seconds. Serve in tall glasses. Top with maraschino cherry. Yield: 3 servings.

Nancy B. Goshin, New City, N. Y.

 ### Pretty Pink Champagne

1 gal. sauterne
4 qt. soda water
4 bottles pink champagne
1 fifth brandy

Freeze one large mold of ice made of water, pink vegetable coloring and fresh mint leaves. Place mold in punch bowl when ready to serve punch and quickly pour all ingredients over ice mold. The very cheapest domestic ingredients are just as good as the expensive brands. This is a very clear, bubbly punch and can easily be refilled. Yield: 120 cups.

Mrs. K. R. Klofkorn, Pres., Officers' Wives' Club, Oakland, Calif.

Spiced Fruit Cooler

4 c. boiling water
8 tea bags or 8 tsp. (rounded) tea
½ tbsp. ground allspice
¼ tbsp. ground nutmeg
¼ tbsp. ground cinnamon
1 pkg. pineapple-grapefruit soft drink powder
1 ½ c. sugar
1 6-oz. can frozen lemonade concentrate
1 6-oz. can cold water
1 c. pineapple juice

Pour boiling water over tea bags and spices; steep 5 minutes. Remove tea bags; pour liquid through strainer if loose tea is used. Cool. Strain through cheesecloth. Chill. Prepare soft drink powder, using sugar and 1 ½ quarts cold water. Blend in remaining ingredients and chilled tea. Pour punch over ice in punch bowl. Yield: 18-20 servings.

Mrs. Gordon Buttenhoff, Grangeville, Idaho

Rum Punch

1 ½ bottles Puerto Rican rum
6 oz. pineapple juice
10 oz. orange juice
10 oz. lime juice
1 ½ qt. ginger ale or soda
1 pt. strawberries, sliced
Lemon slices
Lime slices

Combine rum and juices; let steep for 1 hour. Add ginger ale. Pour over block of ice in large punch bowl and stir. Decorate with 1 pint sliced strawberries, lemon and lime slices. Yield: 12 servings.

Mrs. James E. Ainley, Reno, Nev.

 ## Wassail

1 c. sugar
2 sticks cinnamon
16 cloves
¾ c. unsweetened orange juice
¼ c. unsweetened lemon juice
½ c. unsweetened grapefruit juice
2 c. apple cider
24 maraschino cherries

Boil sugar and 2 cups water with cinnamon and cloves tied in a cheesecloth bag for 5 minutes in 10-quart container. Remove bag of cinnamon and cloves; add orange, lemon and grapefruit juices. Add apple cider and 4 cups water; bring to a boil. Add 2 cherries to each cup; serve warm. Yield: 12 cups.

Mrs. W. F. Giles, Loveland, Colo.

 ## Candy Cane Surprise

2 10-oz. jars strawberry jelly
14 bottles 7-Up
4 pt. soft peppermint stick ice cream
Candy canes

Beat jelly until smooth; add 2 bottles boiling 7-Up, mixing until smooth. Chill. Before serving, spoon 3 pints ice cream into punch bowl. Add jelly mixture, stirring lightly. Pour remaining chilled 7-Up in slowly. Float scoopfuls of re-

(Continued on next page)

maining ice cream on top. Serve with a candy cane in punch glass. Yield: 45 servings.

Jeanette Bazemore, Hixson, Tenn.

 ## Coffee Punch

> 1 gal. strong coffee
> 2 pt. coffee ice cream
> 3 pt. vanilla ice cream
> 1 c. sugar
> 1 tsp. vanilla extract
> 1 pt. cream, whipped (opt.)

Chill coffee; pour over ice cream cut in blocks in punch bowl. Add sugar and extract. Top punch with whipped cream before serving. Yield: 20 servings.

Mrs. John A. Suiter, Garysburg, N. C.

 ## Orange Blossom Punch

> 1 6-oz. can frozen orange concentrate
> 1 pt. orange sherbet
> 1 qt. plus 1 pt. ginger ale
> 1 whole orange, sliced thin
> Maraschino cherries

Place orange juice and sherbet in punch bowl; slowly add ginger ale. Float slices of orange with a maraschino cherry in the center in the punch bowl. Add ice cubes. Yield: 15-20 servings.

Mrs. Alfred C. Smith, Claremont, N. H.

 ## Reception Punch

> 3 or 4 bottles chilled ginger ale
> 1 pt. vanilla ice cream
> 1 pt. pistachio ice cream
> 1 pt. orange sherbet
> 1 lge. can crushed pineapple
> 2 bottles cherries
> 1 pkg. frozen or 1 basket fresh sliced strawberries

(Continued on next page)

Fill punch bowl half full with ginger ale. Add remaining ingredients and serve when ice cream starts to melt. Yield: 25 servings.

Bernadette Voytek, Bridgeport, Conn.

 ## Chocolate Surf Punch with Ice Cream Islands

1 1-pound box quick chocolate-flavored mix
2 quarts cold milk
2 quarts vanilla ice cream
2 1-quart bottles chilled carbonated water

Put chocolate-flavored mix in large mixing bowl; stir in milk. Beat with rotary beater until blended. Pour into punch bowl. Add scoops of ice cream to chocolate mixture. Pour in carbonated water. Yield: 48 ½ cup servings.

Photograph for this recipe below.

Peachy Cooler

>   4 eggs, separated
>   ⅛ t. salt
>   ¼ c. sugar
>   1 12-oz. pkg. frozen sweetened sliced peaches, thawed or 1½
>   c. sweetened sliced fresh peaches, finely chopped or mashed
>   1 tbsp. lemon juice
>   ⅛ to ¼ tsp. almond extract
>   2 c. chilled milk
>   1 pt. vanilla ice cream
>   Whipped cream
>   Peach slices (opt.)

Beat egg whites and salt until soft peaks form. Add sugar gradually; continue beating until stiff and glossy. Combine egg yolks, peaches, lemon juice and almond extract; mix well. Add milk and ice cream; beat until smooth. Fold in egg whites. Serve in tall chilled glasses. Garnish with whipped cream and peach slices, if desired. Yield: 8-10 servings.

Photograph for this recipe on page 9.

 ## Mint Tea

>   1 c. washed mint leaves, firmly packed
>   1 tea bag of orange pekoe
>   3 c. sugar
>   1 stick cinnamon
>   ½ gal. boiling water
>   Juice of 8 large lemons

Place mint leaves, tea bag, sugar and cinnamon stick in large container; add ½ gallon boiling water. Let steep 1 hour, keeping container covered; strain. Add lemon juice and enough water to make 1 gallon. Serve hot or cold. Yield: 16 servings.

Mrs. Thomas J. Boyd, Amarillo, Tex.

Russian Tea

>   4 qt. hot strong tea
>   ¾ tsp. cloves
>   1 ½ tsp. cinnamon
>   Juice of 2 lemons
>   Juice of 4 oranges
>   2 c. sugar

Combine first 3 ingredients; add remaining ingredients. Strain; serve hot. Yield: 5 quarts.

Mrs. W. H. Porter, Bessemer, Ala.

Cakes

STEPS TO A PERFECT CAKE

1. Follow the recipe exactly.

2. Measure accurately.

3. Be sure to use the size and type cake pans specified in the recipe.

4. Fill cake pans one-half to two-thirds full. Pour the batter into the pans, spreading to the sides, and filling all corners so that the baked cake will be even. Tap the batter-filled pans lightly on the table to break up air bubbles that form.

5. Space oven racks so that the cake pans will be almost in the middle of the oven. Stagger layer pans so no pan is directly over another and they do not touch each other or the sides of the oven.

6. Bake in a preheated oven at the temperature specified in the recipe.

7. Test for doneness at the end of the minimum baking time. Don't peek at the cake before this time.

8. Let cake stand in pans for 5 minutes before removing. Loosen the edge of the cake with a knife and turn out onto a rack. Remove paper.

9. Cool cake completely before frosting.

Pans To Use

A cake recipe calling for 2 cups of flour should be baked in two 8-inch round pans that are 1½ inches deep. A cake recipe calling for 2½ to 3 cups of flour should be baked in two 9-inch round pans that are 1½ to 2 inches deep, or in two 8-inch square pans that are 2 inches deep.

A recipe for two 8-inch layers will make:

Two 8-inch layers that are 1½ inches deep

One loaf cake that is 9 x 5 x 5 inches

One oblong cake that is 13 x 9½ x 2 inches

Two square layers that are 8 x 8 x 2 inches

1½ dozen large (3 x 1½-inch) cupcakes

2 dozen medium (2½ x 1¼-inch) cupcakes

2½ dozen small (1½ x ¾-inch) cupcakes

Preparing The Pans

Grease the bottom of baking pans for any cake made with shortening except chiffon types. Line the pan with waxed paper that has been cut to fit the bottom exactly. Grease the paper. Do not, however, grease the baking pans for sponge and angel cakes. If the pans are greased, the batter can't cling to the sides of the pans as it bakes and the cake won't reach full volume.

COMMON CAUSES OF CAKE FAILURES

If This Happens	It May Be Caused by This in Butter-Type Cakes	It May Be Caused by This in Sponge-Type Cakes
CAKE FALLS	1. Too much sugar, liquid leavening or shortening 2. Underbaking 3. Oven temperature too low 4. Not enough flour	1. Egg whites overbeaten 2. Egg yolks underbeaten 3. Greased pans were used 4. Too much sugar 5. Underbaking
CAKE CRACKS OR HUMPS	1. Overmixing 2. Oven temperature too hot 3. Too much flour or not enough liquid 4. Batter uneven in pan	1. Too much flour or sugar 2. Oven temperature too hot
HARD TOP CRUST	1. Overbaking 2. Oven temperature too hot	Same as for butter-type cakes
STICKY TOP CRUST	1. Too little baking 2. Too much sugar	Same as for butter-type cakes
HEAVY, COMPACT	1. Too many eggs 2. Too little leavening or flour 3. Too much mixing 4. Too much shortening or liquid 5. Oven temperature too hot	1. Egg yolks underbeaten 2. Too much mixing 3. Egg whites overbeaten
HEAVY, STICKY BOTTOM LAYER	1. Eggs underbeaten 2. Underbaking 3. Too much liquid 4. Undermixing 5. Shortening too soft	1. Not enough mixing 2. Too many eggs or egg yolks

HIGH ALTITUDE CHANGES

	3,000 Feet	5,000 Feet	7,000 Feet
Liquid: add for each cup	1-2 tbsp.	2-3 tbsp.	3-4 tbsp.
Baking powder: decrease for each teaspoon	⅛ tsp.	⅛-¼ tsp.	¼-½ tsp.
Sugar: decrease for each cup	no change	usually no change	1-2 tbsp.

31

Penuche Applesauce Cake

2 ½ c. sifted flour
1 ½ c. sugar
¼ tsp. baking powder
1 ½ tsp. soda
1 ½ tsp. salt
¾ tsp. cinnamon
½ tsp. cloves
½ tsp. allspice
½ c. butter or oleo
½ c. water
2 c. sweetened applesauce
2 eggs
1 c. raisins, ground
¾ c. nuts, chopped

Sift dry ingredients together 3 times. Add shortening, water and applesauce. Beat 2 minutes at medium speed with mixer. Add eggs; beat 2 more minutes. Add raisins, making sure they are well blended. Fold in nuts. Bake in greased 13 x 9-inch pan 45 to 50 minutes at 350 degrees. When cool, frost with Easy Penuche Icing.

EASY PENUCHE ICING:

⅓ c. butter, melted
1 c. brown sugar
½ c. cream
Confectioners' sugar

Combine butter and sugar in saucepan. Bring to a boil; add cream. Remove from heat; cool to lukewarm. Add enough confectioners' sugar for spreading consistency. Yield: 12 servings.

Mrs. Gloria Shaw, Sedan, Kan., Chautauqua County Fair

Apple Cake

2 cups finely diced apples
1 cup sugar
1 egg
1 cup flour
1 ½ teaspoon cinnamon
1 teaspoon soda
¾ cup nuts
1 teaspoon vanilla

Mix apples and sugar together. Let stand until sugar is thoroughly dissolved. Add egg and beat well. Sift dry ingredients together. Stir into apple mixture.

(Continued on next page)

Add nuts and vanilla. Pour into one 8 x 8-inch pan. Bake at 375° for 40 to 45 minutes or until done.

TOPPING:

> ½ cup brown sugar
> ½ cup granulated sugar
> 2 tablespoons flour
> 1 cup water
> ¼ lb. butter
> 1 teaspoon vanilla

Cook sugars, flour and water until clear. Add butter and vanilla. Stir until butter thoroughly melts. Pour over cake while both are hot. Yield: 6 servings.

Mrs. Roger Branigin, Wife of Governor, Indianapolis, Ind.

Tropical Banana Cake

> 2 ½ c. sifted cake flour
> 1 ⅔ c. sugar
> 1 ¼ tsp. baking powder
> 1 tsp. soda
> 1 tsp. salt
> ⅔ c. shortening
> 1 ¼ c. sieved bananas
> ⅔ c. buttermilk
> ½ c. eggs
> 1 tsp. vanilla

Sift together into large bowl flour, sugar, baking powder, soda and salt. Add shortening, bananas and 1/3 cup buttermilk. Stir to dampen flour. Beat with electric mixer 2 minutes. Add remaining buttermilk, eggs and vanilla. Beat 2 minutes. Pour into 2 paper-lined 9-inch pans. Bake 30 to 35 minutes in 350-degree oven. Frost with following frosting.

LEMON-BANANA FROSTING:

> ⅓ c. butter or oleo
> 2 c. powdered sugar
> 3 tbsp. mashed banana
> 1 tbsp. lemon juice

Cream butter and sugar; add banana and lemon juice. Mix until smooth.

Mrs. Sherron T. Lee, Ralls, Tex., South Plains Fair

Boston Cream Pie

4 eggs
1 cup sugar
1 grated lemon rind
1 tsp. vanilla extract
1 cup flour
¼ cup butter, melted

Beat eggs and sugar in double boiler until creamy and fluffy. Place in mixer bowl and beat until cold on medium speed. Fold in alternately, lemon rind, vanilla, flour and melted butter until well blended. Grease and dust two 9-inch pie pans. Pour mixture in pans. Bake in 350-degree oven 40 minutes. Cool on rack.

FILLING:

2 c. milk
1 c. sugar
4 egg yolks
1 tbsp. flour
1 tsp. cornstarch
1 tsp. vanilla

Heat milk. In a bowl mix sugar, egg yolks, flour and cornstarch. Gradually add boiling milk with vanilla. Cook until thickens, stirring constantly. Cool and spread between 2 layers.

TOPPING:

1 8-oz. pkg. cream cheese
1 ½ c. confectioners' sugar
2 sq. semisweet chocolate

Cream package of cream cheese; mix in confectioners' sugar and chocolate and spread over top.

Mrs. Hulett C. Smith, Wife of Governor, Charleston, W. Va.

Burnt Sugar Cake

½ c. butter
1 c. sugar
3 eggs
2 ¼ c. flour
3 tsp. baking powder
1 tsp. salt
¾ c. cold water
4 tbsp. burnt sugar syrup

Cream butter and sugar; separate eggs. Add well beaten yolks and stir thoroughly. Sift dry ingredients together; add alternately with water and syrup.

(Continued on next page)

Beat thoroughly. Fold in stiffly beaten egg whites. Divide batter between 2 greased and floured layer pans. Bake at 375 degrees about 25 minutes.

BURNT SUGAR SYRUP:

> 1 ⅓ c. sugar
> ½ c. water

Put sugar in heavy pan. Cook over low fire and stir constantly until melted and brown. Add ½ cup water and continue cooking until lumps are dissolved. Cool.

BURNT SUGAR ICING:

> 6 tbsp. burnt sugar syrup
> 4 tbsp. butter
> 3 c. confectioners' sugar
> 1 tsp. vanilla

Heat syrup and butter until butter is melted. Beat in sugar and flavoring slowly until icing is of good spreading consistency. Frost cake.

Mrs. Laurine Sorensen, Pueblo, Colo., Pueblo Fair

Caramel Cake

> 3 c. sugar
> ¾ lb. Crisco
> 5 eggs
> 3 c. flour
> ¼ tsp. salt
> ½ tsp. baking powder
> 1 ¼ c. milk
> 1 tsp. vanilla

Cream sugar and Crisco; add eggs, one at a time. Sift together dry ingredients 3 times; add alternately with milk to creamed mixture. Add vanilla. Pour into 4 greased and floured 9-inch pans. Bake at 325 degrees until cake tests done.

CARAMEL FILLING:

> 2 c. brown sugar
> 2 sticks margarine
> ½ c. milk
> 4 c. confectioners' sugar
> 2 tsp. vanilla
> Pecan halves

(Continued on next page)

Blend brown sugar and margarine over medium heat; bring to a boil. Add milk; boil for 5 minutes. Cool; add confectioners' sugar. Add vanilla. Frost cake; decorate top and sides with pecan halves.

Carrie Funderburk, Lancaster, S. C., Lancaster County Fair

 ## Lazy Daisy Cake

> 2 eggs
> 1 c. sugar
> 1 tsp. vanilla
> 1 c. cake flour
> 1 tsp. baking powder
> ¼ tsp. salt
> ½ c. milk
> 2 tbsp. butter

Combine eggs, sugar and vanilla and beat until thick. Add sifted dry ingredients. Heat milk and butter to boiling point; add to sugar mixture. Bake in buttered 8 x 8-inch pan in a 350-degree oven 30 to 40 minutes. Remove from oven.

FROSTING:

> ¾ c. brown sugar
> ½ c. butter, melted
> 1 c. cream
> 1 c. coconut

Combine all ingredients, blend well. Frost cake, return to hot oven or broiler to brown.

Mrs. Warren P. Knowles, Wife of Governor, Madison, Wis.

Centennial Cream Cake

*3 cups sifted cake flour
1 ½ cups sugar
4 ½ teaspoons baking powder
¾ teaspoon salt
1 ½ cups heavy cream, chilled
1 ½ teaspoons vanilla extract
3 eggs*

Lightly grease cake pans, then line bottom with waxed paper and lightly grease waxed paper. Sift flour, sugar, baking powder and salt together twice. Pour well-chilled cream and vanilla extract into a deep 1-quart bowl; beat with electric mixer or rotary beater until just stiff, about 1 ½ minutes. Add eggs and beat until just blended. Add flour mixture and beat until batter is blended. Turn into pans. Bake in 350 degree oven until center tops of cakes spring back when lightly touched with finger, about 25 to 30 minutes. Cool cakes in pans on rack for 10 minutes. Remove cakes from pans; peel off waxed paper and turn cakes right side up on cake rack and finish cooling.

WHIPPED CREAM FROSTING:

*2 cups heavy cream, chilled
1 teaspoon vanilla extract
¼ cup sugar*

Combine well-chilled cream and vanilla in deep bowl. Gradually beat in sugar; continue beating until stiff. Spread between layers, on top and sides of cake. Chill until ready to serve. Keep unused portion in refrigerator.

Photograph for this recipe on page 29.

Cherry Cake

*¾ c. soft butter
1 ½ c. sugar
3 eggs
1 tsp. soda
½ c. sour milk
½ tsp. allspice
½ tsp. cloves
1 c. cherries, canned or fresh
2 c. sifted flour*

Cream butter; add sugar and cream until smooth. Add eggs; beat well. Add soda to sour milk; add to creamed mixture and beat well. Add spices and cherries. Add flour; mix well. Pour into 13 x 9-inch pan. Bake for 35 to 40 minutes at 350 degrees. Yield: 12-15 servings.

Mrs. Elmer Gellerman, Otoe, Neb., Otoe County Free Fair

Carrot Cake

1 ½ c. salad oil
2 ½ c. sugar
4 egg yolks
5 tbsp. hot water
2 ½ c. sifted flour
1 ½ tsp. baking powder
½ tsp. baking soda
¼ tsp. salt
1 tsp. nutmeg
1 tsp. cinnamon
1 tsp. ground cloves
1 ½ c. grated raw carrots
1 c. chopped black walnuts
4 egg whites

Preheat oven to 350 degrees. Grease 9-inch tube pan and dust lightly with flour. Cream oil and sugar until well mixed. Beat in egg yolks, one at a time. Beat well after each addition. Beat in hot water. Sift together flour, baking powder, baking soda, salt, nutmeg, cinnamon and cloves; beat into egg mixture. Stir grated carrots into batter; add walnuts. Beat egg whites until soft peaks form; fold into batter. Turn into prepared pan. Bake 60 to 70 minutes or until cake tests done.

CREAM CHEESE FROSTING:

¾ stick margarine
1 4-oz. pkg. cream cheese
2 tsp. vanilla
1 box powdered sugar

Cream margarine and cream cheese together until soft and smooth. Add vanilla. Add sugar gradually and beat until of spreading consistency. Spread on cake. Yield: 16 servings.

Sharon A. Longaker, Louisville, Ky., Kentucky State Fair

Chocolate Cake

1 ½ sticks butter
1 lb. box light brown sugar
3 eggs
3 squares melted unsweetened chocolate
2 teaspoons vanilla
2 ¼ cups sifted cake flour
2 teaspoons baking soda
¾ teaspoon salt
½ cup sour milk
1 cup boiling water

(Continued on next page)

Cream together butter, brown sugar and eggs until light and fluffy. Add melted chocolate and vanilla. Sift together flour, salt and soda and add alternately with sour milk. Stir in boiling water. Pour in 2 layer cake pans or one 9 x 13-inch pan lined with greased waxed paper. Bake at 350° for 35 to 40 minutes.

FROSTING:

> 1 pound box powdered sugar, sifted
> ½ stick butter
> 1 egg
> 2 teaspoons of vanilla
> Pinch of salt
> 4 squares melted unsweetened chocolate
> ¼ c. (about) hot water

Cream all ingredients together, adding hot water slowly until frosting is thin enough to spread. Beat until light and fluffy. Swirl on cool cake.

Mrs. John A. Burns, Wife of Governor, Honolulu, Hawaii

 ## German Chocolate Cake

> 1 pkg. sweet chocolate
> ½ c. boiling water
> 1 c. butter
> 2 c. sugar
> 4 egg yolks, unbeaten
> 1 tsp. vanilla
> Pinch of salt
> 1 tsp. soda
> 2 ½ c. sifted cake flour
> 1 c. buttermilk
> 4 egg whites

Melt chocolate in boiling water. Cool. Cream butter and sugar until light and fluffy. Add egg yolks, one at a time, beating after each. Add vanilla to chocolate mixture. Add chocolate mixture to batter. Sift together salt, soda and flour. Add alternately with buttermilk to chocolate batter, beating well after each addition. Beat until smooth. Beat egg whites until stiff peaks form. Fold into batter. Pour into three 8 or 9-inch greased pans, lightly lined on the bottom with paper. Bake at 350 degrees for 30 to 40 minutes. Cool. Frost with following frosting.

COCONUT-PECAN FROSTING:

> 1 c. evaporated milk
> 1 c. sugar
> 3 egg yolks
> ¼ lb. margarine

(Continued on next page)

1 tsp. vanilla
1 ⅓ c. coconut
1 c. pecans, chopped

Combine evaporated milk, sugar, egg yolks, margarine and vanilla in a saucepan. Cook and stir over medium heat until mixture thickens, about 12 minutes. Add coconut and chopped pecans. Beat until frosting is cool and thick enough to spread on cake. Yield: 12 servings.

Mrs. Joseph R. Miller, Orangeburg, S. C.

 Marble Cake

½ lb. butter or margarine
2 c. sugar
4 eggs, separated
2 tsp. vanilla
3 c. sifted cake flour
3 ¼ tsp. baking powder
½ tsp. salt
1 c. milk
1 c. chocolate syrup

Cream butter and sugar. Add egg yolks one at a time; beat well. Add vanilla. Alternately add sifted dry ingredients and milk. Fold in stiffly beaten egg whites. Pour half the batter into a greased angel food pan. Add chocolate syrup to remaining batter and mix well. Pour over batter in pan. Bake at 350 degrees for 1 hour. Yield: 12-14 servings.

Mrs. H. R. Greene, Officers' Wives' Club, Spokane, Wash.

 Red Velvet Cake

1 c. plus 1 tsp. shortening
1 ½ c. sugar
2 eggs
2 1-oz. bottles red food coloring

(Continued on next page)

2 tbsp. cocoa
1 c. buttermilk
1 tsp. salt
2 ¼ c. cake flour
1 tsp. vanilla
1 tsp. soda
1 tbsp. hot water
1 tbsp. vinegar

Cream shortening, sugar and eggs. Make a paste of food coloring and cocoa; add to creamed mixture. Add buttermilk and salt alternately with flour. Add vanilla. Dissolve soda in hot water; mix with vinegar, holding over bowl as it will foam. Quickly add mixture to batter. Pour into three 9-inch pans. Bake at 350 degrees for 30 minutes.

FROSTING:

3 tbsp. flour
1 c. milk
1 c. sugar
1 tsp. vanilla
1 c. butter

Cook flour and milk until very thick, stirring constantly; chill thoroughly. Cream sugar, vanilla and butter until fluffy. Blend in flour mixture. Beat until of spreading consistency. Frost cake. Store, covered, in refrigerator. Yield: 12-15 servings.

Mrs. John B. Wallace, Orlando, Fla.

Coconut Cake

½ c. shortening
1 c. sugar
2 eggs
½ tsp. salt
2 c. sifted cake flour
2 tsp. baking powder
⅔ c. milk
½ tsp. coconut flavoring

Cream shortening; add sugar gradually, beating well. Add eggs, one at a time; beat well. Add sifted dry ingredients alternately with milk to which flavoring has been added. Beat well. Pour batter into 2 greased and slightly floured 8-inch layer cake pans. Bake at 375 degrees for 25 to 30 minutes.

FROSTING:

½ c. oleo
½ c. flour

(Continued on next page)

> 1 c. milk
> 1 c. sugar
> 2 tbsp. Crisco
> ½ tsp. coconut flavoring
> Shredded coconut

Melt oleo; add flour and stir. Add milk, continuing to stir until mixture thickens. Remove from heat and cool. Put sugar and Crisco in bowl; beat until creamy. Add cooked mixture; keep beating until consistency of whipped cream. Add coconut flavoring. Frost cake and sprinkle on shredded coconut. Yield: 12 servings.

Judy Heil, Carson City, Mich., Gratiot County Fair for Youth

 ## Date-Orange Cake

> 1 c. Crisco
> 2 c. sugar
> 4 eggs
> 1 ½ cups buttermilk
> 1 tsp. soda
> 1 tsp. salt
> 4 cups sifted flour
> 1 cup chopped dates
> 1 tsp. grated orange rind

Cream together Crisco, sugar and eggs. Add remaining ingredients. Mix well. Put in large greased angel food cake pan or small ones. Bake at 350° for 1 hour and 15 minutes to 1 hour and 30 minutes.

SAUCE:

> 2 c. sugar
> 1 c. orange juice
> Grated rind of 1 orange

Combine and bring to boil. Pour hot sauce over hot cake. Let set until cold or overnight.

Mrs. Daniel J. Evans, Wife of Governor, Olympia, Wash.

 ## Delicious White Cake

> 3 c. cake flour
> 3 tsp. baking powder
> ½ c. butter
> 2 c. sugar

(Continued on next page)

1 ½ c. cold water
1 tsp. vanilla
4 egg whites, stiffly beaten

Sift flour and baking powder together. Cream butter and sugar; add flour and water alternately to sugar mixture. Add vanilla. Fold in egg whites. Bake at 350 degrees for 30 minutes in 8-inch pans. Top with Seven-Minute icing. Yield: 16 servings.

Mrs. Helen Renoe, Home Economics Teacher, Decatur, Ill.

Blackberry Jam Cake

3 c. all-purpose flour
1 tsp. soda
1 tsp. cinnamon
½ tsp. salt
⅔ c. shortening or butter
1 ½ c. sugar
4 eggs
1 c. buttermilk
1 c. blackberry jam

Heat oven to 375 degrees. Line three 8-inch layer pan bottoms with wax paper. Sift together flour, soda, cinnamon and salt. In large mixing bowl, cream shortening and sugar until creamy and smooth. Add eggs; beat well. Add sifted dry ingredients alternately with buttermilk to creamed mixture. Stir in jam. Pour into greased pans. Bake in 375-degree oven 25 to 30 minutes or until done. Cool on rack 10 to 15 minutes. Remove from pan; remove paper. Place on large cake plate; cover with Sauce Icing.

SAUCE ICING:

½ c. sugar
1 ½ c. sweet milk
1 egg

Boil together sugar and milk in saucepan until it becomes thick and will coat a spoon. Remove from heat. Add beaten egg and stir until cool. Put generously between layers, allowing time for them to absorb the sauce.

Mrs. Billy W. Jones, Springer, Okla., Carter County Free Fair

Gingerbread

½ c. butter
1 c. sugar
1 c. molasses, dark
2 eggs, separated
3 c. cake flour
1 tsp. salt
1 tsp. soda
2 tsp. ginger
2 tsp. cinnamon
1 c. buttermilk

Cream butter; add sugar and cream until light and smooth. Add molasses and beaten egg yolks and mix thoroughly. Sift flour, measure; sift with salt, soda and spices. Add flour mixture alternately with buttermilk. Fold in stiffly beaten egg whites. Turn batter into well-greased and floured mold or 9-inch square pan. Bake in 350° oven for 30 to 40 minutes. Serve hot topped with hard sauce. Yield: 9 servings.

HARD SAUCE:

½ c. butter
1 ½ c. sifted confectioners' sugar
1 egg, separated
2 teaspoons grated lemon rind

Cream butter and sugar. Add egg yolk, beating constantly. Blend in lemon rind. Fold into stiffly beaten egg white; chill. Yield: 2 cups.

Photograph for this recipe below.

Peach Preserve Cake

¾ c. butter
1 c. sugar
3 eggs, separated
2 c. sifted flour
⅛ tsp. salt
1 tsp. soda
½ c. buttermilk
1 c. peach preserves

Cream butter; add sugar slowly, beating constantly. Stir in well-beaten yolks. Sift flour and measure. Add salt to flour. Stir soda into buttermilk. Immediately add flour mixture alternately with buttermilk to the creamed mixture. Begin and end with flour mixture. Lightly fold in peach preserves. Fold in stiffly beaten egg whites. Turn into 9-inch round layer cake pans, lined on the bottom with waxed paper. Bake in 350-degree oven for 25 to 30 minutes. Turn at once onto cake rack. Cool completely before frosting.

ICING:

2 c. sugar
1 c. milk
1 c. coconut
1 c. crushed pineapple, drained
1 orange, ground and drained
1 c. chopped nuts

Cook sugar and milk to hard ball stage. Stir in coconut, pineapple, orange and nuts. Assemble cake. Sprinkle top and sides with coconut and cherries.

Mrs. W. M. Robinson, Memphis, Tenn., Mid-South Fair

Lady Baltimore Cake

¾ c. butter
2 c. sugar
3 ½ c. flour
3 ½ tsp. baking powder
1 c. milk
1 tsp. lemon flavor
8 egg whites, stiffly beaten

Cream butter; add sugar gradually. Sift baking powder and flour 3 times. Add to butter and sugar alternately with milk; add flavoring. Fold in egg whites. Pour in 3 layers. Bake at 350 to 375 degrees until cake tests done.

(Continued on next page)

ICING:

 3 c. sugar
 1 c. boiling water
 3 egg whites, stiffly beaten
 1 c. citron, chopped
 1 c. chopped raisins
 ½ c. candied cherries, cut fine
 1 c. chopped nuts

Stir sugar and water until sugar is dissolved; let boil, without stirring, until syrup spins a thread. Pour over egg whites, beating constantly, until stiff. Continue beating until icing is cold; add fruits, nuts and lemon juice. Spread on cake.

Mrs. R. E. Chappell, Dothan, Ala.

Angel Dream Cake

 1 ¼ c. sifted cake flour
 Sifted sugar
 1 ½ c. egg whites
 ¼ tsp. salt
 1 ¼ tsp. cream of tartar
 1 tsp. vanilla
 ¼ tsp. almond extract

Preheat oven to 375 degrees. Measure sifted flour; add ½ cup sugar. Sift together 4 times. Combine egg whites, salt, cream of tartar and flavorings in large bowl. Beat with sturdy beater until moist peaks form. Add 1 1/3 cups sugar in 4 additions, beating until blended each time. Stir in flour mixture in 4 additions, folding in with large wire spoon. Pour into ungreased 10-inch tube pan. Run spoon around edge 2 times to get rid of bubbles. Bake for 35 to 40 minutes at 350 to 375 degrees. Cool cake upside down in pan resting on cake rack. Yield: 16 servings.

Mrs. Lola Young, Almena, Kan., Rooks County Fair

Pineapple Upside-Down Cake

 ⅓ c. butter
 ½ c. brown sugar, packed
 1 1-lb. 4-oz. can sliced pineapple
 1 ½ c. cake flour or 1 ⅓ c. all-purpose flour
 1 c. sugar
 2 tsp. baking powder
 ½ tsp. salt

(Continued on next page)

⅓ *c. soft shortening*
⅔ *c. milk*
1 *tsp. vanilla*
1 *egg*

Heat oven to 350 degrees. Melt butter in 8-inch pan. Sprinkle brown sugar evenly over butter. Arrange pineapple on butter-sugar mixture. Decorate with cherries if desired. Stir flour, sugar, baking powder and salt in mixer bowl. Add shortening, milk and flavoring. Beat 2 minutes at medium speed or 300 vigorous strokes by hand. Add egg. Beat 2 minutes. Pour batter over fruit. Bake 40 to 50 minutes. Immediately turn upside-down on serving plate. Yield: 8 servings.

Kathy Poe, Placerville, Cal., El Dorado County Fair

Velvet Cake

¾ *lb. butter*
2 ¼ *c. sugar*
6 *eggs*
3 ½ *c. flour*
2 *tsp. baking powder*
1 *c. milk*

Cream together butter and sugar until creamy. Add eggs, 1 at a time; mix well. Add flour mixed with baking powder and milk. Bake at 350 degrees until done. Frost with favorite icing.

Mrs. Sessie Cowine, Silver City, N. C., Chatham County Fair

Pound Cake

1 *lb. butter*
1 ¼ *lb. sugar*
1 *tsp. lemon flavoring*
1 *tsp. vanilla flavoring*
10 *eggs, unbeaten*
1 *pound flour*
½ *teaspoon salt*

Cream butter and sugar well. Add flavorings. Add eggs, 2 at a time and small amounts of flour alternately, beating well after each addition. Add salt. Bake in stem pan at 350 degrees for about 15 minutes. Reduce oven to 325 degrees and bake 45 minutes or longer until done.

Mrs. Dan K. Moore, Wife of Governor, Raleigh, N. C.

Lemon-Apricot Cake

1 box Lemon Supreme cake mix
1 ¼ c. apricot nectar
½ c. Wesson oil
½ c. sugar
4 eggs
1 c. confectioners' sugar
Juice of 1 lemon

Mix first 4 ingredients together. Add eggs, 1 at a time; beat well. Pour into well-greased 9-inch tube pan. Bake in 325-degree oven for 1 hour. Mix well confectioners' sugar and lemon juice; pour over cake while still warm. Yield: 20 servings.

Mrs. Ellen Hurd, Pikeville, Tenn., Bledsoe County Fair

Dark Fruitcake

1 c. soft shortening
2 c. brown sugar, packed
5 eggs
3 c. sifted flour
1 tsp. baking powder
1 tsp. salt
1 tsp. cinnamon
¼ tsp. cloves
1 c. orange juice
1 lb. mixed candied peel
1 lb. candied cherries
1 lb. candied pineapple
1 lb. bleached seedless raisins
½ lb. candied citron
½ lb. each walnut pieces, almond slivers and pecans
2 c. moist shredded coconut

Cream shortening and sugar thoroughly; add eggs and beat well. Add dry ingredients alternately with liquid. Stir in fruit and nuts. Spoon into six 1 ½-pound cake pans lined with waxed paper. Bake 1 hour and 30 minutes to 1 hour and 45 minutes at 300 degrees. Allow to cool in pans 10 to 15 minutes; turn out on rack and remove waxed paper. When cold, wrap in Saran Wrap and store in a cool place. If desired, the tops of the cakes may be decorated when the cakes are about half done. Yield: 9 pounds.

Personal Comment: I began developing this recipe a number of years ago while living in Nigeria as a missionary. We lived 400 miles from the nearest store so it was necessary to make substitutions and make the candied fruits in my own kitchen.

Lucile Heckman, La Verne, Cal., Los Angeles County Fair

Orange Chiffon Cake

2 ¼ c. sifted cake flour
1 ½ c. sugar
3 tsp. baking powder
1 tsp. salt
½ c. Wesson oil
5 medium egg yolks, unbeaten
Grated rind of 2 oranges
Juice of 2 medium oranges
1 c. egg whites
½ tsp. cream of tartar

Sift together first 4 ingredients into mixing bowl. Make well in center of flour mixture; add oil, egg yolks and orange rind. Add water to orange juice to make ¾ cup liquid; add. Beat with spoon until smooth. Pour egg whites into large mixing bowl with cream of tartar; whip until whites form very stiff peaks. Pour egg yolk mixture gradually over egg whites, folding gently just until blended. Do not stir. Pour into ungreased 10-inch tube pan. Bake at 325 degrees for 65 minutes. Turn pan upside down, placing tube on a funnel, until cooled. Frost with favorite icing or serve plain. Yield: 12-15 servings.

Mrs. Harold Snodgrass, Salmon, Idaho, Lemhi County Fair

Banana Chiffon Cake

2 ¼ c. sifted cake flour
1 ½ c. sugar
3 tsp. baking powder
1 tsp. salt
½ c. cooking oil
5 egg yolks, unbeaten
⅓ c. cold water
1 c. mashed ripe bananas
1 tsp. vanilla
1 c. egg whites
½ tsp. cream of tartar

Sift together first 4 ingredients into mixing bowl. Make a well in center of flour mixture; add oil, egg yolks, water, bananas and vanilla. Beat until smooth. In separate bowl, beat egg whites and cream of tartar until very stiff. Pour egg yolk mixture in thin stream over entire surface of egg whites, gently cutting and folding in. Pour into ungreased 10-inch tube pan. Bake at 325 degrees for 55 minutes; increase heat to 350 degrees and continue baking for 10 to 15 minutes or until cake tests done.

Mrs. Henry Becker, Waukesha, Wis., Wisconsin State Fair

Orange Sponge Cake

6 egg yolks
1 ½ c. sugar
1 c. potato flour
2 tbsp. baking powder or cornstarch
½ tsp. salt
4 tbsp. water
1 tbsp. lemon flavoring
6 egg whites
1 c. orange juice

Beat egg yolks until pale yellow color. Gradually add 1 cup sugar, a little at a time and beat well. Mix and sift dry ingredients; add to yolks. Add water and flavoring. Beat thoroughly. Beat egg whites until stiff, but not dry; fold into cake mixture. Pour batter into ungreased 9-inch tube pan. Bake in preheated 300-degree oven for 1 hour. Do not open oven door. Cool. Remove from pan. Combine orange juice and ½ cup sugar; pour over cake. Yield: 8-10 servings.

Mrs. Donna M. Hayes, Florence, Ala., North Alabama State Fair

Sunshine Sponge Cake

7 egg whites
1 tsp. cream of tartar
½ tsp. salt
Sugar
7 egg yolks
¼ c. cold water
1 tsp. vanilla
1 tsp. lemon extract
1 ¼ c. sifted cake flour
½ tsp. baking powder

Beat egg whites with cream of tartar and salt in large mixing bowl until soft mounds form. Add ½ cup sugar, a tablespoon at a time. Continue beating until very stiff, straight peaks form. In small mixing bowl, combine egg yolks, water and flavorings. Add flour, 1 cup sugar and baking powder to yolk mixture. Beat for 1 minute at medium speed. Fold ¼ the batter at a time into beaten egg whites using wire whisk or spatula. Blend gently but thoroughly after each addition. Pour into ungreased 10-inch tube pan. Bake at 350 degrees for 40 to 50 minutes. Invert pan immediately; cool in pan. Yield: 12-16 servings.
Personal Comment: This recipe has won 9 blue ribbons.

Mrs. Elmer Grindahl, Roseau, Minn., Roseau County Fair

Frostings, Fillings and Toppings

KINDS OF FROSTING

A frosting is a thick sugar-liquid mixture used for cakes. All frostings may be used to cover a cake, but special ones are used for decorating it.

An icing is a mixture of confectioners' sugar and liquid. An icing is thin enough to be brushed on with a pastry brush or thick enough to spread. It is usually used on pastries, rolls, and coffee cakes. An icing is sometimes used on simple cakes.

A glaze is a mixture of sugar and a liquid that is thin enough to be poured. A glaze is about the consistency of thin corn syrup. It is used to coat cupcakes, fruit cakes and pieces of cake which are to be used as petit fours and tea cakes.

A filling is a thick mixture which is used to hold the layers of a cake together. A filling may be a frosting to which fruits, marshmallows or nuts are added. Whipped cream and custard mixtures are sometimes used for fillings.

 Hints For Making Frostings

Some frostings call for brown sugar. To measure brown sugar, pack into a dry measuring cup firmly enough so that it holds the shape of the cup when turned out. Crush the lumps from brown sugar with a rolling pin, then press it through a coarse sieve. Store any left-over brown sugar in a tightly covered container to prevent it from becoming lumpy.

Sift confectioners' sugar by pressing it through a wire strainer onto a piece of waxed paper. Then simply spoon the sifted sugar into a dry measuring cup and level off with a spatula.

If frosting is too thin, add a little confectioners' sugar at a time until the desired consistency is obtained. Variations in the weather, temperature or the size or freshness of eggs can cause variations in the consistency of frosting.

If frosting becomes too thick, add more liquid, just a drop at a time, until the desired consistency is reached.

Place a small amount of frosting in a cup if you plan to tint it. Add enough pure food coloring to give it a rather bright color. Blend this frosting into the rest of the mixture, a little at a time, until you get the desired color. Tint frosting delicately . . . too much color may give it a cheap, unappetizing appearance.

To keep frosting from crusting over, keep the bowl of frosting covered with a damp cloth when not in use.

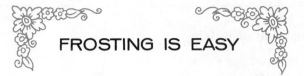

FROSTING IS EASY

It's easy to frost a cake. All you need are a few basic pieces of equipment. To make the task easier, you need a flexible spatula (8 inches long), waxed paper, scissors, wooden toothpicks and a sharp knife.

Cool Cake And Frosting

Allow the cake and frosting to cool. If both are not cool, the cake will be soggy. Frosting the cake as soon as it is cool will help keep the cake fresh and moist. For easier application, frost cake in a cool room.

Prepare The Cake For Frosting

Carefully brush away any loose crumbs and trim ragged edges of cake with scissors. Place strips of waxed paper under the edges of the cake to catch drippings. As soon as the cake is frosted, remove these strips of paper.

Frosting Single Layer Cakes

Place one-layer cakes or sheet cakes right side up on the cake platter. Frost the sides of the cake and finish with the top. Frostings spread more easily on top side of the cake than on bottom.

Frosting Two-And Three-Layer Cakes

Place first layer upside down on the cake plate. Spread with filling or frosting and let set. Top with second layer, right side up. If a two-layer cake, frost sides and finish with top. If cake is to have three layers, place third layer right side up on top of second layer. Frost sides and top.

Frosting Cakes Baked In Tube Pans

Turn cake upside down on plate. The cake may be cut into layers and filled. Use a thin sharp knife to cut. Place toothpicks in the sides of cake as a guide when cutting. Spread inside of hole with frosting.

Frosting Side And Top

Apply frosting to sides of cake by spreading with a spatula. Hold spatula in a vertical position. As you go around the cake, pull up toward the top to keep frosting on the sides. Top cake with plenty of frosting. The frosting should be smooth if cake is to be decorated. If not, make swirls and ridges in frosting.

Easy Caramel Icing

3 c. brown sugar
1 c. water
1 tbsp. butter
1 tsp. vanilla
Cream

Boil sugar and water until syrup spins a thread, 230 degrees. Add butter and vanilla and remove from heat. When cold beat until thick and creamy; thin with cream until consistency to spread.

Mrs. Elmo Farrar, Ashville, N. Y.

Never-Fail Caramel Icing

3 tbsp. butter
6 tbsp. brown sugar
6 tbsp. white sugar
½ c. sweet cream
9 lge. marshmallows
1 ½ tsp. vanilla
1 ½ c. powdered sugar

Mix butter, brown and white sugars and cream. Bring to a boil and cook rapidly for 2 minutes. Remove from heat and add marshmallows. When marshmallows have melted, add vanilla and powdered sugar. Stir until thick enough to spread over layers.

Ina Kimbal, Topeka, Kan.

Chocolate Filling For Angel Food Cake

⅓ c. flour
⅓ c. sugar
2 c. milk
1 c. butter
1 c. confectioners' sugar
2 tbsp. cocoa
1 ½ tsp. vanilla
1 angel food cake

Place flour, sugar and milk in double boiler; cook over boiling water until thick. Cool. Cream butter, confectioners' sugar, cocoa and vanilla in mixer; add cooled milk mixture. Beat thoroughly. Cut cake in 3 horizontal layers; spread filling between layers. Yield: 16 servings.

Mary T. Drazer, Home Economics Teacher, Kouts, Ind.

Chocolate Frosting

1 ½ c. sugar
2 tbsp. cocoa
3 tbsp. syrup
½ c. sweet cream
Pinch of salt
1 tsp. vanilla

Mix in saucepan all ingredients except vanilla. Cook until forms a soft ball in water. Remove from heat; add vanilla. Cool and beat.

Helen Londagin, Gentry, Ark.

 ## Chocolate Glaze Frosting

¼ c. cocoa
3 tbsp. water
2 tbsp. shortening
2 tbsp. light corn syrup
2 c. confectioners' sugar
¼ tsp. vanilla

Combine cocoa, water, shortening and corn syrup in medium saucepan. Stir over low heat until shortening melts and mixture is smooth. Remove from heat; beat in sugar and vanilla. Pour over top of cake allowing to run over sides. If mixture is too thick to pour easily, blend in 1 additional tablespoon water.

Mrs. Lora Hash, Filer, Idaho

 ## Laplander Frosting

1 egg
1 c. sugar
2 squares semisweet chocolate, chopped fine
2 tbsp. butter
2 tbsp. milk
½ tsp. vanilla

In saucepan, beat egg with fork; add sugar, chocolate, butter, milk and vanilla. Mix well. Cook over low heat until mixture comes to a gentle bubbling action. Stir constantly until of spreading consistency. Spread frosting over layer cake. Yield: 1 layer cake.

Alice Lasher, Hyde Park, N. Y., Dutchess County Fair

Fudge Frosting

¾ c. sugar
¼ c. cocoa
2 tbsp. cornstarch
1 c. milk
1 tbsp. butter
1 tsp. vanilla

Mix sugar, cocoa, cornstarch and milk. Cook until thick. Add butter and vanilla.

Mrs. William B. Farrar, Beaver Crossing, Neb.

 ### Minute Fudge Frosting

2 c. sugar
⅛ c. light corn syrup
½ c. milk
7 tbsp. margarine
2 sq. chocolate
¼ tsp. salt
1 tsp. vanilla

Mix all ingredients except vanilla in saucepan. Stir over low heat until chocolate and margarine melt. Bring to full boil, stirring constantly. Boil 1 minute at 225 degrees. Remove from heat and beat until lukewarm. Add vanilla. Beat until a smooth spreading consistency is reached.

Mrs. Dudley Tapp, Springfield, Ky., Washington County Fair

 ### Creamy Coconut Frosting

1 c. evaporated milk
1 c. sugar
3 egg yolks, slightly beaten
½ c. butter or margarine
1 tsp. vanilla
1 ½ c. coconut
1 c. chopped pecans

Combine milk, sugar, egg yolks, butter and vanilla in saucepan. Cook over medium heat, stirring constantly, about 12 minutes or until mixture thickens. Remove from heat. Add coconut and pecans. Beat until cold and of spreading consistency. Yield: 2½ cups.

Rita Bartel, Mason City, Iowa, North Iowa Fair

Coffee Divinity Frosting

    1 c. dark brown sugar
    ⅓ c. coffee or water
    2 tbsp. powdered coffee
    ⅓ tsp. cream of tartar
    2 egg whites
    1 ½ tsp. vanilla

Boil first 4 ingredients slowly until syrup spins a 2 or 3-inch thread or until thermometer reads 242 degrees. Keep saucepan covered first 3 minutes to prevent crystals from forming on sides of pan. While syrup is cooking, beat egg whites. Pour hot syrup very slowly in a thin stream into egg whites, beating constantly. Add vanilla. Beat until frosting holds its shape. Spread between layers and on top and sides of cake.

Sister Mary Clare, O.S.B., Evansville, Ind.

 ## Custard Cream Filling

    ½ c. sugar
    Dash of salt
    4 tbsp. cake flour
    1 ½ c. milk
    2 egg yolks, slightly beaten
    1 tsp. vanilla

Combine sugar, salt and flour in double boiler. Add milk and egg yolks. Cook 10 minutes or until thick. Stir in vanilla.

Mrs. Bertha L. Platt, Waterbury, Conn.

Date Cream Filling

    1 c. milk
    ½ c. chopped dates
    1 tbsp. flour
    ¼ c. sugar
    1 egg, beaten
    ½ c. chopped nuts
    1 tsp. vanilla

Combine milk and dates in top of double boiler. Combine flour and sugar and add beaten egg, blending until smooth. Add to hot milk; cook, stirring, until thick. When cool, stir in nuts and vanilla. Spread between layers of cake.

Edna Parsons, Johnstown, Ohio

Date Filling

1 ½ tbsp. cornstarch
½ c. corn syrup
¼ tsp. salt
⅓ c. warm water
1 tbsp. Spry
2 tsp. lemon juice
2 tsp. grated lemon rind
½ c. chopped dates
¼ c. chopped cherries

Mix cornstarch, corn syrup, salt and warm water together. Add Spry and lemon juice; cook in a saucepan over medium heat for 3 to 5 minutes, stirring constantly. Add lemon rind, chopped dates and chopped cherries. Remove from heat and stir until well blended and slightly cooled. Spread between two 8-inch layers and frost top with same, if desired. Stays moist for a long time. Yield: Frosting and filling for 1 layer cake.

Mrs. Elizabeth Russell, Skowhegan, Maine

Dabbling Frosting

1 lb. box powdered sugar
2 c. Crisco or butter
3 egg whites
1 c. granulated sugar
1 tsp. vanilla

Sift powdered sugar in large mixing bowl. Add shortening; set aside. Place egg whites and granulated sugar in top of double boiler over boiling water. Beat until the mixture holds a peak and is thick. Add to powdered sugar mixture with vanilla. Beat on high speed until light and creamy. Yield: 2 small or 1 large cake.

Sara E. Peabody, Placerville, Cal., El Dorado County Fair

Fig and Pear Cake Filling

7 lb. peeled and cored pears
1 lb. figs
4 lb. sugar

Grind the pears and figs through a food chopper. Add sugar and cook over low heat until thick. Stir frequently while cooking to prevent sticking and scorching. Put in sterilized jars while hot and seal with paraffin. This filling is good between layers of white cake.

Mrs. Arnold Rock, Worcester, N. Y.

Frosting For Angel Food Cake

2 lge. or 3 sm. eggs, separated
½ c. milk
½ c. sugar
1 pkg. strawberry Jell-O
1 c. cream, whipped

In double boiler beat egg yolks slightly and add milk and sugar; when hot add Jell-O and cook until thick. Remove from heat; cool. Add beaten egg whites. When mixture begins to set, fold in whipped cream. Slice cooled angel food cake into 3 layers; fill and frost.

Mrs. Francis Waggener, Halsey, Ore.

Lemon Filling

Juice and grated rind of 1 lemon
1 apple, grated
1 c. sugar
1 egg

Combine the juice and rind of lemon and apple with sugar and egg. Beat and cook until it thickens. Cool and spread between cake layers.

Mrs. Elsie Hadsell, Angelica, N. Y.

Lemon Jelly Filling

1 c. sugar
1 tbsp. butter
2 eggs
Juice and rind of 2 lemons

Combine all ingredients; boil until thick. Spread over and between cake layers.

Mrs. Margaret Thornton, Home Economics Teacher, Crystal City, Tex.

Lemon Butter

Juice of 6 lemons
Grated rind of 4 lemons
2 lb. sugar
¼ lb. butter
6 eggs, slightly beaten

(Continued on next page)

Pour lemon juice and grated rind over sugar. Add butter and eggs. Stir mixture over low heat until it thickens. Cook until sugar is dissolved and mixture begins to bubble.

Personal Comment: This recipe came from England and has been in my family for several generations.

Mrs. Andrew Ellis, St. Petersburg, Fla., Pinellas County Fair

Maple Frosting

½ c. white sugar
½ c. maple sugar
½ c. heavy coffee cream
1 c. broken walnuts

Dissolve sugars in cream before mixture begins to boil; boil until mixture forms a soft ball in cold water. Beat until cool; add walnuts just before spreading on cake. Yield: Frosting for 2 layers or medium square cake.

Ruth M. Palmer, Shelburne, Vt.

Marshmallow Frosting

¼ c. sugar
3 tsp. water
1 egg white
¼ tsp. cream of tartar
6 lge. marshmallows, cut up
½ tsp. vanilla flavoring

Place sugar, water, egg white and cream of tartar in double boiler. Cook, beating constantly, until it peaks. Remove from heat; add marshmallows and vanilla. Stir until cool enough to hold shape.

Gladys Martin, Alma, Kan.

Nut Cake Filling

1 c. sugar
1 c. rich milk
4 egg yolks, well beaten
1 tbsp. cornstarch
⅛ tsp. salt
1 c. rolled nuts
½ tsp. vanilla

Combine sugar and milk; heat just to boiling point. Add egg yolks, cornstarch, salt, nuts and vanilla; cook until thick. Cool and frost medium 2-layer cake.

Mrs. Sue Smith, Elkton, Ore.

 ## Orange Filling

½ c. sifted flour
1 c. sugar
¼ tsp. salt
¼ c. water
1 ¼ c. orange juice
¼ c. lemon juice
Rind of 1 lemon and 1 orange
3 egg yolks
1 c. coconut (opt.)

Mix flour, sugar and salt together. Add water and mix. Add orange juice, lemon juice and rind of orange and lemon. Cook on low heat until thick and mixture becomes translucent. Beat egg yolks. Add some hot mixture to yolks; add to mixture in saucepan, stirring constantly. Return to heat and cook slowly until thick. Add 1 cup coconut if desired. Yield: Filling for 3-layer cake.

Jo Nell Hollingsworth, Home Economics Teacher, Glen Allen, Ala.

Penuche Frosting

1 c. packed, light brown sugar
¼ c. milk
¼ c. vegetable shortening
¼ tsp. salt
½ tsp. vanilla
½ c. chopped pecans

(Continued on next page)

Bring sugar, milk, shortening and salt to a boil; let boil 1 minute and 30 seconds, then beat occasionally until lukewarm. Add vanilla and nuts and continue beating until of spreading consistency.

Mrs. Charles H. Swinehart, Jr., Ontonagon, Mich.

 ## Peppermint Seven-Minute Icing

> ¼ lb. peppermint stick candy
> 6 tbsp. water
> 1 ¼ c. sugar
> ¼ tsp. salt
> ¼ tsp. cream of tartar
> 2 egg whites, unbeaten

Crush candy; add water. Let stand until candy dissolves. Put remaining ingredients in top of double boiler. Add dissolved candy; stir well. Beat with rotary beater over hot water about 7 minutes or until mixture stands in peaks. Spread on cooled cake or cup cakes.

Mrs. Rosa Lee Muehr, League City, Tex.

 ## Seven-Minute Frosting

> 2 egg whites, unbeaten
> 1 ½ c. sugar
> 5 tbsp. water
> 1 ½ tsp. light corn syrup
> 1 tsp. vanilla

Combine egg whites, sugar, water and syrup in top of double boiler; beat with rotary beater or mixer until thoroughly mixed. Place over rapidly boiling water; cook, beating constantly, for 7 minutes or until frosting will stand in peaks. Remove from heat; add vanilla and beat until thick enough to spread. Spread on tops and sides of two 9-inch layers.

Mrs. Malio Liotti, Canton, Ohio

 ## Society Filling

> 5 egg yolks, unbeaten
> 1 c. coconut
> ½ c. butter or margarine
> ½ c. sweet milk

(Continued on next page)

1 c. chopped dates
1 c. chopped pecans
2 c. sugar

Mix all ingredients together and cook on low heat until thick enough to spread. Spread between and on top of white or angel food cake layers.

Mrs. Eugene Albright, Clarksville, Tenn.

Sour Cream Icing

1 c. sugar
1 c. sour cream
1 tbsp. flour
1 egg
1 tsp. vanilla
1 c. nuts

Mix first 4 ingredients and boil until thick; add vanilla and nuts. Spread on cake while still hot.

Mrs. Richard C. Engler, Ignacio, Colo.

Butter-Coconut Icing

3 tbsp. butter
1 tsp. vanilla
1 lb. confectioners' sugar
½ c. coconut flakes
Nuts (opt.)
Milk

Melt butter in saucepan over low heat until lightly browned. Remove from heat; add vanilla, confectioners' sugar, coconut, nuts and enough milk to obtain desired spreading consistency. Beat well and spread over favorite cake. Yield: Frosting for large loaf or layer cake.

Mrs. Dorothy Faust, Richland, Kan.

Butter Cream Frosting

4 tbsp. butter
2 c. powdered sugar
1 tsp. vanilla
½ tsp. almond extract
3 tbsp. cream

(Continued on next page)

Cream butter until soft; gradually add 1 cup powdered sugar. Beat in flavorings; after 1 cup sugar has been thoroughly worked in, begin to add cream with remaining sugar, a little at a time until of spreading consistency. For a milk chocolate frosting, add a few grains of salt and 2 tablespoons dried cocoa. Spread frosting over cake. Yield: Frosting for 1 cake.

Linda Dee Watson, Tallahassee, Fla., North Florida Fair

 ### Butter Frosting

> 1 lb. confectioners' sugar
> ¼ lb. butter or soft margarine
> ⅛ tsp. salt
> 1 tsp. vanilla extract
> 3 to 4 tbsp. milk

Cream 1/3 sugar with butter and salt. Blend extract, 2 tablespoons milk and remaining sugar into mixture. Gradually stir remaining milk into frosting until of desired spreading consistency. Spread over cake. To make frosting for 9-inch cake, increase ingredients by ¼. Yield: Frosting for two 8-inch layer cakes.

Mrs. Barbara Megna, Franklin, Wis., Wisconsin State Fair

 ### Brown Beauty Icing

> 1 c. confectioners' sugar, sifted
> ¼ tsp. salt
> 1 egg, small
> 3 tbsp. milk
> 3 tbsp. soft shortening
> 2 squares unsweetened chocolate, melted
> ¾ tsp. vanilla

Combine ingredients in medium bowl; place bowl in ice water. Beat with beater 3 to 5 minutes or until of spreading consistency. Yield: Frosting for one 2-layer cake or 13 x 9-inch cake.

Lynette Michaud, Old Town, Maine

 ### Chocolate-Cream Cheese Frosting

> 2 pkg. German's sweet chocolate
> 2 pkg. cream cheese
> 2 tbsp. light cream

(Continued on next page)

2 c. confectioners' sugar, sifted
¼ tsp. salt
1 tsp. vanilla

Place chocolate in small bowl and set over hot water until melted. Cool slightly. Add cream cheese and cream; blend. Add sugar gradually, mixing well. Add salt and vanilla. Yield: Frosting for two 8 or 9-inch layers or 30 cupcakes.

Margaret Domenico, Egg Harbor City, N. J.

 ### Chocolate-Rum Icing

4 squares chocolate
3 tbsp. butter
1 lb. powdered sugar
Dash of salt
4 tbsp. milk
3 tbsp. rum

Melt chocolate and butter together; add sugar and salt. Stir to blend; stir in milk and rum, a tablespoonful at a time, until creamy and smooth. Add more rum or milk if needed. Let stand 1 minute, then spread on cake.

Mrs. Marion Popham, Home Economics Teacher, Charleston, Ill.

 ### Mocha Frosting

6 tbsp. cocoa
6 tbsp. hot coffee
6 tbsp. butter or margarine
1 tsp. vanilla

3 c. sifted confectioners' sugar

Combine cocoa and coffee; add butter and vanilla. Beat until smooth; add sugar gradually, until of spreading consistency. Yield: Frosting for tops and sides of two 9-inch layers.

Mrs. Warren Smith, Powell, Wyo.

 ### Spicy Chocolate Frosting

1 1-lb. box confectioners' sugar
½ c. shortening
¼ c. plus 1 tbsp. milk

(Continued on next page)

  1 1-oz. envelope unsweetened chocolate
 ½ c. peanut butter
  1 tsp. cinnamon
  1 tsp. nutmeg
 ½ tsp. cloves
  3 tbsp. honey

Cream confectioners' sugar with shortening until mixed. Add milk and chocolate. Beat with electric mixer until fluffy. Add peanut butter, cinnamon, nutmeg, cloves and honey. Beat 2 to 3 minutes until fluffy and mixed well. Yield: Frosting for one 2-layer cake.

Mrs. Darro F. Fails, Home Economics Teacher, Millsap, Tex.

Sweet Chocolate Frosting

  2 6-oz. pkg. semisweet chocolate bits
 ½ c. butter
  1 c. confectioners' sugar
  2 eggs
  2 tsp. vanilla
 ½ c. chopped pecans

Melt chocolate bits in top of double boiler; cool. Cream butter and sugar together; add eggs and beat well. Combine vanilla and chocolate mixture; beat until thick and smooth. Add ¼ cup pecans. Frost cake and garnish with remaining pecans. Yield: Frosting for two 8-inch layers or loaf cakes.

Mrs. Viola Joslin, Oakfield, N. Y.

Cream Cheese Frosting

  1 stick margarine
  1 box confectioners' sugar
  1 8-oz. pkg. cream cheese
  2 tsp. vanilla
  1 c. chopped nuts

Mix first 4 ingredients and beat well. Add nuts; spread on cake.

Mrs. Alice Nason, Farmington, N. H.

Decorator's Frosting

  4 c. powdered sugar
 ¼ c. egg whites

(Continued on next page)

1 tsp. vanilla
⅛ tsp. salt
1 tbsp. water
⅓ c. Crisco

Combine all ingredients in mixer bowl. Blend at low speed, then beat at high speed until smooth and fluffy, about 5 minutes. If too stiff, beat in a few drops of water. Spread over cake. Yield: frosting for two 8 or 9-inch layers.

Mrs. Robert L. Peterson, Albert Lea, Minn., Freeborn County Fair

Lemon Fluff Frosting

½ c. margarine
Dash of salt
4 c. confectioners' sugar
3 tbsp. lemon juice
2 tsp. grated lemon rind

Cream margarine; add salt and part of sugar. Cream well. Add remaining sugar alternately with lemon juice. Cream until light and fluffy. Add lemon rind and mix until thoroughly blended.

Daisie W. Pollock, Gaithersburg, Md., Montgomery County Fair

Pineapple Cream Frosting

½ c. oleo or butter
1 lb. confectioners' sugar
1 8-oz. pkg. cream cheese
1 tsp. vanilla
3 to 4 tbsp. drained crushed pineapple

Combine all ingredients except pineapple. Beat until fluffy with portable beater. Fold in pineapple and spread on cake.

Mabel Jump, Pittsburg, Kan.

Basic Dessert Sauce

⅓ c. sugar
⅛ tsp. salt
1 tsp. cornstarch
2 tbsp. butter or oleo
1 c. water

(Continued on next page)

1 ½ tsp. vanilla extract
½ tsp. cinnamon (opt.)
¼ tsp. nutmeg (opt.)

Mix sugar, salt and cornstarch in saucepan; add butter and water. Cook, stirring until slightly thickened; add vanilla and spices. Serve warm on apple dumplings, gingerbread, plain cakes or fruit cobblers. For variety omit spices and add 2 tablespoons lemon juice and grated rind of ½ lemon. Will keep well for a week if kept tightly closed in jar in refrigerator. Yield: 1 cup.

Ann Flickinger, North Lima, Ohio

 ## Butterscotch Topping

1 ½ c. brown sugar, firmly packed
⅔ c. white corn syrup
¼ c. butter
¾ c. evaporated milk

Combine brown sugar, corn syrup and butter in heavy saucepan. Place over medium heat; stir until butter melts and ingredients are well mixed. Bring to a boil; cook to soft-ball stage, 325 degrees. Remove from heat. When partially cooled, add evaporated milk slowly, stirring until well blended. Store in refrigerator. This will keep indefinitely and makes a delicious topping for ice cream.

Ruth Schwendemann, Lehigh, Iowa

 ## Caramel-Cream Sauce For Ice Cream

1 egg
1 c. whipping cream
2 c. light brown sugar
2 tbsp. butter

Beat egg slightly; put in top of double boiler. Add remaining ingredients; cook until thick. Pour into dish; cover and refrigerate. Yield: 10-12 servings.

Mrs. T. O. Van DeGrift, Nampa, Idaho

 ## Chocolate Sauce

1 6-oz. pkg. chocolate bits
1 c. sugar
1 c. Milnot
1 stick butter or margarine

(Continued on next page)

Mix all ingredients well in a saucepan. Heat, stirring often, until sugar is dissolved and bits are melted. Pour into a jar; cover and store in refrigerator until ready to use. Yield: 1 ½ pints.

Mrs. Laura T. Russell, Home Economics Teacher, Freelandville, Ind.

 ## Versatile Custard Sauce

> 1 c. instant nonfat dry milk
> ¼ tsp. salt
> ¼ c. sugar
> 1 tsp. cornstarch
> ½ c. cold water
> 1 egg
> 2 egg yolks
> 1 ½ c. hot water
> 1 tsp. vanilla

In a heavy saucepan mix dry milk, salt, sugar and cornstarch. Add cold water, egg and egg yolks and beat until smooth. Gradually pour in hot water. Place in heavy saucepan over low heat and cook while stirring until smooth and mixture coats spoon. Remove from heat; stir in vanilla. Chill.

Photograph for this recipe below.

Custard Sauce

1 c. milk
1 c. medium cream
3 tsp. cornstarch
3 egg yolks
¾ c. sugar
½ tsp. vanilla

Heat milk and cream in double boiler. Wet cornstarch in a little milk; add egg yolks and sugar, beaten together. Cook until mixture coats a spoon; remove from heat. Add vanilla; cook. Serve over pudding. Yield: 10 servings.

Mrs. M. E. Hartley, Falls Church, Va.

Hard Sauce

1 stick butter
1 ½ c. confectioners' sugar
1 tsp. brandy, 2 tsp. sherry or 1 tsp. vanilla
Sprinkle of nutmeg

Cream butter thoroughly; beat in confectioners' sugar gradually. Add brandy, drop by drop. Place in serving dish; sprinkle with nutmeg. Refrigerate at least 1 hour. Will keep 1 week or may be frozen. Yield: 18-24 servings.

Mrs. Alice Hastings, Atlanta, Ga.

Key Lime Fruit Sauce

1 pkg. key lime flavor pie filling
½ c. sugar
2 ½ cups cold water
3 ½ c. pineapple chunks
2 tbsp. margarine
Fresh or well-drained canned fruits, cut up

Empty pie filling into saucepan. Mix in sugar. Gradually add water, stirring to keep smooth. Cook over medium high heat, stirring constantly, until mixture comes to a full boil. Remove from heat. Drain pineapple chunks, reserving 1 cup liquid. Add reserved liquid and margarine to lime mixture. Chill thoroughly. Prepare fruit cup from pineapple chunks and other fresh or well-drained canned fruits. Serve with sauce. Yield: 1 quart.

Photograph for this recipe on page 51.

Lemon Sauce

½ c. sugar
1 tbsp. cornstarch
1 c. boiling water
2 tbsp. butter
2 tbsp. lemon juice
Pinch of salt
Nutmeg to taste (opt.)

Mix sugar and cornstarch in heavy saucepan. Gradually add boiling water, stirring constantly. Boil 5 minutes. Remove from heat. Add butter, lemon juice, salt and nutmeg. Serve warm. This is especially good served over hot gingerbread or hot spice cake. Yield: 4-6 servings.

Mrs. G. K. Robinson, Jr., Colts Neck, N. J.

 ## Velvet Hot Fudge Topping

2 squares chocolate
16 marshmallows
½ c. water
½ c. sugar
¼ tsp. salt
½ tsp. vanilla

Melt chocolate, marshmallows and water together in saucepan over low heat. Stir in sugar, salt and vanilla. Cool slightly. Serve over ice cream. Yield: 6 servings.

Mrs. Nellie Boyles, Tenants Harbor, Maine

 ## Never-Fail Meringue

½ c. sugar
1 tbsp. cornstarch
½ c. water
3 egg whites
⅛ tsp. salt
½ tsp. vanilla extract

Combine 2 tablespoons sugar and cornstarch in small saucepan. Add water. Cook over medium heat, stirring constantly, until soft mounds form. Add 6 tablespoons sugar gradually to egg whites, beating well after each addition. Add cornstarch mixture, salt and vanilla. Continue beating until meringue stands in stiff peaks. Cover pie with meringue; brown in oven. Yield: 6 servings.

Janice Lynn Hopkins, Lancaster, Cal., Antelope Valley Fair

Meringue

    3 egg whites
    6 tbsp. sugar

Beat egg whites until stiff; add sugar, 2 tablespoons at a time. Place meringue over pie filling; bake meringue until brown in 350-degree oven. Yield: 6-8 servings.

Homoiselle House, Home Economics Teacher, Hempstead, Tex.

 ### Orange Sauce

    6 egg yolks
    1 c. sugar
    1 c. orange juice
    1 tbsp. grated orange rind
    1 pt. whipping cream
    1 c. pecans

Combine egg yolks, sugar, juice and rind in upper part of double boiler. Place over hot water and cook until thickened; stir occasionally. Set aside to cool. Whip cream; add cooled mixture. Fold in nuts. Serve on angel food cake. Yield: 6 servings.

Mrs. Verna Wright, Home Economics Teacher, Russellville, Ark.

 ### Mocha Sauce

    ¼ tsp. salt
    1 c. hot coffee
    1 6-oz. pkg. semisweet chocolate chips

Blend all ingredients until thick and smooth. Serve over cake or ice cream.

Mrs. Leo Depuydt, Whitewater, Mont.

 ### Praline Crunch Topping

    ½ c. butter
    1 c. brown sugar
    ½ c. broken pecans
    2 ½ c. cornflakes

Boil butter and sugar for 2 minutes. Remove from heat. Add pecans and cornflakes; toss with fork to coat. Spread on foil to cool. Break up and store in a jar. Serve over vanilla ice cream. Yield: 10 servings.

Mrs. John G. Long, Honolulu, Hawaii

Fudge Sauce

  4 *squares unsweetened chocolate*
  1 *can evaporated milk*
  1 *box confectioners' sugar*
  ½ *tsp. salt*
  2 *tsp. vanilla*
  2 *tbsp. butter*

Combine first 4 ingredients in top of double boiler. Cook over medium heat until well blended. Remove from heat; add vanilla and butter. Beat with rotary or electric beater until smooth. This will keep for a month or more in tightly covered container in refrigerator. Yield: 25 servings.

Mrs. Anne Seger, Collinsville, Conn.

 ### Macaroon-Ice Cream Topping

  ½ *lb. marshmallows*
  ½ *c. bourbon*
  24 *almond macaroons*
  1 *pt. heavy cream, whipped*
  Vanilla ice cream

Cut marshmallows into quarters; soak in bourbon until dissolved. Crush macaroons; fold into whipped cream. Add marshmallow mixture. Chill before serving over vanilla ice cream. Yield: 8-10 servings.

Mrs. Ralph D. Peters, Fort Leavenworth, Kans.

 ### Spicy Chestnut Fruit Sauce

  1 *tbsp. butter*
  1 *5-oz. can water chestnuts, cut in half*
  1 *No. 2 can pineapple juice*
  1 *can condensed tangerine or orange juice*
  2 *sticks cinnamon*
  ½ *c. sugar*
  ¼ *c. cornstarch*
  ½ *tsp. ginger*
  2 *tbsp. lemon juice*
  2 *tsp. grated lemon rind*

(Continued on next page)

Heat butter in skillet; add chestnuts and brown. Set aside. In large saucepan mix pineapple juice, tangerine juice, cinnamon and ¼ cup water; bring to boil. Combine sugar, cornstarch and ginger; add small amount of hot juice to cornstarch mixture. Stir until smooth; return to juice in saucepan. Cook, stirring constantly, until thick; add lemon juice and rind. Cool and chill. Remove cinnamon sticks; add chestnuts and serve over canned or fresh melon balls, grapes or strawberries.

Mrs. E. V. Haines, Springfield, Mo.

Magic Chocolate Topping

1 ⅓ c. sweetened condensed milk
2 oz. unsweetened chocolate
⅛ tsp. salt
½ to 1 c. hot water
½ tsp. vanilla

Place milk, chocolate and salt in saucepan. Cook over low heat, stirring constantly, until thick about 5 minutes. Remove from heat. Slowly stir in water, amount depending upon consistency desired. The topping thickens upon cooling but may be thinned, if desired, by adding more hot water. Stir in vanilla. Serve hot or cold on cake, ice cream or pudding.

Mrs. Mildred L. Clark, Home Economics Teacher, Fillmore, Cal.

Pineapple Topping

1 No. 1 can crushed pineapple
1 pkg. vanilla pudding, not instant
½ pt. heavy cream
½ c. chopped nuts
12 maraschino cherries, cut in quarters

Combine crushed pineapple with vanilla pudding and cook over medium heat until pudding comes to a boil. Remove from heat and cool. Whip cream until stiff; fold into pudding mixture and add nuts and cherries. This is delicious served on wedges of angel or chiffon cake. Can be made in advance and kept under refrigeration. Yield: 10-12 servings.

Mrs. Christina Cutter, Arlington, Mass.

Candy

EQUIPMENT

Always use standard measuring spoons and cups. A cooking pan four times the volume of the ingredients or a 3-quart capacity for each 1½ pounds of candy is necessary. This lets the candy boil up without overflowing the pan.

MEASURING

Always measure carefully. Sift granulated sugar into a standard dry measuring cup and level off with a spatula. Sift confectioners' sugar and dip into cup with a spoon; level off. Pack brown sugar firmly into a cup and level off.

MAKE ACCURATE TESTS

The temperature at which candy is considered done is known as the "finish point."

1. Cold Water Test—This test is fairly accurate for experienced candy makers, but is best used in combination with the candy thermometer. Fill a cup with cold water and drop about ½ teaspoon of the boiling candy syrup into the water. Form into a ball with your fingers, keeping the candy under the water. Pick up the ball to judge its consistency as to the stage of cooking.

2. Candy Thermometer—The candy thermometer gives the most accurate results. Under normal conditions water boils at 212° F. The altitude and atmospheric pressure affects candy making. Use the chart on the next page as a guide to success in making candy.

CRYSTAL CONTROL

The proper control of the crystals affects the quality of candy. There should be small crystals in fondants and fudges and none in caramels.

For fondants, mix ingredients thoroughly. Cover and bring slowly to a boil, stirring as needed. Remove the cover and increase the heat to cook more rapidly to the finish point. For fondant, wipe the crystals from the edges of the pan. Place pan of candy in cold water or pour into pans to cool

CANDY

quickly. Let cool to room temperature before stirring. When the bottom of the pan can be held comfortably in the hand, stir vigorously until creamy.

Fudge may be poured into a buttered pan to harden, or like fondant, poured onto a buttered surface and kneaded. It may be kneaded immediately or covered with a damp cloth and left for 20 minutes.

Candy is kneaded to make it creamier; however, it must not be overkneaded. Press the candy into a buttered pan or dish; cover with waxed paper and let stand until firm.

Avoid tough, hard or chewy caramels by increasing the amount of fat in cream or butter and by not overcooking. Crystallization may be controlled by increasing the amount of corn syrup and by stirring the cooking mixture only enough to thoroughly mix the ingredients.

TEMPERATURE TEST FOR CANDY MAKING AT VARIOUS ALTITUDES

| Candy | Test in cold water | Degrees F. on Candy Thermometer | | | |
		SEA LEVEL	2,000 ft.	5,000 ft.	7,500 ft.
FUDGE, FONDANT	SOFT BALL (can be picked up but flattens)	234-240	230-236	224-230	219-225
CARAMELS	FIRM BALL (holds shape unless pressed)	242-248	238-244	232-238	227-233
DIVINITY, TAFFY, CARAMEL CORN	HARD BALL (holds shape though pliable)	250-268	246-264	240-258	235-253
BUTTERSCOTCH, ENGLISH TOFFEE	SOFT CRACK (separates into hard threads but brittle)	270-290	266-286	260-280	255-275
BRITTLES	HARD CRACK (separates into hard, brittle threads)	300-310	296-306	290-300	285-295

Apricot Fingers

12 to 16 oz. dried apricots
1 medium seedless orange
1 ½ to 2 c. sugar

Grind apricots and orange, including peeling. Mix with sugar in top part of double boiler. Cook over hot water until sugar is dissolved and mixture is no longer grainy, about 8 minutes. Cool. Drop by spoonfuls into additional granulated sugar and form into desired shapes. Top with pecan half, if desired. May be stored in a covered container in the refrigerator for several days.

Mrs. Maurine M. Perkins, Home Economics Teacher, Lake Arthur, La.

Black Walnut Creme Delight

¼ c. oleomargarine
1 c. brown sugar
¾ c. sour cream
1 c. white sugar
1 tsp. vanilla
½ c. finely chopped black walnuts

Melt oleomargarine in heavy 2-quart saucepan. Add brown sugar and heat until sugar has melted and begun to brown, stirring constantly. Add sour cream and white sugar. Stir until sugar is melted. Continue to cook slowly, without stirring, until candy reaches soft-ball stage or 236 degrees. Remove from heat and cool without stirring to 110 degrees or until you can hold hand on bottom of pan. Beat until mixture holds its shape. Add vanilla and black walnuts. Spread in greased 8-inch square pan. Cut into squares when cool. Yield: 1 ½ pounds.

Lillian Cunningham, Mahone, W. Va., Ritchie County Fair

Butterscotch Bonbons

1 6-oz. pkg. butterscotch chips
½ c. peanut butter
1 ½ c. cornflakes
1 c. miniature marshmallows
½ c. chopped candied fruit, raisins or unsalted nuts

Melt butterscotch chips and peanut butter over hot water. Add remaining ingredients; mix until well coated. Chill until set. Drop by teaspoonfuls on cookie sheets lined with waxed paper or use bonbon papers.

Mrs. Joe Ann Killebrew, Durant, Miss.

Butterscotch Tam 'O' Shanters

> 2 c. granulated sugar
> 1 c. light brown sugar, firmly packed
> ½ c. water
> ¼ c. light corn syrup
> 1 tsp. vinegar
> ½ tsp. salt
> 1 6-oz. pkg. butterscotch flavored morsels
> 1 c. coarsely chopped walnuts
> ¼ c. hot water

Combine sugars, water, corn syrup, vinegar and salt in a 2-quart saucepan and cook about 15 minutes over moderate heat, stirring up from bottom constantly to completely dissolve sugar. Boil over high heat 3 minutes; do not stir. Remove from heat. Add butterscotch morsels and beat by hand approximately 3 minutes. Let stand for 15 minutes or until lukewarm. Add walnuts and water; stir to blend. Drop by tablespoons on waxed paper-lined cookie sheet. Decorate with walnut halves. Chill until firm. Yield: Approximately 3 dozen.

Photograph for this recipe on page 75.

Easy Almond Brittle

> 1 c. almonds
> ½ c. sugar
> 2 tbsp. butter

Mix all ingredients; cook over medium heat, stirring until color changes, 10 to 12 minutes. Spread on foil. Salt lightly; break in pieces.

Mrs. O. S. Dews, Pres., Officers' Wives' Club, Defense Depot, Ogden, Utah

 ## Smooth Peanut Brittle

> 1 ½ c. sugar
> 2 c. peanuts
> ½ c. Karo
> 1 16-inch square paraffin
> 2 tsp. soda

Put sugar, peanuts, Karo and paraffin in iron skillet. Turn heat on high until ingredients melt; turn heat on medium and stir constantly for about 12 minutes. Add soda and remove from heat. Stir fast until soda is evenly distributed. Spread on well-buttered cookie sheet. Cool.

Phyllis Shaull, Tulsa, Oklahoma, Tulsa State Fair

Tasty Peanut Brittle

3 c. sugar
¾ c. water
1 c. light corn syrup
2 c. raw peanuts
1 tbsp. vanilla
2 tbsp. butter
2 tbsp. soda

Mix sugar, water and corn syrup in saucepan; cook to 245 degrees on candy thermometer. Add peanuts and continue cooking over medium heat until mixture reaches 310 degrees. When this temperature is reached, remove at once from heat. Add vanilla and butter; stir in. Add soda and stir just enough to mix soda in well. Mixture will foam. Pour onto greased cookie sheet or cooling slab. Break into pieces when cold.

Georgia A. Cool, Lewisburg, Ohio

 ## Candied Orange Peel

6 oranges
1 ½ c. sugar

Scrub oranges. Cut peel away in ¼-inch strips and remove white membrane. Cover with cold water. Bring to boil; drain. Repeat twice. Combine drained peel with sugar and 1 ½ cups water reserved from third cooking of peel. Cook almost dry, about 45 minutes. Watch carefully to prevent scorching. Roll in additional sugar.

Sallie McCracken, Home Economics Teacher, Helen, Md.

Caramel Apples

6 med. red apples
1 c. sugar
¾ c. dark corn syrup
1 c. light cream
2 tbsp. butter
1 tsp. vanilla flavoring
Chopped nuts (opt.)

Stick wooden skewers into stem-end of apples. Combine sugar, corn syrup, cream and butter; cook over low heat until sugar is dissolved. Continue cooking until small amount of mixture forms a hard ball when dropped in cold water. Remove from heat; add vanilla flavoring. Dip apples into syrup quickly; roll in chopped nuts, if desired. Place on well buttered cookie sheet to cool.

Mrs. George Romney, Wife of Governor, East Lansing, Mich.

Chewy Caramels

2 c. white sugar
1 ¾ c. white Karo
1 cube butter
2 c. whipping cream
1 c. chopped pecans (opt.)

Boil sugar, Karo, butter and 1 cup cream briskly. Add rest of cream. Boil until hard ball stage or 235 degrees. Add nuts and pour into 9 x 13-inch buttered pan. Let cool. Cut into small squares and wrap each piece in waxed paper. May be kept in freezer.

Mrs. Dale Scott, Colorado Springs, Colo., Carbon County Fair

Caramel-Walnut Roll

½ c. light brown sugar
¼ c. white sugar
⅔ c. dark corn syrup
3 tbsp. butter
½ c. evaporated milk
¼ tsp. vanilla
1 pinch of salt
1 c. black walnuts

Combine sugars and syrup in heavy 2-quart saucepan. Bring to boil over medium heat, stirring constantly. Cook until syrup reaches 245 degrees and is thick. Add butter, stirring to melt. Slowly add evaporated milk so mixture continues to boil, stirring constantly. Continue cooking until mixture again reaches 245 degrees. Remove from heat; add vanilla and salt. Pour into greased 11 ¼ x 7 ¼ x 1 ⅜-inch pan. Cool until candy is firm enough to handle. Spread 1/3 cup finely chopped walnuts on waxed paper measuring the same size as pan. Turn candy out on top of walnuts; add remaining 2/3 cup broken walnut pieces on top of candy. Roll as for jelly roll, pressing walnuts into candy. Yield: 15-20 pieces.

Mrs. Bessie Haught, Middlebourne, W. Va., Tyler County Fair

Chinese Peanut Candy

1 c. light brown sugar
1 c. light corn syrup
½ c. peanut butter
6 c. dry rice cereal
1 c. salted peanuts
¼ c. sesame seeds, toasted

(Continued on next page)

Combine sugar and syrup in 3-quart saucepan. Cook over moderate heat, stirring frequently until mixture boils. Remove from heat; stir in peanut butter and mix well. Add cereal, peanuts and half the toasted sesame seeds. Stir until well blended. Press into a 13 x 9-inch pan. Sprinkle remaining toasted sesame seeds on top. Cool until firm and cut. Yield: 48 bars.

Ann Bilsborrow, Coldwater, Mich., Branch County 4-H Fair

Black Walnut-Chocolate Candy

1 ½ c. milk
3 c. white sugar
3 tbsp. butter
3 tbsp. white corn syrup
½ c. black walnuts, chopped fine
2 tbsp. shaved parowax
1 lb. milk chocolate or 1 lb. semisweet chocolate bits

Cook milk and sugar for 10 minutes after mixture starts to boil. Add butter and syrup, a spoonful at a time. Cook 10 minutes, stirring constantly. Add nuts and boil to soft-ball stage or 238 degrees. Remove from heat; cool until warm. Stir with wooden spoon until mixture starts to hold its shape. Put on waxed paper. With buttered hands work like bread dough. Divide in half. Roll half between waxed paper until ⅜ inch thick. Slice in ¾ inch squares. Place on waxed paper-lined cookie sheet. Work remainder until smooth. Pinch off ¾-inch ball. Roll in buttered hands and flatten into a patty. While walnut mixture is cooling, put parowax in top of double boiler to melt. Add milk chocolate and melt over hot water, not boiling. Start dipping first squares made. If chocolate gets too stiff, put back on hot water. Dip with 2 forks.

Mrs. Walter Barnhart, Friendly, W. Va., Pleasant County Fair

Bourbon Balls

1 lge. box vanilla wafers, crushed
½ c. cocoa
1 c. chopped nuts
2 tbsp. light Karo syrup
½ c. bourbon
1 ½ c. powdered sugar

Mix wafers with cocoa and nuts. Dissolve syrup with bourbon; blend all together. Chill. Form into small balls; roll in powdered sugar. Chill for 2 hours. Yield: 2 ½ dozen balls.

Mrs. W. A. McCormack, La Verne, Cal.

Bon Bons

> 1 stick margarine, melted
> 2 3½ oz. cans flaked coconut
> 2-4 c. chopped nuts
> 1 6-oz. can evaporated milk
> 2 boxes sifted powdered sugar
> ½ sq. paraffin
> 2 c. semisweet chocolate pieces

Pour margarine over coconut; stir until blended. Add nuts and milk; blend sugar in gradually. Mix well and chill. Form into 1-inch balls; chill at least 3 hours. Melt paraffin and chocolate in double boiler. Using a toothpick as holder, dip coconut balls into chocolate mixture; set on waxed paper, carefully removing toothpick. Yield: 50 servings.

Mrs. Gerald L. Ramsden, Oak Harbor, Wash.

 Martha Washington Candy

> 2 boxes confectioners' sugar
> ¼ lb. butter
> 1 can sweetened condensed milk
> 2 tsp. vanilla
> 4 c. pecans
> 1 box chocolate
> 1 box paraffin

Combine sugar, butter, milk and vanilla; mix thoroughly. Add nuts. Form mixture into balls. Melt chocolate and paraffin in top of double boiler. Dip balls in chocolate-paraffin mixture. Refrigerate. Yield: 20 balls.

Donna Gabriel, Greensboro, Ga., Greene County Fair

Almond Toffee

> 1 lb. butter or margarine
> 2 c. sugar
> 1 c. (heaping) unsalted almonds, unblanched
> 1 lb. semisweet chocolate or 1 12-oz. pkg. chocolate pieces
> Chopped pecans

Cream butter and sugar; add almonds. Cook to 290 degrees, stirring constantly. Pour onto a baking sheet with edges. Melt chocolate in double boiler; spread half of chocolate over candy. Sprinkle top with pecans. When cold and chocolate has hardened, turn over and spread chocolate and nuts on other side. Break into pieces.

Mrs. Sidney A. Stephens, Pres. Officers' Wives' Club, Carswell AFB, Fort Worth, Tex.

English Toffee

   1 c. butter, no substitute
   1 c. sugar
   ⅓ c. chopped almonds
   4 sm. chocolate candy bars
   ⅓ c. finely chopped walnuts

Cook butter and sugar over medium heat until it turns color of caramel, stirring constantly. Remove from heat; stir in almonds. Pour into greased 8 ½ x 8 ½-inch pan. Place candy bars on top; melt and spread. Sprinkle walnuts on top. Cool before cutting.

Mrs. Edward Larson, Bangor, Maine

 ### Traditional English Toffee

   2 c. chopped nuts
   1 box brown sugar
   1 lb. butter
   ½ lb. bar sweet chocolate, grated

Butter a large cookie sheet; line with 1 cup nuts. Combine sugar and butter in heavy saucepan; cook for 12 minutes or to hard ball stage in cold water. Spread candy on cookie sheet. Immediately spread grated chocolate on top until it melts. Sprinkle nuts over top. Mark for cutting before candy hardens. Yield: 2 ½ pounds.

Mrs. Oliver J. Pickard, Fort Belvoir, Va.

 ### Date-Pecan Loaf

   2 ½ c. sugar
   1 c. milk
   1 pkg. dates, finely cut
   2 c. pecans, finely cut

Cook sugar and milk to soft ball stage, about 20 minutes. Beat in dates and pecans. Roll in wet cloth; cool for about 1 hour. Slice and serve.

Mrs. Hubert E. Herrod, Pres. Officers' Wives' Club, 439th USAF Hosp., Japan

Filbert Confection Creams

   1 c. chopped filberts
   ½ c. butter

(Continued on next page)

¼ c. sugar
2 tbsp. cocoa
2 tsp. vanilla
¼ tsp. salt
1 egg
1 ¾ c. vanilla wafer crumbs
½ c. flaked coconut
Icing

Spread filberts in shallow pan; toast in 350°-oven 5 to 10 minutes, stirring occasionally, until lightly browned. In saucepan, combine butter, sugar, cocoa, vanilla, salt and egg. Cook over low heat until mixture thickens and becomes glossy. Combine crumbs, filberts and coconut; add to cocoa mixture. Pack evenly in pan and spread with Icing. Yield: 6 dozen.

ICING:

⅓ c. butter
1 egg
½ tsp. peppermint extract
2 c. sifted confectioners' sugar
4 sq. semisweet chocolate

Cream butter; add egg and extract, beating well. Beat in sugar until smooth and creamy. Spread over chocolate base. Chill until icing is firm. Melt chocolate over hot water; spread over icing. When partially set, cut into small oblong bars. Refrigerate until ready to serve. Yield: 1 cup.

Photograph for this recipe below.

Almond Divinity Candy

    4 c. cane sugar
    ⅔ c. white Karo corn syrup
    1 c. water
    Dash of salt
    2 lge. egg whites
    1 tsp. vanilla
    ½ tsp. almond extract
    ¾ c. chopped walnuts

Mix first 4 ingredients well; place on low heat and keep covered until mixture starts to boil and all crystals disappear from sides of pan. Cook to 253 degrees or until a little syrup dropped from the edge of a spoon will form a hair. Just before syrup finishes cooking, beat egg whites until stiff but not dry. Using electric mixer at fast speed, add hot syrup to beaten whites in a thin stream and continue beating until candy loses gloss. Add flavorings; stir in nuts or candied fruit. Pour into buttered pan or platter; when set, mark into squares. A teaspoon may be used to drop candy onto waxed paper. Yield: 60 pieces.

Mrs. Kathryn M. Goddard, Pasadena, Cal., Los Angeles County Fair

Cherry-Honey Divinity

    2 c. sugar
    ⅓ c. honey
    ⅓ c. water
    2 egg whites, well beaten
    ¼ c. candied cherries, cut

Boil sugar, honey and water until syrup spins a thread, 278 degrees. Pour syrup over egg whites, beating continuously. Just before mixture starts to set add cherries. Drop with spoon on waxed paper. NOTE: For variations use candied rhubarb or chopped nuts.

Mrs. Harold E. Hughes, Wife of Governor, Des Moines, Iowa

Peanut Butter Divinity

    3 c. sugar
    1 c. white corn syrup
    1 c. water
    Dash of salt
    3 egg whites
    1 c. peanut butter

Mix sugar, syrup, water and salt; stir over medium heat until it comes to full boil. Turn down heat to low; put lid on saucepan. Boil 3 minutes; take lid off.

(Continued on next page)

Cook until spins a thread. Beat egg whites until stiff and stand in peaks; add half the syrup, beating continually. Return other half of syrup; cook until it forms firm ball when tested in cold water. Add to syrup mixture; beat until creamy. Rub waxed paper with butter; pour Divinity on paper. Leave until firm. Dampen hands with cold water; pat candy until about ¾ inches thick. Spread peanut butter about ¼ inch thick over entire candy. Roll as for jelly roll; cut in slices.

Mrs. Gordon L. Cowby, St. Johns, Ariz.

Perfect Divinity

    2 *c. sugar*
½ *c. light corn syrup*
½ *c. hot water*
¼ *tsp. salt*
    2 *egg whites*
    1 *tsp. vanilla*
½ *c. chopped nuts*

Combine sugar, syrup, water and salt in 2-quart saucepan. Cook and stir till sugar dissolves and mixture comes to boil. Cook to hard-ball stage or 250 degrees without stirring. Wipe crystals from sides of pan with fork wrapped in damp cloth. Remove from heat. Immediately beat egg whites stiff. Pour hot syrup slowly over beaten whites, beating constantly at high speed about 5 minutes. Add vanilla and beat till mixture forms soft peaks and begins to lose its gloss. Add nuts. Drop by teaspoonfuls, pushing off with a second spoon, onto a cookie sheet covered with waxed paper. Yield: 25 pieces.

Vikki Jones, Crosbyton, Tex., Panhandle South Plains Fair

Dream Balls

    1 *stick oleo*
¾ *c. sugar*
    1 *pkg. chopped dates*
    2 *egg yolks, beaten*
    1 *c. pecans*
    2 *tbsp. marshmallow creme*
    1 *tsp. vanilla*
    2 *c. Rice Krispies*

Cook oleo, sugar, dates, egg yolks, pecans and marshmallow creme in a skillet on low heat from 5 to 10 minutes. Add vanilla and Rice Krispies. Shape into balls. Roll in powdered sugar or flaked coconut, if desired. Yield: 25-30 balls.

Sarah Elizabeth Yarbrough, Home Economics Teacher, Hattiesburg, Miss.

Basic Fondant

⅔ c. water
2 c. sugar
⅛ tsp. cream of tartar
2 tbsp. light corn syrup or honey

Place all ingredients in heavy small saucepan over low heat; stir mixture gently until almost all sugar is dissolved. Avoid splashing on sides of saucepan above the level of the mixture. Cover and boil gently about 3 minutes; do not stir. Remove cover; continue boiling gently to 238 degrees. Remove from heat and pour on a large platter, wet with cold water. Do not scrape syrup from saucepan; cool to lukewarm. Stir until syrup begins to change from a clear syrup to a creamy white mass; knead until smooth and creamy. Small lumps may be disregarded since they disappear during the ripening of the fondant. Store in a tightly covered jar at room temperature. Let stand 2 days before using. Yield: ½ pound fondant.

Mrs. Marguerite K. German, Home Economics Teacher, Copperhill, Tenn.

 ## Fondant For Mints

2 c. granulated sugar
1 c. water
Pinch of cream of tartar

Mix sugar, water and cream of tartar in boiler; cover for 3 minutes. Bring to boil; uncover. Place thermometer in syrup; cook to 238 degrees. Pour out and cool; beat or work on marble slab until creamed. Let stand in covered container overnight; melt and pour or shape as desired.

Mrs. R. S. Clark, Home Economics Teacher, La Grange, Ga.

Quick Fondant

⅔ c. sweetened condensed milk
1 tsp. vanilla extract
4 ¾ c. sifted confectioners' sugar
Ground nuts or grated semisweet chocolate

In medium-sized mixing bowl blend together condensed milk and vanilla extract; gradually stir in sugar. Continue to stir until candy is smooth. Form into small balls and roll in ground nuts. May use as filling for pitted dried dates or uncooked prunes.

Mrs. Tiras Gray, Home Economics Teacher, Fulton, Miss.

No-Cook Fondant Bonbons

1 stick butter
⅓ c. light corn syrup
½ tsp. salt
1 tsp. vanilla extract
4 ½ c. confectioners' sugar
Food coloring
Flavoring to taste
Walnuts, pecans or almonds

Add first 5 ingredients together in large bowl. Work with hands until well blended. Divide into smaller bowls; add color and flavor to each bowl. Again work with hands to make uniform color or marbelized effect. If mixture seems sticky, add small amount powdered sugar. Add nuts by pressing one nut into center of formed ball. Yield: 8 dozen.

Mrs. Felix W. Cary, Alameda, Cal., Alameda County Fair

Brown Sugar Fudge

1 c. light brown sugar
1 c. granulated sugar
¾ c. milk
1 tbsp. butter
1 tsp. vanilla
½ c. chopped walnuts

Combine sugars and milk in saucepan; cook over medium heat to soft ball stage, stirring occasionally. Remove from heat; add butter and vanilla. Cool in sink with cold water; beat until very thick. Add nuts; pour into greased 9-inch square pan. Refrigerate until set. Cut in squares. Yield: 36 squares.

Mrs. Neale O. Westfall, Portsmouth, Va.

Quick Caramel Fudge

1 6-oz. pkg. caramel chips
Pinch of salt
½ c. chopped nuts

Melt caramel chips in top of double boiler. Add salt and nuts. Stir and drop onto waxed paper by spoonfuls. Let cool. Yield: 3 dozen pieces.

Judith Irvin, Home Economics Teacher, Richlands, N. C.

Cherry Creme Fudge

4 c. sugar
1 c. half and half
1 c. butter
½ c. light corn syrup
½ tsp. salt
2 tsp. vanilla
½ c. marshmallow creme
1 c. pecan halves (opt.)
½ c. coarsely chopped candied cherries (opt.)

Combine sugar, half and half, butter, corn syrup and salt in heavy 4-quart saucepan. Bring to boil over moderate heat, stirring constantly until sugar is dissolved. Remove from heat; set pan in cold water and cool to lukewarm. Add vanilla and marshmallow creme; beat until mixture is at setting stage. Pour into well-buttered 8 or 9-inch square pan. Cut into squares when firm. Decorate squares with pecan or cherry halves. Yield: 25 pieces.

Mrs. Jo Anne Tuttle, Home Economics Teacher, Spencer, Iowa

Butter-Rum Fudge

4 c. sugar
1 lge. can evaporated milk
1 c. butter or half margarine
2 6-oz. pkg. semisweet chocolate pieces
1 pt. marshmallow creme
1 tsp. rum flavoring
1 ½ c. broken walnuts and pecans

Mix sugar, milk and butter; cook to soft ball stage, 236 degrees, stirring frequently. Remove from heat; add chocolate pieces, marshmallow creme, rum flavoring and nuts. Beat until chocolate is melted and well blended. Pour into buttered 9 x 9 x 2-inch pan or large cookie sheet. Score immediately into squares. After fudge is cool, cut squares. Yield: 4 dozen.

Mrs. Frank G. Scarborough, Norfolk, Va.

Chocolate-Nut Fudge

2 c. sugar
4 tbsp. cocoa
½ c. milk
¾ c. white Karo
½ tsp. salt
2 tbsp. butter

(Continued on next page)

1 tsp. vanilla
1 ½ c. pecans

Combine first 5 ingredients in saucepan and cook until mixture forms a soft ball when tried in cold water. Cool until tepid; add butter, vanilla and nuts. Beat until thick; pour into well-oiled 8 x 10-inch pan. Cut into squares while still warm.

Mrs. J. R. Julian, Lubbock, Tex., Panhandle South Plains Fair

Fantasy Fudge

3 c. sugar
⅔ c. evaporated milk or 1 c. light cream
¾ c. margarine
2 6-oz. pkg. semisweet chocolate pieces
1 jar marshmallow creme
1 tsp. vanilla
1 c. chopped nuts

Combine sugar, milk and margarine; bring to boil. Cook to soft ball stage, 238 degrees, stirring frequently. Remove from heat; add chocolate pieces, marshmallow creme, vanilla and nuts. Beat until well blended. Pour into greased 12 x 9 x 2-inch pan; cool and cut.

Mrs. Warren E. Hearnes, Wife of Governor, Jefferson City, Mo.

Mrs. Hill's Chocolate Fudge

⅔ c. milk
1 to 2 oz. unsweetened chocolate, cut up
2 c. sugar
1 tsp. corn syrup
Dash of salt
2 tbsp. butter
1 tsp. vanilla
1 c. broken nuts

Place milk and chocolate over low heat, stirring until chocolate melts and mixture is smooth. Stir in sugar, syrup and salt. Cook gently to 236 degrees, stirring from the bottom occasionally. Remove from heat. Add butter; cool, without stirring, to lukewarm. Add vanilla. Beat until thick and no longer glossy. Stir in nuts. Turn onto waxed paper and shape into 12-inch roll; chill and slice. Mixture may be spread in buttered pan and cut into squares. Yield: 1 ¼ pounds.

Linda Hill, Des Moines, Iowa, Iowa State Fair

Old-Time Fudge

2 c. sugar
¾ c. milk
2 1-oz. squares unsweetened chocolate
Dash of salt
1 tsp. corn syrup
2 tbsp. butter or margarine
1 tsp. vanilla

Butter sides of heavy 2-quart saucepan. In it combine sugar, milk, chocolate, salt and corn syrup. Heat and stir over medium heat till sugar dissolves and mixture comes to boil. Cook to soft-ball stage or 234 degrees, stirring only if necessary. Immediately remove from heat; add butter and cool to lukewarm or 110 degrees without stirring. Add vanilla. Beat vigorously until fudge becomes very thick and starts to lose its gloss. Quickly spread in buttered shallow pan. Score while warm; cut when firm. Yield: 24 pieces.

Robert Anderson, Grand Rapids, Minn., Itasca County Fair

Maple Sugar Fudge

2 c. maple syrup
1 tbsp. light corn syrup
¾ c. thin cream
1 tsp. vanilla
¾ c. walnuts or butternuts, coarsely chopped

Combine syrups and cream in saucepan; heat to boiling over low heat, stirring constantly. Continue cooking without stirring to soft ball stage. Remove from heat; cool to lukewarm. Beat mixture until it thickens and loses its gloss. Add vanilla and nuts; pour immediately into 8-inch square buttered cake pan. Cool; cut into squares.

Mrs. Philip H. Hoff, Wife of Governor, Burlington, Vt.

Opera Fudge

2 c. sugar
⅔ c. milk
2 tbsp. light corn syrup
¼ tsp. salt
2 tbsp. butter
1 tsp. vanilla

Combine sugar, milk, corn syrup and salt in a saucepan. Stir over medium heat until sugar dissolves. Cook to 234 degrees or soft-ball stage. Remove

(Continued on next page)

from heat. Add butter and cook to lukewarm, without stirring. Add vanilla; beat until thick and no longer glossy. Pour into a buttered 8 or 9-inch square pan. When set, cut into squares. Yield: 36 pieces.

Melissa Rowland, Kingsport, Tenn., Gray Station Fair

Peanut Butter Fudge

⅓ c. butter
½ c. light corn syrup
¾ c. peanut butter
½ tsp. salt
1 tsp. vanilla
1 1-lb. box confectioners' sugar, sifted
¾ c. chopped nuts

Soften butter into sides of bowl with wooden spoon. Blend in corn syrup; peanut butter, salt and vanilla. Mix till creamy. Stir in confectioners' sugar. Turn candy onto pastry board and knead with hands till blended and smooth. Add nuts gradually, pressing and kneading them into dough. Grease an 8-inch square pan. Press candy out in pan with hands. Cut into small pieces after chilling 1 hour. Yield: 2 pounds.

Mrs. Mary Rogers, Jackson, Mich., Jackson County Fair

 ## Pineapple Fudge

2 c. sugar
1 c. brown sugar
½ c. light cream
1 No. 2 can crushed pineapple, drained
2 tbsp. butter or margarine
2 tsp. ginger
2 tsp. vanilla
1 c. walnuts, broken

(Continued on next page)

Combine sugars, cream and pineapple; cook, stirring occasionally, to soft-ball stage, 236 degrees. Remove from heat. Add butter, ginger and vanilla. Cool at room temperature without stirring until lukewarm. Beat until mixture loses its gloss. Add nuts. Pour into buttered 8 x 8 x 2-inch pan. Score candy in squares. Press walnut half on each. Finish cutting when firm.

Mrs. Edna Empson, Rossville, Ga.

 ### Hard Candy

> 2 *c. sugar*
> ½ *c. water*
> ½ *c. corn syrup*
> 15 *drops cinnamon, anise or clove oil*
> *Food coloring*
> *Powdered sugar*

Bring the first 3 ingredients to a boil at 300 degrees. Remove from heat; add flavoring and desired amount of food coloring. As candy sets, it becomes a lighter color. Pour into buttered 9 x 13-inch pan. When candy starts to border or harden around edges, cut into pieces with scissors. Candy will still be quite hot as cutting begins. Work quickly as candy hardens very rapidly. Put on waxed paper, covered with powdered sugar. May use wintergreen or peppermint oil. Oils may be bought from pharmacist.

Mrs. Joyce Owens, Appleton, Wis.

 ### Hard Sauce Apples

> ¼ *c. butter*
> ¾ *c. confectioners' sugar*
> ¼ *tsp. vanilla*

Beat butter with mixer until soft; add confectioners' sugar slowly, add vanilla. Form into apples, about 1 heaping teaspoon per apple. Poke slivers of green gumdrops in top for stem. Refrigerate several hours. Yield: ½ cup or 14 to 16 apples.

Mrs. Philip H. Hoff, Wife of Governor, Montpelier, Vt.

 ### Hard Mint Candy

> 1 *c. sugar*
> ⅓ *c. white Karo*
> ½ *c. water*

(Continued on next page)

4 or 5 drops of oil flavoring, anise, wintergreen,
* peppermint or clove*
Food coloring

Put first three ingredients in a 2-quart pan and cook to 300 degrees. Remove from heat. Add oil flavoring and color. Pour hot mixture into buttered pie pan; leave until mixture pulls away from pan easily. Pour out on powdered sugar on table top and knead; pull until stiff, then put into long rolls and cut with kitchen shears. Use gloves for kneading or dough will burn hands.

Mrs. Josephine Hively, Home Economics Teacher, Larwill, Ind.

Party Mints

1 lb. powdered sugar
⅓ c. oleo
⅓ c. white syrup
Pinch of salt
1 tsp. mint flavoring or ½ tsp. wintergreen and
* ½ tsp. peppermint*

Put powdered sugar in big bowl; add remaining ingredients. Mix thoroughly. Roll in small balls and lay on waxed paper. Press down with a dish or glass dipped in sugar. Layer in box between waxed paper. May be frozen. Yield: 125 mints.

Mrs. Viola Bartlett, Sac City, Iowa, Sac County Fair

Peanut Butter Candy

2 c. sugar
½ c. white syrup
½ c. water
2 egg whites, beaten stiff
1 c. peanut butter

Combine sugar, syrup and water in a 1-quart saucepan. Bring to boil, stirring constantly; reduce heat and cook to hard-ball stage. Pour hot syrup over beaten egg whites in a thin stream, beating until candy loses gloss and holds shape. Toss on a floured board; pat and roll lightly to ¼ inch thickness. Spread with peanut butter and roll like jelly roll. Cut in 1-inch slices. Yield: 60 pieces.

Personal Comment: This recipe has also won a ribbon at the Anderson County Fair.

Mrs. Kelly Lewis, Powell, Tenn., T. V. A. and I. Fair

Peanut Butter Crunch

2 c. sugar
½ c. milnot
½ c. butter or margarine
1 c. peanut butter, crunchy or plain
2 c. quick-cooking oats, uncooked
2 c. miniature marshmallows
1 tsp. vanilla

Cook sugar, milnot, butter and peanut butter over medium heat until mixture boils. Boil 2 minutes, stirring constantly. Remove from heat; add oats, marshmallows and vanilla. Stir mixture until well blended and slightly thickened. Drop by teaspoonfuls on waxed paper. Let cool. Yield: 50 servings.

Mrs. Chester Mason, Harris, Mo., North Central Missouri Fair

Creamy Peanut Butter Fudge

2 c. sugar
⅔ c. milk
1 c. crunchy peanut butter
1 pt. jar marshmallow creme

Cook sugar and milk to soft ball stage. Add peanut butter and marshmallow creme; stir until melted. Pour into buttered 9-inch pan. Yield: 6 servings.

Karen McKennon, Shallowater, Tex., South Plains Fair

Pecan Roll

2 c. sugar
½ c. water
½ c. light corn syrup
1 sm. can evaporated milk
3 tbsp. butter
1 tsp. vanilla flavoring
1 c. chopped pecans
1 c. broken pecans

Boil sugar, water and syrup to hard ball stage or until candy thermometer reaches 248 degrees. Remove from heat; add milk and butter. Boil again, stirring constantly, until candy thermometer reaches 238 degrees or to soft ball stage. Remove from heat; add flavoring. Beat until nearly hard; add chopped pecans. Butter hands and knead; shape into roll. Roll in broken pecans, coating well.

Mrs. Hulett Smith, Wife of Governor, Charleston, W. Va.

An unusual dish that calls for an extra bit of care and proves well worth it—that's Raisin Swirl Steamed Pudding. Picture a cold night, with swirls of snow flying past the frosted window of a cozy kitchen—and your family enjoying this delicious hearty dessert.

RAISIN SWIRL STEAMED PUDDING

$\frac{1}{2}$ c. shortening
1$\frac{1}{4}$ c. sugar
1 tsp. nutmeg
1 tsp. rum flavoring
2 eggs, beaten
2 c. sifted flour
1$\frac{1}{2}$ tsp. baking powder
$\frac{1}{4}$ tsp. soda
1$\frac{1}{2}$ tsp. salt
$\frac{2}{3}$ c. milk
1$\frac{1}{2}$ c. dark seedless raisins
$\frac{1}{2}$ c. walnuts, chopped
$\frac{1}{2}$ c. flake coconut
1 1-oz. square unsweetened chocolate, melted

Beat shortening, sugar, nutmeg and flavoring until fluffy. Blend in beaten eggs. Sift flour with baking powder, soda and salt; add alternately with milk to sugar mixture. Stir in raisins, walnuts and coconut. Divide batter into two parts. To one-half of batter, add melted chocolate. Spoon light and dark batters alternately into well-greased 2-quart mold. Swirl batters lightly with knife. Cover tightly; place on rack in large kettle. Add boiling water to come halfway up mold. Cover tightly; steam in boiling water for 2 hours and 30 minutes. Let pudding stand, uncovered, in mold for 10 minutes before turning out. Serve warm with favorite sauce. Yield: 8-10 servings.

See photograph on reverse side.

Candied Pecans

1 c. sugar
5 tbsp. cold water
¼ tsp. salt
1 tsp. cinnamon
1 tsp. vanilla
2 c. pecan halves, toasted

Combine sugar, water, salt and cinnamon. Cook over low heat until mixture forms a soft ball, about 10 minutes. Do not stir while cooking. Remove from heat; add vanilla and pecans. Stir until nuts are well-coated with mixture. Pour onto waxed paper and gently separate with fork.

Mrs. Barry Shiftlett, Jr., Montgomery, Ala.

Pecan Log

6 oz. butterscotch bits
1 can sweetened condensed milk
1 tsp. vanilla
⅓ c. pecans, chopped

Melt bits over water; remove from heat and stir in milk. Add vanilla and pecans; chill. Roll into log. Press whole pecan meats on log. Yield: 2 logs.

Sharlene Ann Wheeler, Pikeville, Tenn., Bledsoe County Fair

Sugared Pecans

1 egg white
1 tbsp. water
1 lb. pecan halves
1 c. sugar
1 tsp. salt
1 tbsp. cinnamon

Place egg white and water in bowl. Beat until frothy but not stiff. Pour pecans into egg white; stir until nuts are coated. In second bowl, sift sugar, salt and cinnamon. Pour sugar mixture over pecans; stir until coated. Spread pecans on cookie sheet. Bake at 300 degrees for 45 minutes, stirring every 15 minutes.

Marjorie Ross, Paragon, Ind.

Mrs. Jones' Penuche

2 c. brown sugar
½ c. evaporated milk
¼ c. water
1 tsp. vanilla
2 tbsp. butter
½ c. finely cut nuts

Butter 8-inch square pan. Mix brown sugar, evaporated milk and water in a heavy 2-quart saucepan. Cook and stir over medium heat until mixture comes to a boil and sugar is dissolved. Boil until candy reaches soft ball stage or 234 degrees on candy thermometer, stirring often. Remove from heat; add vanilla, butter and nuts. Beat until candy is thick and creamy and starts to lose its shine. Quickly spread in prepared pan. Cool and cut into squares. Yield: 25 pieces.

Mrs. Betty Jones, Home Economics Teacher, Cedarville, Mich.

Penuche

2 c. brown sugar
1 c. sugar
1 c. cream
2 tbsp. light corn syrup
¼ tsp. salt
2 tbsp. butter
1 tsp. vanilla
½ c. chopped nuts

Combine sugars, cream, corn syrup and salt in saucepan; stir over heat to dissolve sugar. Cook to 234 degrees. Stir occasionally. Remove from heat. Add butter and let stand without stirring until bottom of pan is lukewarm or 120 degrees. Add vanilla and beat until creamy. Mix in nuts. Pour into greased 9-inch square pan. Cut into squares. Yield: 36 1½-inch pieces.

LaVon Huizenga, Huron, S. D., South Dakota State Fair

 ## Creamy Pralines

3 c. sugar
1 c. evaporated milk
Pinch of salt
⅛ stick butter or margarine
Pecans

(Continued on next page)

Dissolve 1 cup sugar in skillet. Boil 2 cups sugar, milk and salt in heavy kettle; add butter. Add dissolved sugar. Cook to soft ball stage. Remove from heat; beat well. Add pecans. Drop on waxed paper. Pralines may be flattened or left in mounds.

Mrs. C. L. Frisbie, Mobile, Ala.

 ### Praline Louisiane

> 3 c. sugar
> 1 ½ c. hot water
> 1 tsp. maple extract
> 1 ½ c. sm. pecans
> ¼ tsp. cream of tartar

Cook all ingredients to 234 degrees, stirring occasionally. Remove from heat. Stir with wooden spoon for 5 to 6 minutes or until mixture begins to lose its gloss and appears slightly granular. Spoon onto a well oiled or buttered pan. Pralines are more uniform and attractive when poured into buttered praline molds or into 3 to 4-inch foil pie plates. If mixture becomes too thick, reheat slowly. Yield: 2 pounds.

Mrs. John C. Hix, Watertown Arsenal, Mass.

 ### Rock Candy

> 2 c. sugar
> ½ c. water
> ½ c. clear syrup
> ¼ tsp. oil of cinnamon flavoring
> Food coloring

Cook first three ingredients without stirring to hard crack stage; remove from heat. Add flavoring and coloring. Pour into ungreased square pan; cool. When cold, turn pan upside down and hit bottom a little. Break into pieces.

Sandra Birk, Gridley, Kan.

 ### Seafoam Candy

> 1 1-lb. box light brown sugar
> ½ c. white sugar
> 2 tbsp. dark corn syrup
> ½ c. water

(Continued on next page)

2 *egg whites*
1 *tsp. vanilla*

Combine sugars, corn syrup and water in saucepan; bring to boil. Add 4 table-spoons boiling syrup to unbeaten egg whites, beating while adding hot syrup. Boil remaining syrup until mixture strings a thread about 6 inches long; beat while adding. Add vanilla. Beat until mixture stands in peaks; drop onto waxed paper with 2 spoons. Yield: 30 pieces.

Mrs. W. P. Fulton, Stuart, Va.

Pull Taffy

2 *c. sugar*
1 *tbsp. white vinegar*
1 *c. water*

Combine ingredients; stir until sugar is dissolved. Cook to hard crack stage or until it will spin a thread, 375 degrees. Pour out on cold buttered platter. Pull edges to center and center out. Pull until white; cut into portions.

Mrs. Edward T. Breathitt, Wife of Governor, Frankfort, Ky.

Salt Water Taffy

2 ½ *c. sugar*
1 ¼ *c. white syrup*
2 *c. water*
1 *tbsp. butter*
2 *scant tsp. salt*
Food coloring
2 *drops oil of spearmint or peppermint*

Put sugar, syrup and water in saucepan; stir until boiling begins. Cover with lid for a few minutes until steam washes down sides of pan. Continue boiling without stirring, until temperature reaches 254 degrees on candy thermometer. Remove from heat; add butter and salt. Pour out onto buttered platters. When cool enough to handle, drop coloring and flavoring on top and pull until candy glistens and gets hard. Cut into kisses and wrap in squares of waxed paper.

Hilda G. Rohlf, Home Economics Teacher, Tallmadge, Ohio

Cookies

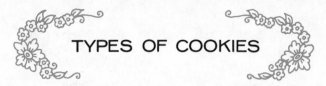

TYPES OF COOKIES

The six basic types of cookies are: refrigerator, molded, dropped, rolled, pressed and bars.

REFRIGERATOR—Refrigerator cookies are made by rolling the dough into a thick bar. Then it is placed in the refrigerator and chilled until ready to bake. To cut the dough, use a sharp knife and make thin slices.

MOLDED—Almost all molded cookies are round and are formed by rolling the dough with your hands.

DROPPED—Dough is dropped by the teaspoonful onto the cookie sheet.

ROLLED—Rolled cookies have a rather stiff dough. The dough is rolled on a lightly floured board and cut with a cookie cutter.

PRESSED—A cookie press is used to make pressed cookies. The dough should be soft enough to be put through a cookie press but must be stiff enough to hold a shape.

BARS—A softer type of cookie, bars and squares are more like cake. Bake these cookies in a baking pan with sides. As soon as the bars are done, they are cut into squares.

Preparing Sheets or Pans

Don't grease the cookie sheets or pans if your cookies contain a considerable amount of shortening. For all other cookies, grease the sheets with a bland fat that contains no salt.

If cookie bars are to be made, grease the baking pan and line it with waxed paper. Grease the waxed paper. Bake macaroons on heavy plain paper.

STORE COOKIES PROPERLY

Crisp cookies are stored in a different manner from soft cookies. To insure freshness, store each kind correctly.

Store soft cookies in a tightly covered container. Bars and squares can be stored in the baking pan and covered with foil. Store crisp cookies in a container with a loose-fitting cover. Soft and crisp cookies should never be stored together.

To keep soft cookies from becoming dry, add an apple, an orange or a piece of bread to the container in which the cookies are stored. Be sure though that the apple, orange or piece of bread does not come into direct contact with the cookies. If crisp cookies become limp, freshen them by putting in a 300-degree oven for about five minutes before serving.

Cookies Take A Journey

It's always great to be on the receiving end especially when the package contains cookies.

If you are mailing cookies, be sure to mail only those which will stand the trip. Soft cookies are better for mailing than crisp ones. Crisp cookies will crumble easily.

The proper package is also necessary when you are mailing cookies. Cookies must be carefully wrapped for them to stay fresh.

Package With Care

A sturdy container is needed for mailing cookies. This can be a strong cardboard box or a metal container.

Before packing the cookies, line the box or container with waxed paper or foil. Put a layer of crumpled paper in the bottom of the box for a cushion.

Wrap cookies in pairs with their backs together. The wrapper should be vapor-proof material. Place heavier cookies in the bottom of the box. To keep cookies from getting jumbled during travel, stuff popcorn, crushed paper, puffed cereal or miniature marshmallows between the packages of cookies. A cushion is needed on top of the cookies, also.

Be sure you take extra care in taping the box and putting the name and address on the package. Wrap the box in heavy brown paper and tie carefully. Label the package "Fragile, Handle with Care."

Apricot Gems

⅔ c. dried apricots
½ c. soft butter
¼ c. white sugar
1 ⅓ c. sifted flour
1 tsp. baking powder
¼ tsp. salt
1 c. brown sugar, packed
2 eggs, well beaten
½ tsp. vanilla
½ c. nuts
Confectioners' sugar

Rinse apricots; cover with water. Boil for 10 minutes; drain, cool and chop. Grease 8 x 8 x 2-inch pan. Mix butter, white sugar and 1 cup flour until crumbly; pack into pan. Bake at 375 degrees for 25 minutes or until light brown. Sift together remaining flour, baking powder and salt. Gradually beat brown sugar into eggs; add flour mixture. Mix in vanilla, nuts and apricots; spread over baked layer. Bake 30 minutes or until done; cool in pan. Cut into bars; roll in confectioners' sugar.

Mrs. Terry Komar, Oceanside, Cal., Del Mar Fair

Brown Sugar Brownies

1 c. (firmly packed) dark brown sugar
¼ c. melted butter or margarine
1 tsp. orange extract
1 egg, beaten
1 c. sifted flour
1 tsp. baking powder
¼ tsp. salt
¾ c. chopped nuts

Cream together sugar and butter; add orange extract and egg. Sift together flour, baking powder, and salt; fold into creamed mixture. Stir in nuts; pour into greased 8-inch square pan. Bake at 350° for 20 to 25 minutes. Cut in squares while warm. Yield: 16 brownies.

Photograph for this recipe on page 101.

Black Walnut-Butterscotch Squares

1 6-oz. pkg. butterscotch morsels
¼ c. butter or margarine
1 c. light brown sugar, firmly packed

(Continued on next page)

2 eggs
½ tsp. vanilla
1 tsp. baking powder
¾ c. flour, sifted
1 c. black walnuts, chopped

Melt butterscotch morsels and butter in saucepan. Remove from heat; stir in sugar until all sugar is melted. Cool 5 minutes; beat in eggs and vanilla. Sift together baking powder and flour; add to other ingredients. Add black walnuts; spread mixture in well-greased 13 x 9 x 2-inch baking pan. Bake approximately 25 minutes at 350 degrees. Cut into squares while warm. Yield: 2 dozen squares.

Mrs. Grace Haught, Grantsville, W. Va., Calhoun County Fair

Applesauce-Chocolate Brownies

½ c. shortening
½ c. cocoa
2 eggs
1 c. sugar
½ c. sweet applesauce
1 c. flour
½ tsp. soda
⅛ tsp. salt
½ tsp. baking powder
½ c. black walnuts
1 tsp. vanilla

Melt shortening; add cocoa. Add beaten eggs and sugar; beat. Add applesauce; beat well. Add flour, soda, salt and baking powder; beat. Add walnuts; mix well. Add vanilla; pour into greased and floured pan. Bake for 25 minutes in a 350-degree oven. Cool; cut into squares.

Mardell Walters, Anita, Iowa, Iowa State Fair

Brownies

½ c. shortening
7 tbsp. cocoa
¾ c. flour
½ tsp. baking powder
½ tsp. salt
2 eggs
1 c. sugar
1 tsp. vanilla
1 c. nuts

(Continued on next page)

Melt shortening and cocoa over hot water; cool. Sift flour with baking powder and salt. Beat eggs until light; add sugar. Add chocolate mixture; blend. Add flour, vanilla and nuts; mix well. Pour batter into 8-inch square waxed paper-lined pan. Bake in 350-degree oven 30 to 35 minutes. Cool; cut into squares. Yield: 16 brownies.

Mrs. A. C. Robertson, Augusta, Ky., Germantown Fair

Frosted Brownies

½ c. oleo
1 c. sugar
4 eggs
1 1-lb. can Hershey's chocolate syrup
1 c. flour
½ c. nuts

Cream shortening; add sugar. Beat; add eggs. Blend in chocolate syrup; stir in flour and nuts. Bake in greased 11 x 16-inch pan at 350 degrees for 25 minutes or until done. Cool.

FROSTING:

1 ⅓ c. sugar
6 tbsp. milk
6 tbsp. butter or oleo
1 c. chocolate chips

Combine sugar, milk, and butter. Boil 1 minute, no longer. Add chocolate chips; stir until chocolate chips have melted. Spread on brownies. Yield: 24 brownies.

Betty Billerbeck, Randolph, Neb., Cedar County Fair

Lunchbox Brownies

4 squares baking chocolate
¾ c. melted butter or margarine
6 eggs
3 c. sugar
2 c. sifted flour
½ tsp. salt
½ c. nuts, chopped
2 tsp. vanilla

Melt chocolate in butter. Beat eggs; add sugar. Sift flour with salt; add to sugar mixture. Add chocolate mixture, nuts and vanilla; turn into 2 oiled 10 x 14-inch pans. Bake in a 450-degree oven for 12 to 15 minutes. Just before

(Continued on next page)

brownies are done, place under broiler flame to give a rich brown. Cut into squares while warm. Yield: 48 brownies.

Carol Ramsay, Waveland, Ind., Indiana State Fair

Fudge-Nut Layer Bars

½ c. butter
1 c. brown sugar
1 egg
1 tsp. vanilla
1 ¼ c. flour
½ tsp. soda
½ tsp. salt
1 ½ c. rolled oats
¼ c. chopped walnuts

Cream together first 4 ingredients. Stir in flour, soda and salt; blend in oats and walnuts. Reserve two-thirds cup mixture for topping; press remaining mixture in greased 9 x 9 or 11 x 7-inch pan.

FUDGE LAYER:

1 c. chocolate chips
1 tbsp. butter
½ c. condensed milk
¼ tsp. salt
½ c. chopped walnuts
1 tsp. vanilla

Combine first 4 ingredients in saucepan. Place over low heat, stirring constantly, until chocolate is melted. Remove from heat; add nuts and vanilla. Press mixture over oatmeal layer. Crumble remaining oatmeal mixture over fudge layer. Bake at 350 degrees for 25 to 30 minutes or until lightly browned. Cool; cut into bars. Yield: 12 bars.
Personal Comment: This recipe won me a trip to the Pillsbury's 14th Grand National 1962 Bake-Off in New York.

Mrs. Joseph A. Trejo, Chula Vista, Cal., San Diego County Del Mar Fair

Sherried Fudge Bars

½ c. flour
½ tsp. baking powder
½ tsp. soda
¼ tsp. salt
2 eggs

(Continued on next page)

1 c. (firmly packed) brown sugar
⅓ c. melted butter or margarine
2 1-oz. sq. chocolate, melted
¼ c. med. or sweet sherry
1 c. chopped walnuts or pecans

Sift together first 4 ingredients. Beat eggs until light; add sugar gradually, beating well. Stir in butter and chocolate; add dry ingredients. Add sherry and nuts; blend well. Pour into greased and floured 8 x 8-inch pan. Bake in 325-degree oven for 45 minutes or until toothpick inserted in center comes out clean. Cool slightly; cut into squares. Roll in powdered sugar, if desired. Yield: 12-14 bars.

Mrs. R. H. Baker, San Antonio, Tex.

 ## Coconut Brownies

½ c. butter or margarine
1 c. sifted flour
1 ¾ c. (firmly packed) light brown sugar
½ tsp. baking powder
½ tsp. coconut flavoring
2 eggs
1 c. shredded coconut
1 c. pecans, chopped

Combine butter, flour and ¼ cup sugar; turn into greased 9-inch square pan. Bake at 375° for 20 minutes. Mix remaining sugar and baking powder with coconut flavoring and eggs; add coconut and pecans. Spread evenly over top of first mixture. Bake at 375° for 30 minutes. Cut brownies while warm; cool and remove from pan. Yield: 2 dozen brownies.

Photograph for this recipe on page 101.

Date Sticks

1 c. sifted flour
⅔ tsp. baking powder
½ tsp. salt
1 c. sugar
2 eggs, well beaten
1 tsp. melted butter

(Continued on next page)

½ *c. nuts*
2 *c. dates, chopped*
1 *tbsp. hot water*
Confectioners' sugar

Sift flour, baking powder and salt together 3 times. Add sugar gradually to eggs. Add butter; beat in nuts and dates. Add flour alternately with hot water, beating well after each addition. Spread batter thin in greased 7 ½ x 12-inch baking dish. Bake at 325 degrees for 30 to 35 minutes. Cool; cut in bars. Remove from pan and roll in confectioners' sugar.

Mrs. W. J. Terwort, Kiowa, Kan., Barber County Fair

 ## Filled Date Bars

¾ *c. soft shortening, part butter*
1 *c. brown sugar, packed*
1 ¾ *c. flour*
½ *tsp. soda*
1 *tsp. salt*
1 ½ *c. quick-cooking rolled oats*
Date Filling

Preheat oven to 400 degrees. Mix shortening and sugar. Blend flour, soda and salt; stir into sugar mixture. Mix in oats; flatten half of mixture into bottom of greased 13 x 9 ½ x 2-inch pan. Spread with cooled Date Filling. Top with remaining crumb mixture, patting lightly. Bake for 25 to 30 minutes. While warm, cut into bars and remove from pan.

DATE FILLING:

3 *c. cut-up dates*
¼ *c. sugar*
1 ½ *c. water*

Mix dates, sugar and water in saucepan. Cook over low heat, stirring constantly, until thickened, about 10 minutes; cool.
Personal Comment: This recipe won blue ribbons at the Minnesota and South Dakota State Fairs.

Mrs. R. J. Mentzel, Huron, S. D.

 ## Gumdrop Jewels

2 *eggs*
1 *c. sugar*
1 *tsp. vanilla*

(Continued on next page)

    1 c. flour
    ½ tsp. salt
    ½ c. cut-up walnuts (opt.)
    ½ c. cut-up gumdrops

Beat eggs well; add sugar and vanilla. Stir in flour and salt, mixing well; add nuts and gumdrops. Spread in well-greased and floured 9-inch square pan. Sprinkle additional gumdrops over top of batter. Bake in 325-degree oven for 30 to 35 minutes or until top has a dull crust. Cut into squares when warm; remove from pan. Yield: 1 ½ dozen bars.

Carolyn M. Mackintosh, Fremont, Cal., Alameda County Fair

 ## Maple Munchies

    1 ½ c. flour
    1 tsp. salt
    1 tsp. baking powder
    3 eggs
    1 ½ c. sugar
    1 c. melted shortening
    1 tsp. maple flavoring
    1 c. walnuts
    1 c. raisins
    Confectioners' sugar

Sift first 3 ingredients. Beat eggs; slowly mix in sugar. Slowly add shortening and dry ingredients; mix well. Add maple flavoring, nuts and raisins. Bake at 350 degrees about 25 minutes. Let stand 5 minutes on rack after removing from oven. Cut in squares; roll in confectioners' sugar. Cool thoroughly before storing. Yield: 1 dozen bars.

Mrs. John W. Hill, Sr., Glynco, Ga.

 ## Lemon-Coconut Treats

    1 ½ c. sifted flour
    1 ½ c. brown sugar
    ½ c. butter or margarine

Mix together flour, sugar and butter; pat down well in buttered 9 x 13-inch pan. Bake at 275 degrees for 10 minutes.

FILLING:

    2 eggs, beaten
    1 c. brown sugar, firmly packed

(Continued on next page)

1 ½ c. flaked or shredded coconut
1 c. chopped nuts
2 tbsp. flour
½ tsp. baking powder
¼ tsp. salt
½ tsp. vanilla

Combine ingredients; spread on top of baked mixture. Bake for 20 minutes at 350 degrees.

FROSTING:

1 c. confectioners' sugar
1 tbsp. melted butter or margarine
Juice of 1 lemon

Combine ingredients; spread on warm cookies. Cut in squares. Yield: 24 squares.

Mrs. Robert T. Brown, Sr., Brookeville, Md., Montgomery County Fair

Orange Slice Bars

1 c. brown sugar
½ c. shortening
2 eggs
1 tsp. baking powder
1 tbsp. hot water
1 ¾ c. flour
1 tsp. salt
2 tbsp. hot milk

Cream sugar and shortening; add eggs. Beat well. Dissolve baking powder in hot water; add to creamed mixture with remaining ingredients. Pour half of dough in 9-inch loaf pan.

FILLING:

½ lb. dates, cut up
2 tbsp. flour
½ c. white sugar
¾ c. water
1 ½ c. nuts
12 to 15 candy orange slices

Cook first 4 ingredients; cool. Add nuts and candy. Cover dough in pan with filling; pour remaining dough over top. Bake at 350 degrees 45 minutes. Cut into bars.

Mrs. Paul Jokinen, Richland, Mich., Kalamazoo County Fair

Pecan Slices

2 eggs
1 c. brown sugar
1 c. white sugar
¾ c. melted butter or margarine
1 ¼ c. sifted flour
1 c. chopped pecans
1 tsp. vanilla

Lightly grease pan with fat on a piece of waxed paper or paper towel. Beat eggs with beater for about 1 minute; add brown sugar to eggs. Mix well; add white sugar and mix well. Melt butter. Pour over sugar mixture; blend. Add flour, nuts and vanilla; mix well. Pour into pan. Bake about 35 minutes in preheated 350-degree oven. Cut into bars or squares while slightly warm. Cool; store in container with tight lid. Yield: 3 dozen bars.

Maryetta Chapman, Bloomingdale, Ind., Parke County 4-H Fair

Pineapple Secrets

1 c. white sugar
2 tbsp. cornstarch
1 No. 2 can crushed pineapple and juice
1 ¾ c. flour
1 c. brown sugar
½ tsp. baking soda
1 tsp. salt
1 ½ c. rolled oats
¾ c. butter or margarine

For filling, combine white sugar and cornstarch in small saucepan; add pineapple. Cook over medium heat until thick; set aside. Combine flour, brown sugar, soda, salt and oats; cut in butter until mixture is crumbly. Place half of crust mixture in greased 9 x 13-inch pan; pat down firmly. Spread filling evenly on top; add remaining crust and pat down as firmly as possibly. Bake in 400-degree oven for 25 to 30 minutes. Cool; cut into bars. Yield: 20 bars.

Mrs. Antone Zelasko, Tamaroa, Ill., Illinois State Fair

Raisin Bars

2 c. dark raisins
1 ½ c. water
4 ½ c. flour
1 tsp. baking powder
1 tsp. soda

(Continued on next page)

1 tsp. salt
1 ¼ c. margarine
2 c. sugar
3 eggs
1 tsp. vanilla extract
1 tsp. ground cinnamon
¼ tsp. ground nutmeg
¼ tsp. ground allspice
1 c. chopped walnuts

Combine raisins and water in saucepan. Bring to boiling; simmer 5 minutes. Set raisins and liquid aside to cool. Blend flour, baking powder, soda and salt; set aside. Cream margarine, sugar, eggs and vanilla together using electric beater; beat until creamy and fluffy. Add dry ingredients; add raisins and liquid, spices and nuts. Mix well. Bake in large loaf cake pans in 375-degree oven until top of dough springs back when touched lightly at center. Remove to cooling rack; cool and frost. Yield: 72 bars.

Mrs. Albert Kitterman, Doland, S. D., South Dakota State Fair

Rhubarb Squares

1 c. sifted flour
¾ c. oatmeal
1 tsp. cinnamon
1 c. brown sugar
½ c. melted butter
4 c. rhubarb, cut up
1 c. white sugar
1 c. water
2 tbsp. cornstarch
1 tsp. vanilla

Crumble first 5 ingredients together; press half of mixture into an 8-inch cake pan. Cover with rhubarb. Cook remaining ingredients until very thick; pour over rhubarb. Sprinkle with remaining oatmeal mixture. Bake at 350 degrees for 1 hour. Serve warm or cold. Top with vanilla ice cream, if desired. Yield: 9 squares.

Rosanne Hanson, Onalaska, Wis., Lacrosse Interstate Fair

 ### Anise Cookies

3 eggs, at room temperature
1 c. sugar
1 ½ c. cake flour
½ tsp. baking powder
1 tbsp. anise seed, finely rolled

(Continued on next page)

Beat eggs until very light. Add sugar; beat until fluffy. Add flour which has been sifted with baking powder. Add anise seed; beat for 3 to 4 minutes or until light and fluffy. Drop dough 1-inch apart from a teaspoon onto well-greased and floured pans. Let stand overnight or about 10 hours at room temperature to dry. Bake at 350 degrees for 10 to 15 minutes. Yield: 3-4 dozen cookies.

Mrs. A. P. Rush, Fort Plain, N. Y.

Applesauce Cookies

1 c. sugar
½ c. shortening
1 egg
1 ½ c. unsweetened applesauce
2 tsp. soda
2 ¼ c. flour
½ tsp. ground cloves
1 tsp. cinnamon
½ tsp. salt
1 c. raisins
½ c. nuts

Cream together sugar, shortening and eggs; add applesauce in which soda has been dissolved. Sift in flour, spices and salt; add raisins and nuts. Drop several inches apart onto greased baking sheet. Bake at 300 degrees about 15 minutes. Yield: 30 cookies.
*This recipe also won ribbons at the Pendleton Co. Fair.

Rose Armentrout, Cabins, W. Va., Tri-County Fair

Carrot Cookies With Orange Icing

⅔ c. shortening
¾ c. sugar
1 egg
1 c. cooked mashed carrots
2 c. sifted flour
¼ tsp. salt
2 tsp. baking powder
1 tsp. vanilla
¼ c. hot orange juice
1 ½ tbsp. butter
Grated rind of 1 orange
2 c. powdered sugar

(Continued on next page)

Cream shortening and sugar; add egg and blend. Add carrots. Sift flour, salt and baking powder; add to creamed mixture. Add vanilla; drop by teaspoonfuls onto greased baking sheet. Bake for 8 to 10 minutes at 350 degrees. Mix remaining ingredients; ice cookies while warm. Yield: 3 dozen cookies.

Mrs. Hazel Gilson, Toledo, Ore., Lincoln County Fair

Caramel Drops

2 c. brown sugar
1 c. shortening
3 eggs
1 c. sweet milk
1 tsp. vanilla flavoring
3 c. sifted flour
1 tsp. soda
Dash of salt

Cream sugar and shortening together; add eggs and beat well. Add remaining ingredients in order listed; mix well. Drop by spoonfuls on slightly greased cookie sheets. Bake in 350-degree oven until done.

ICING:

¼ c. butter
2 tbsp. cold water
1 tsp. maple flavoring
1 egg, beaten
¾ lb. powdered sugar

Brown butter; add water, flavoring, egg and enough powdered sugar to thicken. Mix well until smooth; spread on warm cookies.

Mrs. Donald K. McCloskey, Fargo, N. D., Red River Valley County Fair

Cashew Cookies

½ c. butter
1 c. brown sugar
1 egg
½ tsp. vanilla
2 c. sifted flour
¾ tsp. baking powder
¾ tsp. soda
¼ tsp. salt
⅓ c. sour cream
1 ¾ c. salted cashew nuts

Cream butter, sugar, egg and vanilla. Add dry ingredients with sour cream; mix well. Fold in nuts. Drop by teaspoonfuls onto cookie sheet. Bake at 375 degrees for 10 minutes. Cool.

FROSTING:

½ c. butter
1 tbsp. coffee cream
¼ tsp. vanilla
2 c. powdered sugar

Combine all ingredients; frost cookies.

Mrs. Francis Adamo, Newark, N. J.

 ## Chocolate Chip-Oatmeal Cookies

½ c. shortening
½ c. brown sugar
½ c. white sugar
1 egg
1 tbsp. water
½ tsp. vanilla
¾ c. sifted flour
½ tsp. soda
½ tsp. salt
1 ½ c. rolled oats
1 c. semisweet chocolate chips
¼ c. chopped nuts

Cream shortening; add sugars gradually and cream well. Beat in egg until fluffy; stir in water and vanilla. Sift together flour, soda and salt; add to creamed mixture. Add oats, chocolate chips and nuts; drop from a teaspoon onto greased baking sheet. Bake in a 375-degree oven for 12 minutes. Yield: 3 ½ dozen cookies.

Mrs. Archie Gubbrud, Wife of Governor, Pierre, S. D.

Chocolate Chip Cookies

½ c. butter or margarine
½ c. white sugar
½ c. brown sugar
1 egg, well beaten
1 c. plus 2 tbsp. sifted flour
½ tsp. soda
½ tsp. salt
¼ tsp. hot water
1 6-oz. pkg. semisweet chocolate pieces
½ c. chopped nuts
½ tsp. vanilla

Cream butter and sugars; add egg and beat well. Sift together dry ingredients; add to creamed mixture. Add hot water; mix until well blended. Add chocolate pieces, nuts and vanilla. Drop from teaspoon onto greased cookie sheet. Bake in 375-degree oven for 10 to 12 minutes. Yield: 3 ½ dozen cookies.

Mrs. Paul Fannin, Wife of Governor, Phoenix, Ariz.

 ## Chocolate Drops

½ c. soft shortening, part butter
1 c. sugar
1 egg
2 oz. melted chocolate
¾ c. buttermilk or sour milk
1 tsp. vanilla
1 ¾ c. flour
½ tsp. soda
½ tsp. salt
1 c. chopped pecans or other nuts

Preheat oven to 400 degrees. Mix shortening, sugar, egg and chocolate thoroughly; stir in buttermilk and vanilla. Blend flour, soda and salt; add. Mix in nuts; chill for at least 1 hour. Drop by rounded teaspoonfuls 2 inches apart onto lightly greased baking sheet. Bake 8 to 10 minutes or until cookie springs back when lightly touched. Cool.

FROSTING:

1 tbsp. butter
1 square unsweetened chocolate
1 ½ tbsp. warm water
1 c. sifted confectioners' sugar

Blend butter, chocolate and warm water over hot water; beat in confectioners' sugar. Spread over cookies. Yield: 3 ½ dozen cookies.

Mrs. Clinton Tweeten, Turtle Lake, N. D., McLean County Fair

Cranberry Kitchen Cookies

½ c. butter or margarine
1 c. white sugar
¾ c. (packed) brown sugar
¼ c. milk
2 tbsp. orange juice
1 egg
3 cups sifted flour
1 tsp. baking powder
¼ tsp. baking soda
½ tsp. salt
1 c. chopped nuts
2 ½ c. coarsely chopped cranberries

Cream butter and sugars together; beat in milk, orange juice and egg. Sift together flour, baking powder, baking soda and salt; add to creamed mixture. Blend well; stir in nuts and cranberries. Drop by teaspoonfuls onto greased cookie sheet. Bake at 375 degrees for 10 to 15 minutes. If desired, 1 teaspoon orange extract may be substituted for orange juice; milk must then be increased to 1/3 cup. Yield: 12 dozen cookies.

Photograph for this recipe below.

Favorite Lace Cookies

1 c. sifted flour
1 c. flaked coconut
½ c. brown sugar
½ c. clear corn syrup
½ c. butter
1 tsp. vanilla

Mix flour and coconut; set aside. Combine sugar, syrup and butter in heavy saucepan; bring to a boil over low heat, stirring constantly. Remove from heat; gradually blend in flour mixture. Add vanilla. Drop dough onto a foil-covered cookie sheet by scant teaspoonfuls about 3 inches apart. Bake at 350 degrees for 8 to 10 minutes. Cool cookies 3 to 5 minutes on a rack till foil can be removed easily. Yield: 4 dozen cookies.

Kathi Scott, Rixeyville, Va., Culpeper County Fair

Lizzies

1 c. butter
1 c. brown sugar, packed
4 eggs
3 tbsp. milk
1 c. sherry, fruit juice or bourbon
3 c. flour
3 tsp. (scant) soda
1 tsp. each cloves, nutmeg and cinnamon
1 ½ lb. shelled pecans
1 lb. raisins, cut in half
1 lb. candied cherries, cut up
½ lb. candied pineapple, cut up

Cream butter and sugar. Add eggs, milk and sherry; mix well. Sift flour, soda and spices together several times; add to creamed mixture. Add nuts, raisins and fruit; mix well. Drop by teaspoonfuls on greased cookie sheet. Bake in 300-degree oven about 30 minutes. Yield: 200 Lizzies.

Mrs. E. Orlo Davis, Montague, Cal., Siskiyou County Fair

Hawaiian Cookies

1 c. white sugar
1 c. brown sugar
1 c. shortening
2 eggs
1 c. drained crushed pineapple

(Continued on next page)

    1 c. nuts
    1 c. flaked coconut
    4 c. flour
    2 tsp. baking powder
    1 tsp. soda
    ¼ tsp. salt
    1 tsp. vanilla
    ¼ tsp. banana flavoring

Beat sugars and shortening till creamy; add eggs and beat well. Add pineapple, nuts and coconut. Sift dry ingredients and add; add flavorings. Mix well; drop by teaspoonfuls onto baking sheet. Bake for 12 minutes at 350 degrees. Cool.

DECORATOR ICING:

    ¾ c. shortening
    1 box powdered sugar
    1 tsp. cream of tartar
    ½ tsp. salt
    ½ c. water
    1 tsp. vanilla
    Flaked coconut
    Maraschino cherry halves

Combine all ingredients except coconut and cherries; beat about 10 minutes till fluffy. Frost cookies. Cover with coconut; garnish with cherry half in center of each cookie.

Mrs. D. J. Scott, Sheridan, Ark., Grant County Fair

 Molasses Cookies

    1 c. butter or margarine
    1 c. sugar
    2 eggs
    1 c. molasses mixed with 1 tsp. soda
    4 c. flour
    2 tsp. ginger
    1 tsp. cinnamon
    ½ tsp. salt
    1 c. sour milk mixed with 1 tsp. soda

Cream shortening and sugar until fluffy; add eggs and molasses-soda mixture. Sift dry ingredients together; add alternately with sour milk-soda mixture. Drop by teaspoonfuls on greased baking sheet. Bake at 375 degrees for 10 to 12 minutes. Yield: 6 dozen cookies.

Personal Comment: This recipe won a blue ribbon at the New York State Fair.

Patty Ann McCulley, Camillus, N. Y.

Mincemeat Nuggets

¾ c. shortening
1 ½ c. sugar
3 well-beaten eggs
3 c. flour
¾ tsp. salt
1 tsp. baking soda
1 tsp. cinnamon
1 9-oz. pkg. dry mincemeat
Grated rind of 1 lemon
3 tbsp. water
1 c. nuts

Cream shortening and sugar. Add eggs; beat well. Sift together flour, salt, baking soda and cinnamon. Add half the sifted dry ingredients to creamed mixture. Add finely crumbled mincemeat, lemon rind and water; stir until blended. Add nuts and remaining flour mixture; mix well. Drop from a teaspoon onto cookie sheet. Bake at 350 degrees for 10 to 15 minutes. One cup canned mincemeat may be used. Yield: 4 dozen cookies.

Mrs. Mary C. Zwick, Sunbury, Ohio, Delaware County Fair

Margaret's Peanut Cookies

1 c. butter
2 c. brown sugar
2 eggs
2 c. (or more) flour
1 tsp. soda
1 tsp. cream of tartar
1 tsp. vanilla
1 7¼-oz. can salted Spanish peanuts
2 c. oatmeal
1 c. corn flakes

Cream butter and sugar; add eggs and beat well. Add remaining ingredients; drop by small spoonfuls onto greased baking sheet. Bake at 325 degrees for 12 minutes or until light brown. Do not overbake.

Mrs. William A. Egan, Wife of Governor, Juneau, Alaska

Oatmeal Cookies

½ tsp. salt
½ tsp. soda
1 c. flour

(Continued on next page)

½ c. shortening
6 tbsp. brown sugar
6 tbsp. white sugar
1 egg
Vanilla to taste
1 c. oatmeal
½ c. chopped nuts (opt.)

Sift salt, soda and flour together; set aside. Cream shortening; add sugars, a little at a time. Cream after each addition until mixture is fluffy; add eggs and vanilla. Beat well; add sifted ingredients and mix. Add oatmeal and nuts; mix well. Drop by rounded teaspoonfuls about 2 inches apart on greased cookie sheets. Bake at 350 degrees for 10 to 13 minutes or until firm and slightly browned. Let cookies cool on cookie sheets about 1 minute. Remove to cooling rack. Store in a tight covered cookie jar or can. Yield: 2½ dozen cookies.

Teri Lynn Turpin, Naytahwaush, Minn., Mahnomen County Fair

Florida Cookies

½ c. butter
1 c. sugar
Grated rind of 2 oranges
1 egg, slightly beaten
½ c. orange juice
3 c. sifted flour
½ tsp. cinnamon
4 tsp. baking powder

Cream together butter, sugar and orange rind; gradually add egg, orange juice, flour, cinnamon and baking powder. Mix thoroughly; drop from teaspoon onto ungreased cookie sheet. Bake in 325-degree oven for 12 minutes until light brown.

Mrs. Farris Bryant, Wife of Governor, Tallahassee, Fla.

Orange Blossoms

2 ½ c. sugar
1 c. vegetable shortening
2 eggs
2 tsp soda
1 c. sour milk
4 ½ c. flour
Juice and grated rind of 4 oranges
1 pkg. confectioners' sugar
¼ c. butter, melted

(Continued on next page)

Mix sugar and shortening; add eggs and beat well. Dissolve soda in sour milk. Add flour and sour milk alternately to sugar mixture. Add half of juice and rind; drop onto greased cookie sheet. Bake at 375 degrees until done. Cool; frost with mixture of confectioners' sugar, butter and remaining juice and rind.

Mrs. W. S. Avery, Jackson, Mich., Jackson Fair

Peach Seed Nut Cookies

1 ½ c. sugar
½ c. shortening
2 eggs
3 c. flour
½ tsp. soda mixed with 3 tbsp. flour
½ c. sour milk or buttermilk
Dash of nutmeg
¼ to ½ c. peach seed nuts, chopped fine
⅛ tsp. salt

Cream sugar and shortening; beat in eggs. Add flour and soda mixture alternately with milk; mix until light and fluffy. Add remaining ingredients; drop from teaspoon onto cookie sheet. Bake at 350 degrees 12 to 15 minutes, until light in color. Let cookies mellow in tightly covered can for 1 week. Yield: 4-5 dozen cookies.

Eva B. Kling, York, Pa., York Inter-State Fair

Peanut Butter Drop Cookies

2 c. brown sugar
2 eggs
1 ¼ c. shortening
1 tsp. vanilla
½ c. water
4 c. flour, sifted
1 tsp. soda
1 tsp. salt
Crunchy peanut butter

Cream sugar, eggs and shortening; add vanilla and water. Add sifted dry ingredients. Drop by spoonfuls onto greased cookie sheet; place ½ teaspoon peanut butter on top of each. Cover each with ½ teaspoon cookie dough. Bake at 350 degrees until done. Yield: 5 dozen cookies.

Mrs. Arend Volker, Goodland, Minn.

Pear Drops

½ c. butter
¾ c. brown sugar
½ c. sour cream
1 egg
½ tsp. peppermint flavoring
1 ⅓ c. sifted flour
1 tsp. baking soda
½ tsp. salt
1 c. chopped canned pears
1 c. walnuts
¼ c. chopped maraschino cherries

Cream butter and sugar; blend in sour cream, egg and flavoring. Mix dry ingredients; blend into sour cream mixture. Add well-drained pears, nuts and cherries; mix. Drop from a teaspoon onto greased cookie sheets. Bake at 375 degrees for 15 to 18 minutes. Yield: 2 ½ dozen cookies.

Mrs. J. D. Rives, Jr., New Haven, Conn.

 ### Persimmon Cakes

1 c. sugar
½ c. shortening
1 egg, beaten
1 tsp. soda
1 c. persimmon pulp
2 c. flour
1 tsp. salt
½ tsp. cinnamon
⅛ tsp. cloves
⅛ tsp. nutmeg
1 c. chopped nuts

Cream ½ cup sugar with shortening. Mix remaining sugar with egg; add to creamed mixture. Dissolve soda in persimmon pulp; beat into sugar mixture. Mix dry ingredients and add; mix in nuts. Drop from a spoon onto baking sheet. Bake at 375 degrees for 10 to 15 minutes.

Mrs. Charles L. Peckham, San Diego, Cal.

 ### Pineapple Cookies

1 c. shortening
1 c. brown sugar
1 c. white sugar

(Continued on next page)

1 c. crushed pineapple
1 c. nuts
2 eggs
4 c. sifted flour
½ tsp. salt
½ tsp. soda
2 tsp. baking powder
1 tsp. vanilla

Combine all ingredients in order given; beat until well mixed. Drop by teaspoonfuls onto lightly greased pan. Bake at 350 degrees until lightly browned. Remove from oven; let cool for 5 minutes before removing from pan.

Mrs. Grant Sawyer, Wife of Governor, Carson City, Nev.

Pumpkin Cookies

1 ½ c. pumpkin
½ c. oleo
1 c. sugar
½ tsp. salt
1 tsp. vanilla
1 c. chopped walnuts
1 egg
2 c. unsifted flour
1 tsp. soda
1 tsp. baking powder
1 tsp. cinnamon
1 pkg. butterscotch morsels

Mix all ingredients in order given; drop by spoonfuls onto greased cookie sheet. Bake in 375-degree oven for 12 to 14 minutes. Raisins, pecans or coconut may be substituted for the butterscotch chips. Yield: 4 dozen cookies.

Mrs. Charles H. Thayer, Whitefield, Maine, Pittston Fair

Raisin Chews

1 c. raisins
½ c. water
½ c. shortening
1 c. sugar
2 eggs
1 tsp. vanilla
½ c. chopped nuts
2 c. flour
1 tsp. salt

(Continued on next page)

1 tsp. baking powder
½ tsp. soda
1 tsp. cinnamon
⅛ tsp. nutmeg
⅛ tsp. allspice

Add raisins to water and boil for 5 minutes. Cream shortening and sugar; add eggs and vanilla. Add cooled raisins and nuts. Sift dry ingredients together; add to raisin mixture and blend well. Drop by teaspoonfuls onto greased cookie sheet. Bake at 400 degrees for 12 to 15 minutes. Yield: 3 dozen cookies.

Cheryl Hextell, Lengby, Minn., Mahnomen County Fair

 ## Sesame Seed Wafers

1 stick butter
2 c. brown sugar
1 egg
1 c. flour
¼ tsp. salt
½ tsp. baking powder
1 tsp. vanilla
¾ c. sesame seed, toasted

Cream butter and sugar. Add egg, flour, salt and baking powder; mix well. Add vanilla and sesame seed; blend. Drop about ½ teaspoon at a time onto greased cookie sheet. Bake at 325 degrees for 8 to 10 minutes. Cool about 1 minute before removing from sheet. Wafers burn easily, so watch closely. Yield: 8 ½ dozen wafers.

Mrs. J. C. Hogue, Philadelphia, Pa.

 ## Tart Lemon Drops

2 c. sifted flour
3 tsp. baking powder
¾ tsp. salt
1 tbsp. grated lemon rind
½ c. shortening
1 c. sugar
1 egg
¼ c. lemon juice
¼ c. cold water

Sift flour, baking powder and salt. Blend rind and shortening; add sugar gradually, creaming well. Add egg, lemon juice and water; beat well. Add dry

(Continued on next page)

ingredients; mix thoroughly. Drop by level tablespoonfuls onto greased cookie sheet. Bake at 400 degrees for 8 minutes. Yield: 5 dozen cookies.

Mrs. Michael Vrabel, Salem, Ore.

 ## Almond Gingersnaps

1 c. butter
½ c. dark syrup
1 c. sugar
1 tbsp. ginger
2 tsp. cinnamon
2 tsp. cloves
1 tsp. soda
1 c. blanched almonds
3 ½ c. flour

Work butter until creamy; add syrup, sugar, spices, soda, almonds and flour. Knead until smooth; shape into roll. Wrap in waxed paper and refrigerate. When cold, cut into thin slices; place on cookie sheet. Bake at 450 degrees for 8 to 10 minutes. Yield: 20 cookies.

Evelyn Lucas, Morrill, Maine

Butterscotch Thins

1 c. shortening
2 c. brown sugar
2 eggs, unbeaten
1 tsp. vanilla
3 ½ c. sifted flour
1 tsp. soda
1 tsp. cream of tartar
½ tsp. salt
1 c. broken nutmeats

Cream shortening; add sugar gradually. Cream together until light; add eggs, 1 at a time. Add vanilla. Sift flour, soda, cream of tartar and salt together; stir into creamed mixture with a wooden spoon. Blend in nutmeats; shape into long rolls. Wrap in waxed paper; chill thoroughly or overnight in refrigerator. Slice in ⅛-inch slices; place on ungreased baking sheet ½ inch apart. Bake at 375 degrees for 8 to 10 minutes. Remove cookies from pan; cool on rack. Store in tightly covered jar. Yield: 9 dozen cookies.

Marion Bisek, Mahnomen, Minn., Mahnomen County Fair

Cherry-Pecan Fancies

¾ c. Crisco
1 egg
1 tsp. vanilla
1 c. brown sugar
½ c. chopped nuts
¼ c. maraschino cherries, chopped
2 c. sifted flour
½ tsp. soda
½ tsp. salt
½ tsp. cream of tartar

Place first 4 ingredients in mixing bowl; beat well. Add nuts and cherries. Sift dry ingredients; add half at a time to sugar mixture and beat well. Shape into rolls; wrap in waxed paper and chill until firm. Cut into ⅛-inch slices; place on ungreased baking sheet. Bake at 400 degrees for 6 to 8 minutes. Cool 1 to 2 minutes before removing from pan. May freeze dough wrapped in foil. Yield: 5 dozen cookies.

Jana Spruiell, Abernathy, Tex., Panhandle South Plains Fair

Date and Nut Pinwheels

¼ c. butter
¼ c. oleo
½ c. Crisco
1 ½ c. white sugar
1 c. brown sugar
3 eggs
3 ½ c. sifted flour
½ tsp. baking powder
½ tsp. soda
½ tsp. salt
1 tsp. vanilla
½ lb. dates
1 c. water
½ c. nuts, chopped fine

Cream butter, oleo and Crisco; add 1 cup white sugar and brown sugar gradually. Add eggs, 1 at a time. Add sifted dry ingredients in small amounts; add vanilla. Set aside in refrigerator until chilled or overnight. Cook dates, water and remaining white sugar until thickened over low heat; add nuts and cool. Roll dough in small amounts in rectangular shape. Spread on date filling and roll up; chill again. Slice and bake at 400 degrees for 15 minutes. Yield: 10 dozen cookies.

Mrs. Louis W. Baum, Tiffin, Ohio, Seneca County Fair

Peach Refrigerator Cookies

¾ c. butter
1 ½ c. dark brown sugar
1 egg
2 ½ c. flour
3 tsp. baking powder
1 tsp. salt
1 tsp. cinnamon
¼ c. milk
1 c. chopped nuts
1 c. chopped dried peaches

Cream butter, sugar and egg. Sift dry ingredients; add to creamed mixture alternately with milk. Add nuts and peaches; mix well. Shape into rolls; wrap in waxed paper and place in freezer until ready to bake; slice thin. Bake in 400-degree oven for 12 to 15 minutes. Yield: 5 dozen cookies.
Personal Comment: Mrs. Sanders invented these peachy morsels to accompany her famed Peach Punch.

Mrs. Carl Sanders, Wife of Governor, Atlanta, Ga.

Fancy Tea Cookies

½ c. butter
½ c. shortening
3 tbsp. sugar
1 tsp. vanilla
2 c. flour
1 c. coconut

Combine butter, shortening and sugar, creaming until light and fluffy; add vanilla. Work in flour and coconut gradually until well blended. Form 2 rolls; chill in refrigerator overnight. Slice dough ¼-inch thick. Slices may be cut in fancy shapes. Bake for 35 to 45 minutes at 275 degrees.

Mrs. Lyle Prater, Eugene, Ore., Lane County Fair

 ## Golden Nuggets

½ c. butter
1 c. sugar
2 eggs, beaten
Grated rind of 1 lemon
Grated rind of 1 orange
2 tbsp. orange juice
2 tbsp. lemon juice
3 c. flour

(Continued on next page)

1 tsp. baking powder
¼ tsp. soda
½ tsp. salt

Cream butter and sugar thoroughly; add eggs. Beat hard; add grated rinds and fruit juices. Sift dry ingredients together; add to creamed mixture. Shape mixture into rolls 2 inches in diameter; wrap in waxed paper. Chill; slice very thin. Bake cookies on oiled sheets 10 to 12 minutes at 375 degrees. Yield: 3 dozen cookies.

Mrs. B. G. Wynne, Wytheville, Va.

Icebox Cookies

2 c. brown sugar
1 ½ c. shortening
3 eggs
1 tsp. soda
¼ tsp. salt
1 tsp. cream of tartar
1 tsp. cinnamon
Flavoring
½ c. nuts
5 c. flour

Cream sugar, shortening and eggs; add soda, salt, cream of tartar, cinnamon, flavoring and nuts. Add flour, working in a little at a time. Shape in 2 rolls; chill overnight. Slice; bake at 425 degrees for about 10 minutes. Dough may be divided into parts and different nuts or fruits added to each. Yield: 4-5 dozen cookies.

Jackie Hardee, Austwell, Tex., Refugio County Fair

Lemon-Caraway Favorites

1 c. sugar
1 egg, well beaten
2 tbsp. lemon juice
½ c. shortening, softened
2 tsp. caraway seeds
3 c. cake flour
½ tsp. soda
½ tsp. salt

Add sugar gradually to egg, beating well; add lemon juice, shortening and caraway seeds. Sift dry ingredients; add to mixture. Make into roll; wrap in waxed paper. Chill until firm; slice thin. Bake at 400 degrees for 10 minutes. Yield: 4 dozen cookies.

Mrs. Norman G. Barfoot, Officers' Wives' Club, Eureux, France

Chinese Almond Cookies

1 c. sugar
1 ½ c. shortening
3 c. pastry flour
¼ tsp. baking soda
½ tsp. salt
1 tsp. almond extract
1 egg, beaten
½ c. finely chopped nuts

Cream sugar and shortening. Add flour, soda and salt; mix well. Blend in extract, egg and nuts; shape into round balls and flatten. Dot center of each cookie with a small cork that has been dipped in red food coloring. Bake at 350 degrees for 10 to 12 minutes or until lightly browned. Cool a few minutes before removing from pan.

Mrs. John Burns, Wife of Governor, Honolulu, Hawaii

Mexican Wedding Cakes

1 c. soft butter or margarine
½ c. sifted powdered sugar
1 tsp. vanilla
2 ¼ c. sifted flour
½ tsp. salt
¾ c. finely chopped nuts

Mix butter, sugar and vanilla thoroughly. Sift together flour and salt; add nuts; chill dough. Roll into 1-inch balls; place on ungreased baking sheet. Bake in 400-degree oven until set but not brown. Roll warm cookies in additional powdered sugar; cool. Roll in powdered sugar again. Yield: 4 dozen cookies.

Mrs. Mildred Clement, Pico Rivera, Cal., Los Angeles County Fair—Pomona

Pecan Sandies

1 c. butter or margarine
¼ c. confectioners' sugar
2 tsp. vanilla
1 tbsp. water
2 c. sifted flour
1 c. chopped pecans

Cream butter with sugar; add vanilla, water and flour. Mix well; add pecans. Form into small balls. Bake in 300-degree oven for 20 minutes. While still hot, roll in additional confectioners' sugar. When cool, roll again in sugar. Yield: 3 dozen cookies.

Mrs. J. C. Royalty, Springfield, Ky., Washington County Fair

Pecan Crescents

  1 *c. butter or margarine*
  ¾ *c. confectioners' sugar*
  2 *c. pecans, coarsely chopped*
  1 *tsp. vanilla*
  2 *c. flour*
  1 *tbsp. ice water*
  ⅛ *tsp. salt*

Cream butter and sugar; add remaining ingredients. Roll with palms of hands into finger lengths; shape into crescents. Bake on greased cookie sheet in 325-degree oven for 15 to 20 minutes or until firm, but not brown. Immediately roll in additional confectioners' sugar while still hot, then again when cooled. Yield: 3 dozen cookies.

Mrs. Louise Dean, Lexington Park, Md., St. Mary's County Fair

Peanut Butter Supremes

  1 *c. shortening*
  1 ¼ *c. peanut butter*
  1 *c. white sugar*
  1 *c. brown sugar, packed*
  2 *eggs*
  2 ½ *c. flour*
  Salt
  ½ *tsp. baking soda*

Mix shortening and peanut butter; add sugars. Beat well; beat in eggs. Mix flour, salt and soda; stir into peanut butter mixture. Make dough into small balls; put on baking pan. Flatten with a fork. Bake at 375 degrees for 10 to 15 minutes. Yield: 4-5 dozen cookies.

Mrs. Clytee Thomas, Ecru, Miss., Pontotoc County Fair

Jelly Butterballs

½ lb. butter
⅔ c. sugar
2 egg yolks
2 c. sifted flour
¼ tsp. salt
1 tbsp. vanilla
Tart currant jelly

Cream butter with sugar until smooth; beat in egg yolks, 1 at a time, until smooth. Resift flour twice with salt; gradually add to butter mixture. Beat well; beat in vanilla. Roll ½ teaspoon dough at a time between palms into small balls. Place about 1 inch apart on greased and floured cookie sheet. With the tip of a finger, form a depression on the top of each ball; fill each depression with a small amount of jelly. Bake in 325-degree oven for 12 to 13 minutes or until sand colored.

Mrs. Donald Russell, Wife of Governor, Columbia, S. C.

Old-Fashioned Sugar Cookies

1 ½ c. sifted flour
½ tsp. baking powder
½ tsp. salt
½ tsp. soda
¾ c. sugar
½ c. shortening
1 egg
2 heaping tsp. milk
1 tsp. vanilla

Sift together flour, baking powder, salt, soda and sugar. Cut in shortening until mixture resembles coarse meal. Blend in egg, milk and vanilla; roll out on floured board. Cut with cookie cutter; place on ungreased cookie sheets. Bake at 375 degrees for about 8 minutes. Yield: 3 dozen cookies.

Mrs. Kenneth G. Mang, Trenton, N. J., North Central Missouri State Fair

Orange Sugar Cookies

½ c. shortening
½ tsp. salt
1 tsp. grated orange or lemon rind
1 ½ c. sugar
1 egg
2 tbsp. milk

(Continued on next page)

    2 c. sifted flour
    1 tsp. baking powder
    ½ tsp. soda
    ¾ tsp. nutmeg

Blend together shortening, salt, grated rind and 1 cup sugar; beat in egg and milk. Stir in flour, baking powder and soda which have been sifted together. Chill; form in small balls about the size of walnuts. Roll in a mixture of remaining sugar and nutmeg. Place on lightly greased baking sheet; press each ball down with bottom of glass dipped in additional sugar. Bake 8 to 10 minutes in 400-degree oven. Yield: 3 dozen cookies.

Ann Green, Culpeper, Va., Culpeper County Fair

 ## Butterscotch Cookies

    1 ⅓ c. margarine
    2 c. brown sugar
    2 eggs, well beaten
    2 c. flour
    2 ½ tsp. baking powder
    ½ tsp. salt
    2 tsp. vanilla
    1 ⅓ c. chopped pecans

Cream margarine and sugar; add eggs. Sift together flour, baking powder and salt; add to creamed mixture. Add vanilla and pecans. Mix well; roll into balls and flatten with spoon. Bake in 350-degree oven until done.

Mrs. John Connally, Wife of Governor, Austin, Tex.

Snickerdoodles

    1 c. soft shortening
    1 ½ c. plus 2 tbsp. sugar
    2 eggs
    2 ¾ c. sifted flour
    2 tsp. cream of tartar
    1 tsp. soda
    ½ tsp. salt
    2 tsp. cinnamon

Blend together shortening, 1 ½ cups sugar and eggs. Sift together flour, cream of tartar, soda and salt; add to creamed mixture. Roll dough into balls the size of walnuts. Roll in mixture of cinnamon and remaining sugar. Place balls 2 inches apart on ungreased cookie sheet. Bake in 400-degree oven for 8 to 10 minutes. Remove to rack to cool.

Mrs. Frank G. Clement, Wife of Governor, Nashville, Tenn.

Thumbprint Cookies

  1 c. margarine
¾ c. brown sugar
  2 eggs, separated
  2 tsp. vanilla extract
  2 c. flour
½ tsp. salt
  Finely chopped nuts or grated coconut
  Red or green jelly

Mix margarine, sugar, egg yolks and vanilla thoroughly. Sift together and stir in flour and salt. Make into balls; dip into slightly beaten egg whites. Roll in finely chopped nuts. Bake 5 minutes in 375-degree oven. Remove from oven; press thumb gently into center of each cookie. Return to oven for 8 to 10 minutes. Immediately place jelly in thumbprint. Yield: 40 cookies.

Opal C. McWilliams, Kalispell, Mont., Northwest Montana Fair

Almond Crescents

  1 c. butter
  2 tsp. vanilla
¼ c. confectioners' sugar
  1 tbsp. water
  2 c. flour
  1 c. blanched chopped almonds

Cream butter, vanilla and sugar; add water and flour. Mix thoroughly; stir in almonds. Form dough into 2-inch crescents; place on ungreased sheet. Bake in 300-degree oven for 20 minutes or until delicately browned. Roll hot cookies in additional confectioners' sugar. May be decorated with red hots before baking, if desired. Yield: 2 ½ dozen cookies.

Mrs. J. M. Brown, Providence, R. I.

Chocolate-Spice Cookies

  1 c. shortening
  2 c. milk
1 ¾ c. sugar
  1 tbsp. cloves
  1 tbsp. nutmeg
  1 tbsp. cinnamon
  1 tbsp. baking powder
  6 tbsp. cocoa
  8 c. (about) flour

(Continued on next page)

Melt shortening; cool. Add milk alternately with remaining ingredients; blend well. Knead for 10 minutes. Roll into a ball; shape cookies using about a teaspoonful of dough or shape into desired cookies. Bake on ungreased cookie sheets for 12 to 15 minutes in 375-degree oven.

FROSTING:

>2 tbsp. margarine or butter
>1 box confectioners' sugar
>1 tsp. vanilla
>¼ tsp. salt
>Milk

Melt margarine with sugar, vanilla and salt; add milk to make frosting of spreading consistency. Dip warm cookies into frosting; let dry on cake racks. Personal Comment: This cookie was entered in the cookie jar contest and presented to Governor Rockefeller on Governor's Day at the New York State Exposition in 1966.

Carmella Bartolomeo, Camillus, N. Y., New York State Exposition of 1966

 Date Stacks

>¾ c. butter
>1 ½ c. flour, sifted
>1 ½ c. quick oatmeal
>1 c. brown sugar
>4 tbsp. milk
>1 tsp. soda
>2 tsp. baking powder

Blend all ingredients as for pie crust. Roll out thin on lightly floured board; cut with cookie cutter.

FILLING:

>1 c. sugar
>½ tsp. vanilla
>1 8-oz. pkg. pitted dates
>1 c. water
>1 tsp. vanilla

Combine all ingredients except vanilla; cook until thick. Cool; add vanilla. Place teaspoon of filling on each cookie; cover with dough cut with slightly smaller cookie cutter. Yield: 2 dozen cookies.

June Rehklau, Camden, Mich., Hillsdale County Fair

Meringues
and Tortes

Black Forest Dream

1 c. egg whites
1 ½ c. sugar
¾ c. toasted almonds
2 tbsp. flour
1 tsp. vanilla
2 envelopes Dream Whip
1 tbsp. rum flavoring
1 6-oz. bar sweet chocolate, shaved

Beat egg whites until foamy; add sugar gradually until peaks form. Cover almonds with flour. Fold nuts and vanilla into egg whites; spread into 3 layers on cookie sheet covered with waxed paper. Bake for 45 minutes at 250 degrees. Chill. Prepare Dream Whip according to package directions, adding rum flavoring; spread between meringue layers. Sprinkle each layer with chocolate; spread remaining Dream Whip over top and sides; sprinkle chocolate on top. Chill thoroughly. Yield: 16 servings.

Mrs. Rubye Shepherd, Wills Point, Tex., Favorite Recipes Food Fair

Dark Delight

3 egg whites
¼ tsp. cream of tartar
1 c. sugar
½ tsp. vanilla

Beat egg whites until frothy; add cream of tartar. Gradually beat in sugar, 2 tablespoons at a time. Add vanilla; beat until stiff and glossy. Drop 1/3 cup meringue for each shell on heavy brown paper on baking sheet; shape as desired with back of spoon. Bake in 225-degree oven for 1 hour and 30 minutes. Turn off heat; let meringues stand in oven until cool.

FILLING:

2 4-oz. squares German's sweet chocolate
¼ c. water
5 eggs, separated
1 tsp. vanilla
½ c. sugar

Melt chocolate with water in top of double boiler, stirring constantly; beat in egg yolks, 1 at a time, beating well after each addition. Add vanilla. Beat egg whites until foamy; gradually add sugar. Beat until stiff, not dry; fold carefully into chocolate mixture. Refrigerate about 1 hour. Pile lightly into meringue shells; chill. Serve with whipped cream and sprinkle with grated chocolate, if desired.

Mrs. B. Eugene Ungleich, Cazenovia, N. Y.

Caramel-Yam Surprise

    4 egg whites
    ½ tsp. cream of tartar
    ½ c. sugar
    ½ tsp. cinnamon
    ¼ tsp. nutmeg
    ¼ tsp. cloves
    1 tsp. vanilla
    1 c. chopped nuts
    ½ c. Ritz cracker crumbs
    1 c. cooked yams, mashed
    20 caramels
    ½ c. cream
       Whipped cream

Beat egg whites with cream of tartar until stiff peaks form; beat in sugar gradually. Fold in spices and vanilla; fold in nuts, cracker crumbs and yams. Turn into 2 well-greased 8-inch pie pans. Bake at 350 degrees for 30 minutes. Cool. Combine caramels and cream; cook over low heat, stirring occasionally, until caramels are melted and mixture is creamy and smooth. Remove meringue layers from pans; pour half the caramel sauce over 1 layer. Top with chopped nuts; top with remaining meringue and sauce. Serve with whipped cream and additional chopped nuts on top.

Wanda Taylor, Grayson, La.

Mocha Cloud

    2 tsp. vanilla
    ¼ tsp. cream of tartar
       Dash of salt
    4 egg whites, at room temperature
    1 ¼ c. sugar
    2 6-oz. Pkg. semisweet chocolate pieces
    1 tbsp. powdered instant coffee
    1 c. whipped cream

Add 1 teaspoon vanilla, cream of tartar and salt to egg whites; beat until frothy. Gradually add sugar; beat until very stiff peaks form. Spread mixture on paper-covered baking sheets in four 7 ½-inch circles. Bake 1 hour at 275 degrees. Turn off oven; let circles dry in oven for 1 hour. Melt chocolate over hot water; stir in coffee and ¼ cup boiling water. Beat until creamy and slightly cooled; fold in whipped cream and remaining vanilla. Stack meringue circles together with filling between each, spreading filling to edge. Chill; cut into wedges to serve. Yield: 6 servings.

Beverlee Morotto, Plantsville, Conn.

Mrs. Moran's Squares

    4 egg whites
    ¼ tsp. salt
    1 c. sugar
    1 c. graham cracker crumbs
    ½ c. semisweet chocolate pieces
    ½ c. coconut
    ½ c. chopped walnuts
    1 tsp. vanilla
    9 whole graham crackers

Beat egg whites with salt until foamy; gradually add sugar, beating until stiff peaks form. Fold in cracker crumbs, chocolate pieces, coconut, nuts and vanilla. Line bottom of 8-inch square pan with whole graham crackers; spread with meringue mixture. Bake in 350-degree oven for 30 minutes. Cool; cut in squares. Serve with vanilla ice cream. Yield: 9 servings.

Mrs. Richard C. Moran, Fort Leavenworth, Kan.

Mardi Gras Circles

    3 egg whites
    ½ tsp. almond extract
    ¼ tsp. salt
    ¾ c. brown sugar
    ½ c. chopped pecans

Beat egg whites, almond extract and salt until peaks form; gradually beat in sugar. Fold in nuts; spread on four 8-inch circles drawn on brown paper. Place on ungreased cookie sheet. Bake at 300 degrees for 35 to 40 minutes. Turn off heat; let meringue circles remain in oven until oven is cool. Remove from oven and peel off paper.

FILLING:

    1 6-oz. pkg. chocolate pieces
    1 8-oz. pkg. cream cheese, softened
    1 tbsp. milk
    ¾ c. brown sugar
    Dash of salt
    1 c. heavy cream, whipped
    1 tsp. vanilla
    ½ c. almonds, toasted

Melt chocolate over hot water; cool. Blend cream cheese and milk; gradually beat in sugar and salt. Fold cream cheese mixture, whipped cream and vanilla into chocolate. Spread filling between meringue layers and on sides; sprinkle top with almonds. Chill; slice and serve. Yield: 12-16 servings.

Mrs. W. H. Huber, Officers' Wives' Club, Amarillo, Tex.

Cereal Kisses

¼ tsp. salt
2 egg whites
1 c. sugar
1 tsp. vanilla or orange rind
3 c. dry cereal

Add salt to egg whites and beat until foamy; add sugar, 2 tablespoons at a time, beating until mixture will stand in stiff peaks. Add vanilla; fold in cereal. Drop by teaspoonfuls onto greased baking sheet. Bake at 350 degrees for 15 minutes or until firm. Yield: 3 dozen kisses.

Sharon Thomas, Proctor, Ark.

 ## Cherub Puffs

⅛ tsp. salt
½ tsp. vanilla
½ tsp. vinegar or ¼ tsp. cream of tartar
2 egg whites, at room temperature
½ c. sugar
1 6-oz. pkg. chocolate pieces
¼ -½ c. chopped nuts

Cover baking sheet with brown paper or aluminum foil. Add salt, vanilla and vinegar to egg whites; beat until soft peaks form. Gradually add sugar; beat until very stiff. Fold in chocolate pieces and nuts. Drop from a spoon onto sheet. Bake for 25 to 30 minutes in 300-degree oven. Yield: 4 dozen cookies.

Mrs. H. P. Knutty, Pres., Officers' Wives' Club, Sacramento, Cal.

 ## Coconut Macaroons

8 egg whites
1 c. sugar
Almond flavoring to taste
2 c. coconut

Beat egg whites until peaks form; gradually add sugar. Beat until stiff; add flavoring. Stir in coconut; drop by spoonfuls onto brown wrapping paper. Bake for 2 minutes at 400 degrees. Reduce heat to 350 degrees; continue baking until golden brown. Turn upside down; brush back of paper with water; peel off cookies.

Mrs. R. H. Jones, Portland, Ore.

Chocolate Meringue Cookies

> 3 egg whites
> 1 c. sifted confectioners' sugar
> ⅓ c. crumbled saltine crackers
> 1 pkg. semisweet chocolate bits, melted

Beat egg whites until stiff but not dry; add sugar slowly, beating constantly. Fold in saltines and chocolate; drop by teaspoonfuls on ungreased cookie sheet, 2 inches apart. Bake at 350 degrees for 5 to 10 minutes or until firm to touch. Yield: 3 dozen cookies.

Mrs. John Hicks, Dallas, Tex.

 ### Forgotten Kisses

> 2 egg whties
> ¾ c. sugar
> 1 lb. chocolate mints

Preheat oven to 350 degrees. Beat egg whites until stiff; add sugar gradually. Chop chocolate mints with sharp knife; add to egg whites. Drop by spoonfuls on brown paper. Place in oven; turn oven off. When oven is cool, cookies are done. Yield: 60 small cookies.

Mrs. G. R. Read, Lincoln City, Ore.

 ### Date Drops

> 2 egg whites
> 1 c. powdered sugar
> 1 c. chopped dates
> 1 c. chopped nuts

Beat egg whites until frothy; gradually add sugar, beating until very stiff. Fold in dates and nuts; drop from spoon onto greased baking sheet. Bake at 300 degrees until light brown. Yield: 36 cookies.

Mrs. Kenneth Fallang, White Sulphur Springs, Mont.

Jesse Fox Meringues

> 2 egg whites
> ⅛ tsp. salt
> ⅔ c. fine white sugar

(Continued on next page)

1 tsp. vanilla
¼ tsp. almond flavoring
Mint jelly

Add salt to egg whites; beat until frothy. Add sugar slowly, 1 tablespoon at a time, beating until stiff. Beat in flavorings. Using a pastry tube with small decorating attachment, make a tiny spiral, beginning with a dab of meringue for a bottom and continue, making 3 coils, one on top of each other. Meringues should be about the size of a quarter. Place on greased cookie sheet. Bake at 225 degrees for 30 minutes. Fill decorating tube with jelly; press jelly into each meringue spiral.

Mrs. Sam H. Roberson, Maryville, Tenn.

 ## Pecan Seafoam Cookies

2 c. brown sugar
3 egg whites
3 c. pecans

Beat together sugar and egg whites until texture is like cream; fold in pecans. Drop from spoon onto ungreased foil. Bake at 375 degrees for 15 minutes or until brown. Yield: 12 cookies.

Mrs. J. W. Simmons, Haynesville, La.

 ## Pineapple Kisses

2 egg whites
½ c. sugar
½ tsp. vanilla or almond extract
1 dozen canned pineapple gems, drained
Slivered almonds or chopped walnuts

Beat egg whites until stiff; add sugar gradually, beating constantly. Add extract. Rinse cookie sheet, leaving surface damp; cover with unglazed brown paper.

(Continued on next page)

Spread 1-inch rounds of meringue about 2 inches apart on brown paper. Top each round with 1 pineapple gem; cover each gem with meringue. Sprinkle with almonds. Bake in 300-degree oven 45 to 50 minutes. Yield: 1 dozen kisses.

Betty Dine, Golden, Colo.

 ## Schaum Meringue Torte

> 6 egg whites
> ¼ tsp. salt
> 1 ½ tsp. lemon juice
> 1 ¾ c. sifted sugar
> 1 tsp. vanilla

Beat egg whites until stiff, adding salt and lemon juice. Gradually add sugar, beating until very stiff. Add vanilla. Line bottom of two 9 x 9-inch round cake pans with brown paper. Butter sides of pans well. Turn mixture into pans. Bake for 1 hour in 300-degree oven. Cool; cut around sides of pan and remove.

FILLING:

> 1 ¾ c. heavy cream
> 1 tsp. vanilla
> 2 tbsp. sugar
> 1 ½ c. drained frozen or fresh strawberries

Whip cream stiff; add vanilla and sugar. Fold berries into whipped cream; spread on top of 1 meringue. Top with remaining meringue; refrigerate for 6 to 8 hours. Yield: 6-8 servings.

Edith Leadbetter, Morgantown, W. Va.

 ## Glace Delight

> 3 egg whites
> ⅛ tsp. cream of tartar
> Dash of salt
> ¾ c. sugar
> ½ tsp. vanilla
> Ice cream
> Custard sauce
> Kahlua

Beat egg whites with cream of tartar and salt until stiff but not dry; add sugar, 1 tablespoon at a time, beating until very stiff. Fold in vanilla; drop by tablespoonfuls onto baking sheet covered with heavy ungreased paper. Bake at

(Continued on next page)

275 degrees for 40 to 60 minutes. Place meringues on dessert plates; place 1 scoop ice cream on each plate. Pour Custard Sauce and Kahlua over ice cream and meringues. Serve.

CUSTARD SAUCE:

> 3 egg yolks
> ¼ c. sugar
> ⅛ tsp. salt
> 2 c. scalded milk
> ½ tsp. vanilla
> ½ to 1 c. heavy cream, whipped

Beat egg yolks slightly; add sugar and salt. Gradually add hot milk, stirring constantly; cook over hot water, stirring constantly, until mixture thickens and coats a spoon. Cool; add vanilla. Fold in whipped cream. Yield: 10-12 servings.

Mrs. S. T. Tisdale, Greenfield, Mass.

 Date-Coconut Cream

> 3 egg whites
> ½ tsp. salt
> ½ tsp. vanilla
> 1 c. sugar
> 1 c. coconut
> 1 c. shredded dates
> 1 c. whipping cream
> 1 tbsp. sherry

Beat egg whites until stiff but not dry; add salt and vanilla. Beat in sugar in 3 additions; fold in coconut and dates. Place in shallow greased pan. Bake at 300 degrees for 30 minutes. Cool; break in small pieces. Whip cream; add sherry. Fold in broken meringue. Serve in sherbet glasses. Yield: 5 servings.

Mrs. A. W. Hodgkiss, Jr., Petoskey, Mich.

 Lemon Cream In Meringue Nests

> ½ c. egg whites
> Dash of salt
> ¾ c. sugar
> 4 drops of lemon extract

Beat egg whites with salt until stiff; add sugar; 1 tablespoon at a time, beating well after each addition. Add extract. Drop by spoonfuls onto cookie sheet which has been lined with 2 layers of heavy brown paper; shape into nests.

(Continued on next page)

Bake at 300 degrees for 10 to 15 minutes or until a delicate brown. Reduce heat to 250 degrees; continue to bake for 30 to 40 minutes or until dry. Cool slightly; remove from paper.

FILLING:

> *3 egg yolks*
> *Grated rind of 1 lemon*
> *¼ c. lemon juice*
> *⅔ c. sugar*
> *2 c. whipped cream*

Combine yolks, lemon rind and juice; stir in sugar. Cook in double boiler until thick. Cool; fold in whipped cream. Fill nests with mixture. Refrigerate for at least 2 hours before serving. Top with additional whipped cream. Yield: 12 servings.

Mrs. Doyal Keller, Officers' Wives' Club, Limestone, Maine

 ## Nesselrode Meringue Torte

> *3 egg whites*
> *½ tsp. vinegar*
> *¼ tsp. vanilla*
> *1 c. plus 3 tbsp. sugar*
> *1 package Nesselrode or spumoni pie filling mix*
> *¼ c. margarine, melted*
> *2 c. cold milk*

Combine egg whites, vinegar and vanilla; beat until foamy. Gradually beat in 1 cup sugar and continue beating until stiff peaks form. Spread on baking sheets covered with aluminum foil, forming three 8-inch circles. Bake in 300 degree oven for 15 minutes. Cool thoroughly. Remove from aluminum foil. Combine package graham cracker crumbs, 3 tablespoons sugar and melted margarine. Pour milk into small deep mixing bowl. Add pie filling; beat at medium speed with electric mixer or rotary beater for 3 minutes, scraping bowl occasionally. Stir in package of candied mixed fruit. Starting with a meringue layer, top with 1/3 of the filling, then 1/3 graham cracker crumbs. Repeat layers ending with filling and graham cracker crumbs. Chill at least 1 hour before serving. Yield: 8-10 servings.

Photograph for this recipe on page 137.

 ## Meringue Chantilly

> *8 egg whites, at room temperature*
> *¼ tsp. salt*

(Continued on next page)

¼ *tsp. cream of tartar*
2 *c. sugar*
1 *tsp. vanilla*
2 *c. heavy cream*
Confectioners' sugar
Large fresh strawberries

Lightly grease and flour 2 large baking sheets; line with waxed paper. Pencil two 9-inch circles on each sheet. Beat egg whites until frothy; add salt and cream of tartar, beating thoroughly. Add sugar, 1 tablespoon at a time, beating constantly. Add vanilla; beat until meringue is stiff and glossy. Divide meringue into 4 parts; fill pastry bag with meringue. Press out a pencil-thick strip of meringue around rim of each circle. Make a lattice by pressing 4 strips of meringue horizontally and 4 strips vertically across circle, touching meringue rim. Bake at 225 degrees for 45 minutes or until firm and dry, but still white. Cool slightly; remove from paper with broad spatula. Whip cream until stiff, sweetening to taste with confectioners' sugar. Place 1 meringue lattice on serving dish; spread lightly with whipped cream. Repeat, but do not spread whipped cream on top layer. Fill pastry bag with remaining whipped cream; pipe decorative swirls on sides and a row of rosettes around top. Fill lattice cavities with strawberries. Serve as soon as possible. Yield: 8 servings.

Mrs. William D. Mallard, Jr., Favorite Recipes Food Fair, Anniston, Ala.

 ## Fruit And Nut Macaroon Pie

18 *soda crackers*
6 *dates, chopped*
8 *maraschino cherries, chopped*
½ *c. chopped nuts*
1 *c. sugar*
¼ *tsp. baking powder*
3 *egg whites, beaten*
1 *tsp. almond flavoring*

Crush soda and crackers very fine; add fruits, nuts and sugar. Add baking powder to egg whites; beat until stiff. Fold in flavoring and crumb mixture; turn into buttered pie pan. Bake at 400 degrees for 15 to 20 minutes. Serve topped with whipped cream or ice cream. Yield: 6 servings.

Mrs. General Casteel, Madison, Tenn.

 ## Charm Meringue

6 *egg whites*
2 *c. sugar*
2 *tsp. baking powder*
Whipped cream
Strawberries

(Continued on next page)

Beat egg whites until very stiff, adding sugar and baking powder slowly. Bake in 250-degree oven for 1 hour. Cool. Cut off top; fill with whipped cream and strawberries. Replace top; garnish with whipped cream and strawberries.

Mrs. Colon Neeley, Shelbyville, Tenn.

 ## Macadamia Nut Pie

>   3 egg whites
>   ½ tsp. baking powder
>   Dash of salt
>   1 c. sugar
>   11 crushed graham crackers
>   1 8-oz. can crushed pineapple, drained
>   ½ c. chopped macadamia nuts

Beat egg whites with baking powder and salt until foamy; gradually add sugar, beating until mixture is stiff. Gently fold in crumbs, pineapple and nuts; turn into greased 8-inch pie pan. Bake at 350 degrees for about 30 minutes. Cool. Cut in wedges; top with whipped cream or ice cream. Yield: 6-8 servings.

Mrs. Bonnie Tucker, Portland, Ore.

 ## Strawberry Cream In Meringue Shells

>   6 egg whites, at room temperature
>   1 ¼ tsp. salt
>   1 ½ tsp. cream of tartar
>   Sugar
>   1 pt. whipping cream
>   3 tbsp. Cointreau
>   1 qt. strawberries

Beat egg whites with salt and cream of tartar until almost stiff. Gradually add ¾ cup sugar; beat until sugar is dissolved. Shape into cups on baking sheet which has been lined with ungreased brown paper. Bake at 250 degrees for 1 hour. Turn off heat; cool meringues in oven. Whip cream until stiff, adding sugar to taste and Cointreau. Fill meringue shells with crushed strawberries; top with whipped cream. Yield: 8 servings.

Mrs. Joe L. Moody, Pres., Officers' Wives' Club, Wheelus AFB, Tripoli, Libya

Coffee-Butter Torte

>   12 eggs, separated
>   3 c. granulated sugar
>   4 tbsp. water

(Continued on next page)

148

3 tbsp. sifted flour
2 tsp. baking powder
16 oz. ground nuts, saving some for top
12 oz. soft butter, unsweetened
3 c. powdered sugar
3 tbsp. coffee

Preheat oven to 350 degrees. Beat 9 egg yolks with granulated sugar, adding sugar gradually and stirring until thick and yellow. Add water to beaten yolks. Mix flour with baking powder; add to beaten yolks. Beat 12 egg whites stiff. Add egg whites and nuts gradually to yolk mixture, 1 tablespoon egg whites and 1 tablespoon nuts at a time. Mix well. Pour mixture into 2 round pans; bake 40 to 50 minutes. Remove from oven; let cool completely. Cream butter and powdered sugar, adding sugar gradually. Add 3 egg yolks, 1 at a time and stir well. Prepare very strong coffee; cool completely. Add coffee to creamed butter, little by little, continuing to stir until coffee is absorbed. Divide filling into 4 equal parts. Slice cakes in 2 layers. Spread filling between layers and on top. Strew ground nuts over top of cake.
Yield: 20 servings.

Beulah Gambold, Coatesville, Ind.

 ## Date Torte

3 egg yolks
½ c. powdered sugar
1 tsp. baking powder
2 tbsp. bread crumbs
½ c. walnuts
1 box dates
2 egg whites
½ tsp. vanilla

Beat egg yolks; add sugar and beat until well mixed. Add baking powder, crumbs, nuts and dates. Beat egg whites very stiff; add vanilla. Fold yolk mixture into whites. Bake in shallow pan for 30 minutes at 250 degrees. Serve with whipped cream. Yield: 8 servings.

Mrs. W. H. Cook, Jr., Charleston, S. C.

 ## Graham Cracker Torte

2 ½ c. sugar
2 tsp. vanilla
5 eggs, separated
1 ½ tsp. baking powder
24 single graham crackers, rolled fine

(Continued on next page)

> 1 c. chopped nuts
> 1 tbsp. cornstarch
> 1 egg, beaten
> 1 c. milk

Add 2 cups sugar and 1 teaspoon vanilla to beaten egg yolks. Mix baking powder with cracker crumbs; add crumbs to egg yolk mixture. Add chopped nuts; fold in beaten egg whites. Pour into 9-inch cake pans lined with foil or with removable bottom. Bake about 20 minutes in 350-degree oven. Combine remaining ingredients for custard filling; cook until thick. Cool and spread between layers. Serve with whipped cream. Yield: 6 servings.

Mrs. Nanette Rothacker, Wadsworth, Ohio

 ## Gypsy Torte

YELLOW LAYERS:

> 8 eggs, separated
> 8 tbsp. sugar
> ½ tsp. lemon juice
> 1 tsp. baking powder
> 8 tbsp. sifted all-purpose flour

Beat egg yolks with sugar and lemon juice until thick and lemon colored. Add baking powder and flour; mix well. Fold in stiffly beaten whites. Pour into two 9-inch round pans greased and lined with brown paper. Bake in preheated 325-degree oven until cake tests done. Cool; remove carefully.

NUT LAYERS:

> 8 eggs, separated
> 8 tbsp. sugar
> ½ tsp. lemon juice
> 1 tsp. baking powder
> 8 tbsp. ground walnuts

Beat egg yolks with sugar and lemon juice until thick and lemon colored. Add baking powder and nuts; mix well. Fold in stiffly beaten egg whites. Pour into two 9-inch round pans greased and lined with brown paper. Bake in 325-degree oven until cake tests done. Cool; remove carefully.

COFFEE FROSTING:

> 1 lb. sweet butter
> 4 c. confectioners' sugar
> 5 tbsp. strong coffee

Beat butter until creamy. Slowly add sugar and strong coffee. Beat until smooth.

(Continued on next page)

Alternate yellow and nut layers, frosting between each. Frost outside of cake and sprinkle with ground nuts. May be made the day before. Refrigerate for several hours before serving. Yield: 8 servings.

Mrs. M. Paul Hunt, Marion, Ohio, Favorite Recipes Food Fair

 ## Hazelnut Torte

> 1 ½ c. granulated sugar
> 8 eggs
> 1 tsp. vanilla flavoring
> 1 ¾ c. sifted cake flour
> ½ c. melted butter
> 2 ½ c. whole shelled hazelnuts
> 2 c. heavy cream
> 2 c. sifted confectioners' sugar
> 3 tbsp. water

Combine 1¼ cups granulated sugar, eggs and vanilla in mixing bowl. Set mixing bowl in bowl of hot tap water; beat at high speed for 20 minutes. Remove from water. Add flour alternately with melted butter, beating at low speed. Turn into buttered and floured waxed paper-lined pan. Bake in preheated 350-degree oven for 45 minutes or until cake tests done. Cool in pan for 10 minutes. Loosen cake around edges; remove pan. Remove paper and cool. Cut cake into three crosswise layers. Place nuts in shallow pan; roast at 350 degrees for 25 minutes. Remove loose skins and grind. Whip cream until slightly thick; gradually add remaining granulated sugar. Beat until stiff; fold in 2 cups nuts. Spread between layers. Combine confectioners' sugar with water; stir until smooth. Spread over top and sides. Sprinkle with remaining nuts. Yield: 16 servings.

Mrs. Minnie R. James, Dayton, Ohio

 ## Chocolate-Walnut Torte

> 6 eggs, separated
> 1 c. powdered sugar
> 1 pkg. German's sweet chocolate
> ¼ lb. finely grated walnuts
> ½ tsp. vanilla

Beat egg yolks well; add sugar. Beat again. Melt chocolate in double boiler; while warm, add to egg yolks. Beat well; add walnuts. Add beaten egg whites and vanilla; pour batter into a fluted pan. Bake for 50 minutes in 350-degree oven. Serve with rum-flavored whipped cream. Yield: 8 servings.

Mrs. Dale E. Jordan, Ellsworth, Maine

151

Cynthia's Mocha Torte

> 4 oz. German's sweet chocolate
> 1 tbsp. strong coffee
> ⅛ lb. butter
> ½ c. sugar
> 6 eggs, separated
> ½ tsp. baking powder
> Pinch of salt
> 3 tbsp. sifted flour

Melt chocolate in coffee. Cream butter and sugar; add egg yolks, 1 at a time, beating constantly. Add cooled chocolate. Sift dry ingredients; add alternately with beaten egg whites to chocolate mixture. Bake in 2 buttered and floured cake pans about 25 minutes at 350 degrees. Cool; turn out carefully.

FROSTING:

> 5 oz. chocolate
> 3 tbsp. sugar
> Pinch of salt
> 3 tbsp. water
> 3 beaten egg yolks
> ¾ pt. whipped cream

Combine chocolate, sugar, salt and water; cook until smooth. Cool slightly; add egg yolks, 1 at a time. Cool thoroughly; add whipped cream. Spread between layers and on top of torte. Chill 4 to 8 hours. Yield: 6-8 servings.

Frances Judson Goodwig, Rochester, Minn.

 ### Kremel Torte Mountain

> 6 eggs
> ½ lb. powdered sugar
> 3 tbsp. bread crumbs
> ½ lb. chopped dates
> ½ lb. chopped hickory nuts
> 1 tsp. baking powder
> 1 pt. whipping cream, whipped

Beat eggs until light; add sugar gradually. Add crumbs, dates and nuts; add baking powder. Pour into greased and floured large cake pan or 2 small square cake pans. Bake at 350 degrees for 35 minutes or more. Cool and break into bite-sized pieces. Mound pieces in shape of mountain on a large plate; cover with whipped cream. Serve by spooning on plates.

Mrs. Robert Bauman, Burlington, Wis.

Toasted Mixed Nut Torte

1 tbsp. confectioners' sugar
1 9½-oz. jar dry toasted mixed nuts
6 eggs, separated
6 tbsp. sugar
1 tsp. grated lemon rind
2 tsp. lemon juice
2 tbsp. dry bread crumbs
2 c. heavy cream

Preheat oven to 325 degrees. Grease two 8-inch layer cake pans. Dust lightly with confectioners' sugar. Grind 1½ cups mixed nuts. Set aside. Beat egg yolks until thick and lemon-colored. Gradually, add sugar, about 2 tablespoons at a time, to beaten egg yolks and beat well after each addition. Add lemon rind, lemon juice, 1 cup ground mixed nuts and bread crumbs to egg yolks. Mix well. Beat egg whites until stiff peaks form. Fold egg yolk mixture into beaten egg whites. Spoon into prepared cake pans. Bake for about 40 minutes or until top springs back when touched gently with finger. Remove cake pans to wire rack and cool cake layers in pan completely before removing. Whip cream until stiff. To ½ the whipped cream, stir in ½ cup ground mixed nuts. Spread between layers of cake. Spread remaining whipped cream on top. Garnish top with remaining whole dry nuts. Yield: 8-10 servings.

Photograph for this recipe below.

Vanilla Torte

4 med. eggs, separated
1 c. sugar
1 c. ground, dried bread crumbs
1 tsp. baking powder
1 c. ground walnuts

Preheat oven to 375 degrees. Grease and line bottoms of two 8-inch layer pans with waxed paper. With electric mixer at high speed, beat egg whites until soft peaks form; gradually add ½ cup sugar, beating until stiff. Beat egg yolks; gradually add remaining sugar until very thick and light colored. At low speed, blend in combined bread crumbs, baking powder and walnuts. With spoon, mix in egg whites. Bake 20 minutes; cool on wire racks. When cool, cut layers in half. Fill with Filling between layers and favorite jam in middle. Sprinkle top with powdered sugar.

FILLING:

Vanilla pudding mix
1 c. milk
1 stick butter

Cook pudding in 1 cup milk; cool. Whip butter and pudding together until very light. Yield: 10-12 servings.

Mrs. Gerda Forsten, Dayton, Tenn.

Wine Torte

6 eggs, beaten
2 c. sugar
1 box zwieback, grated or pulverized
1 c. pecan meal
2 tsp. baking powder
½ tsp. salt
1 tsp. vanilla
1 pt. whipping cream
½ c. sweet wine

Beat eggs with sugar until light in color. Add crumbs, pecan meal, baking powder, salt and vanilla. Place 2 sheets of waxed paper in pans, greasing between layers. Spoon batter into pans. Bake for 25 minutes at 350 degrees. Turn cakes out; remove waxed paper before cakes cool. Whip cream; add sweet wine. Ice cakes and place in refrigerator overnight. Pecan meal is found with envelopes of nuts.

Mrs. C. R. Mayers, Jr., Pompano Beach, Fla.

154

Pastries and Pies

A RECIPE
FOR BASIC PASTRY

(Will make pastry for one 9-inch pie)

1 c. sifted all-purpose flour
½ tsp. salt
⅓ c. shortening
3 tbsp. cold water

Be sure ingredients are chilled. A cold, solid fat and ice water are absolutely necessary.

1. Sift the measured flour and salt together. Cut in the shortening with a pastry blender or two knives until the mixture is the size of small peas. Sprinkle water, a tablespoon at a time, over the mixture while tossing quickly with a fork, until the particles stick together. Usually no definite amount of water can be specified since this varies with the dryness of the flour and the amount of shortening used. Usually 2 to 4 tablespoons of water are required for 1 cup of flour.

2. Form pastry into a smooth ball. Wrap dough in waxed paper and chill in the refrigerator. Sprinkle flour lightly on the board and rolling pin and rub into the wood. A kitchen towel dusted with flour can take the place of a pastry board.

Lightly roll the pastry into a circle 1-inch larger than the pie plate. Lift loosely into the pie plate. Pat out air. Fold edges under and crimp.

3. Prick the entire crust throughly before baking. This prevents bubbles and excess shrinkage.
Bake in a 450° F. oven for about 12 minutes or until golden brown. Cool and fill.

PASTRY TIPS

IF THIS HAPPENS	IT MAY BE CAUSED BY THIS	TRY THIS
Dry Dough Hard To Work With	1. Incomplete mixing 2. Not enough water	1. Don't worry about over-mixing. Final mixing or shaping of dough may be done with the hands. 2. Use level measures of water.
Tough Pastry	1. Not enough shortening or too much flour	1. Use at least 1/3 cup of shortening for each cup of sifted all-purpose flour. Use very little flour on board for rolling.
Shrinking or Buckling of Pastry	1. Pastry stretched during fitting into pie pan 2. Pastry shell not adequately pricked on sides and bottom before baking	1. Use large enough recipe to fit pan without stretching. Don't stretch dough when fitting to pie plate. 2. Prick pastry generously over bottom and sides of pie plate.

Pastry for one single 8-inch crust will make:
    Six or seven 4-inch tart shells
    Topping for a deep dish pie
    Four to six 4-inch turnovers

Pastry for one double 8-inch crust will make:
    Eight or nine 4-inch tart shells
    Two single 8-inch crusts
    Latticed pie
    Ten or twelve 4-inch turnovers

MEASURE INGREDIENTS—DON'T GUESS—WHEN YOU WANT A GOOD PIE CRUST

Butterscotch Cream Puffs

½ c. butter
1 c. boiling water
1 c. flour
½ tsp. salt
4 eggs

Add butter to water; heat until butter melts. Add flour and salt; cook, stirring vigorously until mixture leaves side of pan. Remove from heat; cool 1 minute. Add eggs, 1 at a time, beating after each addition. Drop by heaping teaspoonfuls 2 inches apart on buttered baking sheet. Bake in a 450-degree oven 10 minutes. Reduce heat to 400 degrees; bake for 25 minutes. Do not open oven door during first 30 minutes of baking time. Cool. Split and fill, if desired. Top with sauce.

FILLING:

1 c. sugar
½ c. flour
⅛ tsp. salt
3 c. milk, scalded
3 eggs
1 ½ tsp. vanilla
1 c. cream, whipped

Combine first 3 ingredients in top of double boiler; add hot milk gradually, stirring constantly. Add eggs; cook 3 minutes. Cool; add vanilla and cream. Top with sauce.

BUTTERSCOTCH SAUCE:

1 c. brown sugar
¼ c. rich milk
2 tbsp. white corn syrup
3 tbsp. butter

Combine all ingredients in saucepan. Bring to a boil, stirring constantly; simmer for 3 minutes. Yield; 20 cream puffs.

Mrs. Charlotte Brainerd, Home Economics Teacher, Fennimore, Wis.

Cream Puffs

¼ c. butter
½ c. boiling water
½ c. flour
¼ tsp. salt
2 eggs
Chocolate syrup

(Continued on next page)

Melt butter in boiling water over high heat. Reduce heat; add sifted dry ingredients immediately. Cook until spoon pressed in dough leaves a deep clear mark; remove from heat. Beat in eggs, 1 at a time; beat until stiff. Drop onto ungreased cookie sheet. Bake 10 minutes at 450 degrees; reduce temperature to 400 degrees and bake 25 minutes. Cool; Cut off top of each puff. Fill; replace tops. Pour chocolate syrup over puffs; serve.

FILLING:

> 2 tbsp. flour
> 4 to 6 tbsp. sugar
> Dash of salt
> ¾ c. milk
> 1 square chocolate
> 1 tbsp. butter
> 1 tsp. vanilla
> ½ c. whipping cream
> ½ c. walnuts, finely chopped

Mix flour, sugar and salt; add milk and chocolate. Cook in double boiler over low heat, stirring constantly, until thick. Add butter and vanilla; cool. Add whipped cream and nuts. Yield: 8 cream puffs.

Mrs. Louise Conroy, Roggen, Colo.

 Elegant Eggnog Eclairs

> ½ c. water
> ¼ c. butter
> ½ c. sifted flour
> ⅛ tsp. salt
> 2 eggs

Bring water and butter to a boil; stir until butter is melted. Add flour and salt, all at once; continue cooking, stirring constantly, until mixture forms a ball and no longer clings to side of pan. Remove from heat. Add eggs, 1 at a time; beat well after each addition. Continue beating until mixture has a silky sheen, about 5 minutes. Place about 1 tablespoon mixture on a greased baking sheet; spread into oblong shape until about 4 inches long. Repeat 9 times. Bake in 400-degree oven 30 minutes. Cool; slice off tops with sharp knife. Remove bits of soft dough from inside eclair shell. Fill with Eggnog Filling. Serve with butterscotch or chocolate sauce or top with whipped cream and dribble with sauce.

EGGNOG FILLING:

> 2 ½ tbsp. cornstarch
> 2 c. bottled eggnog
> 1 tbsp. rum (opt.)

(Continued on next page)

Place cornstarch in small saucepan; gradually stir in eggnog. Cook over medium heat, stirring constantly, until mixture thickens and boils. Remove from heat; cool, stirring occasionally. Stir in rum. Refrigerate until thoroughly chilled. Yield: 10 eclairs.

Mrs. Paul R. Beauchamp, New Orleans, La.

 ### St. Joseph's Cream Puffs

  1 c. hot water
 ½ c. butter
  1 c. sifted flour
  4 eggs
 ½ tsp. grated lemon rind
 ½ tsp. grated orange rind
 24 candied or maraschino cherries

Boil water and butter in a saucepan; add flour, stirring constantly, until smooth. Cook over medium heat for 2 minutes or until mixture leaves sides of pan, stirring constantly. Remove from heat; allow to cool slightly. Add eggs, 1 at a time, beating well after each addition. Add grated rinds and cherries; blend. Drop by tablespoonfuls onto ungreased cookie sheet, 2 inches apart. Bake at 350 degrees for 30 minutes or until puffs are light. Remove from oven; cut opening in middle of top. Cool thoroughly.

FILLING:

  2 eggs, slightly beaten
  3 tbsp. sugar
  1 tbsp. cornstarch
  1 c. milk
 ½ tsp. almond flavoring

Mix all ingredients except flavoring in saucepan; cook over low heat, stirring constantly, for 10 minutes or until thick. Cool slightly. Add flavoring; fill puffs. Refrigerate until serving time. Yield: 24 cream puffs.

Mrs. Mary C. Antonellis, Hobe Sound, Fla.

 ### Tiny Coffee Cream Puffs

 ½ c. butter
  1 c. sifted flour
  Few grains of salt
  4 eggs
  1 c. whipping cream
 ⅓ c. sugar

(Continued on next page)

> 2 tbsp. instant coffee
> 1 c. confectioners' sugar

Place butter and 1 cup boiling water in saucepan; bring to boiling point. Combine flour and salt; add all at once. Mix well; cook, stirring constantly, until mixture forms smooth, compact mass. Remove from heat; add eggs, 1 at a time, beating vigorously. Drop by teaspoonfuls onto greased baking sheet, 1 inch apart. Bake at 400 degrees for 25 minutes or until puffs are brown and set. Cool. Make a slit in each puff. Whip cream; add sugar slowly, beating constantly. Combine instant coffee with ½ cup boiling water to make coffee essence; fold 1 tablespoon coffee essence into whipped cream. Fill puffs with whipped cream. Add 1 tablespoon coffee essence to confectioners' sugar; mix well. Spread over cream puffs. Yield: 3 dozen miniature cream puffs.

Mrs. Charles R. Davidson, Emporia, Va.

 ## Danish Almond Puffs

> 1 c. plus 1 tbsp. margarine
> 2 c. sifted flour
> 1 tsp. almond flavoring
> 3 eggs
> 2 c. sifted powdered sugar
> 4 tbsp. cream
> 1 tsp. vanilla
> ⅛ tsp. salt

Cut ½ cup margarine into 1 cup flour until mixture resembles coarse meal; add 2 tablespoons cold water and stir until well blended. Divide dough in half; press each half into 3 x 12-inch rectangle on ungreased baking sheet. Place 1 cup boiling water and ½ cup margarine in saucepan; bring to boil. Add almond flavoring; remove from heat. Stir in remaining flour; add eggs, 1 at a time, beating well. Spread over pastry rectangles. Bake at 400 degrees 50 minutes. Combine remaining margarine, powdered sugar, cream, vanilla and salt; beat until smooth. Frost hot pastry. Cut into slices. Yield: 8-10 servings.

Mrs. Thomas B. Michna, Officers' Wives' Club, Pearl Harbor, Hawaii

 ## Apple Dumplings With Ginger Sauce

> 1 recipe pastry
> 4 or 5 lge. tart apples pared, cored and sliced
> 3 tbsp. hot water
> 1 c. sugar
> 3 tbsp. butter

(Continued on next page)

Roll out pastry into six or seven 4-inch squares; place apples in center of each pastry square. Wet edges of pastry; bring together to form a triangle. Press edges with fork and prick top. Put water in large greased baking dish; place dumplings in water. Sprinkle with sugar and dot with butter. Bake at 400 degrees for 35 to 45 minutes.

GINGER SAUCE:

> 1 c. sugar
> 2 tbsp. flour
> 2 tbsp. butter
> 3 tbsp. crystallized ginger or 1 tsp. ground ginger
> ¾ c. milk or water

Combine all ingredients except milk; stir in milk. Cook until thick; serve hot or cold with dumplings. Yield: 6-7 servings.

Mrs. B. C. Blake, Laurinburg, N. C.

 ## Caramel Dumplings

> 1 ½ c. sugar
> 1 ½ c. boiling water
> 1 tbsp. butter
> Sprinkle of salt
> ½ tsp. vanilla extract

Caramelize ¼ cup sugar in iron skillet; gently stir and shake skillet constantly until lumps disappear. Add remaining sugar; add remaining ingredients. Simmer.

BATTER:

> 1 c. sifted self-rising flour
> ¼ c. sugar
> ¼ c. milk
> 1 tbsp. melted butter
> ½ tsp. vanilla

Preheat oven to 400 degrees. Combine flour and sugar; stir in remaining ingredients. Drop by teaspoonfuls into hot syrup. Bake for 25 minutes. To serve, place upside down in dessert dish. Spoon syrup over each serving.

Mrs. Cortez Stewart, Paris, Miss.

 ## Goulbourn Pear Dumplings

> 1 ¾ c. all-purpose flour
> ⅔ tsp. salt

(Continued on next page)

⅔ c. shortening
5 to 6 tbsp. cold water
2 15-oz. cans pear halves, drained
Butter
Mixed spices
Milk
Sugar
Glace cherries

Place flour and salt in bowl; cut shortening into flour until particles are the size of small peas. Add water and mix until mixture forms a ball; flatten pastry and chill. Divide pastry; roll out thinly in squares or circles large enough to coat 2 pear halves. Trim and brush edges with water. Place pear half on each pastry square; dot pear cavities generously with butter. Sprinkle liberally with mixed spices; top with second pear half. Wrap in pastry, sealing edges well. Stand dumplings on a greased baking sheet. Roll out trimmings to make leaves to decorate pears. Brush dumplings with milk and sprinkle with sugar. Bake at 425 degrees for 35 minutes. Decorate with halved glace cherries. Yield: 8 servings.

Mrs. L. P. Royce, Concord, N. H.

  ## Orange Dumplings

⅔ c. plus 1 tbsp. sugar
Salt
1 tbsp. oleo
Grated rind of 2 oranges
Juice of 1 orange plus water to equal ¾ cup
¾ c. flour
1 tsp. baking powder
¼ c. milk

Combine 2/3 cup sugar, dash of salt, oleo, orange rind and orange juice; boil for 3 minutes. Pour into shallow baking dish. Sift flour, 1 tablespoon sugar, baking powder and ⅛ teaspoon salt together; add milk. Mix well; drop into syrup. Bake at 400 degrees for 20 minutes.

Mrs. George W. Clark, Douglasville, Ga.

  ## Dried Peach Pies

1 lb. dried peaches
Sugar to taste
1 recipe biscuit dough
Shortening
Butter

(Continued on next page)

Soak fruit in water to cover for several hours or overnight. Cook over medium heat until very tender, adding more water if needed. Stir occasionally. Mash well with potato masher; sweeten to taste. Remove from heat; let cool. Roll out biscuit dough as for pie crust. Using a saucer as a pattern, cut moon-shaped pieces. Fill half each pastry piece with peach filling to within ½ inch of edge. Fold over; crimp edges together with a fork. Prick with a fork; fry in shortening over medium heat until brown, turning once. Remove from heat; butter and stack.

CREAM SAUCE:

> ¼ c. butter
> 1 c. powdered sugar
> ½ tsp. vanilla
> ¼ c. heavy cream, whipped

Cream butter; add sugar gradually. Add vanilla and whipped cream. Mix well; serve on warm pies.

Mrs. Dorsey Davis, Athens, Ga.

 Delicious Fritters

> ⅓ c. milk
> 1 egg, beaten
> 1 tsp. melted fat
> 1 c. flour
> 1 tsp. sugar
> 1 tsp. baking powder
> ½ tsp. salt
> 1 c. diced fresh peaches

Combine milk, egg and fat. Stir dry ingredients together; add to egg mixture. Stir until mixture is thoroughly blended. Stir in fruit. Drop by spoonfuls into deep fat; fry until brown, about 2 minutes. Drain on absorbent paper. Yield: 12 servings.

Mrs. Hugh Young, Perryville, Ark.

 Peach Fritters

> ½ c. plain flour
> ½ tsp. salt
> 2 tsp. baking powder
> 1 egg, beaten
> ⅔ c. milk
> 2 tbsp. powdered sugar
> Fresh firm peaches, peeled and sliced

(Continued on next page)

Combine dry ingredients. Mix egg with milk; stir in dry ingredients. Batter should be thick enough to coat fruit. Sprinkle sugar over peaches; dip into batter. Fry in deep 370-degree fat until peaches are tender.

Mrs. T. W. Nicholson, Eastman, Ga.

 ## Pineapple Fritters

> 1 c. sifted all-purpose flour
> 1 tbsp. sugar
> 1 tsp. baking powder
> ¼ tsp. salt
> 1 egg
> ½ c. milk
> 2 tbsp. melted shortening
> 1 c. drained, crushed pineapple
> Powdered sugar

Sift flour, sugar, baking powder and salt together. Combine egg and milk; stir into dry mixture. Add melted shortening and pineapple to batter. Drop by spoonfuls into deep hot shortening. Fry for 3 to 5 minutes or until golden brown. Drain on absorbent paper. Sprinkle with powdered sugar.

Mrs. Henry Deese, Jefferson, S. C.

 ## Fresh Pear Strudel

> 1 ½ c. plus 2 tbsp. sifted flour
> ½ tsp. salt
> ¼ c. shortening
> 1 egg
> 3 tbsp. cold water
> ½ c. sugar
> 1 tsp. nutmeg
> 4 c. peeled, cored and thinly sliced pears
> 3 tbsp. butter

Sift together 1½ cups flour and salt; cut in shortening until mixture resembles coarse meal. Beat egg and water together slightly; stir into flour mixture to make a soft ball of pastry. Wrap pastry in waxed paper; chill for about 1 hour. Roll out pastry on lightly floured board into a 15 x 12-inch rectangle. Blend together sugar, remaining flour and nutmeg; sprinkle half the mixture over pastry. Cover pastry with pears; sprinkle with remaining sugar mixture. Dot with butter; roll tightly like a jelly roll. Set roll in shallow pan. Bake at 350 degrees for 50 to 60 minutes. After roll has baked for 20 minutes, brush the surface occasionally with syrup that forms at the bottom of the pan.

(Continued on next page)

PEAR SAUCE:

> 1 pear, peeled, cored and diced
> ½ c. water
> ½ c. sugar
> 2 tsp. cornstarch
> ¼ tsp. nutmeg
> 1 pinch of salt
> 3 tbsp. butter

Simmer pear in water for 15 minutes. Mix together sugar, cornstarch, nutmeg and salt; stir into cooked pears. Add butter; cook over low heat, stirring constantly, until sauce thickens slightly. Serve warm over slices of warm pear roll. Yield: 6-8 servings.

Mrs. Donald S. Hawkins, Home Economics Teacher, Butler, N. J.

 ### Rhubarb Rosettes

> ¼ c. margarine
> Sugar
> 1 c. flour
> 1 ½ tsp. baking powder
> ¼ tsp. salt
> ⅓ c. milk
> 2 c. rhubarb, cut up
> Butter

Put 2 tablespoons margarine in 8-inch square pan; melt and sprinkle with ¼ cup sugar. Sift flour, baking powder, salt and 1 tablespoon sugar; cut in remaining margarine. Add milk and stir; turn out on floured board. Knead 4 or 5 times; roll out to ¼-inch thickness. Mix rhubarb and ¾ cup sugar; spread on dough and dot with butter. Roll as for jelly roll; cut into 1-inch slices. Place in butter-sugar mixture pan. Bake at 400 degrees for 30 minutes.

Mrs. Louis Ivanish, Malta, Mont.

 ### Chess Tarts

> 1 c. butter
> 1 c. sugar
> 1 tsp. flour
> ¼ c. milk
> 3 egg yolks, well beaten
> 1 c. light raisins
> 1 c. water
> 1 c. walnuts, chopped
> Baked tart shells

(Continued on next page)

Cream together butter, sugar and flour in heavy saucepan. Add milk and egg yolks; mix well. Cook over medium heat until mixture coats spoon. In separate pan, cook raisins and water until water is absorbed. Combine cooked mixture, raisins and nuts. Fill tart shells with filling. If desired, filling may be stored in covered container in refrigerator and used as needed. Yield: 8 servings.

Mrs. Don F. Lynde, Hugoton, Kan.

 ## Great Lakes Blueberry Tarts

> *2 c. fresh cultivated blueberries*
> *1 c. sugar*
> *Few drops of lemon juice*
> *1 tbsp. cornstarch*
> *12 baked tart shells*

Rinse 1 cup blueberries in colander; let drain thoroughly. Cook remaining blueberries in 1 cup water for 15 minutes or until mushy; strain through very fine sieve. Add sugar and lemon juice to sieved blueberries. Return to heat; cook for 10 minutes or until consistency of syrup. Add cornstarch dissolved in 2 tablespoons water; cook, stirring constantly to prevent lumps, until thick. Remove from heat; cool slightly. Fill tart shells with uncooked blueberries. Pour warm glaze carefully over blueberries in each tart. Chill. Serve plain or with ribbon of whipped cream around edge. Yield: 12 tarts.

Photograph for this recipe below.

Currant Tarts

    1 11-oz. box currants
    Standard pastry for two-crust pie
    2 eggs
    1 tbsp. butter
    2 c. brown sugar
    1 tsp. vanilla
    1 c. chopped walnuts

Cover currants with boiling water; set aside. Divide pastry into 24 equal parts; roll each into 3½ to 4-inch circle. Line 24 tiny tart or small muffin cups with pastry. Drain currants; mix with remaining ingredients. Fill shells. Bake 30 minutes at 350 degrees. Serve warm or cold. May be served with whipped topping. Yield: 2 dozen tarts.

Mrs. Peggy Brian, Elkland, Pa.

 ## English Date Tarts

    1 3-oz. pkg. cream cheese
    1 stick oleo
    1 c. flour
    Dash of salt
    ¾ c. brown sugar
    ½ c. pecans, chopped
    ½ c. dates, chopped
    1 egg
    1 tsp. vanilla

Blend cheese and oleo into flour and salt. Roll into small balls; press into muffin cups to shape pastry shells. Mix all remaining ingredients together well with fingers; fill shells. Bake at 350 degrees for 15 minutes; reduce heat to 250 degrees and bake 10 minutes. Yield: 8 to 12 tarts.

Mrs. E. E. Tumlinson, West Point, Miss.

Lemon Curd Tarts

    3 c. sifted flour
    1 ½ tsp. salt
    1 c. shortening
    6 tbsp. cold water
    Grated rind of 2 med. lemons
    ½ c. lemon juice
    2 c. sugar
    1 c. butter or margarine
    4 eggs, well beaten

(Continued on next page)

Sift flour and salt; cut in shortening until mixture resembles large peas. Sprinkle water over mixture; mix thoroughly until a smooth dough is formed. Roll on floured surface to ⅛-inch thickness. Cut into 2½-inch rounds; fit into 1¾-inch muffin cups; prick. Bake at 450 degrees for 10 to 12 minutes or until golden brown. Combine lemon rind, lemon juice and sugar in top of double boiler; add butter. Heat over boiling water, stirring, until butter is melted. Stir in eggs. Continue cooking, stirring constantly, for 15 minutes or until mixture is thick enough to pile slightly. Cool thoroughly. Spoon filling into cooled tart shells. Yield: 4 dozen tarts.

Mrs. David Bruce, Jr., Boise, Idaho

 ## Pecan Tassies

¼ lb. plus 2 tbsp. butter
1 3-oz. pkg. cream cheese
1 c. sifted flour
2 eggs
1 ½ c. light brown sugar
Pinch of salt
1 tsp. vanilla
1 c. chopped pecans

Blend ¼ pound butter, cream cheese and flour to make pastry dough. Press about 1½ tablespoons dough into each of 12 muffin cups. Break up eggs with fork; add sugar, remaining butter, salt and vanilla. Spoon filling into pastry shells; cover with pecans. Bake at 350 degrees for 30 minutes. Cool before removing from pan. Yield: 12 servings.

Mrs. Chester H. Cain, Cincinnati, Ohio

 ## Apple Strudelems

2 eggs, separated
1 c. (firmly packed) brown sugar
1 c. finely chopped pared apples
1 tsp. vanilla
½ c. nutmeats (opt.)
2 tbsp. plus 1 tsp. lemon juice
2 sticks pie crust mix
1 tsp. grated lemon or orange rind

Beat egg whites until soft peaks form; gradually add sugar, beating constantly until thick and glossy. Fold in apples, vanilla, nutmeats and 1 teaspoon lemon juice. Mash pie crust mix with fork; add egg yolks slightly beaten with remaining lemon juice and rind. Mix until dough can be easily handled; form into 2 balls. Divide each ball into 10 or 12 pieces. Roll each piece on floured board into 4 or 5-inch circles. Place a spoonful of apple filling in center of

(Continued on next page)

each circle; pinch dough up around filling. Place on ungreased cookie sheet. Bake at 350 to 375 degrees for 12 to 15 minutes. Yield: 20-25 apple strudelems.

Mrs. Henry G. Schurr, Jr., New Orleans, La.

Cherry-Cheese Turnovers

    1 c. grated cheese
    1 stick butter, softened
    2 c. flour
    ⅛ tsp. salt
    1 c. drained dark red sweet canned cherries or frozen pitted
      cherries

Blend cheese, butter, flour and salt; roll out dough. Cut into 2-inch squares. Place 1 tablespoon cherries in center of each square; fold over corners to seal. Bake at 375 degrees until slightly brown.

M. K. Brown, Pegram, Tenn.

Cranberry Bags

    1 c. flour
    ½ c. butter
    ½ lb. creamed cottage cheese
    Cranberry sauce

Sift flour; cut in butter with pastry blender. Mix in cottage cheese. Form a ball; knead until smooth. Roll out ¼ inch thick; cut into 3-inch squares. Put about 1 teaspoon cranberry sauce into middle of each square. Squeeze 4 corners together to resemble a small bag. Bake at 400 degrees until done. Serve warm.

Mrs. T. R. Williams, Portland, Maine

Graham Cracker Pie Crust

    1 ⅓ c. graham cracker crumbs
    ⅛ tsp. cinnamon
    ¼ c. brown sugar
    ⅓ c. soft butter or margarine

Combine crumbs, cinnamon and sugar; blend in butter. Press mixture firmly against sides and bottom of 9-inch pie plate. Bake at 375 degrees for 8 to 10 minutes or until edges brown slightly. Remove to cooling rack.

Madeline Abraham, Williamson, W. Va.

Cheese Pastry

1 c. sifted flour
¼ tsp. salt
½ c. grated sharp natural cheddar cheese
¼ c. vegetable shortening
2 to 3 tbsp. cold water

Sift flour with salt; add cheese and toss with a fork to mix thoroughly. Cut in shortening until mixture resembles small peas. Sprinkle water over mixture, 1 tablespoon at a time, until dough will hold together. Shape into a ball with hands; roll out. Fit into 8 or 9-inch pie pan. Prick surface ¼ to ½-inch apart. Bake at 450 degrees from 10 to 15 minutes or until pie shell is lightly browned. Cool before filling.

Mrs. Doris Swinehart, Home Economics Teacher, Necadah, Wis.

Egg Yolk Pastry

5 c. sifted flour
4 tsp. sugar
½ tsp. salt
½ tsp. baking powder
1 ½ c. lard
2 egg yolks

Combine dry ingredients; cut in lard. Place egg yolks in measuring cup and stir with fork until smooth. Add enough cold water to make 1 scant cup liquid. Sprinkle liquid over dry ingredients; toss with fork until mixture forms a smooth soft dough. Yield: Pastry for three 9-inch 2-crust pies.

Mrs. Elah Wilkinson, Lexington, Tenn.

 ## Flaky Pie Crust

3 c. flour
1 tsp. salt
1 c. (scant) shortening
6 tbsp. water

Mix flour, salt and lard together with pastry blender until mixture holds firmly together. Add water, stirring mixture into a ball, making sure flour is moistened. Divide dough into 3 parts. Roll out dough 2 inches larger than pie plate; fit in pan. Fold up extended 2 inches of pie crust to edge of pan; flute between thumbs and forefingers. Prick crust with fork. Bake 8 to 10 minutes at 425 degrees until golden brown. Yield: Three 9-inch pie shells.

Carol Fusek, Grass Valley, Cal., Nevada County Fair

Oil Pastry

2 c. sifted flour
1 tsp. salt
½ c. oil
5 tbsp. (about) ice water

Sift flour with salt; stir in oil until thoroughly mixed. Add enough water to moisten; mix as little as possible. Roll half the dough at a time between 2 pieces of waxed paper; dampen bottom piece of waxed paper very slightly. Peel off top paper; flip onto pie plate. Yield: Pastry for one 2-crust pie.

Mrs. James Alexander, Pierre, S. D.

 ## Apple Cider Pie

1 c. sugar
1 c. apple cider
6 c. sliced apples
2 tbsp. cornstarch
1 tbsp. lemon juice
1 tbsp. butter
1 tsp. vanilla
Pastry for 2-crust pie

Bring sugar and cider to a boil; add apples. Cook, uncovered, until apples are tender. Remove apples; add remaining ingredients except pastry to syrup. There should be 1¼ to 1½ cups syrup; if less, add additional cider. Cook until smooth and thickened, about 3 minutes. Fill pie shell with apples and sauce. Cover with top pastry crust; seal edges tightly. Bake at 450 degrees for 10 minutes. Reduce temperature to 375 degrees until crust is lightly browned. Yield: 6 servings.

Mrs. Marvin G. Hansen, Hoquiam, Wash.

 ## Crumbly Apple Pie

½ c. white sugar
¾ tsp. cinnamon
⅛ tsp. salt
5 c. thin apple slices
1 unbaked 9-in. pie shell
¾ c. (firmly packed) brown sugar
¾ c. sifted flour
⅓ c. butter or margarine

Mix white sugar, cinnamon, salt and apple slices in mixing bowl. Arrange in pie shell. Blend brown sugar and flour; cut in butter or margarine with pastry

(Continued on next page)

blender until crumbly. Sprinkle over apples. Bake at 400 degrees on bottom shelf for 35 minutes. Serve plain or with cream, whipped cream or cheese. Yield: 6 servings.

Personal Comment: This recipe received Grand Prize.

Mrs. J. W. Blount, Peru, Kan., Chatauqua County Fair

 ## Ozark Pie

> 1 egg
> ¾ c. sugar
> ¾ c. flour
> ⅛ tsp. salt
> 1 ¼ tsp. baking powder
> 1 c. pared, diced apple
> 1 c. chopped nuts
> 1 tsp. vanilla flavoring

Beat egg and stir in sugar. Add flour, salt and baking powder; stir about 1 minute. Add remaining ingredients; stir until blended. Spread mixture into a greased pie pan. Bake at 350 degrees for 30 to 35 minutes or until brown. Especially good when topped with ice cream or whipped cream. Yield: 6-7 servings.

Mrs. N. B. Kightlinger, Port Clinton, Ohio

 ## Apricot Pie

> ¾ c. plus 1 tbsp. cold margarine
> 2 c. flour, chilled
> Ice water
> 1 c. sugar
> ⅛ tsp. salt
> ¼ tsp. nutmeg
> ¼ tsp. cinnamon
> 2 ½ tbsp. Minute tapioca
> 3 c. fresh apricots, pitted

Cut ¾ cup margarine into flour with pastry blender until particles are very fine. Sprinkle with just enough ice water to make dough hold together. Roll half the dough on lightly floured board to fit 8-inch pie pan. Mix in small bowl the sugar, salt, spices and tapioca. Sprinkle 1 tablespoon mixture in unbaked pie shell. Fill with apricots. Cover with remaining sugar mixture. Dot with remaining butter. Roll out remaining crust. Cut in ½-inch strips with pastry wheel; arrange over fruit in lattice effect. Sprinkle with sugar. Bake in 400-degree oven 15 minutes. Reduce heat to 375 degrees and bake an additional 30 minutes. Yield: 6 servings.

Mrs. Mary Woitt, Merced, Cal., Chowchilla Jr. Fair

Banana Cream Pie

½ c. sugar
4 tbsp. flour
¼ tsp. salt
2 c. milk
2 egg yolks, slightly beaten
2 tbsp. margarine
1 tsp. vanilla
2 bananas
1 9-in. pastry shell
Meringue topping

Mix dry ingredients with a small amount of milk. Add remaining milk; cook over boiling water, stirring, until thick. Cover and cook for 15 minutes longer, stirring occasionally. Add a small amount of hot mixture to egg yolks. Return to hot mixture and cook a few minutes longer. Add margarine and vanilla. Slice bananas into pie shell. Pour filling over bananas. Cool slightly. Cover top of pie with meringue. Bake at 425 degrees for 4 minutes.

Mrs. Ina Moore, Ringgold, La.

 ### Blackberry Pie

Pastry for 2-crust pie
1 pt. frozen or fresh blackberries
Flour
1 c. sugar
¼ tsp. salt
¼ c. water
4 tbsp. butter

Line 10-inch pie plate with pastry. Place berries in pan; slightly dredge with flour. Sprinkle sugar and salt over berries. Add water; dot with butter. Cover with top crust. Bake at 375 degrees until brown.

Mrs. Charles E. Barnes, Marion, Ala.

 ### Blueberry Pie Deluxe

4 c. fresh blueberries
1 c. water
1 c. sugar
3 tbsp. cornstarch
Juice of ½ lemon
1 c. heavy cream, sweetened
1 baked cooled pie shell

(Continued on next page)

Boil 1 cup blueberries with water and sugar; strain. Add cornstarch to liquid; boil until thick. Place remaining blueberries in large bowl. Add lemon juice; pour boiling mixture over berries and let cool. Put layer of whipped cream in pie shell. Put berry mixture over whipped cream; chill for several hours. Yield: 8 servings.

Mrs. Bernard S. Waterman, Officers' Wives' Club, Fort Totten, N. Y.

 ## Butterscotch Deluxe Pie

> 1 c. uncooked oats
> ¼ c. (firmly packed) brown sugar
> ⅓ c. butter or margarine, melted

Heat oats in shallow baking pan in preheated 350-degree oven about 12 minutes. Combine oats and brown sugar. Add butter; mix well. Press firmly onto bottom and sides of 8-inch pie plate. Chill for 1 hour.

FILLING:

> ¾ c. (firmly packed) brown sugar
> ⅓ c. sifted all-purpose flour
> ¼ tsp. salt
> 1 ½ c. milk
> 3 tbsp. butter or margarine
> 1 ½ tsp. vanilla
> ¾ c. whipping cream, whipped
> 6 pecan halves

Combine brown sugar, flour, salt and milk in a saucepan. Cook over medium heat until thick, stirring constantly. Remove from heat. Stir in butter and vanilla. Place in a medium bowl. Cover with foil. Refrigerate 1 hour or until cold. Fold in ½ cup whipped cream. Pour into pie shell. Chill until set. Top pie with dollops of ¼ cup whipped cream and pecan halves. Yield: 6 servings.

Mrs. A. A. Brune, Van Horn, Tex.

 ## Caramel Pie

> 2 c. (heaping) golden brown sugar
> 1 stick margarine
> ½ c. half and half
> ⅛ tsp. salt
> 1 c. hot milk

(Continued on next page)

> 5 tbsp. flour
> 4 tbsp. cornstarch
> 1 c. cold sweet milk
> 4 beaten egg yolks
> Vanilla
> 1 lge. pastry shell, baked

Combine first 4 ingredients; cook for 5 minutes, being careful not to let stick. Add hot milk slowly. Continue cooking for 3 minutes. Slowly add flour and cornstarch, mixed and beaten with cold sweet milk; be sure there are no lumps. Reduce heat to simmer; cook until thickened. Add hot mixture to egg yolks; return to heat. Continue cooking until thickened; remove from heat. Add vanilla to taste. When cool, pour in large baked pie shell. Cover with Meringue.

MERINGUE:

> 4 egg whites
> 1 tsp. vanilla
> ½ tsp. cream of tartar
> 8 tbsp. sugar

Beat egg whites with vanilla and cream of tartar; when peaks form, gradually add white sugar. Spread over pie. Bake in oven at 375 degrees for 12 to 15 minutes. Yield: 8 servings.

Mrs. Beth Ghormley Spurling, Madisonville, Tenn., Sweetwater Valley Fair

 ### Cherry Schaum Torte

> 3 egg whites
> 1 tsp. vanilla
> Dash of salt
> 1 c. sugar
> 2 ½ c. cherries
> ¾ c. cherry juice
> 2 tbsp. cornstarch
> 1 c. heavy cream, whipped

Beat egg whites with vanilla and salt until foamy. Gradually add ¾ cup sugar; beat until stiff peaks form. Spread in a well-greased 9-inch pie pan, building up sides. Bake at 400 degrees for 40 minutes. Let cool in oven for at least 1 hour or more. Slivered almonds may be added to meringue, if desired. Drain cherries; reserve juice. Combine ½ cup reserved cherry juice with sugar. Heat to boiling. Add drained cherries; cook for 10 minutes. Mix cornstarch with remaining cold cherry juice. Add to hot mixture. Cook, stirring constantly, until thickened and clear; cool. Line baked shell with whipped cream; fill with cherry mixture. Top with remaining cream. Yield: 8 servings.

Jo Roxanne Ognibene, Gasport, N. Y., Niagara Co. Fair

Cheery Cherry Pie

    1 c. sugar
    2 c. plus 4 tbsp. flour
    ½ tsp. cinnamon
    ½ tsp. almond extract
    1 No. 2 can cherries and juice
    1 tsp. salt
    ⅔ c. lard
    4 tbsp. water
    1 tbsp. butter

Mix sugar, 4 tablespoons flour, cinnamon, extract and cherries together in saucepan; cook over moderate heat, stirring constantly, until thick. Combine remaining sifted flour, salt, lard and water as for pie crust. Pour cherry mixture into pastry-lined pan. Dot with butter; cover with top crust. Bake at 450 degrees for 10 minutes, then at 350 degrees for 25 minutes. Yield: 6 servings.

Mrs. Maynard C. Nolting, Redwood Falls, Minn., Redwood Co. Fair

Cheese Pie

    1 ½ c. vanilla wafers, crushed
    ½ c. melted butter
    2 eggs
    ½ lb. cream cheese
    1 ½ tsp. vanilla
    ½ c. plus 2 tbsp. sugar
    ½ pt. sour cream

Combine crushed wafers and butter. Line pie plate by pressing crushed mixture with fingers. Chill. Beat thoroughly eggs, cream cheese, 1 teaspoon vanilla and ½ cup sugar; pour into chilled crust. Bake at 375 degrees for 20 minutes. Cool. Beat sour cream, 2 tablespoons sugar and ½ teaspoon vanilla. Pour on top of cooled pie. Bake at 475 degrees for 5 minutes. When cooled, place in refrigerator until ready to serve.

Mrs. H. H. Eggner, Jr., Tampa, Fla.

Chess Pie

    1 tbsp. cornmeal
    1 ¼ c. sugar
    2 tbsp. flour
    3 eggs, beaten
    ¼ lb. oleo, melted
    1 tbsp. vanilla
    1 tbsp. vinegar
    1 unbaked pie shell

(Continued on next page)

Mix cornmeal, sugar and flour; add to eggs. Add oleo; cream thoroughly. Add vanilla and vinegar; pour into pie shell. Bake at 350 degrees for 45 minutes. Yield: 6 servings.

Mrs. W. G. Byrd, El Reno, Okla.

 ### Black Bottom Pie

   1 envelope unflavored gelatin
¼ *c. cold water*
   1 c. sugar
   1 tbsp. cornstarch
Dash of salt
   2 c. milk
   4 eggs, separated
   2 squares unsweetened chocolate
   1 tsp. vanilla
   1 baked pie crust
   1 tbsp. rum
⅛ *tsp. cream of tartar*
   1 c. whipping cream

Soften gelatin in water. Mix ½ cup sugar, cornstarch and salt in medium pan. Stir in milk. Cook, stirring constantly, over low heat until mixture thickens. Beat egg yolks. Stir in hot cornstarch mixture. Remove from heat and add gelatin. Strain into a 4-cup measure. Spoon 1 cup back into saucepan; blend in melted chocolate and vanilla. Pour chocolate mixture into pie crust. Chill. Stir rum flavoring into remaining custard. Cool. Beat egg whites with cream of tartar; add remaining sugar. Add to custard. Spoon over chocolate mixture in crust. Chill 2 hours. Top with whipped cream. Yield: 6 servings.

Mrs. Okey Patteson, Mount Hope, W. Va.

 ### Chocolate Pie

¼ *lb. unsweetened chocolate*
½ *lb. sweet chocolate*
   5 tbsp. water
½ *c. white sugar*
   6 egg yolks, beaten
   6 egg whites, stiffly beaten
   1 9-in. pie shell or crumb crust

Heat chocolates, water and sugar in double boiler; stir until smooth. Cool. Beat in egg yolks; fold in egg whites. Pour into pie shell. Chill overnight in refrigerator. Serve with whipped cream on top. Yield: 8 servings.

Edna M. Burgstabler, Delton, Mich.

Coconut Custard Pie

1 ½ c. sugar
5 eggs
4 level tbsp. flour
5 tbsp. melted butter
4 c. cold milk
Pastry for two 9-in. pies
1 c. coconut

Combine sugar, eggs and flour. Add butter and milk. Pour into pie shells. Put ½ cup coconut on top of each pie. Bake at 425 degrees for 20 minutes, then reduce heat to 350 degrees for 25 minutes or until done. Yield: Two 9-inch pies.
Personal Comment: This recipe also won a ribbon at the New Holland Fair.

Mrs. Charles L. White, Akron, Pa., Ephrata Fair

Cointreau Chiffon Pie

1 envelope unflavored gelatin
¼ c. cold water
4 eggs, separated
¾ c. sugar
⅓ c. orange juice
¼ tsp. salt
2 tbsp. Cointreau
1 tbsp. grated orange peel
1 9-in. baked pie shell

Soften gelatin in cold water. Beat egg yolks until thick and lemon colored. Beat in ½ cup sugar and orange juice. Add salt. Cook over boiling water, stirring constantly until thickened. Add Cointreau and orange peel. Cool until mixture begins to stiffen. Beat egg whites; add remaining sugar gradually. Beat until stiff and glossy. Fold into gelatin mixture. Spoon into baked pie shell. Chill until firm. Garnish with whipped cream sprinkled with mixture of 1 tablespoon grated orange peel and 2 teaspoons finely chopped toasted almonds. Yield: 8 servings.

Mrs. E. J. Mansueto, Pres., Officers' Wives' Club, El Centro, Cal.

Cranberry Pie

1 1-lb. can whole cranberry sauce
1 tbsp. cornstarch
½ c. sugar
1 envelope unflavored gelatin
2 egg whites, stiffly beaten

(Continued on next page)

⅛ tsp. salt
2 tsp. lemon juice
1 tsp. almond extract
1 c. heavy cream
1 9-inch baked pastry shell

Cook cranberry sauce and cornstarch until thickened; cool. Cook sugar and 1/3 cup water to soft ball stage or 238 degrees on candy thermometer. Soften gelatin in ¼ cup water; add to syrup mixture. Pour syrup slowly over egg whites, beating constantly. Add salt, lemon juice and almond extract; continue to beat until cool. Beat cream; combine with egg white mixture. Pour into pie shell; chill. Spread cranberry sauce over top; refrigerate. Yield: 6 servings. Personal Comment: Mrs. Gayoski won a prize at one of the Cranberry Festivals in Massachusetts for this pie.

Mrs. John Gayoski, Rochester, Mass.

 ## State Fair Cranberry-Apple-Nut Pie

1 pkg. pie crust mix
1 1-lb. can whole berry cranberry sauce
½ c. chopped nuts
3 medium apples, cored and finely chopped
½ c. seedless raisins
½ c. sugar
3 tbsp. flour
1 tsp. cinnamon
½ tsp. nutmeg
2 tbsp. butter or margarine, melted

Prepare pie crust according to package directions. Shape 2/3 of the pastry into flat round and roll out to form circle large enough to line bottom and sides of ungreased 9-inch pie pan, allowing pie crust to hang over edge of pan about 1 inch. Combine remaining ingredients and put into pastry-lined pan. Roll out remaining pastry and cut into ½-inch strips. Attach strips to rim of shell; press and twist strips across filling. Press firmly. Fold excess pastry over strips; flute edge. Bake pie in 425-degree oven 40 to 50 minutes or until filling bubbles and crust is browned. Serve warm. Yield: 1 9-inch pie.

Photograph for this recipe on page 155.

 ## Custard Pie

2 ½ c. milk
4 slightly beaten eggs
½ c. sugar
¼ tsp. salt
½ tsp. vanilla
1 9-in. pie shell, unbaked
Nutmeg

(Continued on next page)

Scald milk. Blend eggs, sugar, salt and vanilla. Gradually stir into milk. Pour into pie shell. Sprinkle nutmeg on top. Bake in 400-degree oven 25 to 30 minutes.

Personal Comment: This recipe won the Grand Champion prize.

Mrs. Clarence Schuette, Topeka, Kan., Mid-America Fair

 ### Elderberry-Dutch Pie

1 ¼ c. sugar
⅓ c. flour
⅛ tsp. salt
3 c. shelled elderberries
1 10-in. unbaked pie shell
1 egg white
4 tbsp. thick sour cream
Cinnamon

Mix sugar, flour and salt; pour over elderberries in bowl and toss lightly. Berries should be coated with mixture. Pour into unbaked pie shell brushed with egg white. Spread sour cream over berries and sprinkle with cinnamon. Bake at 450 degrees for 20 minutes. Reduce heat to 325 degrees and bake 30 minutes longer. Juice will bubble. Egg white keeps crust from becoming soggy. Yield: 6 servings.

Mrs. Edwin J. Westrick, Carrolltown, Pa.

Grasshopper Pie

2 c. chocolate wafer crumbs
⅓ c. melted butter
1 tbsp. gelatin
½ c. sugar, divided
⅛ tsp. salt
½ c. cold water
3 eggs, separated
¼ c. creme de menthe
¼ c. creme de cacao
1 c. cream, whipped

Blend 1½ cups crumbs with butter. Press into bottom and sides of a 9-inch pie pan. Dissolve gelatin, ¼ cup sugar and salt in water in top of double boiler. Add well-beaten egg yolks; cook over hot water until thick. Cool; add creme de menthe and creme de cacao. Congeal until mixture is consistency of egg whites. Beat egg whites until stiff, adding remaining sugar. Fold into gelatin mixture. Fold in whipped cream; pour into crust. Top with the remaining crumbs. Chill. Yield: 6-8 servings.

Mrs. E. B. Chancey, Union Springs, Ala.

Heavenly Cream Pie

2 tbsp. cornstarch
1 tbsp. flour
1 c. sugar
1 tbsp. butter or oleo
1 pt. coffee cream
1 tsp. vanilla
1 9-in. baked pie shell
Nutmeg or cinnamon to taste

Mix all ingredients for filling except spice. Cook in a double boiler until thick. Pour into baked pie shell. Sprinkle nutmeg or cinnamon on the top.

Mrs. Gerold N. Fogt, Celina, Ohio

Huckleberry Pie

3 c. huckleberries
1 unbaked pastry shell
3 egg yolks, beaten
1 c. milk
1 c. sugar
Butter
1 tbsp. flour

Clean and wash berries; put into pie shell. Mix remaining ingredients; pour over berries.

MERINGUE:

2 egg whites
3 tbsp. sugar
1 tbsp. vanilla

Beat egg whites, sugar and vanilla until stands in peaks; spread over berries. Bake at 350 degrees until shell is brown around edges and filling thickened.

Mrs. Sibbie Fenley, Springville, Ala.

Lemon Meringue Pie

1 ¾ c. plus 2 tbsp. sugar
3 tbsp. cornstarch
3 tbsp. flour
Dash of salt
1 ½ c. hot water
3 slightly beaten egg yolks
2 tbsp. butter
½ tsp. grated lemon peel
⅓ c. plus 1 tsp. lemon juice
1 9-in. baked pie crust
3 egg whites

Mix 1½ cups sugar, cornstarch, flour and salt; add hot water. Mix well. Bring to a boil, stirring constantly; cook 1 minute. Stir small amount of hot mixture into egg yolks; return to hot mixture in pan. Stir well. Boil 1 minute. Remove from heat. Add butter, 1/3 cup lemon juice and peel. Cool slightly. Beat egg whites with remaining lemon juice till soft peaks form. Gradually add remaining sugar. Beat until stiff peaks form. Pour filling into baked shell; spread meringue over filling, bringing to crust edge. Bake 5 minutes or until brown in a hot oven. Cool before serving. Yield: 6 servings.
Personal Comment: This recipe also won ribbons at Austin and Owatonna Co. Fairs.

Mrs. Ben Dannen, Blooming Prairie, Minn., Mower County Fair

Key Lime Pie

6 egg yolks, slightly beaten
1 15-oz. can sweetened condensed milk
½ c. Key lime juice
1 9-in. baked pie shell
6 egg whites
4 tbsp. sugar

Combine egg yolks and condensed milk; mix well. Add lime juice; blend well. Turn into baked pie shell. Beat egg whites until stiff, but not dry. Gradually beat in sugar just until whites hold firm peaks. Swirl onto pie, spreading to edge of pie shell. Bake in 300-degree oven until meringue is pale honey colored. Refrigerate until served. Yield: 6 servings.

Mrs. J. C. Andrews, Apopka, Fla.

Holiday Cream Pie

1 28-oz. jar mincemeat
1 9-inch pastry pie shell, unbaked

(Continued on next page)

3 tbsp. brown sugar
2 tbsp. flour
1 c. heavy cream
¾ c. chopped pecans

Spread mincemeat in pie shell. Combine sugar and flour; stir in cream. Pour over mincemeat; sprinkle with nuts. Bake at 425 degrees for 40 to 45 minutes.

Mrs. M. S. Gross, Birmingham, Ala.

 ## Old-Fashioned Mincemeat Pie

3 c. mincemeat
1 ½ c. chopped apples
Pastry for 2-crust pie

Mix mincemeat and apples; pour into pastry-lined 9-inch pie pan. Cover with top crust; cut slits in top crust. Bake 40 to 45 minutes in 425-degree oven until crust is browned. Serve warm.

Mrs. Geraldine Mars, Iuka, Miss.

 ## Peach Delight Pie

3 egg yolks
¾ c. sugar
1 can evaporated milk
1 tsp. vanilla
½ tsp. almond flavoring
2 c. mashed cooked dried peaches, sweetened to taste
1 unbaked pie shell

Beat egg yolks thoroughly; add sugar and milk, beating well. Add flavorings and peaches. Pour into unbaked pie shell. Bake at 400 degrees for 15 minutes; reduce heat to 350 degrees and bake until brown and firm.

MERINGUE:

3 egg whites
2 tbsp. sugar
Pinch of cream of tartar

Beat egg whites until stiff; add sugar and cream of tartar. Beat until mixture stands in peaks; spread on pie. Brown lightly in 350-degree oven.

Mrs. E. K. Bullock, Landrum, S. C.

Pear Pie

2 c. chopped pears
Sugar
1 egg, beaten
1 c. cream
⅔ c. plus 1 tbsp. flour
1 tsp. vanilla
⅛ tsp. salt
1 unbaked pastry shell
¼ c. butter

Combine pears, ½ cup sugar, egg, cream, 1 tablespoon flour, vanilla and salt; pour into pastry shell. Bake at 350 degrees for 15 minutes. Combine remaining flour, 1/3 cup sugar and butter; put crumb mixture on top of pie. Return to oven; continue baking for 30 minutes or until browned on top. Yield: 6 servings.

Mrs. Etta McAllister, Dufur, Ore.

 Pumpkin Pie

2 eggs, slightly beaten
2 c. solid pack pumpkin
¾ c. sugar
½ tsp. salt
1 tsp. cinnamon
½ tsp. ginger
¼ tsp. cloves
1 ⅔ c. evaporated milk or light cream
1 9-in. unbaked pastry shell

Mix ingredients in order given; pour into pastry shell. Bake in 425-degree oven for 15 minutes. Reduce heat to 350 degrees; continue to bake for 45 minutes or until knife inserted in center comes out clean.

Rosalyn A. Metzger, Grafton, Wis., Ozaukee County Fair

 Pecan Pie

3 eggs
1 tsp. salt
½ c. brown sugar
1 c. light syrup
1 tsp. vanilla
2 tbsp. melted butter
1 c. pecans
1 ¼ c. flour

(Continued on next page)

½ tsp. white sugar
½ c. lard
3 to 4 tbsp. ice water

Beat eggs lightly; add ½ teaspoon salt and brown sugar. Beat well; add syrup, vanilla and butter. Beat; add pecans. Combine flour, remaining salt and sugar; work in shortening until mixture resembles cornmeal. Add water, a little at a time, until easy to handle. Roll between waxed paper; press dough into pie plate. Pour filling into crust. Bake at 375 degrees for 15 minutes; reduce heat to 325 degrees and continue baking for 35 minutes. Yield: 6-8 servings.
Personal Comment: I won a purple ribbon and $28.50 with this pie recipe in 1965 at Mid-American Fair.

Iva D. Deeringer, Topeka, Kan., Mid-American Fair

Strawberry Pie

1 c. (heaping) flour
½ c. butter
3 ½ tbsp. powdered sugar
1 qt. strawberries
1 c. sugar
3 tbsp. cornstarch

Blend flour, butter and powdered sugar; press in pan with fingers. Bake at 350 degrees until slightly brown, about 20 minutes. Place half of berries in baked crust. Add sugar and cornstarch to remaining berries; boil until clear and thick. Cool slightly; pour over berries in crust. Cool; cover with whipped cream and serve.

Louise H. Brus, Blue Grass, Iowa, Mississippi Valley Fair

Transparent Pie

1 ½ c. sugar
¼ lb. butter
3 eggs, separated
1 tsp. flour
1 c. milk
1 tsp. vanilla
1 9-in. unbaked pie crust

Cream sugar and butter together; add egg yolks, flour, milk and vanilla. Blend well. Beat egg whites until firm; fold into sugar mixture. Pour into pie crust. Bake at 350 degrees for 40 minutes. Yield: 8 servings.

Mrs. Earnest Cole, Germantown, Ky., Robertson County Fair

Puddings

COOKING CUSTARD

Milk, eggs, sugar and flavoring are the basic ingredients for a custard. Custards should always be cooked slowly and carefully.

Failure in custards can be caused by two things: cooking at too high a temperature and cooking too long. A boiled custard is much easier to overcook than a baked custard.

To bake a custard, set filled custard cups in a pan of water. To test for doneness, insert a knife near the edge of the custard. If the blade comes out clean, the custard is thoroughly cooked.

Custard made in the top of a double boiler and cooked over moderate heat is a boiled custard. A boiled custard is done when it is thick enough to coat a spoon.

Savory Steamed Puddings

Steamed puddings are prepared in a different way from other puddings. To steam the pudding, place the filled mold on a rack in a deep kettle. Boiling water should then be added up to about halfway of the mold. Cover tightly and keep water boiling. Steam for the required length of time. Steamed puddings are rich and have a very distinctive flavor.

Cooking With Eggs

Both puddings and custards are made with eggs. They thicken puddings and custards.

Cooking with eggs can sometimes make it difficult to get good results. Steps to follow to success in cooking with eggs:

▲ Store eggs in the refrigerator until needed.

▲ Take eggs from the refrigerator about an hour before needed. It is easier to separate yolks from whites in eggs at room temperature. They will also beat up to a greater volume.

▲ Do not cook eggs at high temperatures. Eggs cooked at high temperatures will water, curdle and be tough.

▲ Take special care in mixing the hot liquid with the eggs if you are making a custard where milk is scalded before being added to the eggs. Add milk slowly, stirring constantly.

Apple Airs

4 egg yolks
4 tbsp. sugar
4 tbsp. flour
½ tsp. salt
1 ¼ c. milk
4 tbsp. butter
1 c. apples, cut in cubes
½ c. chopped nuts
4 egg whites

Beat egg yolks until light and fluffy; gradually beat in sugar, flour and salt. Add milk and heat in top of double boiler. Add butter; stir until thick. Cool slightly; stir in apples and nuts. Fold in stiffly beaten egg whites. Bake in a well-buttered dish at 325 degrees for 30 minutes or until firm. Serve with cream. Raspberries or strawberries may be substituted for apples and nuts. Yield: 6-8 servings.

Alice Atwood, Hanson, Mass.

Bread Pudding Winner

1 egg
3 c. milk
1 tbsp. vanilla flavoring
½ c. raisins
⅔ c. sugar
3 biscuits, crumbled

Beat egg in a 1-quart baking dish; add remaining ingredients. Mix well and bake until light brown at 350 degrees. Yield: 4-5 servings.

Transy Gay Barron, Jonesboro, Tenn., Gray Fair

Hanover Pudding

1 c. fine cake crumbs
2 c. milk, scalded
3 eggs, separated
½ c. sugar
¼ tsp. salt
1 tsp. vanilla
Raspberry jam

Soak crumbs in milk. Beat egg yolks; add ¼ cup sugar, salt and vanilla. Add to crumb mixture; pour into greased baking dish. Set in pan of hot water; bake at 325 degrees for 1 hour and 30 minutes or until custard is firm. Spread thick layer of raspberry jam over top. Beat egg whites with remaining sugar until

(Continued on next page)

stiff. Spread meringue over top of pudding. Return to oven; bake for 10 minutes or until brown. Serve hot, warm or cold. Yield: 6 servings.

Mrs. Harold Arlen, Pacific Palisades, Cal.

 ## Chocolate Elegante

    3 tbsp. butter
    3 tbsp. flour
    1 c. milk
    ½ c. sugar
    ½ tsp. salt
    2 sq. unsweetened chocolate, melted
    3 tbsp. hot water
    1 tsp. vanilla
    3 eggs, separated

Melt butter in top of double boiler; add flour and mix well. Gradually add milk; bring to boiling point, stirring constantly. Add sugar, salt and chocolate mixed with hot water. Cool thoroughly. Add vanilla and well-beaten egg yolks. Fold in stiffly beaten egg whites. Pour into an ungreased 2-quart casserole. Place in pan of hot water; bake at 325 degrees for 50 to 60 minutes.

ICE CREAM SAUCE:

    1 egg
    ¼ c. granulated sugar
    Pinch of salt
    ⅓ c. butter or margarine, melted
    1 tsp. vanilla extract or brandy
    1 c. heavy cream, whipped

Beat egg until light. Add sugar and salt; beat well. Gradually add butter, beating constantly; add vanilla. Fold into whipped cream. Chill. Serve over souffle.

Mrs. J. T. McNarney, LaJolla, Cal.

 ## Date-Nut Pudding

    1 pkg. dates
    1 tsp. soda
    1 c. boiling water
    4 tbsp. shortening
    1 c. sugar
    1 egg
    1 ⅔ c. flour
    ½ tsp. salt
    1 tsp. vanilla
    ½ c. nuts

(Continued on next page)

Pit and quarter dates. Add soda and pour over boiling water. Let cool. Cream shortening; add sugar and egg. Beat; add flour and salt alternately with date mixture. Add flavoring and nutmeats. Pour into a greased and floured pan. Bake for 40 minutes at 350 degrees. Top with whipped cream. Yield: 15 servings.

Mrs. Vernon Carlson, Oakland, Neb., Oakland Fair

 ## Grape Nut Cups

> 1 qt. milk
> 1 c. sugar
> ⅛ tsp. salt
> 1 tsp. vanilla
> 5 eggs
> 1 c. Grape Nuts
> ½ stick butter, melted

Combine milk, sugar, salt, vanilla and eggs; beat well. Add Grape Nuts and butter; stir in. Pour into custard cups. Bake at 450 degrees until firm. Serve at once.

Mrs. Winthrop Rockefeller, Wife of Governor, Little Rock, Ark.

 ## Ginger Dandy

> ½ c. rice
> 5 c. cold milk
> ½ c. sugar
> ½ tsp. salt
> 1 tsp. vanilla
> ½ c. preserved ginger and syrup
> 1 c. heavy cream, whipped

Soak rice for 30 minutes; drain. Add cold milk. Bake at 350 degrees for 1 hour, stirring several times. Add sugar, salt and vanilla. Bake ½ hour without stirring. Chill. Fold in chopped ginger and syrup, and whipped cream. Serve cold. Garnish with whipped cream. Yield: 8 servings.

Mrs. George C. Dewey, Pres. Officers' Wives' Club, Fort George G. Meade, Md.

Simple Rice Pudding

> 1 c. rice
> 1 qt. cold water
> 1 stick margarine

(Continued on next page)

1 ½ c. sugar
½ c. raisins
2 eggs
1 tsp. vanilla
3 c. milk

Cook rice in water until tender; add margarine, sugar and raisins. Take off heat. Add well-beaten eggs, vanilla and milk; stir well. Cook in 325-degree oven 50 to 60 minutes.

Mrs. Bailey L. Clark, Chase City, Va.

 ## Rich Baked Custard

4 eggs, slightly beaten
½ c. sugar
¼ tsp. salt
1 tsp. vanilla
1 qt. rich milk or thin cream, warmed

Combine eggs, sugar, salt and vanilla. Add milk. Strain into buttered baking dish. Bake in a pan of warm water at 300 to 325 degrees until firm. Do not allow water to boil. Pudding is done when knife inserted into center comes out clean. Yield: 6 servings.

Mrs. Burton G. Hatch, Brooklyn, N. Y.

 ## Orange-Frilled Rice Pudding

4 tbsp. rice
1 qt. milk
4 eggs
½ tsp. salt
1 tsp. vanilla
Juice and rind of 1 orange
½ c. sugar

Cook rice in heavy saucepan with half the milk. Pour into a 2-quart casserole with beaten eggs, salt, vanilla, juice and rind of orange. Add remaining milk and sugar. Bake in 350-degree oven for 45 minutes or until set. Cool. Yield: 5 servings.

Mrs. Roy A. Johnson, Lindstrom, Minn., Chisago County Fair

Plump, juicy, red strawberries—who doesn't love them? Here are strawberry recipes which will draw raves and requests for second helpings from guests and family.

STRAWBERRY-RICE CREAM

3 c. water
2 c. milk
¾ c. uncooked rice
¾ tsp. salt
Dash of cinnamon
3 envelopes unflavored gelatin
¾ c. sugar
2 tsp. vanilla
1 c. heavy cream, whipped

Combine first five ingredients in double boiler. Cover and cook over simmering water for 40 minutes or until rice is tender. Stir occasionally. Mix gelatin and sugar; stir into rice until gelatin dissolves. Pour into large bowl; cool. Add vanilla. Chill until slightly thickened. Fold in whipped cream. Turn into 8-cup ring mold. Chill until firm. Unmold.

STRAWBERRY SAUCE

1 10-oz. pkg. frozen sliced California strawberries, thawed but not drained
2 tsp. cornstarch
3 tbsp. sugar
¼ c. water
2 tbsp. orange juice, Strega or orange Curacao
2 tbsp. lemon juice

Puree stawberries. Gradually blend into cornstarch and sugar in saucepan. Add water. Cook, stirring, until sauce boils for 30 seconds. Stir in juices. Chill. Pour over rice cream. Yield: 8-10 servings.

STRAWBERRY WAFFLES

3 10-oz. pkg. frozen sliced California strawberries, thawed and drained
1½ c. (about) milk
3 eggs
⅓ c. salad oil
3 c. buttermilk pancake and waffle mix

Puree strawberries. Combine with milk to measure 3 cups. Add remaining ingredients and beat until batter is smooth. Bake on preheated waffle iron until steaming stops. Yield: 6 large waffles.

See photograph on reverse page.

Spare Pudding

½ c. melted butter
½ c. sugar
½ c. syrup
2 well-beaten eggs
½ c. flour
½ tsp. salt
1 tsp. soda
½ c. sweet milk

Mix butter and sugar; add syrup and beaten eggs. Sift flour, salt and soda; add to mixture. Add milk. Place in well-greased 4 x 8 x 2½-inch loaf pan. Bake in 350-degree oven for 20 minutes.

SAUCE:

3 tbsp. butter
3 tbsp. flour
2 c. boiling water or to suit thickness of sauce
1 c. sugar
2 tsp. vanilla

Melt butter; add flour and boiling water. Cook until thick. Remove from heat and add sugar and vanilla. This dessert is best served warm with whipped cream or sauce. Yield: 8 servings.

Jo Ann Oak, Home Economics Teacher, Long Prairie, Minn.

Sweet Potato Delicacy

2 ½ c. grated coconut
2 c. light cream
4 sweet potatoes
4 tbsp. sugar
2 tbsp. butter

Combine 2 cups coconut and cream in a saucepan. Bring to a boil; remove from heat. Soak for 30 minutes. Press all liquid from coconut and discard pulp. Boil unpeeled sweet potatoes until soft; peel and mash. Add coconut cream and sugar; beat until light and fluffy. Pour mixture into buttered, shallow baking dish. Bake at 400 degrees for 15 minutes. Saute remaining coconut in butter. Sprinkle on top after baked. Serve hot or cold. Yield: 4-5 servings.

Mrs. Jill Kaufman, Home Economics Teacher, Cullom, Ill.

Basic Banana Pudding

6 eggs, separated
3 c. milk

(Continued on next page)

1 ½ c. plus 2 tbsp. sugar
3 tbsp. flour
1 lb. vanilla wafers
6 med. ripe bananas, sliced
Vanilla flavoring to taste

Mix egg yolks, milk, 1½ cups sugar and flour; cook in double boiler until medium thick. Let cool. Put wafers and bananas in large Pyrex dish in alternate layers; pour milk mixture over. Beat egg whites until stiff; add remaining sugar and flavoring. Spread over pudding. Brown in 350-degree oven until golden brown. Yield: 10 servings.

Mrs. Rex L. Phillips, Altoona, Ala., Favorite Recipes Food Fair

 ### Butterscotch Cream

Butter, size of walnut
2 c. brown sugar
Milk
½ c. flour
2 eggs
2 c. milk
Bananas
Nuts

Combine butter, brown sugar and ¾ cup milk in pan; cook for 6 minutes. Mix flour, eggs and 2 cups milk; beat well until smooth. Add to cooked mixture; cook all together until thick. Stir and beat well as mixture thickens. Top with bananas and nuts.

Mrs. Omer J. Miller, Goshen, Ind.

 ### Chocolate Yummy

2 c. milk
1 c. sugar
⅓ c. flour
⅛ tsp. salt
⅓ c. cocoa
1 tsp. vanilla

Heat 1½ cups milk in double boiler. Mix dry ingredients together in bowl pressing the chocolate lumps against side of bowl. When thoroughly mixed, stir in remaining milk. Add to hot milk in double boiler; stir until thickened. Remove from heat; stir in vanilla. Pour into individual containers. Yield: 4 servings.

Mrs. Roy M. Bowen, Woodland, Wash.

Creamy Coconut Pudding

3 tbsp. cornstarch
3 tbsp. sugar
⅛ tsp. salt
2 c. coconut milk

Combine dry ingredients. Add ½ cup prepared coconut milk and blend to a smooth paste. Heat remaining milk on low heat; add to cornstarch mixture, stirring constantly until thickened. Pour pudding into a shallow pan or bowl; allow to cool until firm. Yield: 6 servings.

Personal Comment: Coconut milk as used in Hawaii is extracted from grated coconut and should not be confused with the watery liquid found in a mature coconut. Coconut milk is easily made by either of the following methods: Fresh coconut: Pour 2 cups boiling water over 4 cups freshly grated coconut. Let stand 20 minutes, stirring occasionally. Strain this mixture through a double thickness of cheesecloth, pressing hard to remove all liquid. Prepared coconut: Pour 2 cups of milk over 1 can or package of shredded coconut. Slowly bring to a boil; remove from heat and let stand 20 minutes, stirring occasionally. Strain through a double thickness of cheesecloth, pressing to remove all liquid.

Arlene Lenort, Home Economics Teacher, Pine Island, Minn.

Creme Brulee

3 c. heavy cream
1 1-in. piece vanilla bean
6 egg yolks
6 tbsp. white sugar
½ c. brown sugar

Heat cream and vanilla bean in top of double boiler. Beat egg yolks with white sugar until light and creamy. Remove vanilla bean; carefully and slowly stir warm cream into egg yolks. Return mixture to double boiler over boiling water. Stir constantly until mixture coats spoon. Pour into glass serving dish; chill until firm. Cover top of custard with brown sugar. Place serving dish in a tray of crushed ice; melt and caramelize sugar under broiler. Watch carefully to prevent burning. Serve immediately. Yield: 6 servings.

Mrs. John Fitzgerald Kennedy

Mrs. Livingston's Cranberry Pudding

1 ⅓ c. flour
½ c. molasses
⅓ c. hot water
2 tsp. soda
½ tsp. salt
2 c. raw cranberries, halved
½ c. butter
1 c. sugar
1 tsp. flour
½ c. cream

Combine flour, molasses, hot water mixed with soda, salt and cranberries. Pour into a buttered pan and steam 2 hours. Pudding may be cooked in top half of double boiler or coffee can placed in pan of boiling water and covered. Beat butter, sugar and flour until creamy. Heat in double boiler; add cream. Serve over warm pudding. Yield: 6-8 servings.

Mrs. John W. Livingston, Blytheville, Ark.

 ### Maple Walnut Cream Pudding

2 c. milk
1 c. maple syrup
2 tbsp. cornstarch
¼ tsp. salt
2 eggs
½ c. chopped walnuts
1 c. cream, whipped stiffly

Scald 1¾ cups milk with maple syrup in top of double boiler. Combine remaining milk with cornstarch and salt; add gradually to hot mixture. Stir until mixture thickens. Beat eggs; add slowly to syrup mixture, stirring briskly. Cook 5 minutes longer. Pour into serving dish and sprinkle with chopped nuts while pudding is still hot. When cold, cover with cream and serve.

Mrs. Phillip H. Hoff, Wife of Governor, Montpelier, Vt.

 ### Old-Fashioned Southern Custard

3 qt. milk
1 c. cream
10 eggs, separated
2 c. sugar
1 heaping tbsp. flour

(Continued on next page)

Pinch of salt
1 tbsp. vanilla

Scald milk and cream in a large double boiler. Do not boil. Beat egg yolks. Beat egg whites until stiff. Mix sugar, flour and salt; add to the beaten egg yolks. To the yolk mixture, add several tablespoons of scalded milk and cream, mixing well. Slowly add the yolk mixture to scalded milk mixture. Cook for 10 minutes, stirring constantly. Turn off heat, but leave mixture over boiling water. Beat in egg whites. Add vanilla; cool. Chill. Serve with cookies or cake.

Clara Lee Webb, Amber, Okla.

 ## Orange Custard Pudding

2 oranges
1 qt. milk
3 tbsp. flour
3 egg yolks
1 c. sugar
1 tsp. vanilla extract
3 or 4 egg whites

Peel and skin sections of oranges; marinate in a little sugar. Let set while mixing other ingredients. Simmer milk; do not boil. Mix flour, egg yolks and sugar; add slowly to milk, stirring constantly. Cook to desired thickness. Pour into Pyrex casserole and add vanilla extract. Stir in orange sections. Beat egg whites until stiff; use as topping. Brown quickly in a 450-degree oven. Chill and serve ice cold. For a thicker custard, add another heaping tablespoon of flour.
Personal Comment: This recipe was given to Mrs. Connally by her grandmother and is the first dessert she cooked after she and Governor Connally were married. It is still a favorite of their family.

Mrs. John Connally, Wife of Governor, Austin, Tex.

 ## Pineapple-Crumb Pudding

1 pkg. vanilla pudding mix
Milk
1 c. graham cracker crumbs
¼ c. creamy or chunk-style peanut butter
1 c. drained crushed pineapple
½ c. heavy cream, whipped

Cook pudding with milk according to directions on package. Cool. Blend graham cracker crumbs and peanut butter. Stir pineapple into cooled pudding; fold in whipped cream. Arrange in parfait glasses, beginning and ending with crumbs. Garnish with additional whipped cream, if desired. Yield: 6 servings.

Photograph for this recipe on page 187.

Raisin Duff With Egg Sauce

1 c. flour
½ c. raisins
1 egg
½ c. cold water
2 tsp. baking powder
½ tsp. salt
1 tbsp. butter

Mix together all ingredients; put in double boiler. Cook for 1 hour. Test with cake tester.

EGG SAUCE:

2 eggs, separated
½ c. sugar
1 tsp. cooking sherry or vanilla flavoring
Dash of nutmeg (opt.)

Beat egg whites until stiff; add sugar. Add well-beaten egg yolks. Add cooking sherry and nutmeg. Serve over duff. Yield: 4 servings.

Mrs. Charles T. Howard, Birmingham, Ala.

Rice-Cinnamon Pudding

1 qt. whole milk
Rice
⅛ tsp. salt
1 stick cinnamon
4 tbsp. cream

Heat milk in top of double boiler. Add ⅞ cup rice, salt and cinnamon stick. Cook over hot water, covered, until rice is done, stirring occasionally. Remove cinnamon stick. Stir in cream and pour into large serving bowl. Garnish with cinnamon and raisins, or red and green cherries may be used as garnish for Christmas. Yield: 12-15 servings.

Mrs. Beverly Skrovig, Home Economics Teacher, Baltic, S. D.

Tapioca Magic

2 tbsp. tapioca
2 ripe coconuts
1 c. maple or other fruit syrup

(Continued on next page)

Boil tapioca in fluid extracted from coconuts. Pour boiled mixture into mold to cool and harden. Extract meat from coconuts; grate it finely. Squeeze all its juice through a clean rag sterilized by boiling. Resulting juice forms one of the sauces with which pudding is served. To serve, unmold hardened mixture. Apply maple syrup to pudding first, followed by juice squeezed from coconuts. A distinction is made between liquid occurring naturally in the nut, and the rich flavorful juice extracted by squeezing the grated meat.

Personal Comment: This recipe was sent to me in 1930 by my husband who was then in Nyounghla, Upper Burma.

Mrs. R. E. Leigh, Austin, Tex.

 ## Chocolate Pudding Delicious

    3 *tbsp. shortening*
    ⅔ *c. white sugar*
    1 *egg, well beaten*
    2 ¼ *c. sifted flour*
    3 *tsp. baking powder*
    ¼ *tsp. salt*
    1 *c. milk*
    2 ½ *squares unsweetened chocolate, melted*
    1 *tsp. vanilla*

Work shortening with spoon until creamy and fluffy. Add sugar; work with spoon until light. Stir in egg. Beat well. Sift together flour, baking powder and salt. Add to shortening mixture alternately with milk. Add melted chocolate and vanilla. Pour into 2-quart greased pudding mold. Cover. Place mold in large kettle or trivet or wire rack. Pour in boiling water to cover half of mold. Steam for 1 hour and 15 minutes. Add more boiling water if necessary to keep same level. Three-fourths cup raisins or walnuts may be added, if desired. Serve with hard sauce or ice cream. Yield: 8-10 servings.

Mrs. Daisie L. Mardin, Plymouth, N. H.

 ## Molded Applesauce Pudding

    ½ *c. butter*
    1 *c. sugar*
    1 *egg*
    1 *c. thick aplesauce, unsweetened*
    1 *c. raisins or dates*
    1 *c. nuts*
    1 ¾ *c. flour*
    1 *tsp. baking soda*
    ¼ *tsp. cinnamon*
    ½ *tsp. cloves*

(Continued on next page)

Cream butter and sugar together; add egg, applesauce, fruit and nuts. Mix well. Add dry ingredients which have been sifted together. Pour into steamed pudding mold; cover with waxed paper and steam for 3 hours. Good hot or cold. Serve with favorite caramel sauce. Yield: 12 servings.

Mrs. Dale Stubbendick, Palmyra, Neb.

 ### Harvest Steamed Dessert

1 c. grated apples
1 c. grated carrots
1 c. grated potatoes
1 c. finely ground suet
½ c. white sugar
½ c. brown sugar
2 tbsp. brandy or rum
½ tsp. nutmeg
½ tsp. cinnamon
½ tsp. cloves
1 c. flour
1 tsp. baking powder
1 tsp. salt
1 c. nuts
1 c. raisins
½ c. chopped dates

Mix all ingredients well; put in greased pans. Tie 2 layers waxed paper over pudding pans and steam 3 hours. Remove paper immediately. Serve hot with vanilla sauce or caramel sauce flavored with rum or brandy, whichever was used in pudding. Yield: 8 servings

Mrs. Peter Van Otten, Tooele, Utah

 ### Salim Pudding

3 c. flour
1 c. raisins
⅔ c. molasses
1 c. (scant) milk
⅓ c. butter
½ tsp. cinnamon
¼ tsp. cloves
1 tsp. salt
¼ tsp. nutmeg
1 tsp. soda

Mix all ingredients as given, adding soda last. Pour into greased pan. Steam for 3 hours. May be served with cream. Yield: 8 servings.

Kathleen L. Zehr, Home Economics Teacher, Carthage, N. Y.

Steamed Cranberry Pudding

    1 ½ c. sifted all-purpose flour
    1 tsp. double acting baking powder
    ¼ tsp. salt
    1 ¼ c. fresh cranberries
    ½ c. molasses
    ⅓ c. warm water
    2 tbsp. shortening, melted
    2 tsp. soda

Sift flour, baking powder and salt together. Add cranberries. Mix molasses, water, shortening and soda; add to cranberry-flour mixture. Spoon into greased 1-quart mold and tie waxed paper loosely over top. Steam 2 hours. Unmold onto serving platter.

EASY VANILLA SAUCE

    1 c. sugar
    ½ c. cream
    ½ c. butter, melted
    1 tsp. vanilla or rum flavoring

Mix sugar and cream. Heat; do not boil. When ready to serve, beat in butter with rotary beater. Add flavoring. Serve hot over hot pudding. Yield: 8 servings.

Photograph for this recipe below.

Pumpkin-Spice Pudding

½ c. butter or margarine
1 c. brown sugar, firmly packed
¼ c. white sugar
½ tsp. cinnamon
½ tsp. nutmeg
½ tsp. ginger
2 eggs, well beaten
1 c. chopped walnuts
2 c. sifted all-purpose flour
1 ½ tsp. baking powder
¼ tsp. soda
1 ½ tsp. salt
1 c. canned or cooked pumpkin
½ c. sour cream

Cream butter, brown and white sugar and spices together until light and fluffy. Beat in eggs; stir in walnuts. Sift flour with baking powder, soda and salt. Add to cream mixture alternately with pumpkin and sour cream. Turn into well-greased 1½ to 2-quart mold; cover tightly. Set mold in pan of hot water. Water should come halfway up sides of mold. Cover pan; steam pudding in continuously boiling water about 2 hours. Remove mold from water; let stand 5 minutes before removing pudding. Serve with lemon sauce. Yield: 8 servings.

Mrs. Don Tracy, Lakeview, Ore.

Tangy Fig Pudding

2 lb. dried figs, chopped
½ lb. bread crumbs
½ lb suet, cut fine
6 oz. sugar
4 tbsp. milk
4 eggs
4 tsp. baking powder
½ tsp. cinnamon
½ c. chopped nuts

Mix ingredients together; let stand 1 hour. Steam 4 hours in greased mold. May be reheated.

HOT LEMON SAUCE:

Diluted lemon juice
Small piece of butter
1 tsp. vanilla
Cornstarch

(Continued on next page)

Combine lemon juice, butter, vanilla and enough cornstarch to slightly thicken. Heat until well blended. Serve with pudding. Yield: 10 servings.
Personal Comment: This recipe was brought from Scotland.

Mrs. Andrew J. Snow, St. Petersburg Beach, Fla.

Blind Date

3 c. brown sugar
3 tbsp. butter
1 egg
2 c. flour
2 tsp. baking powder
Dash of salt
1 c. milk
1 c. chopped dates
1 c. raisins
½ c. chopped walnuts
3 c. water

Cream 1 cup brown sugar and 2 tablespoons butter; add egg. Alternate dry ingredients and milk to creamed mixture, beating after each addition. Add dates, raisins and nuts. Pour into greased 13 x 9½ x 2-inch pan. Bring remaining brown sugar, water and remaining butter to a boil; pour over batter. Bake at 375 degrees for 25 minutes. Serve with whipped cream. Yield: 12 servings.

Phyllis Burroughs, Catlin, Ill.

Fruited Pudding-Cake

Fresh or canned fruit, any type
1 ¾ c. sugar
3 tbsp. butter
1 tsp. baking powder
¼ tsp. salt
½ c. milk
1 c. sifted flour
1 tbsp. cornstarch
⅔ c. boiling water

Cover bottom of 8-inch square pan with fruit. Mix ¾ cup sugar, butter, baking powder, salt, milk and flour together; pour over fruit. Mix remaining sugar

(Continued on next page)

and cornstarch; sprinkle over mixture. Pour boiling water over top. Bake at 375 degrees for 45 minutes. Yield: 9 servings.

Alice Knox, Latham, Kan.

Hot Fudge Pudding-Cake

> 1 c. sifted flour
> ¾ c. white sugar
> 6 tbsp. cocoa
> 2 tsp. baking powder
> ¼ tsp. salt
> ½ c. milk
> 2 tbsp. melted shortening
> 1 c. chopped nuts
> 1 c. brown sugar, packed
> 1 ¾ c. hot water

Sift flour, white sugar, 2 tablespoons cocoa, baking powder and salt; stir in milk and melted shortening. Mix until smooth; add chopped nuts. Turn into generously greased and floured 9 x 9 x 2½-inch pan. Sprinkle with a mixture of brown sugar and remaining cocoa. Pour hot water over entire batter. Bake 40 to 45 minutes at 350 degrees. Cut in squares; invert squares on plates. Dip sauce from pan over each. Serve plain or with whipped cream. For butterscotch pudding, omit cocoa and add 1 teaspoon of vanilla to batter.

Mrs. Rena Toole, Gray, Maine, Favorite Recipes Food Fair

Luscious Lemon Cups

> 1 c. sugar
> 4 tbsp. flour
> ⅛ tsp. salt
> 2 tbsp. butter or shortening, melted
> 5 tbsp. lemon juice
> Grated rind of 1 lemon
> 3 eggs, separated
> 1 ½ c. milk

Combine sugar, flour, salt and butter; add lemon juice and rind. Add to well beaten egg yolks and milk; mix well. Fold in stiffly beaten egg whites. Pour into greased custard cups or 2-quart dish. Bake in pan of hot water at 325 to 350 degrees for 45-60 minutes. Cake will be on top and custard on bottom. Serve chilled with whipped cream garnished with additional lemon rind. Yield: 8-10 servings.

Mrs. W. J. Maddocks, Pres. Officers' Wives' Club, Norfolk, Va.

Cobblers, Crisps and Shortcakes

Cinnamon-Apple Cobbler

1 No. 2 can apple pie filling
1 can refrigerated quick cinnamon rolls

Pour apple pie filling into 9-inch pie pan or square cake pan. Separate dough into 8 rolls. Cut each roll in half. Place on pie filling, cinnamon side up. Bake at 350 degrees for 20 to 25 minutes or until golden brown. Spread icing on top; serve warm. Yield: 5 servings.

Mrs. Arizona L. Jackson, Lake Charles La.

 ### New England Apple Cobbler

4 c. thinly sliced McIntosh apples
¾ c. walnuts
1 ½ c. sugar
1 tsp. cinnamon
1 egg
½ c. cream or milk
1 c. melted butter
1 c. sifted all-purpose flour
1 tsp. baking powder
¼ tsp. salt

Place apples in 2-quart buttered casserole. Mix and sprinkle with ½ cup walnuts, ½ cup sugar and cinnamon. Beat egg; add cream and butter. Add dry ingredients and remaining sugar all at once to egg mixture; stir until smooth. Pour over apples. Sprinkle with remaining nuts. Bake at 325 to 350 degrees about 55 minutes. Serve with whipped cream or ice cream. Flavor whipped cream with a little cinnamon, if desired. Yield: 8-10 servings.

Margaret Webster, Oklahoma City, Okla.

Yankee Apple John

6 tart apples, thinly sliced
⅓ c. sugar
½ tsp. nutmeg
¾ tsp. cinnamon
Salt
2 c. sifted flour
3 tsp. baking powder
½ c. shortening
⅔ c. milk or enough for biscuit batter

Fill shallow 12 x 8-inch greased baking dish with sliced apples. Mix sugar, spices and ⅛ teaspoon salt; sprinkle over apples. Sift flour, baking powder

(Continued on next page)

and ¾ teaspoon salt. Cut in shortening; add milk. Roll out to fit dish and place over apples. Cut a few slits in top of crust. Bake in 425-degree oven for 25 minutes.

NUTMEG SAUCE:

>   1 c. sugar
>   ¼ tsp. nutmeg
>   2 tbsp. flour
>   Dash of salt
>   2 c. boiling water
>   1 tbsp. butter
>   1 tbsp. vinegar

Mix sugar, nutmeg, flour and salt. Add boiling water, stirring constantly. Add butter and boil 5 minutes. Remove from fire; add vinegar. Serve hot over Yankee Apple John.

Frances L. Colby, Danville, N. H.

 ## Apricot Cobbler Supreme

>   1 egg
>   1 c. sugar
>   1 c. flour
>   1 tsp. baking powder
>   ½ tsp. salt
>   ¼ c. milk
>   ½ tsp. vanilla
>   1 tbsp. melted shortening
>   2 c. cooked apricots, sweetened

Beat egg and sugar until creamy. Sift flour, baking powder and salt. Add dry ingredients alternately with milk and vanilla to creamed mixture; add shortening. Put fruit in greased baking dish; pour in batter. Bake at 350 degrees for 30 minutes or until batter is done. Serve warm with cream or ice cream. Any type fruit, fresh or canned, may be substituted for apricots. If using fresh fruit, sprinkle with 1 cup sugar and heat before pouring in batter.

Mrs. Ann Stater, Amanda Park, Wash.

 ## Cherry-Cinnamon Cobbler

>   ½ c. white sugar
>   2 to 4 tbsp. cinnamon candy
>   2 tbsp. cornstarch
>   ½ c. water
>   Cherry juice

(Continued on next page)

1 1-lb. can sour cherries, drained
1 ½ c. sifted flour
2 tsp. baking powder
½ tsp. salt
6 tbsp. brown sugar
⅓ c. finely chopped pecans
¼ c. shortening
1 egg, slightly beaten
2 tbsp. milk
1 tbsp. soft butter
¼ tsp. cinnamon
½ c. sifted powdered sugar
1 tbsp. lemon juice

Combine white sugar, cinnamon candy, cornstarch, water and cherry juice in saucepan. Cook over medium heat, stirring occasionally until thickened. Stir in cherries. Pour into 8 x 8-inch pan. Sift flour with baking powder and salt. Add 3 tablespoons brown sugar and pecans. Cut in shortening until fine. Combine egg and milk. Add to flour mixture. Mix until all dry particles are moistened, adding a few drops more milk if necessary. Roll on floured surface to 12 x 14-inch rectangle. Brush with butter. Combine remaining brown sugar and cinnamon. Sprinkle over dough. Roll up, starting with 12-inch side. Cut into ¾-inch slices. Place on cherry filling. Bake at 400 degrees for 25 to 30 minutes. Glaze with mixture of powdered sugar and lemon juice while warm. Yield: 8-10 servings.

Mrs. John Fryer, Milan, Ohio, Favorite Recipes Food Fair

 ## Top O' The Range Cherry Dessert

1 can tart cherries, packed in water
½ c. plus 1 tbsp. sugar
2 tbsp. cornstarch
Red food coloring (opt.)
¼ tsp. almond flavoring
1 c. prepared biscuit mix
⅓ c. milk
2 tbsp. butter

Mix cherries, ½ cup sugar and cornstarch in saucepan. Add food coloring and flavoring. Bring to boil, stirring gently. Remove from heat. Mix remaining ingredients; drop by spoonfuls on cherry mixture. Cover; cook over low heat 20 minutes. Serve hot.

Elaine Duncan, Millport, Ala.

 ## Deep-Dish Cherry Almond Cobbler

¼ c. finely chopped almonds
Sugar

(Continued on next page)

208

　　1 c. biscuit mix
　　2 tbsp. butter or margarine
⅓ c. milk
　　Cherry Filling

Stir almonds and 1 teaspoon sugar into biscuit mix. Cut in butter; add milk and mix to moderately stiff dough. Roll out on floured board to about ⅜-inch thickness. Cut into 4 rounds. Bake in 425-degree oven until golden brown, about 8 to 10 minutes. Sprinkle with sugar; drop on Cherry Filling in serving dishes. Cool before serving. If desired, garnish with whole almonds and pitted cherries.

CHERRY FILLING:
　　　1 1-lb 1-oz. can pitted dark sweet cherries
　¼ c. sugar
　　2 tbsp. cornstarch
　¼ tsp. almond extract
　　2 tsp. lemon juice
　¼ tsp. salt
　　1 tbsp. butter or margarine

Drain cherries, saving syrup. If necessary, add water to syrup to make 1 cup. Stir together sugar and cornstarch; stir into syrup. Bring to a boil; lower heat and cook, stirring until mixture thickens and is smooth. Add remaining ingredients and turn into 4 individual serving dishes. Yield: 4 servings. Pitted sour red cherries may be substituted. If so, increase sugar to ½ cup and add a drop or 2 of red food coloring to sauce.

Photograph for this recipe below.

George Washington's Cherry Treat

⅔ c. sugar
2 tbsp. cornstarch
1 c. cherry juice
2 1-lb. cans red tart cherries, drained
1 tbsp. butter or margarine
¼ tsp. cinnamon
Few drops of red food coloring

Combine sugar and cornstarch; add cherry juice and cook until thick. Stir in cherries, butter, cinnamon and food coloring. Pour into 8-inch square pan.

TOPPING:

1 c. sifted flour
2 tbsp. sugar
2 tsp. baking powder
½ tsp. salt
3 tbsp. shortening
½ c. milk
2 tbsp. sugar

Sift dry ingredients; cut in shortening. Add milk gradually. Mix well with fork. Drop by tablespoonfuls onto cherry mixture. Sprinkle sugar over pastry. Bake at 400 degrees for 30 minutes. Serve hot. Yield: 6 to 8 servings.

Mrs. Ernest Schwabe, Elkhorn, Wis.

Deep-Dish Pear Pie

PASTRY:

1 c. sifted all-purpose flour
½ tsp. salt
⅓ c. shortening
¼ c. grated cheddar cheese
2 to 3 tbsp. water

Sift flour and salt together; cut in shortening until mixture resembles coarse cornmeal. Mix in cheese; stir in 1 tablespoon water at a time until pastry holds together. Chill in refrigerator until ready to use. Preheat oven to 350 degrees.

PEAR FILLING:

2 lb. pears
1 tbsp. lemon juice
3 tbsp. flour
1 c. sugar
Dash of salt
½ tsp. cinnamon

(Continued on next page)

½ tsp. nutmeg
1 tbsp. butter or margarine

Peel pears; cut in halves and core. Arrange in a 1½-quart baking dish. Sprinkle with lemon juice. Mix flour, sugar, salt, cinnamon and nutmeg together; sprinkle over pears. Dot with butter. Roll pastry in a circle a little larger than top of baking dish. Slash in several places and arrange over pears, crimping pastry to edges of dish securely. Bake for 30 to 40 minutes. Serve with cream. Yield: 6 servings.

Cathleen Adams, LaFayette, Ala., Favorite Recipes Food Fair

 ## Fresh Blackberry Cobbler

1 stick margarine or ¼ lb. butter
1 c. milk
1 c. sifted flour
1 c. sugar
1 qt. blackberries

In bottom of baking pan or large baking dish, melt margarine. Add milk; do not stir. Sift flour and sugar; add to dish. Do not stir. Add blackberries. Bake at 325 to 350 degrees until crust rises to top and browns.

Mrs. Mildred Gresham, Cadiz, Ky.

 ## Crusty Peach Dessert

2 ½ c. sliced peaches
1 ½ tsp. lemon juice
½ tsp. grated lemon rind
½ tsp. almond extract
1 c. flour
2 tsp. baking powder
¼ tsp. salt
¼ c. shortening
1 egg, well beaten

Drain peaches, reserving syrup; arrange in greased 8-inch square pan. Combine ¼ cup reserved syrup, lemon juice and rind and extract; sprinkle over peaches. Heat in oven while preparing dough. Sift dry ingredients into bowl; stir in shortening, egg and 1/3 cup peach syrup. Stir until dry ingredients are moistened. Drop dough from tablespoon over mixture and spread with spatula. Sprinkle with 2 tablespoons additional sugar. Bake at 350 degrees for 30 minutes. Serve with plain or whipped cream. Yield: 9 servings.

Mrs. W. B. Watt, Iva, S. C.

Deep-Dish Peach Pie

4 peaches, halved
Pastry
1 ¼ c. white sugar
½ c. brown sugar
1 stick butter or margarine
3 eggs

Place peaches, cut-side up in 2 to 3-inch deep baking dish that has been lined with pastry. Sprinkle a small amount of sugar over peaches. Bake at 400 degrees until peaches are tender and the crust starts to brown. Cream remaining white sugar, brown sugar and butter or margarine; add eggs. Mix well. Pour over peaches and bake until brown.

Mrs. J. T. Sowders, Richmond, Ky.

 ## No-Bake Summer Cobbler

1 recipe for pastry
3 tbsp. melted butter or oleo
Fresh or canned peaches
Seasoning

Prepare pastry; roll ¼ to ⅛-inch thick and cut into desired lengths. Fry in electric skillet with butter. Lay fried crust aside. Place peaches in same skillet with desired seasoning and cook until tender. Put peaches in baking dish; cover with fried crust. If using fresh peaches add 1½ cups water.

Mrs. W. L. Pulley, Riesel, Texas

Peach Treat

2 c. sliced peaches
2 c. sugar
1 stick butter or margarine
¾ c. flour
2 tsp. baking powder
Pinch of salt
¾ c. milk

Mix peaches with 1 cup sugar. Put butter in very deep pan and set in 350-degree oven to melt. Stir batter of remaining sugar, flour, baking powder, salt and milk. Pour over melted butter. Do not stir. Place peaches on top. Bake for 1 hour or until crust is golden brown. Batter rises to top during baking.

Mrs. Harry D. Larson, Officers' Wives' Club, Ogden, Utah

Pineapple-Peach Cobbler

1 stick margarine
1 No. 2½ can sliced peaches
1 sm. can crushed pineapple
1 c. sugar
1 c. flour
1 c. milk

Melt margarine in baking dish or oblong pan. Add peaches and pineapple. Make thin batter of sugar, flour and milk. Mix well; pour over fruit and margarine in dish. Bake in 350-degree oven until golden brown. Serve with whipped cream or ice cream.

Mrs. C. F. Masters, Elizabethtown, Ky.

 ### Plum Pandowdy

2 ½ lb. fresh plums
1 c. plus 3 tbsp. sugar
3 tbsp. quick-cooking tapioca
¾ tsp. salt
½ tsp. ground cinnamon
2 tbsp. butter
1 c. sifted all-purpose flour
2 tsp. baking powder
3 tbsp. shortening
⅓ c. milk

Slice plums; combine with 1 cup sugar, tapioca, ¼ teaspoon salt and cinnamon. Turn into 8 x 6 x 2-inch baking dish; dot with butter and set aside. Combine flour, 3 tablespoons sugar, baking powder and remaining salt; add shortening. Mix to crumb consistency. Stir in milk. Drop 6 mounds from tablespoon over top of plums. Bake in preheated 375-degree oven 50 minutes or until done.

Georgia H. Ward, Neva, Tenn.

Ruby Rhubarb Cobbler

4 c. rhubarb
2 c. sugar
Juice of 1 orange
1 tbsp. butter
½ c. shortening
1 egg
1 c. flour
1 tsp. baking powder
½ c. milk

(Continued on next page)

Cut rhubarb into bite-sized pieces; spread in 8 x 12-inch baking dish. Sprinkle with 1 cup sugar and orange juice; dot with butter. Cream remaining sugar with shortening; beat in egg. Sift together flour and baking powder; add alternately with milk to creamed mixture. Spread batter over rhubarb. Bake at 350 degrees for 45 minutes. Yield: 6-8 servings.

Mrs. Helen Dunn, Home Economics Teacher, Newman, Ill.

Apple Brown Betty

2 ½ c. soft stale bread cubes, firmly packed
4 c. finely chopped tart apples
¾ c. seedless raisins
⅔ c. brown sugar, packed
¼ tsp. nutmeg
½ tsp. cinnamon
¼ c. melted butter or margarine
2 tbsp. lemon juice
⅓ c. water

Sprinkle 1/3 of the bread cubes in greased baking dish. Combine apples, raisins, sugar and spices. Spread ½ of the mixture over bread cubes in baking dish. Repeat layers. Cover with remaining bread cubes; pour butter, lemon juice and water over top. Cover. Bake at 375 degrees for 1 hour; uncover during last 20 minutes of baking. Serve warm with cream. Yield: 6 servings.

Mrs. Walter McBee, Lead Hill, Ark., Favorite Recipes Food Fair

 ## Apple Goodie

3 c. sliced apples
1 c., scant, sugar
1 tbsp., rounded, flour
Salt
Cinnamon
¼ tsp. soda
¼ tsp. baking powder
⅓ c. melted butter
1 c. oatmeal
¾ c. flour
¾ c. brown sugar

Mix apples, sugar, flour, salt and cinnamon; place in pan. Mix remaining ingredients until crumbly; sprinkle over apples. Bake for 30 to 40 minutes at 350 degrees. Cut in squares. Serve with whipped cream or vanilla ice cream. Yield: 6 servings.

Mrs. John Jacobson, Tampa, Fla.

Green Apple Crisp

3 c. green apples, sliced
1 tbsp. plus ⅔ c. sugar
¾ c. flour
¼ tsp. salt
½ tsp. cinnamon
½ c. soft butter or margarine

Arrange apples in buttered baking dish; sprinkle with 1 tablespoon sugar. Combine flour, salt, cinnamon, remaining sugar and soft butter; mix until crumbly. Pour over apples, spreading to edge. Bake at 375 degrees until brown and crisp. Serve warm.

Mrs. Robert W. Russell, Albemarle, N. C.

 ### Dawdler's Delight

2 cans apple, cherry, peach or blueberry pie filling
½ pkg. white cake mix
1 c. shredded coconut
1 c. chopped pecans
¼ lb. butter, melted

Spread pie filling in 14 x 9-inch sheet cake pan. Mix cake mix, coconut and nuts; spread over fruit. Dribble butter over top. Bake at 350 degrees until golden brown and bubbly, about 35 minutes. Serve with vanilla ice cream or whipped cream, if desired. Yield: 12-14 servings.

Mrs. Laura M. Sanders, Great Falls, Va.

 ### Banana-Butter Crackle

3 c. diced bananas
½ c. sugar
½ tsp. nutmeg
1 c. brown sugar, firmly packed
1 ¼ c. sifted flour
1 c. rolled oats
½ tsp. salt
½ c. butter
⅓ c. shortening

Mix bananas, white sugar and nutmeg. Place mixture in bottom of greased 10 x 6 x 1½-inch baking pan. Combine brown sugar, sifted flour, oats and salt in bowl. Cut in butter and shortening as for pastry and sprinkle over bananas. Bake in 375-degree oven 40 minutes or until crisp and browned. Serve warm with cream, if desired. Yield: 6 servings.

Mrs. Sharon Spruell, Stratford, Tex.

Blueberry Dream Dessert

2 c. quick-cooking oats
1 c. sifted flour
¾ c. melted margarine
1 c. light brown sugar
1 can blueberry pie filling

Combine oats, flour, margarine and brown sugar; reserve 1 cup for topping. Spread remaining crumbs in buttered 8-inch square pan; press firmly. Spread pie filling over crust; sprinkle with reserved crumbs. Bake at 325 degrees for 35 minutes. Serve with ice cream. Yield: 6 servings.

Mrs. Rexford S. Holstein, Dunbar, W. Va.

 ## Dutch Blueberry Betty

1 qt. soft bread cubes
1 pt. fresh blueberries
¼ c. melted butter or margarine
¾ c. sugar
2 tbsp. lemon juice
1 tbsp. lemon rind

Combine bread cubes and berries. Combine butter, sugar, lemon juice and rind. Pour over berries and bread, tossing to evenly distribute ingredients. Turn into greased 1½-quart casserole. Bake in 350-degree oven for 30 minutes. Serve hot or cold with milk, cream or whipped cream. Yield: 8 servings.

Ethel S. Moore, Somerville, N. J.

 ## Cherry Delight

¾ stick butter
1 can tart cherries or other fruit
¾ c. sugar
Few drops lemon juice
Few drops red food coloring (opt.)

Mix all ingredients; bring to rapid boil. Pour into baking dish.

TOPPING:

½ c. shortening
1 c. sugar
1 egg
Pinch of salt
1 heaping c. flour

(Continued on next page)

Cream shortening and sugar until fluffy; add egg, salt and flour. Beat with mixer until fluffy; drop by teaspoonfuls over cherries. Completely cover cherry mixture; sprinkle with additional sugar. Bake 30 to 35 minutes at 350 degrees. Serve warm with ice cream, if desired.

Mrs. Espie Loehela, Crossett, Ark.

 ## Cherry Crunch

22 graham crackers, crushed fine
⅓ c. sugar
1 tsp. cinnamon
1 stick margarine, melted
4 tbsp. flour
1 can cherries, sweetened to taste
3 egg whites

Combine crumbs, sugar, cinnamon and margarine. Reserve ¾ cup for top. Press remaining mixture in 1½-quart casserole, covering sides and bottom. Heat flour and cherries until thickened. Pour into crumb-lined dish. Top with meringue made from egg whites. Sprinkle with reserved crumb mixture. Bake at 275 degrees for 35 minutes. Serve with ice cream, if desired. For more servings, use 2 cans cherries; bake in 2-quart casserole.

Mrs. Ivan Kessinger, Morgantown, Ky.

 ## Hawaiian Fruit Crumble

2 c. sliced, pared tart apples
1 tbsp. lemon juice
1 9-oz. can crushed pineapple, drained
1 1-lb. can whole cranberry sauce
1 c. quick-cooking oats
¾ c. brown sugar
½ c. flour
½ tbsp. cinnamon
Dash of salt
⅓ c. butter or margarine

Toss apple slices with lemon juice; place in a 10 x 6 x 1½-inch pan. Spoon pineapple and cranberry sauce evenly over apples. Toss dry ingredients with a fork till evenly mixed. Cut in butter until crumbly. Sprinkle over fruit. Bake at 350 degrees till fruit is done, about 30 minutes. Yield: 6 servings.

Mrs. Richard Grosz, Beulah, N. D.

Lemon Crisp

6 tbsp. butter or margarine
¾ c. brown sugar
1 c. sifted flour
½ tsp. soda
¾ tsp. salt
⅓ c. flaked coconut
¾ c. finely crushed saltine crackers
¾ c. white sugar
2 tbsp. cornstarch
1 c. hot water
2 beaten egg yolks
½ tsp. grated lemon peel
½ c. lemon juice

Cream butter and brown sugar; add flour, soda, ½ teaspoon salt, coconut and crackers. Press half the crumb mixture into 8 x 8 x 2-inch baking pan. Bake at 350 degrees for 10 minutes. In saucepan combine white sugar, cornstarch and remaining salt; gradually stir in water. Bring to boil, stirring constantly; boil about 2 minutes. Remove from heat; stir small amount of hot mixture into egg yolks. Return to pan. Bring to boil, stirring constantly; remove from heat. Stir in lemon peel and juice gradually. Pour over baked crust; top with remaining crumb mixture. Bake at 350 degrees for 30 minutes or until lightly browned. Top with whipped cream. Yield: 8 servings.

Ingvald Vevang, Webster, S. D., Favorite Recipes Food Fair

Oatmeal Peach Betty

1 qt. canned peaches and juice
2 tbsp. lemon juice
¼ tsp. cinnamon
1 tbsp. butter
⅓ c. brown sugar
¼ c. melted shortening
⅔ c. flour
¼ tsp. salt
¼ tsp. baking soda
⅔ c. oats
½ tsp. vanilla

Place peaches in buttered 2-quart casserole. Sprinkle with lemon juice and cinnamon; dot with butter. Mix brown sugar and melted shortening. Sift flour, salt and soda; add oats. Add flour mixture and vanilla to shortening mixture; mix well and spread over peaches. Bake 45 minutes in 375-degree oven. Serve with cream, whipped cream, or vanilla ice cream if desired. Yield: 6-8 servings.

Mrs. Amy Van Hazinga, Fitchburg, Mass.

Panic

  1 can pie filling
  1 sm. box cake mix
  ½ c. melted butter or margarine
  ½ c. chopped nuts (opt.)

Pour pie filling into greased pan. Sprinkle with cake mix. Pour melted butter over cake mix. Top with nuts. Bake at 325 to 350 degrees for 35 minutes to 1 hour, depending on pan size. Serve with whipped cream, half and half or vanilla ice cream. NOTE: Use white cake mix with cherry, blueberry or peach filling; spice cake with apple filling; yellow cake with pineapple filling. Yield: 6-8 servings.

Mrs. Elizabeth Horne, Minneapolis, Minn.

 Peach Crunch

  1 lge. can sliced cling peaches, drained
  ½ c. crushed corn flakes
  ½ c. brown sugar
  ½ tsp. cinnamon
  ⅛ tsp. cardamom
  3 tbsp. butter

Place peaches in shallow baking dish. Mix corn flakes with brown sugar, cinnamon and cardamom; sprinkle over peaches. Dot with butter. Bake at 350 degrees for 25 minutes. Serve plain or with whipped cream. Yield: 4-6 servings.

Mrs. George Paddock, San Diego, Cal.

Peach Pie Crumble

  3 c. fresh peaches, peeled and sliced
  Sugar
  2 tbsp. flour
  ½ tsp. salt
  1 c. water
  Nutmeg
  1 stick pie crust mix
  1 tbsp. oleo

Sprinkle peaches with 6 tablespoons sugar; set aside. Combine flour, salt and water in pint jar; shake until blended. Pour over peaches; sprinkle with nutmeg. Mix pie crust mix, oleo and ½ cup sugar until crumbly; sprinkle over peaches. Bake at 375 degrees about 30 minutes; increase temperature to 400 degrees to brown.

Mrs. John Ezell, Alvarado, Tex.

Pear Crisp

1 qt. pared and sliced fresh pears
1 c. sifted flour
⅛ tsp. salt
1 c. brown sugar
½ c. butter
½ tsp. vanilla

Place sliced pears in buttered deep pie pan. Mix flour, salt and brown sugar. Cut butter-vanilla mixture into flour-sugar mixture with fork or pastry blender. Sprinkle over fruit. Bake in 350-degree oven about 25 to 45 minutes or until fruit is tender and crumb is golden brown. Serve warm with or without cream. If sweetened canned or frozen fruit is used reduce the amount of sugar in crust.

Ruth A. Fanelli, Wimauma, Fla.

 ## Rhubarb Rumble

1 c. flour
1 c. brown sugar
½ c. melted butter
¾ c. oatmeal
1 tsp. cinnamon
4 c. diced rhubarb
1 c. sugar
2 tbsp. cornstarch
1 c. water
1 tsp. vanilla

Mix flour, brown sugar, butter, oatmeal and cinnamon. Press half of mixture into a greased baking pan. If desired, reserve half of mixture for topping. Cover with rhubarb. Cook sugar, cornstarch, water and vanilla. Pour over rhubarb. Top with remaining crumbs. Bake 1 hour at 350 to 375 degrees. Serve warm, topped with whipped cream, if desired. Yield: 9-12 servings.

Mrs. Carol J. Domier, Mayville, N. D.

Strawberry-Rhubarb Crisp

⅔ c. sugar
2 tbsp. arrowroot
⅛ tsp. cloves
Pinch of cardamom
1 10-oz. pkg. frozen strawberries, thawed
3 c. diced rhubarb
Few drops red food coloring
⅓ c. softened butter or margarine
⅔ c., packed, brown sugar
½ c. flour
½ c. quick-cooking rolled oats
Grated rind of 1 lemon
½ tsp. nutmeg
2 tbsp. cinnamon-sugar

Combine sugar, arrowroot, cloves and cardamom. Add fruits and food coloring. Mix and pour into 1½-quart greased baking dish. Mix remaining ingredients with fork until crumbly; sprinkle over fruit. Bake at 350 degrees for 40 to 45 minutes. Serve warm or cooled with whipped cream. If frozen rhubarb is used, reduce sugar to 1/3 cup. Yield: 6 servings.

Mrs. Howard H. Sypher, Tampa, Fla.

 ### Peach Shortcake

3 lb. peaches, pared and sliced
1 c. firmly-packed light brown sugar
½ c. lemon juice
3 ⅓ c. sifted all-purpose flour
1 ½ tsp. salt
1 ¼ c. shortening
7 to 8 tbsp. water
Sugar
1 ½ c. heavy cream

Combine peaches, brown sugar and lemon juice; chill 1 hour. Combine flour and salt in bowl. Cut in shortening with pastry blender or 2 knives until mixture resembles coarse meal. Sprinkle with water; toss with fork and press into ball. Divide dough into 4 parts. On a lightly floured surface, roll out each part into an 8-inch circle, trimming edges even with a 8-inch round cake pan. Place circles on baking sheets. Sprinkle generously with sugar; prick with fork. Bake in 425°-oven for 15 minutes or until golden brown. Cool on racks. Whip cream with 1 tablespoon sugar until soft peaks form. Stack pastry circles on large serving plate, topping each with peaches, then whipped cream. For individual shortcakes, cut pastry into thirty 3-inch circles. Stack in 3 layers with peaches and cream. Yield: 10 servings.

Photograph for this recipe on page 205.

Grandma Byrd's Strawberry Shortcake

1 ½ qt. fresh strawberries, sliced
2 c. sugar
2 c. self-rising flour
⅔ c. shortening
⅔ c. milk
1 stick butter, melted

Blend together sliced fresh strawberries and sugar. Set aside to form juice while making shortcake. Sift flour; cut in shortening until particles are the size of rice. Add milk all at once; mix lightly and quickly with fork. Knead lightly. Pat into 2 thin rounds about 8 inches across. Bake on cookie sheet at 450 degrees until golden brown. To serve, split layers apart; put hot rounds on serving dish. Drizzle with melted butter. Spoon sweetened fresh strawberries and juice generously between layers and on top. Serve warm with cream or plain. Yield: 6 servings.

Mrs. J. D. Driskill, Parrottsville, Tenn.

Strawberry Flans

¾ c. orange juice
6 sponge cake shells
3 c. strawberries, halved
3 tbsp. sugar
1 ½ c. heavy cream
4 ½ tsp. Cointreau

Sprinkle 1 tablespoon orange juice in center of each shell; cover and refrigerate. Combine remaining juice with strawberries and sugar; mix gently. Cover and chill 1 hour. Divide strawberries equally into shells. Pour over any remaining liquid. Whip cream until stiff; fold in Cointreau. Spoon over strawberries. Serve immediately, garnished with whole berries. Yield: 6 servings.

Mrs. Paul H. McConnell, Pres., Officers' Wives' Club, Dover, N. J.

Strawberry Stack Cake

6 canned biscuits
Cooking oil
Sweetened strawberries
Whipped cream

Roll biscuits very thin; stick several times with a fork. Fry in oil until brown and crisp, turning once. Cool. Place one biscuit on shallow platter; cover with berries. Repeat until all biscuits are used, making berries the last addition. Serve with liberal amount of whipped cream.

Mrs. Alice Kinder, Tannersville, Va.

Fruit Desserts

Apple Delight

> 4 med. apples
> 2 tbsp. lemon juice
> 4 to 6 tbsp. powdered sugar
> 2 tsp. rose water
> 4 ice cubes

Pare and grate apples. Sprinkle each apple immediately with lemon juice after grating to prevent apples from darkening. Add sugar and rose water. Stir lightly. Add ice cubes. Serve in dessert dishes. Yield: 4 servings.

Mrs. Margaret McAuliffe, Home Economics Teacher, Bellows Falls, Vt.

 ## Cinnamon-Baked Apples

> 6 lge. apples
> 1 c. brown sugar
> 1 tbsp. butter
> 1 tbsp. flour
> ½ tsp. cinnamon

Remove cores from apples; place apples in baking dish. Cream sugar and butter; add flour and cinnamon. Mix well. Fill center of apples with sugar mixture. Bake at 350 degrees for 30 minutes or until soft. Baste with a little hot water while baking. Yield: 6 servings.

Mrs. Glenn C. Smith, Palisade, Colo.

Molasses Taffy-Spiced Apples

> ¾ c. Grandma's West Indies Molasses
> ¾ c. sugar
> ¾ c. water
> ½ tsp. each cinnamon and nutmeg
> ¼ tsp. each ground cloves and ginger
> 6 tbsp. lemon juice
> 7 to 8 large apples
> Whipped cream

In 10-inch skillet combine molasses, sugar, water, spices and lemon juice; bring to a boil. Peel and core apples. Add to molasses mixture; cover and simmer 15 minutes. Uncover and simmer 30 minutes longer. Spoon syrup over apples frequently. Cool in syrup. Serve with whipped cream. Yield: 6 servings.

Photograph for this recipe on page 223.

Party Apples With Almonds

4 lge. baking apples
8 tbsp. maple syrup
4 tbsp. raisins
4 tbsp. blanched almonds, split
8 tbsp. sweet red wine

Core apples; peel down about 1-inch from bottom end. Set in shallow baking pan, stem down. Fill each cavity with 2 tablespoons maple syrup, 1 tablespoon raisins and 1 tablespoon almonds. Cover bottom of pan with hot water. Cover; bake at 400 degrees for 30 minutes. Remove from oven; pour 2 tablespoons wine over each apple. Bake 10 minutes longer or until apples are done. Baste frequently with pan syrup. Serve with ice cream. Yield: 4 servings.

Mrs. W. B. Jones, Navy Officers' Wives' Club, London, England

Skillet Apple Slices

3 lge. apples
3 tbsp. butter
1/4 c. sugar
1/2 c. muscatel wine
1/2 c. heavy cream
1/8 tsp. cinnamon
Dash of salt

Pare and core apples; cut in thin slices. Place in skillet with butter; sprinkle with 2 tablespoons sugar. Cover; saute over moderate heat about 5 minutes. Turn apples once or twice. Add wine; cover and simmer until tender. Whip cream with remaining sugar, cinnamon and salt. Serve apples warm; top with whipped cream. Yield: 4-5 servings.

Mrs. G. H. Drewry, Dover, N. J.

Bananas A La Cointreau

6 to 8 ripe bananas
2 tbsp. lemon juice
3 tbsp. brown sugar
1/3 c. Cointreau

Bake bananas in skins in 350-degree oven for 30 minutes or until black. Split. Add lemon juice and sugar; let sugar melt. Add Cointreau. Heat for 5 minutes. Serve hot in sherbets. Add more Cointreau, if desired. Yield: 6-8 servings.

Helen D. Humm, Home Economics Teacher, Kalamazoo, Mich.

Bananas Flambe

3 tbsp. butter or margarine
¾ c. brown sugar
¼ c. dark rum
6 med. bananas, sliced lengthwise
2 tbsp. brandy

Heat butter and sugar in chafing dish. Add rum. Place bananas in pan; simmer about 7 minutes. Heat brandy and ignite; pour into pan. Stir gently until flame burns out. Serve over vanilla ice cream. Yield: 6 servings.

Mrs. J. H. B. Smith, Sunnyvale, Cal.

 ### Fried Red Bananas

1 c. flour
½ tsp. sugar
½ tsp. salt
1 beaten egg
1 c. ice water
2 tbsp. vegetable oil
1 ice cube
10 red bananas
Oil

Combine first 6 ingredients; beat until smooth. Add ice to keep cool. Dip sliced bananas into batter and fry in hot oil until lightly browned. Yield: 5 servings.

Grace B. Cowell, Home Economics Teacher, Seattle, Wash.

 ### Blackberry Flummery

1 qt. blackberries
1 c. water
Sugar to taste
Pinch of salt
2 tbsp. cornstarch

Cook berries with water. Bring to boil; simmer until very tender. Press and rub through a fine sieve; sweeten to taste. Mix cornstarch with a little cold water; stir into berries. Stir over fire until thick and free of starchy taste. Pour into a glass bowl; chill thoroughly. Serve with cream. Yield: 4 servings.

Mrs. Hugh Sease, Pensacola, Fla.

Flaming Cherries Jubilee

    1 12-oz. jar red currant jelly
    1 can red tart pitted cherries
    Slivered almonds
    ¾-1 c. brandy

Melt jelly in chafing dish. Stuff cherries with almond slivers. Add to melted jelly with ¼ cup brandy; simmer 6 to 8 minutes. At serving time, heat to gentle simmer; add ½ cup brandy and flame. Serve over vanilla ice cream while flaming. Yield: 10-12 servings.

Mrs. Herbert Dean, Pres., Officers' Wives' Club, Albany, Ga.

 ## Crimson Cranberry Flambe

    1 ½ c. sugar
    2 c. fresh cranberries
    1 c. water
    ¼ to ½ c. brandy or 6 to 8 sugar cubes soaked in lemon extract

Bring sugar and water to a boil. When sugar dissolves, add cranberries; simmer gently until skins pop open, about 5 minutes. When ready to serve, heat sauce in chafing dish. Pour brandy over top or place sugar cubes on top and light. Ladle sauce over scoops of coconut ice cream or coconut ice cream balls. Yield: 6-8 servings.

Mrs. Arthur J. Walsh, Woods Hole, Mass.

 ## Dates Marinade

    2 lb. fresh dates with pits
    2 c. good Tawny port wine

Place dates in dish with tight cover. Pour wine over dates. Cover tightly and refrigerate for at least 24 hours. Will keep indefinitely. Eat as dessert served with dry cheese and crackers. Yield: 10 servings.

Mrs. Richard G. Dougherty, Pres. Officers' Wives' Club, Clark AB, Philippines

 ## Canned Figs In Brandy

    1 can figs
    1 can coconut
    ½ c. chopped walnuts
    ¼ c. brandy

(Continued on next page)

Pour figs into an oven-proof serving dish. Sprinkle ½ cup coconut over figs. Add walnuts and brandy. Cover; bake until heated through. Sprinkle with remaining coconut. Serve hot. Whipped cream may be added. Yield: 6 servings.

Mrs. J. W. Gannon, Moffet Field, Cal.

 ### Figs-A-Flame

> 1 lge. can Kadota figs
> 1 tsp. arrowroot or cornstarch
> 2 thin lemon slices
> ¼ c. plus 2 tbsp. brandy
> ½ pt. coffee or heavy cream
> Lemon wafers

Pour syrup from figs into a chafing dish. Add arrowroot or cornstarch; stir until thickened. Add figs, lemon slices and 2 tablespoons brandy; heat thoroughly. Heat remaining brandy. Just before serving, ignite brandy and pour over figs coating each one. Serve at once with cream and lemon wafers. Yield: 4 servings.

Mrs. Raymond M. Harris, Little Creek, Va.

 ### Grape Brule

> 2 c. seedless grapes
> 1 pt. commercial sour cream
> ¼ c. brown sugar

Wash and stem grapes. Place in a shallow baking dish. Spread sour cream over grapes. Sprinkle brown sugar over the cream. Place under broiler until cream and sugar become bubbly. Yield: 4-6 servings.

Mrs. Laureen Brown, Walnut Creek, Cal.

 ### Butter-Baked Oranges

> 8 lge. oranges
> ½ c. sugar
> 8 tsp. butter

Wash oranges; grate skins slightly. Cover with water; boil 30 minutes. Drain; cool. Cut off small slice at blossom end; remove core. Place 1 tablespoon sugar and 1 teaspoon butter in center of each orange. Place in buttered baking dish; fill two-thirds full of water. Cover; bake in 350-degree oven 2 hours. Yield: 8 servings.

Carol Hughes, Madison, Ind.

Sliced Oranges With Grand Marnier

6 oranges
2 c. sugar
1 c. water
Grand Marnier

Cut skin from oranges, taking it off in tiny julienne strips. Take off as little of the white pulp as possible. Make a sugar syrup by boiling the sugar and water for 5-10 minutes. Add the tiny strips of orange peel; cook until tender. Flavor the orange peel syrup with Grand Marnier to taste. Peel the white pulp from the oranges; cut them in half. Seed the oranges and place cut side down in a serving dish. Spoon the hot orange peel syrup over the oranges; chill. Garnish with candied violets and serve. Yield: 6 servings.

Mrs. Avery R. Kier, Santa Ana, Calif.

 ### Brandy Peaches

4 tbsp. butter
½ c. sugar
¼ c. water
4 fresh peaches
3 oz. brandy

In top of double boiler, melt butter and sugar; blend. Stir in water and add peeled whole peaches. Cook 30 to 35 minutes, turning peaches several times. Add brandy and serve. Yield: 4 servings.

Sue Vedral, Home Economics Teacher, Camp Hill, Pa.

Broiled Peaches

6 or 8 canned peach halves
6 to 8 tsp. oleo
½ tsp. cinnamon
2 tbsp. sugar
½ pt. whipping cream
¼ tsp. nutmeg
½ c. pecan halves

Place peach halves with pitted side up in 8-inch square baking dish. Place 1 teaspoon oleo in center of each peach half. Sprinkle lightly with cinnamon-sugar mixture. Place in oven at broiler temperature; remove when oleo melts. Whip cream and stir in remaining sugar, cinnamon and nutmeg. Spoon over peach halves. Sprinkle with nuts. Serve at once. Yield: 6-8 servings.

Mrs. Judith G. Kashwer, Home Economics Teacher, Stilwell, Okla.

Peach Cordial

¼ c. light corn syrup
5 tsp. frozen concentrated orange juice
1 tbsp. water
4 drops aromatic bitters
4 med. peaches

Mix corn syrup, orange juice, water and bitters in cup and chill. When ready to serve, peel peaches; pit and slice. Place in dessert dishes; top with orange syrup. Garnish with mint, if desired. Yield: 4 servings.

Mrs. Marion D. Fogle, North, S. C.

Stuffed Peaches

6 ripe peaches
½ c. chopped blanched almonds
½ tbsp. sugar
½ tbsp. finely chopped candied orange peel
½ tbsp. finely chopped citron
  Crushed pulp of ½ peach
3 ladyfingers, finely cut
  White wine
  Sugar caramels
3 oz. peach brandy
3 oz. good brandy

Scald peaches in boiling water; slip off skins. Halve lengthwise; remove pits. Pound almonds in a bowl with sugar, adding a few drops cold water. Mix in orange peel, citron, peach pulp and ladyfingers. Pack mixture into peach cavities; rejoin halves, Secure with toothpicks; place in baking dish. Moisten peaches with wine; dust with sugar caramels. Heat brandies; pour over peaches and ignite. Serve. Yield: 6 servings.

Mrs. DeLair A. Clark, Pres., Officers' Wives' Club, Otis, Mass.

 ## Syllabub

1 c. fresh peaches
1 tbsp. lemon juice
½ c. plus 2 tbsp. powdered sugar
1 c. whipping cream
1 egg white
2 tbsp. sherry

Combine peaches, lemon juice and 2 tablespoons sugar; set aside. Whip cream with ¼ cup sugar. Beat egg white until stiff with ¼ cup sugar. Combine,

(Continued on next page)

blending lightly. Add wine and pour over fruit. If desired, pineapple or bananas may be substituted for peaches. Yield: 4 servings.

Nell W. Pantell, Jefferson, Ga., Favorite Recipes Food Fair.

 ## Brandied Pears

12 pears
1 c. light brown sugar
1 c. plus 2 tbsp. white sugar
1 tsp. cinnamon
½ tsp. nutmeg
Brandy
2 sticks butter or oleo
1 egg yolk

Peel pears; leave on stems. Mix brown sugar and 2 tablespoons white sugar with cinnamon and nutmeg; mix well. Roll pears in mixture. Put in a large casserole; pour 1 tablespoon brandy over each pear. Bake 20 minutes in 350-degree oven. If pears are hard, cook covered. Cream butter till fluffy; add remaining sugar at intervals. Add egg yolk. Add 1 wine glass brandy last, a small amount at a time. Serve with pears. Yield: 12 servings.

Mrs. Whitney Edmonson Smith, Webb, Miss.

 ## Pears Armenonville

1 c. sugar
¼ c. lemon juice
2 tbsp. butter
2 c. boiling water
8 ripe pears
2 boxes frozen raspberries, thawed
¼ c. Port wine
Sour cream

Simmer sugar, lemon juice, butter and water for 5 minutes. Pare pears, leaving on stems; arrange in 3-quart casserole. Add lemon mixture. Bake, covered, at 350 degrees for 45 minutes. Cool in liquid; drain. Sieve raspberries; put puree in large bowl and stir in wine. Lay pears in mixture. Refrigerate several hours or overnight, turning occasionally and basting with sauce. Serve pears with sauce and sour cream. Yield: 8 servings.

Mrs. Edward M. Saunders, Wash., D. C.

 Chocolate Pears

¾ c. sugar
1 tbsp. cornstarch
¼ tsp. cloves
1 tsp. cinnamon
1 ½ tsp. cocoa
1 c. water
1 tbsp. butter
Pear halves

Combine first 6 ingredients in saucepan and simmer until syrupy. Add butter, then pear halves and simmer until soft. Serve topped with whipped cream.

Mrs. William A. Fisher, Portland, Ore.

 Stuffed Pears Milanese

6 lge. firm pears
3 oz. powdered sugar
4 Maraschino cherries, finely chopped
¼ lb. shelled toasted almonds, finely ground
¼ tsp. almond extract
½ c. dry sherry

Wash pears; cut in half lengthwise. Scoop out cores. Blend remaining ingredients except sherry. Fill pear halves with mixture. Place in baking dish; pour sherry over pears. Bake at 350 degrees for 15 minutes or until pears are done, but not too soft. Serve hot or cooled. Yield: 6-8 servings.

Mrs. Jack B. Baugh, Ft. Irwin, Cal.

Baked Pineapple

> 1 c. brown sugar
> 1 tbsp. flour
> ½ c. pineapple juice
> 1 can pineapple, 8 or 10 slices

Mix sugar, flour and juice until smooth; add remaining juice. Pour into saucepan; cook until thickened. Place pineapple rings in 12 x 9 x 2-inch baking dish. Pour thick juice sauce over rings. Dot with butter. Bake at 300 degrees about 20 to 25 minutes until pineapple is a delicate brown.

Mrs. William H. Setters, Mount Sterling, Ky.

 ## Raspberry Razzle

> 1 pkg. frozen raspberries, well drained
> ¼ c. powdered sugar
> 1 tbsp. lemon juice
> ¼ c. Cointreau
> 1 c. heavy cream

Combine all ingredients; freeze or chill. Serve in dessert glasses. Yield: 4 servings.

Marilyn Komendarek, Herkimer, N. Y.

 ## California Strawberries With Cream

> 2 pt. fresh California strawberries, halved
> ½ c. sifted confectioners' sugar
> 2 c. sour cream
> ¾ tsp. almond flavoring
> Mint

Mix strawberries and sugar; chill. Mix sour cream and almond flavoring. Put strawberries in parfait glasses or serving dishes; top with sour cream mixture. Garnish with mint. Yield: 4 servings.

Mrs. J. W. Browning, San Diego, Cal.

 ## Strawberries Romanoff

> 1 qt. fresh strawberries
> 1 c. powdered sugar
> ½ pt. heavy cream

(Continued on next page)

¼ to ½ tsp. almond extract
2 tbsp. Cointreau

Wash and stem berries; let set. Sprinkle berries with powdered sugar 1 hour before serving. Fold in cream, whipped and flavored with extract and Cointreau. Spoon into sherbet or parfait glasses and serve immediately. Yield: 6-8 servings.

Mrs. John A. Clapperton, New Martinsville, W. Va.

 ### Brandied Fruit

2 lge. grapefruit
4 lge. oranges
2 c. grapes, halved and seeded
¼ c. blanched almonds
2 tbsp. sugar
3 tbsp. brandy

Peel and section fruit, saving juice. Mound grapes in center of crystal bowl; surround with grapefruit and orange sections. Sprinkle with almonds. Add sugar and brandy to reserved fruit juice; stir to dissolve. Pour over fruit; chill several hours. Yield: 8-10 servings.

Mrs. Albert M. Ward, Officers' Wives' Club, Karamursel Air Sta., Turkey

 ### Friendship Fruit

1 fifth of rum, bourbon or brandy
Rind of 1 orange, cut into spirals
Whole cloves
Cinnamon sticks
Allspice berries
1 lb. pitted cherries
9 c. sugar
1 lb. skinned pitted peaches
1 lb. skinned pitted apricots
1 lb. skinned pitted plums
1 lb. grapes
1 lb. strawberries
1 lb. raspberries
1 lb. pineapple chunks

Scald a 6-quart stone crock with boiling water; dry crock. Pour liquor into crock. Add orange rind, spices, cherries and 1 cup sugar. Place a plate on top of crock; set a weight on plate. Let set for 1 week. Add peaches and 1 cup sugar; let set for 1 week. Add apricots and 1 cup sugar; let set for 1 week. Add plums and 1 cup sugar; let set for 1 week. Add grapes and 1 cup sugar;

(Continued on next page)

let set for 1 week. Add strawberries and 1 cup sugar; let set for 1 week. Add raspberries and 1 cup sugar; let set for 1 week. Add pineapple and 1 cup sugar; let set for 2 to 3 months in dark place to ripen fruit. Serve as dessert or as sauce over ice cream or pound cake.

Mrs. Blanche A. Gore, Home Economics Teacher, Houston, Tex.

Florida Ambrosia

3 *Florida grapefruit*
3 *Florida oranges*
1 *c. fresh strawberries, sliced*
3 *tbsp. sugar, optional*
¼ *c. flaked coconut*

Chill oranges and grapefruit before preparing. Cut slice from top; cut off peel in strips from top to bottom, cutting deep enough to remove white membrane. Cut slice from bottom. Go over fruit again, removing any remaining white membrane. Section grapefruit and 2 oranges by cutting along side of each dividing membrane from outside to middle of core. Remove section by section, over bowl, to retain juice. Slice remaining oranges crosswise, ¼-inch thick. Combine grapefruit, oranges and strawberries; sprinkle with sugar if desired. Turn into serving bowl or individual dishes and sprinkle with coconut. Yield: 6 servings.

Photograph for this recipe below.

Fruit-Almond Treat

> 1 1-lb. 14-oz. can fruit cocktail
> 1 ½ c. sour cream
> 3 tbsp. brown sugar
> ¾ c. cookie crumbs
> ½ c. roasted slivered almonds
> 1 bottle cherries, cut into halves

Drain fruit cocktail. Combine sour cream and brown sugar. In parfait glasses, layer 1 tablespoon sweetened sour cream, 2 teaspoons cookie crumbs, a sprinkle of almonds and 2 tablespoons fruit cocktail mixed with cherries. Repeat twice. Top with spoonful sour cream and garnish with almonds. Yield: 6 servings.

Mrs. Annie R. Davis, Statesboro, Ga.

 ## Fruit Macedoine

> 1 lge. can peach halves
> 1 lge. can sliced pineapple
> 1 lge. can pear halves
> 1 lge. can apricot halves
> 1 lge. can applesauce
> Butter
> Ginger

Strain fruits. Place in large baking dish. Cover with applesauce. Dot with butter. Sprinkle lightly with ginger. Bake in 250-degree oven for about 1 hour or until mixture bubbles up.

Mrs. Rudolph Small, Safford, Ala., Favorite Recipes Food Fair

 ## Fruit Parfait Perfection

> 1 box frozen sliced peaches, thawed
> Brown sugar
> 1 carton sour cream
> 1 box frozen raspberries, thawed

Place a layer of peaches with some of the juice in 6 parfait glasses; sprinkle each with a teaspoon brown sugar. Cover with sour cream. Add a layer of raspberries with some of the juice; sprinkle each with a teaspoon brown sugar. Cover with sour cream. Top with a whole raspberry and a little juice. Be sure peaches are covered with juice or sour cream so they will not turn brown. Yield: 6 servings.

Mrs. William F. Train, Pres. Officers' Wives' Club, Fort Meade, Md.

Georgia Belle's Cherry Dessert

    2 c. cream
    2 c. sugar
    4 tbsp. flour
    1 tsp. almond flavoring
    1 qt. cherries
    4 bananas
    1 c. coconut

Mix cream, sugar, flour and flavoring; cook until thick, stirring constantly. Cool; mix together thoroughly with fruits and coconut. Refrigerate. Yield: 16 servings.

Mrs. Nick Carter, Welsh, La.

Ginger-Fruit Oriental

    1 1-lb. can sliced peaches, drained
    1 c. orange juice
    2 tsp. finely chopped candied ginger
    2 bananas

Combine peach slices, orange juice and candied ginger. Chill several hours to blend flavors. Peel bananas and run fork down sides to flute. Slice diagonally. Add to peach mixture. Heap in serving dishes. Trim with kumquats and sprigs of green leaves. Yield: 4-6 servings.

Sharon Lee Woodbury, Home Economics Teacher, Oakes, N. D.

Grandma's Favorite Ambrosia

    12 oranges, sectioned
    1 No. 2 can pineapple, crushed or tidbits
    1 c. coconut, flaked or fresh grated

Arrange orange sections and pineapple in layers; sprinkle each layer with coconut. Chill. Yield: 8 servings.

Mrs. Billie C. Carver, Woodsdale, N. C.

Hawaiian Ambrosia

    1 fresh pineapple
    3 papayas
    4 mangos

(Continued on next page)

6 bananas
½ c. light honey
½ to ¾ c. Kirsch

Peel and cube fruit. Mix gently in a large bowl with honey. Cover and chill. Just before serving add Kirsch. Yield: 8 servings.

Mrs. Richard W. Sanborn, Navy Wives' Club, Honolulu, Hawaii

 ## Hot Fruit Fantasia

1 1-lb. can apricot halves
1 1-lb. can Elberta peach halves
1 1-lb. can purple plums
1 can figs (opt.)
2 tbsp. butter
1 orange, thinly sliced
½ c. orange juice
¼ c. brown sugar
½ tsp. grated lemon rind
2 tbsp. brandy (opt.)
½ c. shredded coconut

Drain canned fruits well; arrange in a shallow 9 x 13-inch casserole. Dot butter over plums. Place halved orange slices on top. Mix orange juice, sugar, lemon rind and brandy; pour over fruit. Sprinkle coconut over the top. Bake at 425 degrees for 15 minutes. Yield: 10 servings.

Mrs. Wilson Freeman, Pres. Wives' Club, Wash. D. C.

 ## Kirsch Kabobs

6 canned peach halves, drained and cut in half
3 lge. bananas, sliced in 3-in. lengths
2 apples, peeled and cut in wedges
1 fresh pineapple cubed
2 grapefruits, cut in double sections
1 c. grapefruit juice
½ c. honey
2 tbsp. Kirsch
1 tsp. finely chopped fresh mint

Marinate fruits in juice, honey, Kirsch and mint for at least 1 hour at room temperature. Carefully thread on skewers, alternating fruits for color. Broil for 5 minutes, basting frequently with the marinade. Yield: 6 servings.

Mrs. John B. Kohagen, Pres. Officers' Wives' Club, Rhein Main Air Base, Germany

Heavenly Hash

> 1 6-oz. pkg. miniature marshmallows
> 6 med. bananas
> 1 8-oz. bottle red cherries
> 1 lge. can crushed pineapple
> ½ c. chopped pecans
> 1 pt. whipping cream, whipped

Combine all ingredients, including cherry juice; serve. Yield: 8-10 servings.

Mrs. James H. Mann, Columbia, S. C.

 ## Hot Mustard Fruit

> ¼ c. butter, melted
> ½ c. brown sugar, firmly packed
> 2 tbsp. prepared mustard
> 1 1-lb. can sliced peaches, drained
> 1 13½-oz. can pineapple chunks, drained
> 2 lge. bananas, cut in chunks

Preheat oven to 325 degrees. Combine butter, sugar and mustard in small bowl. Mix well. Reserve ¼ cup for topping. Add fruits; toss lightly. Put in 1-quart casserole. Spoon reserved sugar mixture over top. Bake for 40 minutes. Serve warm. Yield: 6-8 servings.

Mrs. J. R. Burrier, Nicholasville, Ky.

 ## Mango Fluff

> 2 c. mangoes
> 1 box dessert topping mix or 1 c. heavy cream plus 2 tbsp.
>   sugar
> 1 med. orange, peeled, seeded and cut in sm. pieces (opt.)
> ½ c. pecans, broken (opt.)
> Maraschino cherries

Peel and slice mangoes. Puree in blender or by pressing through sieve. Prepare dessert topping mix as directed on box, or whip cream and add sugar gradually. Reserve a little topping for garnish. Fold in pureed mangoes, orange pieces and pecans. Pile into sherbet or parfait glasses. Garnish with fluff of dessert topping mix or whipped cream and Maraschino cherry. Yield: 6-9 servings.

Mrs. Edward H. Schmidt, Delray Beach, Fla.

Chilled Melon Balls

> 2 c. water
> 1 c. sugar
> 4 mint leaves
> 4 tbsp. lemon juice
> 2 c. cantaloupe balls
> 2 c. watermelon balls
> 2 c. honeydew melon balls

Mix water, sugar and mint leaves; boil slowly for 2 minutes. Remove leaves; add lemon juice. Cool and chill. Arrange balls in chilled dessert cups. Add chilled sugar mixture; serve. Yield: 8 servings.

Mrs. H. W. Snow, Sunnyside, Wash.

 ## Melon Balls In Mint

> *Papaya balls*
> *Watermelon balls*
> *Cantaloupe balls*
> *Creme de menthe*

Place cold melon balls in sherbet glasses; pour creme de menthe over fruit. For variation serve melon balls in scooped out pineapple or watermelon. Creme de menthe should be served in a bowl with ice cubes; serve with toothpicks for dunking.

Mrs. Paul D. Stroop, San Diego, Cal.

Dried Fruit Compote

> ¾ lb. mixed dried fruits
> 1 c. raisins
> 3 c. water
> ⅓ c. sugar
> Juice of 1 lemon
> 1 orange, peeled and thinly sliced
> Sour cream

Wash and drain mixed dried fruits and raisins; put in baking dish with water. Bake fruits in 325-degree oven for 1 hour. Add sugar and lemon juice; stir fruits until sugar is dissolved. Add orange slices; cool. Chill and serve with sour cream. Yield: 6 servings.

Mrs. John Wilson, West Long Branch, N. J.

Apple-Champagne Compote

    3 Golden Delicious apples
    1 ½ c. champagne
    2 c. frozen sliced strawberries
    1 c. powdered sugar
    Shredded coconut or nuts

Peel, core and slice apples into very thin circles. Cover with champagne and strawberries. Sprinkle with powdered sugar; chill 3 hours. Sprinkle with shredded coconut or nuts. Yield: 6-8 servings.

Mrs. Edward C. Fritsch, Jr., Oak Harbor, Wash.

 ## Olympian Nectar

    1 c. strawberries, fresh or frozen
    1 c. blueberries, cooked
    1 ½ c. pineapple
    1 c. applesauce
    2 c. diced apples
    ⅔ c. raisins
    2 c. grape juice
    1 c. shredded coconut
    4 diced bananas
    2 c. pineapple juice
    1 sm. jar cherries and juice
    1 c. chopped pecans

Combine all ingredients. Mix well. Refrigerate until served. Yield: 6 servings.

Mrs. Harry T. Howle, Galivants Ferry, S. C.

Millionaire Dessert

    2 eggs or 3 egg yolks, beaten
    5 tbsp. sugar
    5 tbsp. lemon juice
    2 tbsp. butter
    1 c. heavy cream, whipped
    1 can white cherries, cut into halves
    1 can sliced pineapple, diced
    ½ lb. colored marshmallows
    ¼ lb. blanched almonds or pecans

Combine eggs, sugar and lemon juice in double boiler; heat, beating constantly, until thick and smooth. Remove from heat; add butter. Cool. Fold in whipped cream and fruits, marshmallows and nuts. Yield: 8-10 servings.

Mrs. John Culbuson, Livingston, Tenn.

Molasses Curried Fruit

> 1 1-lb. can cling peach halves
> 1 1-lb. can pear halves
> 1 1-lb. can whole unpeeled apricots
> 1 20-oz. can pineapple slices
> ½ c. unsulphured molasses
> ¼ c. vinegar
> 1 3-in. stick cinnamon
> 2 tsp. curry powder
> 6 Maraschino cherries

Drain syrup from fruits into saucepan. Bring to a boil; boil rapidly until reduced to ¾ cup. Add unsulphured molasses, vinegar, stick cinnamon and curry powder; bring to a boil. Add fruits; simmer 5 minutes. Garnish with Maraschino cherries. Serve hot or cold. Yield: 12 servings.

Mrs. Augustus T. Terry, San Antonio, Tex.

Baked Fruit Casserole

> 1 can pineapple chunks
> 1 can apricots
> 1 can peaches
> 1 can pears
> 1 sm. can cherries
> ½ c. brown sugar
> 4 tsp. curry powder
> ⅓ c. butter

Cut up fruits; drain overnight. Mix remaining ingredients. Pour over fruits. Bake at 325 degrees for 1 hour. Yield: 8-10 servings.

Mrs. H. E. Shomo, Harrisonburg, Va.

 ## Banana-Apricot Dessert

> 3 tbsp. butter or margarine
> 1 14-oz. can apricot halves
> 1 tsp. cinnamon
> 2 tsp. cornstarch
> ¼ c. water
> 6 firm bananas, halved crosswise
> Whipped cream

Melt butter in skillet; pour in apricots. Sprinkle with cinnamon. Mix cornstarch with water; gradually add to liquid in skillet, stirring constantly. Bring

(Continued on next page)

to a boil; cook for 3 minutes. Place bananas in pan with apricots. Heat enough to warm. Serve hot with whipped cream. Yield: 6 servings.

Luanna Hunt, Blair, Okla.

 ### Bananas Baked In Orange Juice

> 6 to 8 med. underripe bananas
> 1 med. orange, peeled and cut in chunks
> 2 tbsp. orange juice
> 2 tbsp. lemon juice
> 1/3 c. sugar
> Dash of cinnamon
> Dash of nutmeg

Preheat oven to 325 degrees. Peel bananas; arrange in shallow baking dish. Add remaining ingredients. Bake 25 to 30 minutes or until bananas are golden and tender. Serve hot. Yield: 6-8 servings.

Mrs. Mary Jane McNory, Home Economics Teacher, Doleville, Ind.

Spiced Fruit

> 1 1-lb. can each whole apricots, pear halves and
>   greengage plums
> 1 1-lb. can each peach halves and pineapple rings
> 1 tsp. whole aniseed
> 2 cinnamon sticks
> 3 tbsp. lemon juice
> 1/3 c. grenadine
> 1 8¾-oz can each black sweet cherries and grapes, drained

Drain syrup from first 5 ingredients. Add aniseed and cinnamon sticks to syrups and bring to a boil. Simmer, uncovered, 10 minutes. Strain, reserving cinnamon. Add lemon juice and grenadine. Cut pineapple rings in half. Put other fruits in bowl; add drained cherries and grapes. Pour simmered syrup over top. Add cinnamon sticks and a few halved slices of lime. Chill several hours. Yield: 12 servings.

Mrs. Bill Jack Evans, Bowie, Tex.

 ### Strawberries Susan

> 4 bananas, thinly sliced
> 1 qt. strawberries
> 2 tbsp. melted currant jelly

(Continued on next page)

Sugar
1 c. heavy cream
6 almond macaroons, crumbled
Slivered almonds or minced candied fruit (opt.)

Arrange bananas in bottom of a deep crystal bowl. Crush strawberries; add currant jelly and sugar to taste. Spread mixture over bananas. Whip cream with 4 tablespoons sugar until stiff; spread over strawberries. Sprinkle macaroons over cream. If desired, top with almonds or candied fruit. Chill for 1 hour. Yield: 4-6 servings.

Mrs. Donald MacGrain, Pres. Officers' Wives' Club, Seoul, Korea

 Tropical Compote

1 ½ c. cubed fresh pineapple
½ c. cubed cherimoya or 1 banana, sliced
1 c. cubed papaya or 1 c. sliced fresh peaches
½ c. dry white wine

Combine fruit with wine; marinate at room temperature for 1 hour. Chill at least 1 hour. Yield: 6 servings.

Mrs. Noel A. Lucas, Plattsburgh, N. Y.

 Watermelon Outriggers

1 long watermelon, cut lengthwise
1 cantaloupe
1 honeydew melon
1 lb. fresh peaches, peeled and sliced or 1 can peaches, drained
1 pt. fresh strawberries or 2 pkg. frozen strawberries
1 pt. fresh blueberries
1 pineapple, cut into chunks

Scoop out watermelon in chunks, reserving rind. Scoop out cantaloupe and honeydew melon making balls. Mix with watermelon. Add peaches and berries. Scoop into watermelon rind. Cut top from pineapple; scoop out pineapple. Add to fruit mixture. Reserve pineapple shell and top.

SAUCE:
1 c. sugar
2 c. water
½ c. rum

Bring sugar and water to a boil; cook until syrupy. Add rum. Pour into pineapple shell. Cover with pineapple top. Ignite sauce when ready to serve. Dump fruits into sauce. Yield: 20-25 servings.

Mrs. Gloria Commerato, Roselle Park, N. J.

Frozen Desserts

HINTS ON FREEZING DESSERTS

1. Be sure the food is cooled quickly and completely.
2. After cooling, package food in a moisture-vapor-proof paper. Make certain all air is out of the package.
3. Seal the package with care. Improperly packaged food will become dry and will absorb flavors of other foods.
4. Carefully label packages with date and contents. Always use the older packages first.
5. Do not package more than your family will eat in one meal.

Using The Ice Cream Freezer

1. Refrigerate ice cream mixture until chilled. If the freezer can will fit into your refrigerator, it is best to chill the mixture in the can.
2. Fill freezer can no more than two-thirds full; this allows room for expansion.
3. Ice cream freezes as heat is absorbed from it by the ice and salt. Salt is used to lower the temperature of the ice.
4. To freeze the ice cream, use 8 parts of ice to 1 part ice cream salt. Finely crushed ice melts faster and hastens freezing so it is best to crush larger pieces.
5. Turn the freezer slowly at first. After a few minutes you will feel a resistance which means the mixture is beginning to freeze. Then turn more rapidly until the dessert is frozen. This helps to produce a smooth product.
6. Drain all water from the freezer tub before removing the cover, to prevent the brine from entering the can, but do not lift can from ice. Remember to wipe the cover thoroughly before taking it off so that salt will not get into the ice cream.
7. Scrape the ice cream from the dasher and quickly pack it down with a spoon or rubber scraper.
8. As a safety measure, cover the can with a double thickness of waxed paper before replacing the cover. Plug hole of freezer can cover with folded waxed paper as a cork.
9. Drain water from the tub so ice cream will freeze firmly.
10. Now repack the freezer, but this time use a mixture of 4 parts of ice to 1 part ice cream salt. With these proportions the temperature will drop quickly and the ice cream will harden faster. Cover the freezer with a heavy cloth or newspaper and allow to stand at least 2 hours. In this time the ice cream will "ripen" and greatly improve in flavor as well as become a harder, more desirable consistency.

FREEZING CHART

DESSERT	PREPARATION	PACKAGING AND APPROXIMATE STORAGE TIME	SERVING
CAKES			
1. Butter or Sponge	Baking before freezing is recommended. Cool on rack after baking.	Wrap in moisture-vapor-proof paper. Freeze in amounts for meal. Store up to 4 months.	Unwrap frosted cakes while defrosting. Allow 30 minutes for angel or sponge, others 2 hours.
2. Fruit	Bake and age before freezing.	Wrap as above and store up to 1 year.	
3. Frostings	Uncooked or butter icings are recommended.		
COOKIES			
1. Baked	Use desired recipe. Cool before wrapping.	Place in layers with waxed paper between layers. Freeze in container or in freezer wrap. Store up to 6 months.	Thaw at room temperature about 15 minutes.
2. Unbaked a. Rolled	Cut and stack with waxed paper between layers.	Wrap and store as above for 1 to 2 months.	Bake without thawing.
b. Dropped	Shape on cookie sheet and then freeze.	Remove from cookie sheet and store in moisture-vapor-proof box or bag for 1 to 2 months.	Bake without thawing.
FRUITS			
Apples, Baking	Prepare firm, ripe apples; bake according to recipe. Cool quickly.	Wrap in foil or freezer paper. Store 8 to 12 months.	If wrapped in foil, place directly in 300° F. oven for heating.
Other Fruits To Serve Uncooked	Select fully ripened fruit. To prevent light colored fruit from turning brown, when exposed to air, ascorbic acid may be added to the sugar or cool syrup before combining with the fruit.	Package in freezer containers. Store up to 1 year.	Defrost quickly in up-opened container for 30 to 60 minutes. Serve icy cold.
PIES			
1. Baked Chiffon	Prepare filling according to recipe and pour into baked or crumb crust. Cool until set.	Press plastic wrap down on filling. Wrap pie in freezer wrap. Store up to 1 or 2 months.	Defrost in refrigerator 4 to 6 hours before serving.
2. Unbaked: Fruit, Pecan, Mincemeat, Pumpkin, Sweet Potato	It is recommended that these pies be frozen before baking. Prepare according to recipe.	Use metal, foil or glass pie plates. Press plastic wrap on filling of one-crust pies. Wrap in moisture-vapor-proof material. Store up to 6 months.	Remove from freezer and cut steam vent in top crust. Bake, unthawed, in preheated oven. Using dull aluminum or glass pans with sufficient time for baking will prevent an underbaked bottom crust.

Almond Cream Mold

2 eggs
1 tbsp. cornstarch
3 c. light cream
½ c. sugar
⅛ tsp. salt
2 tsp. almond extract
½ c. blanched chopped almonds

Beat eggs in top of double boiler. Mix in cornstarch, then cream, sugar and salt. Place over hot water and cook, stirring constantly until thickened; do not boil. Stir in the almond extract; strain. Cool; then, mix in almonds. Turn into buttered melon mold. Place a piece of buttered waxed paper over top; cover. Freeze 4 hours or until firm. Unmold onto a chilled serving dish. Yield: 6-8 servings.

Mrs. Kay B. Frantz, Home Economics Teacher, Topton, Pa.

 ### Individual Baked Alaska

1 qt. ice cream
6 sm. sponge shortcakes
6 egg whites
½ tsp. cream of tartar
1 c. sugar

Place ice cream in mounds on sponge shortcakes. Put in freezer at least 1 hour. Shortly before serving, beat egg whites and cream of tartar until stiff. Beat sugar in gradually, beating until meringue is stiff and glossy. Place cakes with ice cream on several thicknesses of wrapping paper on a board thoroughly soaked in water. Completely cover ice cream and sides of cakes with thick coating of meringue. Place in 500-degree oven just until delicately browned, 3 to 5 minutes. Serve at once. Yield: 6 servings.

Mrs. Dean Bradley, Manhattan, Ill.

Grapefruit Baked Alaska

3 lge. grapefruits
Sugar
⅛ tsp. salt
3 egg whites
½ tsp. vanilla
1 pt. vanilla ice cream

Cut grapefruit in half; remove core. Cut around each section, loosening fruit from membrane. Sprinkle lightly with sugar; chill. When ready to serve, preheat oven to 500 degrees. Add salt to egg whites; beat until foamy. Gradually add 6 tablespoons sugar, beating until very stiff and glossy; add vanilla. Remove grapefruit halves from refrigerator; place heaping spoonful of ice cream in center of each half. Cover with meringue. Place in oven until lightly

(Continued on next page)

browned, about 1 minute. Serve at once. Yield: 6 servings.

Mrs. Bryce Freds, Bluffton, Ind., Favorite Recipes Food Fair

Royal Baked Alaska

1 pkg. no-bake dutch chocolate pie
½ c. plus 3 tbsp. sugar
¼ c. margarine, melted
1 ½ c. plus ⅓ c. milk
3 egg whites

Combine graham cracker crumbs, 3 tablespoons sugar and melted margarine. Press mixture firmly against sides and bottom of an 8½ x 4½ x 2⅞-inch loaf pan. Refrigerate for 15 minutes. Pour 1½ cups cold milk into small deep mixing bowl. Add no-bake dutch chocolate pie filling and 2 tablespoons sugar; beat at medium speed with electric mixer or rotary beater for 3 minutes, scraping sides of bowl occasionally. Pour into prepared pan. Make a well in center about 1-inch deep and to within 1-inch of all sides; set aside. Pour remaining milk into deep mixing bowl. Add topping package contents. Beat on high speed 3 to 4 minutes, or until soft peaks form. Pour into hollow center of filling. Freeze until firm. Beat egg whites until foamy. Gradually add and beat in remaining sugar. Beat until peaks hold. Unmold frozen loaf onto wooden board. Cover top and sides of mold with meringue mixture sealing to board. Bake in a very hot oven (450°F.) about 5 minutes, or until meringue is lightly browned. Slice and serve immediately. Package contains 1 envelope dutch chocolate filling, 1 envelope topping and 1 envelope graham cracker crumbs. Yield: 10 servings.

Photograph for this recipe below.

Banana Chantilly

    3 egg whites
    ¾ c. sugar
    ½ tsp. vanilla
    ¼ tsp. vinegar
    1 c. banana pulp
    ¼ tsp. salt
    1 ½ tbsp. lemon juice
    1 c. heavy cream, whipped
    ¼ c. confectioners' sugar
    Mint leaves
    Red cherries

Beat egg whites until nearly stiff; add ¾ cup sugar, beating constantly. Add vanilla and vinegar. Beat until well blended. Divide meringue into 2 equal parts. Shape each part to fit a refrigerator ice cube tray. Place shaped meringue on a buttered baking sheet. Bake at 275 degrees for 40 to 45 minutes or until delicately browned. Remove from oven and cool. Combine banana pulp, salt and lemon juice. Sweeten whipped cream with confectioners' sugar; fold into banana mixture. Place baked meringue in refrigerator tray or on aluminum foil; cover with filling. Top with second meringue. Freeze about 3 hours. Slice into serving portions; top each with mint leaves and red cherry. Can be frozen for several days. Yield: 6-8 servings.

Mrs. Allen Londo, White Pine, Mich.

 ## Easy Vanilla Dessert

    ¼ c. sugar
    ¼ c. milk
    ⅛ tsp. salt
    1 tsp. vanilla extract
    1 c. heavy cream, whipped

Combine sugar, milk, salt and vanilla in medium mixing bowl; stir until sugar is almost dissolved. Fold in whipped cream until well blended. Place in fluted cups inserted in muffin pan with the bottom of the pan touching the surface of freezer. Freeze for 1½ to 2 hours. Leave at room temperature 10 to 15 minutes before serving. Yield: 6 servings.

Mrs. R. A. Powell, Navy Officers' Wives' Club, Whidbey Island, Wash.

 ## Fat Man's Misery

    ¾ c. crushed chocolate wafers
    ½ c. butter
    1 c. powdered sugar

(Continued on next page)

1 egg
1 ½ tsp. vanilla
1 c. heavy cream
1 tbsp. sugar
½ c. chopped pecans

Place ½ cup chocolate crumbs on bottom of buttered refrigerator tray. Cream butter with powdered sugar. Add egg and 1 teaspoon vanilla; beat until fluffy. Spread mixture over wafer crumbs. Whip cream, adding sugar and remaining vanilla; spread over butter mixture. Sprinkle pecans over whipped cream. Sprinkle remaining wafer crumbs over pecans. Place in freezing compartment of refrigerator until firm. Remove from freezer 1 hour before serving. Yield: 8-10 servings.

Mrs. Frances McLaughlin, Home Economics Teacher, Connersville, Ind.

 ## Italian Strawberry Water Ice

2 c. sugar
1 c. water
4 pts. fresh strawberries
¼ c. lemon juice
⅓ c. orange juice
Pink champagne (opt.)

Combine sugar and water in medium saucepan. Heat and stir until sugar dissolves; boil 5 minutes. Cool. Force strawberries through food mill or blend in electric blender; strain to remove seeds. Blend strawberry puree, lemon and orange juices into cool syrup. Pour into icecube trays. Wrap trays in aluminum foil. Freeze until firm; twenty minutes before serving, remove from freezer to soften slightly. Serve in sherbet glasses with champagne. Yield: 8-10 servings.

Photograph for this recipe on page 245.

 ## Lemon Ice

2 ½ c. water
¾ c. corn syrup
1 c. sugar
¼ tsp. salt
1 tbsp. grated lemon rind
⅔ c. lemon juice
Yellow food coloring

Combine water, corn syrup, sugar, salt and lemon rind in saucepan. Stir over low heat until sugar is dissolved. Bring to a boil; boil 5 minutes without stirring. Cool. Add lemon juice. Strain mixture to remove lemon rind. Tint a delicate yellow with a few drops of food coloring. Pour into refrigerator tray; freeze

(Continued on next page)

until firm throughout. Remove to chilled bowl. Break into lumps; beat with rotary beater or electric mixer until light. Return to refrigerator to complete freezing.

Dixie Lindsay, Jackson, Tenn.

 ### Paradise Ice

> 1 ½ c. sugar
> 1 ½ c. corn syrup
> 3 c. water
> 1 No. 2 can crushed pineapple
> 3 bananas, mashed
> Juice of 3 oranges
> Juice of 3 lemons
> Juice of 3 limes

Combine sugar, corn syrup and water in saucepan. Heat and stir until sugar is completely dissolved. Cool; add fruits and fruit juices. Mix well; pour into freezing trays. Freeze until firm. Turn into bowl; beat with electric mixer for a few minutes. Return to freezing trays. May pour mixture into freezer can and set in freezer to shorten freezing time. Freeze as for ice cream. Yield: 3 quarts.

Mrs. John H. Mason, Springfield, Va.

 ### Watermelon Ice

> ½ lge. watermelon
> Juice of 4 oranges
> Juice of 2 lemons
> 1 c. sugar
> 1 egg white

Scoop meat from melon; extract juice by putting in a cloth bag and squeezing. To watermelon juice add orange and lemon juice and sugar; stir and freeze. When slightly frozen add beaten egg white and finish freezing. Serve in scooped out melon rind and garnish with watermelon, honeydew or cantaloupe balls, cherries and seedless grapes. Yield: 24 servings.

Mrs. P. S. Stouall, Hollandale, Miss.

 ### Aunt Edna's Chocolate Ice Cream

> 2 lge. cans evaporated milk and 2 cans water
> 5 eggs
> 2 tsp. flour
> 2 c. sugar

(Continued on next page)

5 tbsp. cocoa
1 tsp. vanilla extract
¼ tsp. salt

Combine milk and water. Put milk in large pan over low heat; reserve ½ cup milk. In separate bowl, mix eggs, flour and sugar; add to milk. Cook slowly 20 minutes until becomes a light custard. Cream cocoa with reserved milk; add during last 2 minutes of cooking. Stir; add vanilla and salt. Cool thoroughly; freeze either in hand or electric freezer. Yield: ½ gallon ice cream.

Mrs. E. C. Fremaux, Rayne, La.

Coffee Ice Cream

6 tbsp. ground coffee
3 c. milk
2 eggs
1 ½ c. sugar
2 tbsp. arrowroot
2 c. cream, stiffly whipped

Scald coffee and milk; strain through a cheesecloth. Beat eggs, sugar and arrowroot together. Stir in milk; cook in a double boiler until mixture thickens. Remove from heat; cool. Add cream. Freeze. Yield: 2 quarts ice cream.

Mrs. Arzo Carson, Huntsville, Tenn.

Grandma's Peach Ice Cream

1 ½ c. milk
1 c. sugar
2 tbsp. flour
Few grains of salt
2 eggs
1 ½ tsp. vanilla extract
1 ½ c. heavy cream
1 ½ c. sieved fresh peaches
Almond extract to taste

Scald milk in double boiler. Mix ¾ cup sugar, flour and salt; stir in enough milk to make smooth paste. Stir into rest of milk in double boiler until thickened. Cover and cook 10 minutes. Beat eggs slightly; stir in milk mixture. Return to double boiler; cook 1 minute. Cool; add vanilla and cream. Stir in peaches, remaining ¼ cup sugar and almond extract. Freeze in 2-quart crank freezer until difficult to turn. Yield: 1¼ quarts.

Mrs. J. K. Pirkle, Augusta, Ga., Favorite Recipes Food Fair

Louisiana's Famous French Ice Cream

1 qt. plus 1 tbsp. milk
8 tbsp. sugar
4 tbsp. cornstarch
3 eggs, separated
1 pt. thick sweet cream
Lemon extract

Place 1 quart milk in double boiler to scald; while heating, rub together sugar and cornstarch until free of lumps. Add blended sugar and cornstarch to scalded milk in double boiler; cook until thick enough to coat spoon. Beat egg yolks with 1 tablespoon milk until lemon-colored; add to mixture on stove. Cook 1 minute more. Remove from stove; while still boiling, strain. Add whites of eggs which have been stiffly beaten. Lightly fold egg whites into boiling custard; do not beat into custard. When custard is cooled, add sweet cream; flavor with lemon extract. Freeze. One quart ambrosia added before freezing varies flavor and gives a festive touch. One quart crushed fruit, sweetened, may be poured over ice cream before serving.

Nellie McCollum, Eagle Pass, Tex.

 ## Sunday Dinner Strawberry Ice Cream

1 c. sliced strawberries
1 whole egg
1 tbsp. lemon juice
¾ c. sugar
1 c. heavy cream, whipped

Whip together all ingredients except cream at low speed on mixer for 20 minutes. Fold in whipped cream. Pour into tray and freeze. Yield: 6 servings.

Mrs. B. J. Davis, Officers' Wives' Club, US Naval Sta., Bermuda

Bombe Lucretia

1 qt. chocolate ice cream
2 c. sugar
⅔ c. water
¼ tsp. cream of tartar
8 egg yolks
2 c. whipping cream, whipped
Kahlua liqueur

Line a bombe mold with ice cream about ½-inch thick; freeze. Combine sugar, water and cream of tartar; bring to a boil and cook rapidly until syrup spins a thread, 232 degrees. Beat egg yolks until thick and pale; continue beating,

(Continued on next page)

adding syrup gradually. Cook over hot water, stirring constantly, until thick and smooth. Chill. Add whipped cream. Flavor with Kahlua. Add to bombe and freeze. Yield: 6-8 servings.

Mrs. George B. Norberg, Jr., Tacoma, Wash.

Coffee-Ice Cream Log Roll

½ tsp. salt
4 eggs
¾ c. white sugar
1 tsp. vanilla
¾ c. pancake mix
 Confectioners' sugar
1 qt. coffee ice cream, slightly softened
⅓ c. butter or margarine
 Strong coffee, cold

Add salt to eggs; beat until thick and lemon colored. Add white sugar, a little at a time, beating well after each addition. Add vanilla and pancake mix; stir until smooth. Spread evenly in greased waxed paper-lined 10 x 15-inch jelly roll pan. Bake at 400 degrees for 10 to 12 minutes. Sprinkle dry towel well with confectioners' sugar. Remove cake from oven; loosen edges and turn out on towel. Remove waxed paper carefully; roll cake in towel and let stand 20 minutes. Unroll. Spread ice cream over cake; roll as for jelly roll. Wrap in aluminum foil; freeze several hours. Cream butter and 1½ cups confectioners' sugar. Blend well; add enough additional coffee to make frosting fluffy and of spreading consistency. Spread frosting over frozen cake roll and serve. Yield: 8 servings.

Mrs. Jane Bellefeuille, Conyers, Ga.

Chocolate Ice Cream Roll

6 eggs, separated
½ tsp. cream of tartar
1 c. sugar
½ tsp. vanilla
¼ tsp. salt
4 tbsp. flour
½ c. cocoa
1 ½ to 2 qt. ice cream, softened

Beat egg whites until foamy; add cream of tartar and beat until stiff. Gradually add sugar; beat until creamy. In separate dish, beat yolks and salt until light; fold into egg white mixture. Sift flour and cocoa over mixture; fold in. Pour into a 15 x 10 x 1-inch pan lined with waxed paper and greased. Bake at 350 degrees about 20 minutes. Invert on a tea towel sprinkled with confectioners'

(Continued on next page)

sugar or cocoa. Remove waxed paper; trim off crusty edges. Roll as a jelly roll; cool. Unroll; spread with softened ice cream and reroll. Wrap in foil and store in freezer. Slice and serve with warm chocolate sauce.

SAUCE:

>   1 tbsp. cornstarch
>   3 tbsp. cocoa
>   ⅛ tsp. salt
>   ¾ c. sugar
>   1 c. milk
>   1 tsp. vanilla
>   1 tbsp. butter

Place dry ingredients in a saucepan; gradually add milk while stirring. Cook until thick. Remove from stove and add butter and vanilla.

Mrs. George J. Gast, Osage, Iowa

Frozen Yum Yum

>   ⅔ c. butter
>   2 c. powdered sugar
>   3 eggs, separated
>   2 squares melted chocolate
>   Pinch of salt
>   1 tsp. vanilla
>   ½ c. chopped nuts
>   Graham cracker crumbs
>   1 qt. mint or other ice cream, softened

Cream butter and sugar, add slightly beaten egg yolks, chocolate, salt, vanilla and nuts. Fold in egg whites. Grease 9 x 13-inch pan; place crumbs in bottom. Put egg mixture on top of crust. Freeze for 1 to 2 hours. Spread ice cream on top; sprinkle with graham cracker crumbs. Freeze. This can be made the day before. Take out of freezer 10 to 15 minutes before serving for better results in slicing. Yield: 8-12 servings.

Mrs. Mabel E. Lenz, Lyle, Minn.

Macedoine Francois

>   2 c. green grapes
>   2 c. cubed fresh pineapple
>   2 c. fresh strawberries, halved
>   2 c. melon balls
>   2 c. sliced bananas
>   2 oranges, sectioned

(Continued on next page)

¾ c. sugar
½ c. Madeira
⅓ c. cognac brandy
1 qt. lemon sherbet

Combine fruit in serving bowl. Combine sugar, wine and cognac. Pour over fruit. When ready to serve, add sherbet with ice cream scoop.

Mrs. Charles Balfanz, Chicago, Ill.

 ## Melba Miniatures

1 pkg. frozen raspberries, thawed
2 tbsp. corn syrup
½ tsp., plus 1 tbsp. lemon juice
1 c. milk
2 c. miniature marshmallows
⅛ tsp. salt
1 tbsp. lemon juice
1 14-oz. can crushed pineapple, drained
1 c. heavy cream, whipped
½ c. toasted slivered almonds

Combine raspberries, syrup and ½ teaspoon lemon juice. Spoon mixture into 16 paper cups set in muffin tins. Place in freezer until partially set. Scald milk; add marshmallows and stir until melted. Cool. Add salt and lemon juice. Fold in pineapple, whipped cream and almonds. Spoon mixture over raspberries. Freeze until firm. To serve remove paper cups and invert into sherbet glasses. Yield: 16 servings.

Mrs. Truman Clark, Jacksonville, N. C.

 ## Peach Melba

1 10-oz. pkg. frozen red raspberries, thawed
⅔ c. sugar
Pinch cream of tartar
2 pt. vanilla ice cream
1 1-lb. can cling peach halves, drained

Press raspberries through sieve into small saucepan, discarding seeds; stir in sugar and cream of tartar. Heat quickly, stirring constantly, to boiling; cook, stirring constantly, for 3 minutes. Pour into small bowl. When ready to serve, scoop ice cream into dessert dishes; top each with peach half. Spoon raspberry sauce over each, dividing evenly.

Mrs. Madeleine Newell, Carrollton, Ga.

Frozen Raspberry Parfait

2 c. heavy cream
18 coconut macaroons, crushed
1 c. finely chopped pecans
1 pt. raspberry sherbet
1-2 drops red food coloring
½ c. coconut

Whip 1½ cups cream until stiff. Add crushed macaroons and pecans. Spread half the mixture in loaf pan and freeze until firm. Remove from freezer and spread with raspberry sherbet. Return to freezer to set sherbet firmly. Cover with remaining cream mixture and freeze. Two hours before serving, whip remaining cream and add red food coloring to tint light pink. Remove loaf from freezer; run hot wet rag over outside of pan to loosen. Invert on serving plate and frost with tinted whipped cream. Sprinkle with coconut; freeze until served. Yield: 8 servings.

Mrs. Walter H. Godshall, Officers' Wives' Club, Guam

 ### Biscuit Tortoni

¾ c. sugar
1 c. milk
3 eggs, separated
⅛ tsp. salt
½ c. macaroons, ground
3 tsp. sherry wine
½ c. almonds, finely ground and toasted
1 ½ c. heavy cream, whipped

Heat sugar and milk in top of double boiler; add well-beaten egg yolks gradually. Stir constantly about 5 minutes. Remove custard from heat; pour into bowl to cool. Fold in stiffly beaten egg whites and salt. Add ground macaroons that have been soaked in sherry; add almonds. Fold in whipped cream; ladle into individual souffle cups. Freeze; serve with whipped cream, if desired. Yield: 12 servings.

Mrs. W. Meredith M. Heyl, Philadelphia, Pa.

Rum Tortoni

½ c. finely chopped toasted almonds
½ c. coconut, toasted and crumbled
½ c. seedless dark raisins
1 qt. vanilla ice cream
3 tsp. rum extract
Maraschino cherries or slivered, toasted almonds

(Continued on next page)

Mix almonds, coconut and raisins. Stir ice cream until soft, but not melted to thin consistency. Quickly stir in rum extract and almond mixture. Spoon into paper cups placed in 2½-inch muffin tins. Place in freezer; when slightly frozen, top with Maraschino cherries. Freeze firm. Remove from freezer just before serving. Yield: 12-14 servings.

Mrs. H. C. Bridgers, Jr., Pres. Officers' Wives' Club, Roosevelt Roads, Puerto Rico

 ## Frozen Tortoni With Strawberry Sauce

> 1 pt. vanilla ice cream
> 12 macaroons, crumbled
> 8 tsp. orange juice
> ½ c. heavy cream
> ½ tsp. powdered sugar
> 2 tbsp. chopped toasted almonds
> 1 pt. fresh strawberries, hulled and cut in half or
> 1 10-oz. pkg. frozen sliced berries, thawed

Soften ice cream slightly. Stir in macaroons and 4 tablespoons juice. Whip cream until thick and shiny; fold into ice cream mixture. Spoon into 3-cup metal dish or mold. Sprinkle surface slightly with powdered sugar and almonds. Cover with Saran Wrap. Freeze until firm, about 4 or 5 hours or overnight. To unmold, wrap mold for 4 or 5 seconds in a towel wrung out with hot water. Loosen edge with spatula; turn out onto cold platter. Put berries in saucepan with sugar added to taste. Simmer until soft, but not mushy. Remove from heat; add remaining orange juice. Pour mixture into chafing dish; serve hot over souffle. Yield: 4 servings.

Mrs. H. F. Norcross, Tyronza, Ark.

Peach Cloud

> 1 c. fresh peaches, finely chopped
> ¼ c. plus 2 tbsp. sugar
> 1 c. whipping cream, whipped
> 2 egg whites, beaten
> Dash of salt

Mix peaches and ¼ cup sugar; fold quickly into whipped cream before the peaches become discolored. Add 2 tablespoons sugar and salt to beaten egg whites. Beat until the mixture forms soft peaks. Fold egg whites into cream mixture. Pour immediately into chilled refrigerator freezing trays or molds; freeze until firm. Yield: 6-8 servings.

Mrs. Agnes Hackley, Louisville, Ky.

Cloister Frozen Rum Pie

CRUST:

8 oz. graham cracker crumbs
2 oz. granulated sugar
2 oz. melted butter

Mix all ingredients. Line two 9-inch pie tins, pressing down firmly with fingers. Bake at 300 degrees until golden brown.

FILLING:

3 eggs, at room temperature
4 oz. granulated sugar
¼ oz. gelatin
1 oz. hot water
2 oz. Jamaica rum
1 oz. lemon juice
2 oz. fine cake crumbs
1 pt. heavy cream, whipped
1 oz. brandy

Whip eggs and sugar to 4 times original volume. Mix gelatin, hot water, 1-ounce Jamaica rum and the lemon juice. Blend with egg mixture. Sprinkle cake crumbs with a little Jamaica rum; mix with whipped cream. Blend into egg mixture, adding 1-ounce Jamaica rum and brandy. Fill shells with mixture and put in freezer for 10 to 12 hours. Remove a few minutes before serving.

Mrs. Carl H. Newman, Officers' Wives' Club, Rota, Spain, Favorite Recipes
Food Fair

Frozen Chocolate Pie

⅔ c. plus 1 tbsp. sugar
3 eggs, separated
¼ c. milk
1 tsp. vanilla flavoring
1 square chocolate
1 c. heavy cream, whipped
16 graham crackers, crushed
¼ c. butter or margarine

Combine 2/3 cup sugar, slightly beaten egg yolks, milk, vanilla and chocolate in saucepan; cook until thick. Cool. Fold in whipped cream and stiffly beaten egg whites. Combine cracker crumbs, remaining sugar and butter; pat into 9-inch pie plate. Pour custard into crust. Freeze. Yield: 6 servings.

Mrs. Wade Good, Harrisonburg, Va.

Grasshopper Pie

1 egg white
Dash of salt
2 tbsp. sugar
⅓ c. light corn syrup
½ pt. heavy cream
4 tbsp. green creme de menthe
4 tbsp. white creme de cacao

Beat egg white and salt until peaks form. Add sugar gradually; beat until smooth and glossy. Beat in syrup slowly until mixture holds stiff, firm peaks. Whip cream until stiff; fold in cream de menthe and cream de cacao. Fold into egg white mixture.

CHOCOLATE CRUST:

1 ½ c. chocolate cracker crumbs
¼ c. melted butter
¼ c. brown sugar

Combine all ingredients. Press in pie plate or pan. Bake at 400 degrees for 5 minutes. Cool. Pour filling into shell. Freeze overnight.

Mrs. William Edward Robinson, Jr., Milledgeville, Ga.

Fudge Sundae Pie

1 c. evaporated milk
1 c. chocolate chips
1 c. miniature marshmallows
¼ tsp. salt
Vanilla wafers
1 qt. vanilla ice cream
Pecans

Put milk, chocolate chips, marshmallows and salt into heavy 1-quart saucepan. Stir over medium heat until chocolate and marshmallows melt completely and mixture thickens. Remove from heat and cool to room temperature. Line bottom and sides of a 9-inch pie plate with vanilla wafers; spoon half of ice cream over wafers. Cover with half of chocolate mixture. Repeat layers. Place a few pecans on top. Freeze until firm, 3 to 5 hours. Yield: 8-10 servings.

Mrs. Paul Muehl, Marshfield, Wis.

Mile-High Ice Cream Pie

1 pt. chocolate ice cream, softened
1 baked 9-in. pie shell, cooled
1 pt. strawberry ice cream, softened
4 egg whites
½ tsp. vanilla
¼ tsp. cream of tartar
½ c. sugar

Spread chocolate ice cream in pie shell; top with layer of strawberry ice cream. Place in freezer. Beat egg whites with vanilla and cream of tartar until soft peaks form; gradually add sugar, beating until stiff and glossy. Spread meringue over ice cream, carefully sealing to edge of pastry. Bake in 475-degree oven for 2 to 3 minutes or until meringue is lightly browned. Freeze pie several hours or overnight.

CHOCOLATE SAUCE:

4 squares unsweetened chocolate
¾ c. water
1 c. sugar
Dash of salt
6 tbsp. butter or margarine
1 tsp. vanilla

Heat chocolate and water over low heat in saucepan, stirring constantly until chocolate is smooth and melted. Stir in sugar and salt. Simmer until lightly thickened, about 5 minutes. Remove from heat; blend in butter and vanilla. Serve warm over wedges of pie. Yield: 6 servings.

Mrs. Harry G. Barnett, Greybull, Wyo.

Avocado Sherbet

Sugar
1 c. water
1 c. sieved avocado
½ c. or juice of 2 lemons
1 c. pineapple juice
2 egg whites
4 tbsp. sugar

Mix 1 cup sugar and water together; bring to a boil. Stir until sugar is dissolved; cool. Add avocado and fruit juices; mix thoroughly. May be mixed in blender. Place in refrigerator tray; freeze until mushy. Beat egg whites until stiff. Beat 4 tablespoons sugar into egg whites. Fold into mixture; freeze until firm. Yield: 8 servings.

Mrs. Hunter Daughtrey, Carrsville, Va.

Lime Sherbet

2 marshmallows
1 c. boiling water
1 c. ginger ale
¼ c. fresh lime juice
1 tbsp. lemon juice
½ tsp. green coloring
1 tbsp. sugar
2 egg whites

Melt marshmallows in boiling water. Add ginger ale, fruit juices and coloring; cool. Add sugar to beaten egg whites, beat. Combine with lime mixture; freeze. Yield: 8 servings.

Mrs. Tressie Halman, Chico, Tex.

 Melon Coupe

2 ripe cantaloupes
1 c. sugar
1 c. water
1 envelope unflavored gelatin
Juice of 2 lemons
Juice of 2 limes
2 tbsp. light corn syrup
¼ tsp. salt
2 ripe honey dew melons

Put enough cantaloupe through blender to make three cups puree. Slowly heat sugar, water and gelatin until dissolved, stirring frequently. Remove from heat; add juices, puree, corn syrup and salt. Mix well. Pour into two refrigerator trays; partially freeze. Remove mixture from trays; beat until light and fluffy. Pack into 6-cup melon or fluted mold. Freeze until firm. Unmold on a large plate and surround with honeydew melon balls and fluffs of whipped cream. Center of mold may be filled with lime ice and strawberries. Garnish coupe with crisp mint sprigs. Yield: 8 servings.

*Mrs. Frederic J. Brown, Pres. Wives' Club, San Francisco, Cal., Favorite
Recipes Food Fair*

 Peach Sherbet

1 c. sugar
Juice of 1 orange and 1 lemon
4 peaches sliced with sugar or 1 pt. frozen peaches
1 pt. milk

(Continued on next page)

263

Stir together; put in freezer tray. Stir once after beginning to freeze.

Mrs. D. H. Callender, Jr., Haynesville, La.

 ## Pineapple Sherbet

½ envelope unflavored gelatin
2 tbsp. cold water
2 c. buttermilk
1 c. sugar
1 9-oz. can crushed pineapple
1 tsp. vanilla
1 egg white

Soften gelatin in cold water; dissolve over hot water. Combine buttermilk, ¾ cup sugar, pineapple, vanilla and gelatin; mix well. Pour into refrigerator tray; freeze until firm. Break in chunks and beat smooth. Beat egg white until soft peaks form; gradually add ¼ cup sugar, beating to stiff peaks. Fold into pineapple mixture. Return quickly to cold tray. Freeze firm. Yield: 4-6 servings.

Eva J. Nance, Asheboro, N. C.

 ## Frosty Strawberry Squares

1 c. sifted flour
¼ c. brown sugar
½ c. chopped nuts
½ c. butter, melted
2 egg whites
1 c. white sugar
2 c. sliced fresh strawberries
2 tbsp. lemon juice
1 c. whipping cream, whipped

Stir together first 4 ingredients. Spread evenly in shallow baking pan. Bake at 350 degrees for 20 minutes, stirring occasionally. Sprinkle 2/3 of crumbs in 13 x 9-inch baking pan. Combine egg whites, white sugar, berries and lemon juice in large bowl; with electric beater beat at high speed to stiff peaks, about 10 minutes. Fold in whipped cream. Spoon over crumbs; top with remaining crumbs. Freeze 6 hours or overnight. Cut into 10 or 12 squares. Garnish with whole strawberries. If frozen berries are used, partially thaw and reduce white sugar to 2/3 cup. Yield: 10-12 servings.

Mrs. Elaine Cruikshank, Montrose, Iowa

Chilled Desserts

Almond Supreme

1 pkg. lemon gelatin
2 tbsp. sugar
¼ tsp. salt
1 c. boiling water
½ c. cold water
1 c whipped cream
1 tsp. almond extract
6 macaroons, dried and rolled
6 marshmallows, cut into pieces
3 tbsp. candied cherries, chopped

Dissolve gelatin, sugar and salt in boiling water; add cold water. Chill. When mixture begins to thicken, whip until frothy. Fold in remaining ingredients. Pour into mold; chill. Yield: 6 servings.

Mrs. Agnes Hackley, Louisville, Ky.

 ## Apricot Delight

½ lb. vanilla wafers, crushed
½ c. butter or margarine
½ c. powdered sugar
2 eggs, beaten
1 lge. can apricots, drained and mashed or chopped
½ pt. heavy cream, whipped
½ c. chopped nuts

Line a 7 x 11-inch pan with waxed paper. Place 2/3 the wafer crumbs on bottom of pan. Cream butter and sugar; add eggs, mixing well. Spread mixture over crumbs. Spread with apricots, then whipped cream. Cover with remaining crumbs and nuts. Refrigerate for 24 hours. Yield: 8-10 servings.

Mrs. Paul V. Kiehl, Pres. Officers' Wives' Club, Honolulu, Hawaii

Snowballs

1 lb. apricots
1 to 1½ c. brown sugar
1 8-oz. pkg. almonds, finely ground
1 pt. heavy cream
1 tsp. vanilla or almond flavoring
Sugar to taste
1 box vanilla wafers
2 pkg. flaked coconut

(Continued on next page)

Combine apricots and brown sugar; cook to jam consistency. Blend in almonds; refrigerate for 3 days. Whip cream with flavoring and sugar. Spread apricot mixture between vanilla wafers, sandwich-style, using 4 wafers per stack. Ice generously with whipped cream; coat heavily with coconut. Place in container and cover tightly. Refrigerate for 24 hours before serving.

Mrs. Roy F. Claytor, Grand Forks, N.D.

 ## Apricot Whimsy

>   1 12-oz. box dried apricots
>   2 c. water
>   1 c. butter
>   2 c. sifted confectioners' sugar
>   4 eggs, separated
>   Grated rind and juice of 1 lemon
>   1/3 c. sugar
>   3 doz. ladyfingers
>   3/4 c. heavy cream, whipped
>   Toasted sliced almonds
>   Canned whole apricots
>   Fresh mint sprigs

Stew dried apricots in water until tender and liquid is absorbed; put through ricer or sieve. Cool. Cream butter; add confectioners' sugar and beat till light. Add egg yolks, 1 at a time, and beat well. Beat in apricot pulp, lemon rind and juice. Beat egg whites until stiff; gradually beat in sugar, beating until sugar is dissolved. Fold in apricot mixture. Line deep 9-inch springform pan with ladyfingers; put in alternate layers of 1/3 apricot mixture and 1/3 lady-fingers. Chill overnight or a day or two. Remove sides of pan; garnish with whipped cream and almonds. Arrange whole apricots and mint sprigs around outside. Leftover cake can be stored in refrigerator for a few days or can be frozen. Yield: 10-12 servings.

Mrs. Dorothy Levy, Home Economics Teacher, Floral Park, N. Y.

 ## Banana Cream

>   5 lge. bananas
>   5 tsp. sugar
>   1 c. cream
>   1 pkg. lemon gelatin
>   3/4 pt. boiling water

Peel bananas; rub smooth with sugar. Add cream, beaten to stiff froth. Dissolve gelatin in boiling water; when cold, stir in cream mixture. Pour into mold; set in refrigerator. Serve with whipped cream, if desired.

Onita G. Montfort, Campbellsburg, Ky.

Banana Flip

2 pkg. graham crackers, rolled
¾ c. melted margarine
1 box powdered sugar
2 eggs
1 tsp. vanilla
½ c. soft margarine
8 bananas
Maraschino cherries, chopped
½ pt. whipping cream, whipped and sweetened
¼ c. chopped nuts

Mix cracker crumbs and melted margarine; pack evenly in 9 x 13-inch pan. Refrigerate 1 hour. Combine next 4 ingredients; beat until creamy. Spread on top of crumb mixture; slice bananas lengthwise on top. Sprinkle with a few cherries. Spread cream over cherries; sprinkle with nuts. Refrigerate at least 1 hour and 30 minutes or overnight before serving. Yield: 12 servings.

Mrs. Don Moomaw, Smithville, Ohio

Bavarian Cream

1 c. milk
1 tbsp. gelatin
2 eggs, separated
¼ c. sugar
½ tsp. salt
½ c. heavy cream, whipped
½ tsp. vanilla

Scald milk in top of double boiler with gelatin. Beat egg yolks slightly with sugar and salt. Add hot milk slowly, stirring constantly. Return to double boiler; stir and cook until coating forms on spoon. Strain onto stiffly beaten egg whites. When beginning to thicken, fold in whipped cream and vanilla. Pour into molds and chill. Yield: 4 servings.

Mrs. George B. Dany, Pres., Officers' Wives' Club, Travis AFB, Cal.

Blueberry Treat

½ c. oleo
2 ½ c. crushed coconut bars or graham crackers
1 pkg. Dream Whip
½ pt. whipping cream
2 c. small marshmallows
1 can blueberry pie filling

(Continued on next page)

Mix oleo and crushed coconut bars; press into 9 x 13-inch pan. Beat Dream Whip as directed on package. Whip the whipping cream; fold into Dream Whip. Add marshmallows; put into pan. Spoon and spread pie filling over top; set in refrigerator at least 12 hours. Yield: 12 servings.

Mrs. M. Redman, Home Economics Teacher, Marquette, Mich.

Broken Glass Torte

　1 pkg. of each lemon, orange, lime and cherry gelatin
　1 ½ c. hot water for each package
　1 envelope plain gelatin
　¼ c. cold water
　1 c. hot pineapple juice
　2 c. heavy cream, whipped
　1 c. sugar
　1 tsp. vanilla
　24 graham crackers, crushed
　½ c. soft butter

Dissolve each package gelatin in hot water; chill in separate pans until firm. Cut into ½ inch cubes. Soften plain gelatin in cold water; dissolve in hot pineapple juice. Cool. Whip cream; beat with ½ cup sugar and vanilla. Fold in plain gelatin mixture and cubes of colored gelatin. Mix graham crackers with butter and ½ cup sugar. Line springform pan or angel cake pan with removable bottom with 2/3 of the crumb mixture. Turn filling into pan and top with remaining crumb mixture.

Mrs. Carolyn Gentry, Searcy, Ark.

Charlotte

　3 envelopes unflavored gelatin
　½ c. cold water
　½ c. hot water
　1 c. sugar
　1 qt. whipping cream, whipped stiff
　6 egg whites, beaten stiff
　1 tsp. vanilla
　Pinch of salt

Soak gelatin in cold water; dissolve in hot water. Add ½ cup sugar to warm gelatin. Add remaining sugar to cream. Mix cream and egg whites; add vanilla and salt. Fold into gelatin mixture; pour in large mold. Refrigerate. Yield: 12 servings.

Mrs. Rusl Valentine, Starkville, Miss.

Charlotte Russe

> 1 tbsp. unflavored gelatin
> ¼ c. cold water
> ¼ c. boiling water
> 4 egg whites, stiffly beaten
> 1 c., scant, sugar
> 1 pt. heavy cream, whipped
> Wine

Dissolve gelatin in cold water; add to boiling water. Let cool. Combine stiffly beaten egg whites and ½ cup sugar. Add remaining sugar to whipped cream. Fold together egg whites and whipped cream. Add gelatin flavored with a little wine. Refrigerate at least 2 hours. Yield: 8 servings.

Mrs. William W. Momyer, Randolph, Tex.

 Cherry Coke Dessert

> 1 pkg. cherry gelatin
> 1 sm. can crushed pineapple
> 1 sm. bottle maraschino cherries
> 1 3-oz. pkg. cream cheese
> 1 6-oz. bottle cola beverage
> ½ c. pecans, chopped

Dissolve gelatin in heated pineapple and cherry juice. Stir in cream cheese until smooth. Chill until very thick. Add remaining ingredients and pour into a 1-quart mold. Chill until firm. Lime gelatin and 7-Up may be substituted for cherry gelatin and cola drink if green dessert is desired. Cheese may be folded in last instead of melted in hot juice. Yield: 6 servings.

Governor Lurleen Wallace, Montgomery, Ala.

 Cherry Dandy

> 2 c. graham cracker crumbs
> ½ c. sugar
> ½ c. margarine or butter, melted
> 1 can cherry pie mix
> ½ c. chopped walnuts
> 48 to 50 lge. marshmallows
> 1 c. milk
> 1 c. heavy cream, whipped

Combine cracker crumbs, sugar and margarine. Press half of the mixture into a buttered 9-inch square pan. Mix cherry pie mix and nuts. Melt marshmallows in milk in double boiler. Beat smooth and cool. Fold in whipped cream. Place

(Continued on next page)

cherry mixture on top of crumbs; spread marshmallow mixture over cherries. Sprinkle remaining crumbs on top. Chill 6-12 hours. Yield: 12 servings.

Mrs. Donald M. Alderson, Officers' Wives' Club, MacDill, Fla.

Cherry Ring

> 1 1-lb. can tart, pitted red cherries
> 1 3-oz. pkg. cherry flavored gelatin
> 1 tbsp. kirsch or water
> 1 8-oz. pkg. cream cheese
> 1 c. sugar
> 1 tsp. vanilla
> 3 tbsp. lemon juice
> 1 ⅔ c. evaporated milk, partially frozen

Drain cherries; add enough water to drained juice to measure 1 cup liquid. Heat liquid to boiling; pour over gelatin in small mixing bowl. Stir until dissolved; stir in kirsch. In medium-sized mixing bowl combine cream cheese, sugar, vanilla and lemon juice; beat until well blended. Slowly blend in gelatin, mixing well. Stir in cherries; chill mixture to consistency of unbeaten egg whites. When slightly thickened, whip milk in large mixing bowl at high speed until stiff. Fold in gelatin mixture lightly, but thoroughly. Turn into a lightly oiled mold; chill until firm. If desired, pile into parfait glasses. Yield: 12-15 servings.

Mrs. Grace L. Thompson, Home Economics Teacher, Valdosta, Ga.

Sweet Cherry Mold

> 2 c. fresh dark sweet cherries
> ⅓ c. butter, melted
> 1 ½ c. crushed graham crackers
> 1 tbsp. gelatin
> ¼ c. cold water
> 2 c. milk, scalded and cooled
> ½ c. sugar
> ⅛ tsp. salt
> 3 eggs, separated
> 1 tsp. vanilla
> Whipped cream

Wash cherries. Pit and halve 1½ cups cherries. Set ½ cup aside for garnish. Mix butter and graham crackers. Press around sides and bottom of a 1½-quart bowl; chill. Soften gelatin in cold water. Add to scalded milk in top of double boiler with sugar and salt. Cook, stirring, until .gelatin and sugar are dissolved. Beat egg yolks slightly. Stir in a little hot milk mixture; add remaining milk. Cook over boiling water until slightly thickened, about 10 minutes.

(Continued on next page)

Chill until thickened. Fold in stiffly beaten egg whites, vanilla and cherries. Pour into prepared bowl; chill 2 to 3 hours. Unmold and garnish with whipped cream and remaining cherries. Yield: 8 servings.

Mrs. Richard E. Prouty, Favorite Recipes Food Fair, Tullahoma, Tenn.

Almond Cheesecake

 1 ½ lb. ricotta cheese
 2 tbsp. honey
 1 tbsp. cream sherry or catawba wine
 ½ c. ground almonds

Combine cheese, honey and wine; beat until well blended and soft. Lightly grease 1-quart mold; dust with crushed nuts. Add remaining nuts to cheese. Press cheese mixture into mold; cover. Chill 24 hours. Dip into hot water to unmold. Garnish with seeded grapes or fresh berries. Yield: 6-8 servings.

Mrs. Robert B. Wood, Norfolk, Va.

Creamy Cheesecake

CRUST:

 1 ½ c. graham cracker crumbs
 ⅓ c. brown sugar
 ½ tsp. cinnamon
 ⅓ c. melted butter

Mix all ingredients until crumbly; press evenly over bottom and sides of cheesecake pan.

FILLING:

 2 eggs
 ½ c. sugar
 ½ tsp. vanilla
 1 ½ c. creamed cottage cheese
 1 8-oz. pkg. cream cheese
 1 c. sour cream

Blend eggs, sugar, flavoring, cottage and cream cheese until smooth. Pour into crumb-lined pan. Bake at 350° about 35 minutes. Remove from oven and spread with sour cream while cake is hot.

Dorothy Wynkoop, Home Economics Teacher, Greenville, Ohio

Cheesecake Coup

>   1 envelope unflavored gelatin
>   1 c. cold water
>   1 egg, separated
>   ¼ c. milk
>   ½ c. sugar
>   1 c. cottage cheese
>   1 3-oz. pkg. cream cheese
>   Grated rind and juice of 1 lemon
>   ½ tsp. vanilla
>   ½ c. light cream
>   1 graham cracker pie crust

Soak gelatin in cold water for 5 minutes. Combine slightly beaten egg yolk, milk and sugar; cook for 5 minutes over a low heat, stirring constantly. Remove from heat. Add gelatin; stir until dissolved. Cream the cheeses together; add lemon rind, vanilla and gelatin mixture. Chill until begins to thicken. Beat cream until foamy; add lemon juice. Continue beating until cream thickens. Fold whipped cream and stiffly beaten egg white into gelatin mixture. Pour mixture into crumb crust; chill until firm, preferably 24 hours. Cut into wedge-shaped pieces and serve. Yield: 8 servings.

Mrs. Jesse W. Taft, Sanford, Fla.

 Mandarin Orange Cheesecake

>   1 c. zwieback or graham cracker crumbs
>   2 ¼ c. sugar
>   ¼ c. butter, melted
>   5 8-oz. pkg. cream cheese
>   6 eggs
>   ½ c. heavy cream
>   1 tsp. lemon flavoring
>   ¼ c. flour
>   ¼ tsp. salt
>   1 11-oz. can mandarin orange segments, drained
>   1 small jar apple jelly, melted

Combine crumbs, ¼ cup sugar and butter; press in greased 9-inch springform pan. Beat cheese until fluffy. Add eggs, 1 at a time; add cream and lemon flavoring. Mix remaining sugar with flour and salt; add to mixture, beating until smooth. Pour on crumbs. Bake at 475 degrees for 15 minutes; reduce heat to 250 degrees. Continue to bake for 1 hour and 15 minutes. Remove from oven; cool. Arrange orange segments over top. Spoon jelly over oranges and refrigerate. Other fruits and glazes may be substituted. Yield: 12 servings.

Mrs. Herbert T. King, Key West, Fla.

Pineapple Cheesecake

16 graham crackers, crushed
1 c. drained crushed pineapple
1 ½ lb. cream cheese
1 c. sugar
4 eggs
1 tsp. vanilla
1 pt. sour cream

Pat crumbs in bottom of large angel food cake mold. Top with crushed pineapple. Cream remaining ingredients in order listed. Pour over pineapple and bake at 350 degrees for 1 hour.

Mrs. R. E. Hammond, Pres. Officers' Wives' Club, San Diego, Cal.

Matchless Cheesecake

CRUMB MIXTURE:

¾ c. chocolate cookie crumbs
3 tbsp. sugar
3 tbsp. butter or margarine, melted

Combine all ingredients. Press ½ cup mixture in bottom of 8 or 9-inch spring form pan. Reserve remaining for top.

FILLING:

3 envelopes unflavored gelatin
1 c. milk
2 eggs, separated
¾ c. sugar
3 c. creamed cottage cheese
1 6-oz. can frozen orange juice concentrate, unthawed
1 c. heavy cream, whipped
1 tbsp. grated orange peel (opt.)

Sprinkle gelatin over milk in 2½-quart saucepan to soften. Stir in egg yolks. Place over low heat; stir until gelatin dissolves and mixture thickens slightly, about 3 minutes. Remove from heat; stir in ½ cup sugar. Sieve or beat cottage cheese on high speed of electric mixer until smooth, 3 to 4 minutes. Stir cottage cheese and unthawed concentrate into gelatin mixture. Beat egg whites until stiff; add remaining ¼ cup sugar gradually. Beat until very stiff; fold into gelatin mixture. Fold in whipped cream. Pour into prepared pan; sprinkle with remaining crumbs and grated orange peel. Chill until firm, 2 to 3 hours. Loosen cake from sides of pan with knife; release spring form. If spring form pan is not available, use 8-cup loaf or square pan. Grease pan lightly so waxed

(Continued on next page)

paper cut to fit will cling to pan. To unmold, invert on serving plate; remove waxed paper. Yield: 10-12 servings.

Mrs. Joseph H. Schumacher, Schenectady, N. Y.

No-Bake Miniature Cheesecakes

1 pkg. no-bake cheesecake filling
¾ c. finely chopped pecans
3 tbsp. sugar
⅓ c. margarine, melted
1 ½ c. milk
Maraschino cherry pieces, drained

Combine graham cracker crumbs, chopped pecans, sugar and melted margarine; mix thoroughly. Place 12 paper baking cups in muffin cups. Divide crumb mixture among baking cups and press firmly against sides and bottoms of cups. Refrigerate until firm, about 15 minutes. Pour milk into small mixing bowl. Add cheesecake filling. Beat at low speed with electric mixer or rotary beater until blended, about 1 minute. Beat at medium speed 3 minutes longer. Pour into prepared crusts. Chill at least 1 hour before serving. To serve, garnish cheesecakes with maraschino cherry pieces. The package contains 1 envelope each: cheesecake filling and graham cracker crumbs. Yield: 12 miniature cheesecakes.

Photograph for this recipe below.

Chestnut Cakes

    1 ½ lb. chestnuts
    1 c. sugar
    ½ c. rum
    ½ pt. heavy cream, whipped
    Dash of nutmeg

Shell and skin chestnuts. Cover with boiling water; add sugar and cook until soft. Drain off water; mash and add rum. Chill. Serve with whipped cream and nutmeg on top. Yield: 6 servings.

Mrs. Howard L. Rice, Reno, Nev.

 ## Chocolate Icebox Dessert

    ½ c. butter
    2 c. powdered sugar, sifted
    2 tbsp. cocoa
    ¼ tsp. salt (opt.)
    2 egg yolks, unbeaten
    1 tsp. vanilla
    1 c. nuts, plain or toasted
    2 egg whites
    1 ¾ c. or 1 sm. pkg. vanilla wafer crumbs

Cream butter. Add sugar, cocoa, salt and egg yolks; beat until creamy. Add vanilla and nuts. Fold in stiffly beaten egg whites. Line 9 x 9 or 6 x 9-inch pan with ½ the vanilla wafer crumbs; pour in batter. Add remainder of crumbs on top. Garnish with maraschino cherries. Let set overnight in refrigerator; serve with whipped cream, if desired. Yield: 6-8 servings.

Mrs. Margie R. Gilchrist, Home Economics Teacher, Borger, Tex.

 ## Chocolate Special

    4 eggs, separated
    1 c. sugar
    2 sq. unsweetened chocolate, melted
    1 ½ tsp. gelatin
    1 tbsp. cold water
    5 tbsp. boiling water

Beat egg yolks until light; add sugar and beat again. Add chocolate. Soften gelatin in cold water; add boiling water. Mix with chocolate mixture; beat vigorously. Fold in stiffly beaten egg whites. Chill until set. Serve with whipped cream. Yield: 6 servings.

Mrs. Bryan Gruver, Jr., Fort Devens, Mass.

Chocolate Layer Dessert

1 6-oz. pkg. chocolate chips
2 tbsp. water
2 tbsp. sugar
2 eggs, beaten
2 tbsp. milk
½ c. pecans
1 c. whipping cream
Vanilla wafers

Melt chips in water in double boiler. Add sugar to beaten eggs and milk and blend into hot melted chips. Cook a little more, then cool. Fold cool mixture and nuts into cream. Line an 8 x 8-inch pan with wafers; pour half the chocolate mixture. Add another layer of wafers then cover with remaining chocolate. Let set overnight. Top with whipped cream.

Mrs. Robert E. McNair, Wife of Governor, Columbia, S. C.

English Toff

1 c. butter
2 c. powdered sugar
3 eggs, separated
2 sq. chocolate, melted
1 tsp. vanilla flavoring
1 c. chopped pecans
½ lb. vanilla wafers, crushed

Cream butter; add sugar, well beaten egg yolks and cooled chocolate. Mix well. Fold in vanilla, nuts and stiffly beaten egg whites. Put half the wafer crumbs in bottom of a greased 12 x 8-inch baking dish or a pie pan. Pour chocolate mixture over wafers; sprinkle remaining wafers on top. Chill about 6 hours. Yield: 8-10 servings.

Mrs. Frank L. Gunn, Fort Ord, Cal.

Coffee Melba

32 marshmallows, cut up
1 c. hot coffee
1 c. heavy cream, whipped

Dissolve marshmallows in coffee; cool thoroughly. Stir coffee mixture; fold in whipped cream. Refrigerate in mixing bowl or spoon into sherbet dishes and refrigerate. Top with nuts, if desired. Yield: 8 servings.

Mrs. Johnnie G. Miller, Pres. Officers' Wives' Club, Minneapolis, Minn.

Coffee-Brandy Puff

1 ½ to 2 doz. ladyfingers
1 tbsp. gelatin
¼ c. brandy
1 ¼ c. rich milk
2 tsp. instant coffee powder
½ tsp. salt
¾ c. sugar
1 tsp. vanilla
2 eggs, separated
¼ tsp. cream of tartar
1 c. heavy cream
1 c. chopped walnuts

Split lady fingers; arrange over bottom and sides of buttered 9-inch pie pan, flat side down, making a crust. Soften gelatin in brandy. Combine milk, coffee powder, salt, ½ cup sugar, vanilla and beaten egg yolks in top of double boiler. Cook over hot water until mixture thickens slightly, about 10 minutes. Add gelatin, stirring until dissolved; remove from heat and cool. When mixture begins to jell fold in egg whites beaten to a meringue with remaining ¼ cup sugar and cream of tartar. Fold in stiffly beaten cream and ¾ cup walnuts. Mound filling in ladyfinger crust. Garnish top with ¼ cup chopped walnuts and walnut halves if desired. Chill until firm. Yield: 6-8 servings.

Mrs. Francis E. Naughton, Ft. McPherson, Ga.

Fruited Coffee Cream

½ 9-oz. pkg. condensed mincemeat
¼ c. cold water
2 c., packed, miniature marshmallows
1 c. hot strong coffee
1 c. heavy cream, whipped

Simmer mincemeat in water until all water disappears; watch carefully, as this mixture burns easily. Add marshmallows to hot coffee; stir until dissolved. Chill until mixture starts to set. Fold mincemeat into whipped cream; fold in marshmallow mixture, mixing well. Pile into parfait glasses. Garnish with a dollop of whipped cream; top with a walnut half. Yield: 8 servings.

Rev. Raymond G. J. Decker, Olney, Md.

Mocha Mist

1 tbsp. unflavored gelatin
1 4-oz. pkg. butterscotch pudding mix
1 ½ tsp. instant coffee

(Continued on next page)

1/4 c. sugar
1 2/3 c. evaporated milk
1 c. water
2 tbsp. orange juice

Mix gelatin, pudding, coffee, sugar, 1 cup milk and water in saucepan; cook over low heat until mixture comes to full boil, stirring constantly. Chill until mixture mounds from spoon. Chill remaining milk in refrigerator until soft ice crystals form around edges of tray, 10 to 15 minutes. Whip until stiff, 1 minute; add orange juice. Whip very stiff, about 2 minutes longer; beat into pudding mixture. Spoon into sherbet or parfait glasses; chill until firm, about 2 hours. Garnish with chopped pecans. Yield: 8 servings.

Mrs. Jane Royal, Clearwater, Fla.

Coconut Frappe

1 c. sugar
4 eggs, separated
1 pt. milk
1 tbsp. plain gelatin
1 tbsp. cool water
1 doz. coconut macaroons
1 tsp. sherry flavoring
Whipped cream
Shredded coconut

Add sugar to egg yolks. Let milk come to boil and pour into yolks. Thicken in double boiler slowly. Add gelatin dissolved in cool water. Cool entire mixture. Heat macaroons until crisp; cool. Roll finely and add to mixture. Beat egg whites with sherry; fold into mixture. Pour into mold. Chill 4 hours. When ready to serve, turn out of mold; frost with whipped cream and sprinkle with coconut. Place pieces of cherries among whipped cream to decorate. Yield: 8 servings.

Mrs. Larry Luttrell, Favorite Recipes Food Fair, Mobile, Ala.

Cranberry Whip

1 1/2 c. cranberries
3/4 c. boiling water
3/4 c. sugar
3 egg whites
1 tsp. grated orange rind
1 tsp. lemon juice

(Continued on next page)

Cook cranberries in water until skins burst. Reserve 15 to 18 cranberries for garnish; put the rest through a sieve. Add sugar. Beat egg whites until stiff; add cranberries, orange rind and lemon juice. Beat until glossy and stiff; chill. Garnish with reserved cranberries. Yield: 8 servings.

Mrs. Thelma M. Ash, Home Economics Teacher, Hampton, Va.

 ## Creme De Menthe Dessert

20 marshmallows
½ c. milk·
½ pt. heavy cream, whipped
3 tbsp. creme de menthe
20 chocolate cream sandwich cookies, crushed

Melt marshmallows in milk over low heat. Combine whipped cream and creme de menthe. Fold into marshmallow mixture. Line 12 x 18-inch pan with half the cookie crumbs; cover with marshmallow mixture. Top with remaining crumbs. Chill overnight. Serve topped with whipped cream and cherry. Yield: 10 servings.

Mrs. Edward Wehrs, West Salem, Wis.

Graham-Nut Roly-Poly

1 lb. graham crackers, finely rolled
1 lb. dates, finely chopped
1 lb. marshmallows, finely cut
1 lb. nuts, finely chopped
1 c. pineapple juice or cream

Mix all ingredients and shape into roll. Refrigerate. Slice and serve with whipped cream.

Mrs. Robert G. Frye, Pres. Officers' Wives' Club, Syracuse, N. Y.

 ## Date Roll

1 ¼ c. miniature marshmallows
1 c. chopped nuts
1 ½ c. chopped dates, pitted
2 c. graham cracker crumbs
1 4-oz. bottle maraschino cherries, chopped
1 c. whipping cream

(Continued on next page)

280

Combine all ingredients except cream, reserving ¼ cup graham cracker crumbs. Whip cream; add to other ingredients. Mix and shape into roll 3 inches thick. Roll in remaining graham cracker crumbs. Wrap in foil; let stand 12 hours in refrigerator. Slice and serve with additional whipped cream and maraschino cherry on top. Yield: 6-8 servings.

Mary Jane Bertrand, Home Economics Teacher, Blackfoot, Idaho

 ### Lemon Blocks

        2 pkg. lemon gelatin
    ½ tsp. salt
    ⅔ c. honey
        6 tbsp. lemon juice
        Grated rind of 2 lemons
        2 ½ c. boiling water
        2 13-oz. cans evaporated milk, chilled
        5 c. vanilla wafer crumbs

Combine gelatin, salt, honey, lemon juice and rind with boiling water. Beat evaporated milk until thick. When gelatin slightly hardens, whip it and fold in beaten milk. Alternate layers of vanilla wafer crumbs and gelatin mixture in 15½ x 10½-inch pan, ending with wafer crumbs. Refrigerate overnight. Serve in small squares with whipped cream. Yield: 30 servings.

Mrs. John A. Roberts, Wurtsmith, Mich.

 ### Lemon Lady

        10 eggs
        1 ½ c. sugar
        Juice and grated rind of 4 lemons
        1 ½ tbsp. gelatin
        18 ladyfingers

Beat egg yolks until creamy. Add ¾ cup sugar slowly, beating constantly. Add lemon juice, rind and gelatin which has been dissolved in cold water. Heat in double boiler, stirring constantly until mixture thickly coats a silver spoon. Remove from heat and cool quickly. Beat egg whites until stiff. Add ¾ cup sugar gradually, beating until mixture forms peaks. Fold in lemon mixture. Line a spring form pan with split ladyfingers, using crumbs on bottom of form. Pour in mixture and chill overnight. Yield: 10 servings.

Mrs. Warren E. Walters, Pres. Officers' Wives' Club, San Juan, Puerto Rico

Lime Highbrow

1 c. sugar
1 c. boiling water
1 pkg. lime gelatin
Juice and grated rind of 3 lemons
1 lge. can evaporated milk, chilled
12 macaroon cookies, crushed

Melt sugar in hot water; add gelatin and dissolve. Add lime juice and rind. Chill until partially jelled. Whip evaporated milk until stiff; fold in gelatin mixture. Pour into 11 x 7 x ½-inch pan; top with cookie crumbs. Chill. Yield: 12 servings.

Mrs. Arnold Hackney, Akron, Ohio

Mrs. Eisenhower's Frosted Mint Delight

1 pkg. unflavored gelatin
2 1-lb. cans crushed pineapple
¾ c. mint-flavored apple jelly
1 pt. heavy cream
2 tsp. confectioners' sugar

Chill all ingredients. Dissolve gelatin in 1 cup juice from pineapple. Melt jelly; mix in pineapple. Add gelatin mixture. Whip cream with sugar; fold into gelatin mixture. Pour into mold. Place in freezer until firm, but do not freeze solid. Yield: 10-12 servings.

Mrs. Dwight D. Eisenhower, Gettysburg, Pa.

 ## Pineapple Mousse

1 pkg. lemon gelatin
1 c. warm water
1 No. 2 can crushed pineapple
1 c. honey graham crumbs
½ pt. heavy cream, whipped

Dissolve gelatin in warm water. Drain pineapple; add 1 cup pineapple juice to gelatin. Allow to congeal partially. Spread graham cracker crumbs to 8 x 8 x 2-inch pan, reserving some for top. Whip gelatin; fold in pineapple. Fold in whipped cream. Pour into pan; top with remaining crumbs. Refrigerate 4 to 6 hours. Yield: 10 servings.

Mrs. James A. Hebbeler, Pres., Officers' Wives' Club, Ft. Douglas, Utah

Coconut Mousse

1 ½ pkg. unflavored gelatin
¼ c. cold water
1 ½ c. scalded milk
½ c. sugar
½ can shredded coconut
½ tsp. almond flavoring
1 c. heavy cream, whipped
Strawberries

Dissolve gelatin in cold water; set in pan of hot water. Combine milk and sugar; stir until dissolved. Add gelatin mixture. Remove from heat; add coconut and almond flavoring. Pour into bowl and refrigerate until partially set. Fold in whipped cream. Pour into a ring mold; refrigerate until firm. Unmold; fill center with strawberries.

SAUCE:

1 c. white sugar
1 c. brown sugar
¼ lb. butter or margarine
1 c. heavy cream

Combine sugars, butter and cream in top of double boiler; cook until creamy and smooth. Serve warm over mousse and berries. Yield: 12 servings.

Mrs. James C. Hare, Nellis AFB, Nev.

Strawberry Mousse

1 qt. strawberries, washed and hulled
½ c. sugar
½ c. white wine
2 envelopes unflavored gelatin
½ c. cold water
½ c. boiling water
2 c. heavy cream, whipped

Crush berries; add sugar and white wine. Stir well: chill. Soften gelatin in cold water; add boiling water. Stir to dissolve; cool. Combine gelatin and chilled strawberry mixture; beat with rotary beater until slightly thickened. Fold in whipped cream; turn into 2-quart ring mold. To serve, fill ring with additional strawberries and whipped cream; garnish top with large berries. Yield: 10-12 servings.

Mrs. Guy Wehr, Steubenville, Ohio

Simply Simple Apricot Mousse

    1 28-oz. can apricots
    1 pkg. lemon flavored gelatin
    2 tbsp. brandy
    1 c. heavy cream, whipped
    1 c. crumbled vanilla wafers

Drain and puree apricots. Reserve juice. Add water to apricot juice to make 1¾ cups liquid. Heat to boiling. Add gelatin; stir until dissolved. Cool. Add apricots and brandy; refrigerate until consistency of jelly. Beat slightly; fold in whipped cream. Pour half the mixture into 8-inch square pan. Sprinkle with crumbs; add remaining mixture. Refrigerate until firm. Yield: 6-8 servings.

Mrs. Melvin Harper, Concord, Cal.

 ### Tangerine Cream Mousse

    1 envelope unflavored gelatin
  ¼ c. sugar
  ⅛ tsp. salt
  ½ c. water
    1 6-oz. can frozen tangerine concentrate
    1 c. heavy cream

Mix together gelatin, sugar and salt in saucepan. Add water; place over medium heat, stirring constantly, until gelatin is dissolved. Remove from heat and stir in tangerine concentrate. Chill until consistency of unbeaten egg white. Whip cream and fold into tangerine mixture. Turn into 4-cup mold and chill until firm. Unmold; garnish with tangerine sections. Serve with Tangerine-Orange Sauce.

TANGERINE-ORANGE SAUCE:

    2 tsp. cornstarch
  ½ c. sugar
  ¼ tsp. salt
    1 c. orange juice
    2 tangerines, sectioned and seeds removed

Mix cornstarch, sugar and salt in saucepan. Stir in orange juice. Bring to boil, stirring constantly. Cool; add tangerine sections. Yield: 6 servings.

Mrs. Ralph Keeley, Tucson, Ariz.

Orange Blossom Cake

    2 c. milk
    1 tbsp. cornstarch
    1 c. sugar

(Continued on next page)

4 egg yolks
2 tbsp. gelatin
4 tbsp. cold water
¾ c. orange juice
1 tsp. grated orange rind
1 pt. heavy cream, whipped
1 ½ doz. ladyfingers

Heat milk in double boiler. Mix cornstarch, sugar and egg yolks. Pour hot milk over egg mixture and return to double boiler. Cook until thickened; cool. Add gelatin soaked in cold water, orange juice and rind. Refrigerate until thickened. Fold in whipped cream. Split ladyfingers and cut ¾ inch from end of each half. Stand these around edge of spring form pan; line bottom of pan with cut pieces. Pour whipped cream mixture into lined mold; refrigerate overnight. NOTE: If desired, place halved Maraschino cherries on top for color. Yield: 8-10 servings.

Mrs. Allen J. Jedel, Pres. Officers' Wives' Club, Goose AFB, Labrador

Orange Pastry Squares

1 3-oz. pkg. lemon gelatin
1 3-oz. pkg. orange gelatin
1 c. boiling water
1 16-oz. can evaporated milk, chilled
¾ c. sugar
Juice of 1 orange
1 c. graham cracker crumbs

Blend gelatins and boiling water; set in refrigerator until thickened. Beat chilled milk until it holds its shape; add sugar and orange juice. Continue beating until well blended; add thickened gelatin mixture and beat until mixture will not rise further. Pour into 9 x 14 x 2-inch cake pan, lined with waxed paper scattered with graham cracker crumbs. Keep refrigerated. Cut in squares. Yield: 12 servings.

Mrs. Mary Nicholson, Home Economics Teacher, Denver, Colo.

Peach Glace

1 pkg. raspberry or strawberry gelatin
1 c. hot water
1 c. cold ginger ale
1 c. sweetened peaches

Dissolve gelatin in hot water. Add ginger ale. Chill until slightly thickened. Fold in peaches.

Louise Rushing, Kilmichael, Miss.

Peach Coeur A La Creme

2 envelopes unflavored gelatin
⅓ c. cold water
1 c. light cream
6 3-oz. pkg. cream cheese
2 c. heavy cream
1 c. sugar
1 pkg. frozen sliced peaches, thawed
Few drops red and yellow food coloring

Soften gelatin in cold water. Scald light cream; add gelatin and stir until dissolved. Cool. Soften cream cheese; beat until light. Slowly add heavy cream, beating constantly until mixture is smooth. Add sugar. Mash peaches in blender; add to cheese mixture. Mix well; stir in food coloring for more pronounced peach color. Combine mixtures. Pour into lightly oiled 6-cup mold. Refrigerate several hours. Garnish with more peaches. Yield: 8-10 servings.

Mrs. R. L. Delashaw, Seymour Johnson AFB, N. C.

Peach-Marshmallow Cake

1 tbsp. unflavored gelatin
¼ c. cold water
⅓ c. soft butter
1 c. confectioners' sugar
2 eggs, separated
½ lb. miniature marshmallows
4 c. sliced canned peaches
3 c. vanilla wafer crumbs

Soften gelatin in water 5 minutes. Cream butter; add sugar and blend in egg yolks. Cook over low heat, stirring constantly, until thickened. Remove from heat; add gelatin and stir until dissolved. Add marshmallows; blend and chill until mixture begins to thicken. Fold in sliced peaches and beaten egg whites. Arrange alternate layers of crumbs and peach filling in mold, beginning with filling and ending with cookie crumbs. Chill until firm; unmold and serve with whipped cream. Yield: 8 servings.

Mrs. Sandra Hain, Laramie, Wyo.

Peach Velvet

1 ⅓ c. light brown sugar
1 c. sour cream
1 tsp. maple extract
1 c. heavy cream
3 ¾ c. sliced fresh peaches or well-drained canned peaches

(Continued on next page)

Mix sugar, sour cream and maple extract until sugar is dissolved. Whip heavy cream until stiff. Fold into sour cream mixture; chill until serving time. Fold in sliced peaches; serve immediately.

Mrs. Eugene Moore, Ailey, Ga.

 ### Pear Whip Dessert

> 1 3-oz. pkg. orange Jell-O
> 1 sm. can pears, drained
> 1 envelope Dream Whip

Prepare Jell-O as directed on package; let set until firm. When firm, put in mixing bowl with drained pears. Beat with beater until well blended. Fold in prepared Dream Whip. Serve immediately or refrigerate until needed. Serve with chocolate cake or wafers. Yield: 8 servings.

Mrs. Donald Hyatt, Montrose, Colo.

 ### Mint With Melon Balls

> 1 pkg. lime gelatin
> 1 c. hot water
> 1 c. cold water
> Few drops oil or peppermint or mint extract
> Watermelon and honeydew balls

Dissolve gelatin in hot water. Add cold water and mint extract to flavor delicately. Chill until it begins to thicken; beat with egg beater until frothy and thick. Pour into ring mold which has been rinsed with cold water but not dried. Chill until firm. Unmold and fill center or serve with watermelon and honeydew balls or unhulled strawberries. Garnish with fresh mint. Yield: 8 servings.

Mrs. John J. Hilton, Jr., Glynco, Ga.

 ### Peppermint Candy Dessert

> 1 pt. whipping cream
> 2 c. chopped pecans
> 25 sticks peppermint candy, crushed
> 1 8-oz. bag marshmallows, chopped
> 1 sm. box or pkg. graham crackers
> 1 stick margarine

(Continued on next page)

287

Whip cream until thick but not stiff; fold in nuts, candy and marshmallows. Make a crust of crushed crackers and melted margarine; place in bottom of 9 x 14-inch buttered pan. Pour in the peppermint mixture; chill overnight. Cut in squares to serve. Yield: 15 servings.

Mrs. Eleanor Weatherford, Home Economics Teacher, Tupelo, Miss.

 ## Peppermint Cream

> 24 marshmallows
> ½ c. milk
> 3 drops peppermint flavoring
> 1 tsp. vanilla
> ⅛ tsp. salt
> Few drops green food coloring
> 1 c. heavy cream, whipped

Melt marshmallows in milk over hot water. Remove from heat; cool slightly. Stir in peppermint flavoring, vanilla, salt and food coloring. Cool until mixture mounds slightly when dropped from spoon. Fold in whipped cream. Spoon into parfait or custard cups; chill until firm. Top with green Maraschino cherries and fresh mint leaves. Yield: 4 servings.

Mrs. Henry S. Laurinat, Lakehurst, N. J.

 ## Hawaiian Refrigerator Cake

> 1 15-oz. can sweetened condensed milk
> ¼ c. lemon juice
> 10 marshmallows, quartered
> ½ c. crushed pineapple
> 10 Maraschino cherries, quartered
> ½ c. heavy cream, whipped
> Ladyfingers or coconut bars

Combine condensed milk and lemon juice; stir until thickened. Add marshmallows, fruit and whipped cream. Line 9-inch tube pan with foil; stand ladyfingers around edge. Carefully pour filling into pan so as not to disturb ladyfingers. Cover top with ladyfingers; chill 6 hours or overnight. Yield: 10 servings.

Mrs. H. G. Barber, Joliet, Ill.

Shades of back-on-the-farm and the pleasant smells of Grandma's kitchen! But a modern innovation—dry milk crystals—holds the calorie count down in Spiced Louisiana Yam Pie. Generous spices plus the natural rich goodness of Louisiana yams hold the flavor up.

SPICED LOUISIANA YAM PIE

2 c. mashed cooked yams
¾ c. (firmly packed) dark brown sugar
2 tbsp. butter, melted
½ tsp. salt
1 tsp. cinnamon
½ tsp. nutmeg
½ tsp. ginger
¼ tsp. allspice
3 eggs
⅔ c. instant nonfat dry milk crystals
1 c. water
1 9-in. pie shell, unbaked
1¼ c. whipped instant nonfat dry milk crystals
Chopped candied ginger

Combine yams, sugar, butter, salt, spices and eggs; beat until well blended. Stir milk crystals into water; add to yam mixture. Pour into pie shell. Bake at 375 degrees for 1 hour or until set. Cool thoroughly. Garnish with whipped instant crystals and candied ginger. To whip instant nonfat dry milk crystals, mix ¼ cup instant nonfat dry milk crystals with ¼ cup ice water in bowl. Whip for 3 to 4 minutes or until soft peaks form. Add 1 tablespoon lemon juice. Continue whipping for 3 to 4 minutes longer or until stiff peaks form. Gradually add 2 tablespoonfuls sugar.

See photograph on reverse side.

Make-Ahead Pineapple Delight

> 20 lge. oatmeal cookies or 20 whole cinnamon crisp graham
>   crackers
> ½ c. butter
> 2 eggs
> 1 ½ c. powdered sugar
> 1 can pineapple, well drained
> ½ pt. heavy cream, whipped

Crush cookies; pack half the crumbs in 9-inch cake pan. Combine butter, eggs and powdered sugar; beat until creamy. Spread mixture over crumbs. Add pineapple to whipped cream; spread over butter mixture. Cover with remaining crumbs; refrigerate overnight or longer. Cut into squares to serve. Yield: 6-8 servings.

Mrs. B. J. Berryman, Norfolk, Va.

Pineapple-Mint Supreme

> 1 c. flour
> ¼ c. brown sugar, packed
> ½ c. butter
> ½ c. chopped walnuts
> 1 1-lb. 4-oz. can crushed pineapple
> 1 pkg. lime Jell-O
> 1 c. cream cheese
> 1 c. white sugar
> ⅔ c. evaporated milk
> ⅛ tsp. peppermint extract

Mix first four ingredients until fine grained. Press mixture into greased 12 x 8 x 2-inch pan. Bake at 400 degrees for 10 minutes. Cool. Drain juice off crushed pineapple; bring to boil. Dissolve Jell-O in the hot liquid; cool. Cream the cheese with white sugar; blend in gelatin mixture. Stir in pineapple; chill until thick but not set. Chill evaporated milk and extract in small bowl until ice crystals form; beat until thick. Fold into pineapple-cheese mixture; spoon over baked crust. Refrigerate while preparing glaze.

CHOCOLATE-MINT GLAZE:

> ½ c. chocolate chips
> ⅓ c. evaporated milk
> 1 tbsp. butter
> 1 tsp. peppermint extract

Melt ingredients in saucepan. Spoon hot glaze over dessert; spread carefully. Chill at least 4 hours. Yield: 16 servings.

Mrs. Esther Bennett, Lansing, Mich.

Pineapple Refrigerator Cake

½ c. butter
1 c. sugar
1 egg, well beaten
3 tsp. cream
1 c. crushed pineapple
2 ¼ c. fine graham cracker crumbs
3-4 tbsp. pineapple juice
1 c. chopped walnuts

Cream butter and sugar; add egg, cream and pineapple. Line oblong glass dish with heavy waxed paper; place layer of fine cracker crumbs about ½ inch deep on bottom. Pour pineapple juice and half the pineapple mixture over crumbs. Sprinkle with nuts. Add second layer of crumbs, pineapple and nuts; complete with third layer. Cover with waxed paper. Refrigerate for at least 24 hours. Cut in thick slices and serve with whipped cream. Yield: 8-10 servings.

Mrs. William R. Tubbs, Pres. Officers' Wives' Club, El Centro, Calif.

 ### Queen Charlotte Confection

1 3-oz. pkg. lime Jell-O
1 3-oz. pkg. raspberry Jell-O
3 c. miniature marshmallows
1 c. drained crushed pineapple
1 c. heavy cream, whipped

Dissolve each flavor Jell-O separately in 1½ cups boiling water; pour into two 8-inch square pans. Chill until firm; cut in cubes. Combine marshmallows, pineapple and Jell-O cubes; mix lightly. Fold in whipped cream; pour in bowl. Chill for several hours or overnight. Yield: 8-10 servings.

Mrs. Evelyn Hillmer, Richmond, Va.

Viennese Pineapple Delicacy

6 eggs, separated
Juice and rind of 1 lemon
¼ c. granulated sugar
½ tsp. salt
1 tbsp. cornstarch
2 tbsp. pineapple juice, Curacao, Triple Sec or Grand Marnier
1 c. butter, softened
1 ½ c. sifted powdered sugar
½ c. canned pineapple, drained

2 pkg. ladyfingers
1 pt. heavy cream, whipped and sweetened
Coconut
Orange rind, grated

Beat egg yolks thick; add lemon juice, rind, sugar, salt and cornstarch dissolved in pineapple juice. Cook until thick over hot water in double boiler; cool. Cream butter; add powdered sugar slowly. Add pineapple. Fold in stiffly beaten egg whites. Chill briefly. Line 8 or 10-inch spring form pan with ladyfingers. Put rounded sides out; stand upright on sides. Lay flat on bottom. Pour in custard. Chill overnight. Cover with whipped cream, coconut and grated orange rind before serving. NOTE: Orange liqueur may be added with sweetening to whipped cream. Yield: 12 servings.

Mrs. Robert Cammack, Charlotte, N. C.

 ## Poppy Seed Chilled Dessert

1 ¼ c. graham cracker crumbs
⅓ c. melted butter
2 tbsp. sugar plus 1½ c.
1 ½ c. milk
5 eggs, separated
¼ c. poppy seeds
¼ tsp. salt
2 tbsp. cornstarch
1 envelope gelatin
⅓ c. water
1 tsp. vanilla
1 tbsp. butter
½ tsp. cream of tartar

Mix crumbs, butter and 2 tablespoons sugar together; line 9 x 13-inch pan. Bake for 10 minutes at 325 degrees. Boil milk, 1 cup sugar, beaten egg yolks, poppy seeds, salt and cornstarch together until thick. Remove from heat. Add gelatin softened in water, vanilla and butter. Cool. Beat together egg whites, cream of tartar and ½ cup sugar. Fold into cold custard mixture. Pour into crumb crust. Refrigerate. Top with whipped cream. Yield: 12 servings.

Mrs. Arthur B. Olson, Chicago, Ill.

Black Raspberry Delight

1 10-oz. box butter cookies
¾ c. butter
1 c. powdered sugar
2 eggs, slightly beaten
⅓ c. black walnuts, chopped fine
1 qt. fresh black raspberries, sliced and sweetened
1 c. heavy cream, whipped

Roll cookies into crumbs; line 8-inch square pan with 2/3 the crumbs. Cream butter and sugar; add eggs. Beat well; spread over crumbs. Pat down; sprinkle with about ¾ the nuts. Top with berries; pat down. Top with whipped cream; decorate with remaining crumbs and nuts. Chill 3 hours or until thoroughly chilled. Yield: 10 servings.

Ada W. Goff, Home Economics Teacher, Hinton, W. Va.

 ### Raspberry Creme Dessert

2 c. crushed vanilla wafers
½ c. butter or margarine
1 ½ c. powdered sugar
2 eggs
1 tsp. vanilla extract
2 10-oz. pkg. frozen raspberries, thawed and well drained
1 c. heavy cream, whipped

Place half the wafer crumbs in bottom of 9 x 9-inch glass baking dish. Cream butter and confectioners' sugar until smooth. Add eggs 1 at a time, beating well after each. Add vanilla. Mixture may have curdled appearance. Place butter mixture by spoonfuls on top of crumbs. Spread carefully to avoid disturbing crumbs. Place raspberries in single layer on butter mixture. Top with whipped cream. Sprinkle remaining crumbs on top. Chill 8 to 24 hours. Cut in squares. Yield: 9 servings.

Mrs. Robert Nelson, Gary, Ind.

Rum Dream Creme

6 egg yolks
1 c., scant, sugar
1 tbsp. gelatin
½ c. water
1 pt. heavy cream, whipped
¾ to 1 c. dark Jamaican rum
Grated bitter chocolate

(Continued on next page)

Beat egg yolks well; add sugar. Soak gelatin in water until dissolved; bring to boil, stirring constantly. Add to egg yolk mixture, stirring constantly. Fold in whipped cream and rum. Pour into sherbet glasses and refrigerate until set. Sprinkle tops with grated chocolate. Yield: 12 servings.

Mrs. D. W. Cooper, San Diego, Calif.

 ## Snow Pudding With Vanilla Sauce

    3 envelopes unflavored gelatin
    3 c. water
    1 c. granulated sugar
    ¼ c. fresh lemon juice
    3 egg whites, stiffly beaten

Soak gelatin in ¼ cup cold water; dissolve in boiling water. Add sugar and lemon juice; strain and set aside in cool place. Occasionally stir until mixture is quite thick. Beat with egg beater until frothy; add egg whites. Continue beating until stiff enough to hold shape. Place in mold or pan and refrigerate.

VANILLA SAUCE:

    1 c. sugar
    3 egg yolks
    ½ tsp. salt
    1 c. milk, heated
    1 tsp. vanilla

Mix sugar, egg yolks and salt; beat with egg beater. Add hot milk. Cook in double boiler for 20 minutes; add vanilla. Chill; serve over pudding. Yield: 6 servings.

Mrs. Edmund B. Taylor, Pres. Naval Officers' Wives' Club, Norfolk, Va.

Spanish Cream

    3 eggs, separated
    ½ c. sugar
    ½ pt. milk
    1 pkg. unflavored gelatin

Beat egg yolks with sugar. Heat milk; pour over egg yolk mixture. Stir and cook until thickened. Soften and dissolve gelatin according to directions on package. Stir into custard; cool. Beat egg whites until stiff; fold into custard. Place in mold, refrigerate for several hours. Yield: 6 servings.

Mrs. James E. Dwyer, Camp Douglas, Wis.

Rum Ice Box Cake

    1 pkg. lemon gelatin
    1 c. hot water or pineapple juice
    6 eggs, separated
    1 c. sugar
    4 tbsp. rum
    Juice of 1 med. lemon
    1 c. heavy cream, whipped
    2 doz. ladyfingers

Dissolve gelatin in hot liquid; cool to room temperature. Cream egg yolks and sugar; add gelatin. Add rum and lemon juice. Beat egg whites until stiff; add whipped cream. Carefully fold all together; fill 8-inch spring form pan which has been lined with ladyfingers. Chill 24 hours. Yield: 8 servings.

Mrs. William A. Harris, Pres. Officers' Wives' Club, Fort Sam Houston, Tex.

 ## Seville Cream

    1 envelope unflavored gelatin
    1 qt. milk
    3 eggs, separated
    ½ c. sugar
    1 tsp. vanilla flavoring
    Pinch of salt

Soak gelatin in milk for 10 minutes. Heat and stir until dissolved. Beat egg yolks with 4 tablespoonfuls sugar; add to warm milk. Cook slowly, constantly stirring, until mixture coats a spoon. Cool for 1 hour. Beat egg whites with remaining sugar, vanilla and salt. Fold into custard. Turn into mold; chill overnight. Serve with whipped cream and cherries, if desired. Yield: 10 servings.

Mrs. Rose Slezak, Helmetta, N. J.

 ## Almond Bavarian Souffle

    1 envelope unflavored gelatin
    ½ c. plus 3 tbsp. sugar
    ⅛ tsp. salt
    2 eggs, separated
    1 ⅔ c. milk
    ¼ c. finely chopped toasted almonds
    1 ⅓ c. non-dairy coffee creamer
    1 tsp. almond extract
    20 chocolate wafers

(Continued on next page)

Mix gelatin, ¼ cup sugar and salt in top of double boiler. Beat egg yolks and 1 cup milk; stir into gelatin mixture. Cook, stirring constantly, over boiling water until gelatin dissolves, 5 to 8 minutes. Remove from heat; chill until consistency of unbeaten egg whites. Fold in almonds. Beat egg whites until soft peaks form; gradually add ¼ cup sugar, beating until stiff but not dry. Fold in gelatin mixture. Chill bowl and beaters in refrigerator 15 minutes. Blend coffee creamer with 2/3 cup cold milk, almond extract and 3 tablespoons sugar in chilled bowl. Whip at high speed with electric mixer until thick and creamy, 3 to 5 minutes. Fold into gelatin mixture. Arrange halves of chocolate wafers in bottom of 9 x 5 x 3-inch loaf pan. Pour in 1/3 Bavarian mixture; arrange layer of whole chocolate wafers on top. Repeat. Chill until firm. To serve, unmold on serving platter and slice. Yield: 6-8 servings.

Mrs. V. H. Krulak, Honolulu, Hawaii

 Coffee Souffle Mold

> 1 envelope unflavored gelatin
> ¼ c. milk
> 3 eggs, separated
> 1 ¾ c. milk, scalded
> 2 tbsp. instant coffee
> ¼ tsp. salt
> 6 tbsp. sugar
> ½ tsp. vanilla flavoring

Soften gelatin in milk. Combine slightly beaten egg yolks and scalded milk in saucepan; add coffee, salt and 3 tablespoonfuls sugar. Cook on top burner, set at 190 degrees, stirring constantly, until mixture coats spoon. Add softened gelatin; stir until gelatin is dissolved. Chill until mixture mounds slightly when dropped from spoon. Beat egg whites until foamy; gradually add remaining sugar, beating until mixture stands in soft peaks. Fold in vanilla. Fold gelatin mixture into egg whites. Pour into mold rinsed in cold water. Chill until firm. Garnish with whipped cream and shaved chocolate, if desired. Yield: 6 servings.

Mrs. Riley Franz, Ashland Ky.

Cold Cherry Souffle

> ⅔ c. chopped red maraschino cherries
> ½ c. orange juice or kirsch
> 2 envelopes unflavored gelatin
> Sugar
> ¼ tsp. salt
> 8 eggs, separated
> 1 c. milk
> ½ c. water
> 2 c. heavy cream, whipped
> Red maraschino cherries for garnish

(Continued on next page)

Blend cherries with orange juice in electric blender; set aside. Mix gelatin, 2/3 cup sugar and salt in top of double boiler. Beat in egg yolks until light. Gradually stir in milk and water. Cook over boiling water, stirring constantly until slightly thickened and gelatin dissolved, about 10 minutes. Add cherry mixture. Chill until slightly thickened. Beat egg whites until foamy. Gradually add ½ cup sugar, beating until stiff. Fold with whipped cream into gelatin mixture. Turn into 1½-quart souffle dish with aluminum foil collar. Chill until firm. Remove collar and garnish with maraschino cherries. Decorate with whipped cream and additional cherries. Yield: 10-12 servings.

Mrs. Ruth Halleck, Dayton, Ohio

 ## Cold Mandarin Souffle

¼ c. sugar
1 envelope gelatin
4 eggs, separated
¾ c. tangerine or orange juice
2 tbsp. lemon juice
2 tsp. grated orange peel
2 tbsp. sugar
1 c. heavy cream, whipped
Mandarin orange sections
Sweetened whipped cream

Combine sugar and gelatin in saucepan. Blend in beaten egg yolks, tangerine and lemon juices. Cook and stir over low heat until gelatin dissolves and mixture thickens slightly. Stir in orange peel; cool to room temperature. Beat egg whites to soft peaks, gradually adding 2 tablespoons sugar. Beat to stiff peaks. Fold in gelatin mixture, then whipped cream. Pour into 5-cup mold; chill overnight or until set. Unmold on serving dish; garnish with Mandarin orange sections and sweetened whipped cream. Yield: 6-8 servings.

Mrs. John E. Clark, Pres., Naval Officers' Wives' Club, Pt. Mugo, Cal.

 ## Filbert Souffle

2 envelopes unflavored gelatin
⅓ c. water
2 ¼ c. milk
6 eggs, separated
1 c. sugar
2 tbsp. cognac (opt.)
1 tsp. vanilla flavoring
1 ½ c. ground toasted filberts
1 c. heavy cream, whipped

(Continued on next page)

Soften gelatin in water. Heat milk in medium heavy saucepan; stir in gelatin until dissolved. Beat egg yolks and sugar until light and fluffy; gradually stir into hot milk. Cook over low heat, stirring constantly, until mixture thickens and coats a metal spoon; do not allow to boil. Remove from heat; stir in cognac, vanilla and ground filberts. Stir over ice or chill until mixture begins to set. Beat egg whites until stiff, but not dry. Fold into filbert mixture with whipped cream. Pour into 5-cup souffle dish which has a 4-inch collar of waxed paper around it. Chill until set. Remove collar. Garnish sides of souffle with toasted chopped filberts, as desired. Yield: 8 servings.

Mrs. Catherine Miller, Tucson, Ariz.

Strawberries In A Pink Cloud with Sauce aux Fraises

  1 *pt. fresh strawberries, sliced*
  1 *c. sugar*
  2 *envelopes unflavored gelatin*
  ⅛ *tsp. salt*
  4 *eggs, separated*
  ½ *c. water*
  ¼ *c. Cointreau*
  1 *tbsp. lemon juice*
  1 *c. heavy cream, whipped*

Combine strawberries and ½ cup sugar; chill until berries form a syrup, about 1 hour. Mix gelatin with ¼ cup sugar and salt in top of double boiler. Beat yolks with water; stir into gelatin mixture. Add syrup from strawberries. Cook over boiling water, stirring constantly, until gelatin dissolves and mixture is slightly thickened, 5 to 8 minutes. Remove from heat; stir in strawberries, Cointreau and lemon juice. Chill, stirring occasionally, until mixture forms peaks. Gradually add remaining sugar, beating until stiff, but not dry. Fold into strawberry mixture; fold in whipped cream. Turn into 8-cup mold. Chill until firm. Unmold and serve with Sauce aux Fraises. Yield: 6-9 servings.

SAUCE aux FRAISES

  1 *pt. fresh strawberries*
  ⅓ *c. sugar*
  1 *tbsp. cornstarch*
  ⅛ *tsp. each salt and ground allspice*
  1 *c. water*
  3 *tbsp. Cointreau*
  1 *tsp. grated lemon peel*
  1 *tsp. lemon juice*

Measure 1½ cups strawberries; set aside. Reserve remainder for garnish. Blend sugar, cornstarch, salt and ground allspice in saucepan. Stir in water. Bring to

(Continued on next page)

boil; boil 30 seconds. Add sliced strawberries, Cointreau, lemon peel and lemon juice. Chill. Yield: 2 cups.

Photograph for this recipe on page 265.

 ### Chocolate Icebox Cake

  1 envelope plain gelatin
  ½ c. cold water
  4 eggs, separated
  1 c. confectioners' sugar
  3 squares chocolate
  Dash of salt
  ½ c. boiling water
  2 tsp. vanilla
  ½ c. chopped walnuts
  2 sponge cake layers
  ½ pt. heavy cream whipped

Soften gelatin in cold water. Beat egg yolks until thick; add sugar gradually. Add melted chocolate and salt. Dissolve gelatin in boiling water and add to chocolate mixture. Add vanilla. Fold in stiffly beaten egg whites. Line 9 or 10-inch square pan with waxed paper; sprinkle paper with chopped nuts. Pour half the chocolate mixture into pan. Break sponge cake into 1-inch squares; press squares into chocolate mixture. Pour remaining mixture over top. Cover with waxed paper and refrigerate at least 12 hours. Turn out onto chilled plate; frost with whipped cream and garnish with shaved chocolate. Yield: 10 servings.

Mrs. Pat Conley, South Portland, Maine

Tipsy Parson

  1 sponge cake
  1 c. sherry or rum
  1 c. blanched slivered almonds
  1 recipe of boiled custard
  1 c. heavy cream, whipped

Break cake into bite-sized pieces. Place layer of cake in deep bowl. Sprinkle with sherry and almonds; top with custard. Repeat layers until bowl is almost full. Chill for at least 4 hours. Just before serving, top with whipped cream. NOTE: For a quickie, frozen pound cake and instant vanilla pudding can be substituted. Yield: 8-10 servings.

Mrs. Henry J. Skipper, Richmond, Va.

Dessert Breads

Apple Coffee Cake

 2 eggs
 4 c. diced raw apples
 2 c. sugar
 ½ c. oil
 Dash of salt
 2 tsp. soda
 2 tsp. vanilla
 2 tsp. cinnamon
 2 c. flour
 1 c. chopped nuts

Mix all ingredients; blend well, but do not overbeat. Bake in greased 8 x 16-inch pan at 350 degrees for 45 minutes. Yield: 32 servings.

Mrs. William E. Conniff, Jr., Officers' Wives' Club, Norfolk, Va.

 ## Candy Cane Coffee Cake

 2 c. sour cream
 2 pkg. dry yeast
 ½ c. warm water
 ¼ c. soft margarine
 ⅓ c. sugar
 2 tsp. salt
 2 eggs
 6 c. flour
 1 ½ c. finely chopped dried apricots
 1 ½ c. finely chopped drained maraschino cherries
 2 c. sifted confectioners' sugar

Heat sour cream over low heat just until lukewarm. Dissolve yeast in water in large bowl; add warm cream, margarine, sugar, salt, eggs and 2 cups flour. Beat until smooth; stir in remaining flour. Knead dough on well-floured board until smooth, about 10 minutes. Place in greased bowl; cover. Let rise in warm place about 1 hour or until dough is doubled; divide dough into 3 parts. Roll each third into a 15 x 6-inch rectangle. Place on greased baking sheet; make cuts 2 inches deep from outer edge of 15-inch sides at ½-inch intervals. Mix fruits together; spread one-third of fruit filling down center of each rectangle. Crisscross strips over filling. Stretch cane to 22 inches in length; curve dough to form cane. Bake at 375 degrees 15 to 20 minutes or until golden brown. While warm brush with additional margarine; drizzle with confectioners' sugar mixed with 2 tablespoons water. Yield: 3 canes.

Mrs. Albert J. Heinitz, Many, La.

Cherry Streusel Cake

1 c. plus 2 tbsp. butter or margarine
1 ⅓ c. sugar
2 eggs
2 ⅓ c. flour
2 tsp. baking powder
½ tsp. salt
1 can cherry pie filling

Cream 1 cup butter and 1 cup sugar until light and fluffy. Add eggs; beat. Sift 2 cups flour, baking powder and salt; add gradually to creamed mixture. Continue to beat until light; spread ¾ the mixture in greased 9 x 13-inch pan. Spread pie filling over batter; drop remaining cake batter over filling. Spread out with knife. Blend remaining butter, sugar and flour; sprinkle evenly over batter. Bake at 375 degrees for 45 minutes. Cool in pan; cut into squares. May be served with whipped cream. Yield: 10-12 servings.

Mrs. Frank J. Goossens, Oak Park, Ill.

Heath Bar Coffee Cake

2 c. light brown sugar
2 c. flour
1 stick margarine
1 egg, beaten
1 c. sour milk or buttermilk
1 tsp. vanilla flavoring
1 tsp. salt
1 tsp. soda
6 Heath bars, finely chopped
½ c. chopped nuts

Combine brown sugar, flour and margarine. Mix until crumbly, reserving 1 cup. Add egg, sour milk, vanilla, salt and soda to crumb mixture. Add Heath bars and nuts to reserved crumb mixture; sprinkle over batter. Bake at 350 degrees for 35 to 40 minutes.

Mrs. Claude Czerniak, Maple City, Mich.

Jewish Sour Cream Coffee Cake

1 ½ c. sugar
½ lb. butter
2 eggs, beaten
½ pt. sour cream
Vanilla
2 c. flour
1 tsp. baking powder
1 tsp. soda
Pinch of salt
Dash of cinnamon
½ c. nuts

Cream 1 cup sugar and butter; add eggs. Add sour cream and vanilla to dry ingredients; add to creamed mixture. Combine remaining sugar and nuts. Put half of the batter in well-greased tube pan; pour in half of sugar-nut mixture. Add remaining batter and remaining topping. Bake at 375 degrees for 45 minutes.

Dora Swan, Bane, Mass.

 ### Old-Fashioned Coffee Cake

1 c. sour cream
1 tsp. baking soda
½ c. soft butter
1 c. white sugar
2 eggs, well beaten
1 tsp. vanilla
1 ¾ c. cake flour
2 tsp. baking powder
¼ c. brown sugar
1 tbsp. cinnamon
2 tbsp. finely chopped walnuts (opt.)

Combine sour cream and soda in bowl. Blend butter, sugar, eggs and vanilla; beat well. Add sifted dry ingredients alternately with sour cream. Pour half the batter in tube cake pan or 8-inch pan; sprinkle with half the topping mixture. Pour remaining batter over, then remaining topping. Bake at 350 degrees for 45 minutes.

Mrs. Glen H. Becker, Tucson, Ariz.

Lemon Crumb Coffee Cake

1 ¾ c. sifted flour
1 ¼ c. sugar
½ tsp. salt

(Continued on next page)

1 tsp. grated lemon rind
½ c. shortening
3 tsp. baking powder
2 eggs, well beaten
¾ c. sweet milk
1 tsp. lemon extract

Put flour, sugar, salt and lemon rind in bowl; cut in shortening until mixture is crumbly. Reserve ½ cup crumbs for topping; set aside. Add baking powder to crumbs in bowl. Combine eggs, milk and lemon extract; add to crumb mixture and beat well. Pour into a greased 8 or 9-inch square pan; sprinkle reserved crumbs on top. Bake in 350-degree oven 35 to 40 minutes; cool in pan on cake rack. Serve warm or cold.

Mrs. Irma Claycomb, Bedford, Pa.

 ## Peanut-Y Tea Ring

1 pkg. plain or buttermilk refrigerated biscuits
¼ c. melted butter or margarine
1 c. finely chopped peanuts
½ c. powdered sugar
1 tbsp. water

Separate biscuits. Dip both sides in melted butter, then in peanuts, coating well. Arrange in overlapping circle on greased baking sheet. Bake at 425° for 10 to 15 minutes or until golden brown. Mix powdered sugar and water. Drizzle at once over hot tea ring. Slide onto serving plate and serve warm. Yield: 6-8 servings.

Photograph for this recipe on page 299.

 ## Rhubarb Coffee Cake

½ c. shortening
1 ½ c. brown sugar, firmly packed
1 beaten egg
2 c. sifted all-purpose flour
1 tsp. baking soda
1 c. buttermilk
1 ½ c. cut-up fresh rhubarb
½ c. white sugar
1 tsp. cinnamon

Cream shortening and brown sugar; add egg. Sift flour and baking soda together; add flour alternately with buttermilk. Fold in rhubarb. Pour batter into a greased 9-inch square pan. Sprinkle white sugar and cinnamon over top. Bake in a 350-degree oven 30 to 35 minutes or until cake tests done. Yield: 8-10 servings.

Mrs. Nephi Kuykendall, Redwood City, Cal.

Summer Coffee Cake

⅓ c. plus 4 tbsp. butter
1 c. white sugar
1 egg
2 ¼ c. flour
3 tsp. baking powder
1 tsp. salt
1 c. milk
½ c. brown sugar, packed
2 tsp. cinnamon
½ c. coconut, chopped fine
½ c. walnuts, chopped fine

Cream 1/3 cup butter. Add white sugar; beat well. Add egg; beat well. Sift 2 cups flour, baking powder and salt together; add alternately with milk to creamed mixture. Mix remaining ingredients with fork; sprinkle topping mixture over batter. Bake at 350 degrees 35 to 45 minutes in 8 x 13-inch pan.

Mrs. Anne Rempel, Portland, Ore.

 ## Strudel

STRUDEL DOUGH:

1 c. lukewarm water
½ tsp. salt
1 egg
2 tbsp. cooking oil
3 to 4 c. sifted flour

Combine all ingredients to make a soft dough, using 3 cups flour. Add remaining flour, if necessary. Beat dough on floured board until smooth; keep soft. Grease dough with oil; place in bowl. Cover with waxed paper and cloth; let rest in warm place for 30 minutes. Stretch dough on floured cloth; let rest for a few minutes. Stretch until paper thin. Trim thick edges; let dough dry for a few minutes. Spread with one of the following fillings; roll like jelly roll. Bake at 350 degrees for 1 hour.

CHEESE STRUDEL FILLING:

4 eggs, separated
1 ½ lb. creamed cottage cheese
½ c. sour cream
2 c. sugar
1 c. crushed pineapple (opt.)
⅓ c. farina
½ c. melted butter

Beat egg whites until stiff. Mix cheese, cream, egg yolks, sugar and pineapple. Fold in egg whites. Spread on ¾ stretched dough. Sprinkle farina over filling.

(Continued on next page)

Drizzle butter over filling and part of dough. Roll carefully so that dough does not break through. Place in 15 x 10-inch pan. Bake at 350 degrees for 1 hour.

APPLE STRUDEL FILLING:

> 2 c. bread crumbs
> ½ c. butter
> 3 lb. apples
> 1 ½ c. sugar
> Cinnamon
> 2 tbsp. tapioca

Brown crumbs in butter; cool slightly. Spread over stretched dough. Place apples in row, 6-inches wide along one edge of Strudel Dough. Sprinkle handful of sugar and dash of cinnamon over dough; sprinkle remaining sugar over apples with tapioca and cinnamon. Roll up like jelly roll. Place on greased cookie sheet. Bake at 350 degrees for 1 hour.

Mrs. Helen Snyder, Cleveland, Ohio

Spudnuts

> 1 ¾ c. milk
> ½ c. shortening
> ½ c. sugar
> ½ c. mashed potatoes
> 1 pkg. active dry yeast
> ½ c. warm water
> 2 eggs, beaten
> ½ tsp. vanilla
> 6 ½ to 7 c. sifted flour
> 1 tsp. baking powder
> 2 tsp. salt
> Oil or melted shortening
> Confectioners' sugar

Scald milk; stir in shortening, sugar and mashed potatoes. Cool to lukewarm; blend well. Sprinkle yeast over water and stir until dissolved. Add to lukewarm mixture. Stir in eggs and vanilla. Sift 6½ cups flour with baking powder and salt; add gradually to mixture, mixing well after each addition. Add remaining flour if needed. Turn into greased container; cover. Let rise about 1 hour and 30 minutes until doubled in bulk. On a well-floured board, roll out dough to ½ inch thickness; cut with floured doughnut cutter. Place cut doughnuts on waxed paper; cover with cloth and let rise about 30 minutes until doubled in bulk. Fry spudnuts a few at a time in oil heated to 375 degrees. Drain on absorbent paper. Shake a few doughnuts at a time in bag containing sugar and cinnamon or spread with thin glaze made from confectioners' sugar and additional milk.

Mrs. Hazel Dempsey, Adrian, Mich., Lenawee County Fair

Doughnuts

2 c. sweet milk
1 c. sugar
½ c. shortening
½ tsp. salt
1 c. fresh mashed potatoes, seasoned
2 pkg. yeast
¼ c. water
3 eggs, lightly beaten
½ tsp. lemon flavoring
½ tsp. cinnamon
8 c. sifted flour
1 box confectioners' sugar

Heat milk; do not boil. Add sugar, shortening, salt and mashed potatoes. Cool to lukewarm. Soften yeast in lukewarm water; let stand 5 minutes. Mix in eggs, lemon flavoring and cinnamon. Add flour, part at a time. Work smooth. Cover; let rise in warm place. When double in size work down on floured board; roll to about ¼ inch thick. Cut out with cutter; place on a cloth and let rise again. Drop in deep fat; fry until golden brown. Mix confectioners' sugar with ¼ cup water. Roll doughnuts in sugar mixture. Place on a platter. Yield: 75 servings.

Mrs. Elsie Marvin, Linden, Tenn., Perry County Fair

 ## New Orleans French Market Doughnuts

2 tbsp. shortening
¼ c. sugar
¼ tsp. salt
½ c. boiling water
½ c. evaporated milk
½ pkg. yeast
¼ c. lukewarm water
1 egg, well beaten
3 ¾ c. sifted flour
½ c. confectioners' sugar

Place shortening, sugar and salt in a mixing bowl; stir in boiling water. Add milk and cool to lukewarm. Dissolve yeast in lukewarm water; add sugar mixture to lukewarm water. Stir in eggs; add 2 cups flour. Beat thoroughly; stir in remaining flour. Place in greased bowl; grease top of dough. Cover and chill. Do not let dough rise before frying. Roll chilled dough to ¼-inch thickness; cut into 2-inch squares. Fry, a few at a time, in deep hot fat at 375 degrees. Brown on one side for 2 minutes; turn and brown on other side for 1 minute. Drain. Place confectioners' sugar in a shaker or sifter and sugar-coat each doughnut. Yield: 30 servings.

Barbara Mans Hawkins, Home Economics Teacher, Midland, La.

Golden Bites

1 c. cake flour
¼ tsp. salt
2 tsp. baking powder
¼ c. wheat germ
1 tbsp. oleo (opt.)
⅓ c. milk
Melted butter
Cinnamon and sugar mixture

Sift first 4 ingredients into bowl. Add wheat germ and cut in oleo. Add milk; stir and knead until dough is homogenous. Pull off 1 to 2 teaspoons dough and roll into balls. Place in ungreased frypan; cover with vent open. Bake, turning a few times, at 340 degrees for 15 minutes or until brown. Spear with toothpick, dipping in melted butter, then in cinnamon sugar. Yield: 4-6 servings.

Mrs. W. R. Nummy, Midland, Mich. Midland County Fair

Raised Doughnuts

½ c. milk
3 tbsp. sugar
2 tsp. salt
3 tbsp. oleo or margarine
1 ½ c. warm water
1 pkg. or cake yeast, active dry or compressed
5 ½ c. unsifted flour

Scald milk; stir in sugar, salt and oleo. Cool to lukewarm. Measure warm water into large mixing bowl. Sprinkle or crumble in yeast; stir until dissolved. Add lukewarm milk mixture and 3 cups flour; beat until smooth. Add enough additional flour to make a soft dough. Turn out onto lightly floured board. Knead about 8 to 10 minutes until smooth and elastic. Form into smooth ball. Place in greased bowl, turning to grease top. Cover; let rise about 1 hour in warm place, free from draft, until doubled in bulk. Punch down. Roll out to about ½ inch thickness. Cut with 2½-inch doughnut cutter. Place on greased baking sheets. Cover; let rise about 1 hour in warm place, free from draft until double in bulk. Handle doughnuts as little as possible to prevent falling. Fry in 375-degree deep fat for 2 to 3 minutes or until brown on both sides. Drain on absorbent paper. While warm, dip in glaze or Cinnamon Sugar.

GLAZE:

2 c. sifted confectioners' sugar
⅓ c. milk
1 tsp. vanilla

Blend ingredients together. Dip warm doughnuts into glaze. Drain on rack set over waxed paper or platter to catch icing so it may be reused.

(Continued on next page)

CINNAMON-SUGAR:

    ½ c. sugar
    2 tsp. cinnamon

Combine ingredients. Dip warm doughnuts into mixture.

Janice Hunt, Stockton, Kan., Rooks County Free Fair

 ## French Jam Puffs

    ¼ c. shortening
    ½ c. boiling water
    ½ c. flour
    ⅛ tsp. salt
    2 eggs
    Jam

Bring shortening and water to boiling point in a saucepan. Sift flour and salt; add to water. Beat until mixture is thick and comes away from pan. Remove from the heat. Add eggs, 1 at a time, beating thoroughly after each addition. Drop by teaspoon in hot deep fat and fry until brown. Drain on paper. Slit Puffs and insert jam. Sprinkle with powdered sugar.

Mrs. W. A. Fadgen, Officers' Wives' Club, New Cumberland, Pa.

 ## Fresh Apple Bread

    1 c. plus 3 tbsp. sugar
    ½ c. shortening
    2 eggs
    1 ½ c. grated apples
    2 c. flour
    ½ tsp. salt
    1 tsp. soda
    ½ tsp. vanilla
    1 ½ tbsp. buttermilk
    1 c. pecans
    1 tsp. cinnamon

Cream 1 cup sugar and shortening; add beaten eggs and apples. Mix in dry ingredients, vanilla, buttermilk and floured pecans. Pour into 9⅝ x 5½ x 2¾-inch loaf pan; sprinkle top with mixture of remaining sugar and cinnamon. Bake in 350-degree oven for 1 hour. Yield: 12 servings.

Sharon Hixon, Lewis, Colo., Montezuma County 4-H Fair

Apricot-Nut Bread

½ c. dried apricots
1 beaten egg
¾ c. corn syrup
¼ c. sugar
2 tbsp. melted shortening
2 c. plus 2 tbsp. flour
¼ tsp. salt
3 tsp. baking powder
¼ tsp. soda
½ c. orange juice
¼ c. water
1 c. chopped nutmeats

Soak apricots in water to cover for 30 minutes. Drain; cut finely. Combine egg, corn syrup and sugar; beat well. Add shortening. Add 2 cups flour sifted with salt, baking powder and soda, alternately with orange juice and water. Mix nutmeats, apricots and remaining flour. Add to batter. Pour into a greased 5 x 9-inch loaf pan lined with waxed paper. Bake at 350 degrees for 1 hour. Cool; cover with a thin powdered sugar glaze.

Mrs. Richard E. Cour, St. Louis, Mo., DuQuoin State Fair

 ### Banana Bread

½ c. butter or Crisco
1 c. sugar
2 eggs
3 bananas, riced
2 c. flour
1 tsp. soda
Dash of salt
½ c. walnuts, chopped

Cream butter; add sugar gradually. Beat in eggs; add bananas. Beat well. Add flour sifted with soda and salt; add walnuts. Bake 40 or 50 minutes in bread tin in 350-degree oven.

Nancy Troop, Gardiner, Me., Pittston Fair

Bishop's Bread

3 c. flour
1 lb. brown sugar
1 c. shortening
1 c. sour milk
1 tsp. soda
1 egg
1 tsp. vanilla

(Continued on next page)

Work flour, sugar and shortening into crumbs as for pie crust; reserve 1 cup of crumb mixture to sprinkle on top of cake. To remaining crumb mixture, add sour milk, soda, egg and 1 teaspoon vanilla; stir only to blend. Turn into oblong flat cake pan. Bake at 350 degrees for 1 hour.

Mrs. Paul Sherwood, West Mansfield, Ohio

Patricia's Banana Bread

   1 c. sugar
½ c. shortening
2 eggs, well beaten
2 c. flour
1 tsp. salt
1 tsp. baking powder
½ tsp. soda
3 tsp. sour cream or milk
3 bananas, crushed
1 c. chopped nuts

Cream sugar and shortening; add eggs. Sift flour; measure and sift with salt, baking powder and soda. Add to first mixture. Add remaining ingredients. Pour into greased 5 x 10 x 3-inch loaf pan. Bake in 350-degree oven for 30 to 40 minutes.

Patricia Fairbanks, Mason City, Iowa, North Iowa Fair

Cherry-Nut Bread

   2 c. sifted all-purpose flour
½ tsp. baking powder
1 tsp. soda
½ tsp. salt
¼ c. shortening
1 c. brown sugar
1 egg
¾ c. buttermilk or sour cream
¼ c. maraschino cherry juice
½ c. cherries, cut up
½ c. nuts, chopped

Mix and sift flour, baking powder, soda and salt. Cream shortening and sugar; add egg and mix well. Add dry ingredients alternately with liquid to creamed mixture; add cherries and nuts. Put in bread pan. Bake at 350 degrees for 1 hour.

Janis M. Hine, New Milford, Conn.

Cinnamon Swirl Loaf

1 pkg. or cake yeast
¼ c. water
2 c. milk, scalded
1 ¼ c. sugar
½ c. shortening
2 tsp. salt
7 ½ to 8 c. sifted flour
2 eggs
1 ½ tbsp. cinnamon
Soft butter

Soften dry yeast in warm water or compressed yeast in lukewarm water. Pour scalded milk over ½ cup sugar; add shortening and salt. Stir to dissolve sugar. Cool to lukewarm. Add 3 cups flour; mix well. Stir in softened yeast and eggs; beat well. Add enough of remaining flour to make a soft dough. Turn out on lightly floured surface. Cover and let rise 10 minutes. Knead until smooth and elastic, 8 to 10 minutes. Place in lightly greased bowl, turning once to grease surface. Cover and let rise in warm place until double, 1 hour and 30 minutes to 2 hours. Punch down and let rise again until almost double, about 1 hour. Punch down and divide dough in half. Cover and let rest 10 minutes. Roll each half in 15 x 7-inch rectangle, about ½ inch thick. Mix remaining sugar and cinnamon. Reserve 2 tablespoons mixture; sprinkle remaining mixture over rectangles of dough. Sprinkle about 2 teaspoons water over each; smooth with spatula. Roll each as for jelly roll, beginning with narrow sides seal long edge. Place, sealed edge down, in 2 greased 9½ x 5 x 3-inch loaf pans. Let rise until almost double, 45 minutes to 1 hour. Just before baking, brush loaves with soft butter and sprinkle with remaining cinnamon-sugar mixture. Bake at 375 degrees 35 to 40 minutes or until done. If crust browns too fast, cover with aluminum foil last 10 minutes of baking. Turn out of pans and cool on rack. Yield: 2 loaves.

Colleen Kiemele, Havre, Mont., Hill County Fair

Carrot Bread

1 c. sugar
¾ c. salad oil
2 eggs
1 ½ c. flour
¼ tsp. salt
1 tsp. cinnamon
1 tsp. soda
1 tsp. baking powder
1 c. grated carrots
½ c. nuts

Cream sugar, oil and eggs. Add flour, salt, cinnamon, soda and baking powder. Mix in grated carrots and nuts. Bake in greased loaf pan at 375 degrees for 55 minutes.

Laurie Ann Avery, Jackson, Mich., Jackson Fair

311

Prize Winning Date-Nut Bread

   2 c. sifted flour
   2 tsp. baking powder
  ½ tsp. ground cinnamon
  ¼ tsp. mace
  ½ tsp. salt
   6 tbsp. butter or margarine
  ¾ c. sugar
   2 well-beaten eggs
  ½ c. milk
   1 8-oz. pkg. chopped dates
  ½ c. chopped walnuts
   2 tsp. grated orange rind (opt.)

Sift flour with baking powder, cinnamon, mace and salt. Cream butter until soft; gradually add sugar. Add well-beaten eggs. Add dry ingredients alternately with milk. Fold in chopped dates, chopped walnuts and orange rind. Pour into a greased 9-inch loaf pan. Bake in a preheated oven at 325 degrees 1 hour to 1 hour and 15 minutes or until a cake tester inserted in center comes out clean. Cool in pan 5 minutes; remove and cool completely before slicing. Personal Comment: This recipe also won a ribbon at the Alfalfa Festival

Patsy M. Smutny, Lancaster, Cal., Antelope Valley Fair

 Fruit And Peanut Bread

   6 c. sifted flour
   1 ½ c. sugar
   2 ½ tbsp. baking powder
   1 tbsp. salt
  Grated rind of 1 orange
   1 c. peanut butter
   2 c. chopped diced fruit
   2 eggs
   3 c. milk
   2 tsp. vanilla

Combine flour, sugar, baking powder, salt and orange rind. Cut in peanut butter until particles resemble cornmeal; fold in chopped diced fruit. Beat eggs with milk and vanilla; add all at once to dry ingredients. Stir until well-blended. Spoon batter into 2 greased and floured 9 x 5 x 3-inch loaf pans. Bake in preheated 350-degree oven for 1 hour or until loaves test done. Remove from pans and cool on a rack. Cool thoroughly before cutting into thin slices. This bread will freeze well.

Mrs. Caroline M. Mason, Bristol, N. H.

Fruit Bread

½ c. butter
1 c. sugar
2 eggs
2 well-ripened bananas
2 c. flour
1 tsp. soda
¼ c. coarsely chopped nutmeats
½ c. chocolate chips
¼ c. whole maraschino cherries

Cream butter; add sugar gradually until light. Add eggs; beat until light. Add mashed bananas. Sift flour with soda; stir into batter. Stir in nutmeats, chocolate chips and maraschino cherries. Grease and flour bottoms of 3 round cans. Pour dough evenly in cans. Bake in 350-degree oven for 40 minutes. Set cans on a wire rack. Let cool 10 minutes. Turn out of cans and cool thoroughly.

Mrs. Arthur Haugen, Huron, S. D., South Dakota State Fair

Grape Nut Bread

½ c. Grape Nuts
1 c. buttermilk or sour milk
½ c. sugar
1 egg
2 c. flour
2 tsp. baking powder
½ tsp. soda
½ tsp. salt

Soak Grape Nuts and milk in saucepan 20 minutes. Cream sugar and egg; add Grape Nut mixture. Stir in flour, baking powder, soda and salt. Bake in 350-degree oven in pan for 20 to 25 minutes. Cool and serve.

Alberta Mushrush, Lexington, Ky.

Hawaiian Bread

1 No. 2½ can crushed pineapple, undrained
1 10-oz. pkg. moist flaked coconut
4 eggs, beaten
1 ½ c. sugar
4 c. flour
2 tsp. salt
2 tsp. soda

Combine all ingredients in order given. Bake for 1 hour at 325 degrees in 2 greased loaf pans. Yield: 2 loaves.

Mrs. Vivian DeMartini, Plymouth, Cal., Amador County Fair

Holiday Cranberry Bread

2 c. flour
1 c. sugar
1 ½ tsp. baking powder
1 tsp. salt
½ tsp. soda
1 orange
½ c. boiling water
2 tbsp. shortening
1 egg
1 c. nuts
1 c. raw cranberries, cut in half

Sift flour, sugar, baking powder, salt and soda into large bowl. Grate orange and reserve 1 tablespoon rind. Combine juice of orange and boiling water. Stir in 2 tablespoons shortening and well-beaten egg. Add to dry ingredients. Mix until dry particles are moistened. Stir in chopped nuts, cranberries and reserved orange rind. Turn into greased 9 x 5 x 3-inch pan. Bake at 350 degrees for 55 minutes to 1 hour.

Mrs. Lee Osborn, Chanute, Kan., Neosho and Allan County Fair

Jewish Bread

1 c. sugar
4 eggs
3 c. flour
¾ c. oil or butter
1 sm. bag slivered almonds
½ tsp. vanilla
1 tsp. almond extract

Mix sugar, eggs and 1 cup flour. Mix well and add oil. Add remaining ingredients. Pour into 2 bread pans. Bake at 350 degrees for 30 minutes. Remove from pans and slice. Toast at 300 degrees until brown. Yield: 2 loaves.

Mrs. Jacob Tjepkema, Norwood, Minn.

Lemon Bread

½ c. shortening or margarine
1 ¼ c. sugar
2 eggs, slightly beaten
1 ⅔ c. sifted flour
1 tsp. baking powder
½ tsp. salt
½ c. milk

(Continued on next page)

½ c. nuts, chopped fine
Grated peel and juice of 1 lemon

Cream shortening with 1 cup sugar; add eggs. Sift flour with baking powder and salt. Add to sugar mixture alternately with milk. Mix in nuts and lemon peel. Bake in greased 5 x 9-inch loaf pan in 350-degree oven for 1 hour. Combine remaining sugar with lemon juice. Pour over top of loaf while still hot. Yield: 1 loaf.

Mrs. Don E. Duholke, Seattle, Wash.

Nut Bread

⅓ c. molasses
1 c. brown sugar
1 c. sour milk
1 tsp. soda
1 ¼ c. graham flour or Wheatsworth flour
1 c. white flour
1 tsp. cinnamon
Speck of allspice and cloves
½ tbsp. salt
1 tbsp. shortening
2 eggs
1 c. English walnuts, whole

Combine molasses, brown sugar, sour milk, soda and graham flour; mix. Add remaining sifted dry ingredients. Put an 8 x 8-inch pan in 350-degree oven; melt shortening. Pour excess shortening, eggs and walnuts into mixture. Mix a little. Pour batter into 8 x 8-inch pan. Bake for 45 minutes.

Mrs. Carl F. Palmer, Dresden, Maine, Pittston Fair

Orange-Nut Bread

2 tbsp. shortening
1 c. honey
1 egg, beaten
1 ½ tbsp. grated orange rind
2 ¼ c. flour
2 ½ tsp. baking powder
½ tsp. salt
⅛ tsp. soda
¾ c. orange juice
¾ c. chopped nuts

Cream shortening and honey. Add beaten egg and orange rind. Sift together dry ingredients; add alternately with orange juice. Add chopped nuts. Pour into greased loaf pan in which the bottom has been lined with waxed paper. Bake

(Continued on next page)

in a 325-degree oven 1 hour and 10 minutes or until the loaf is nicely browned and begins to shrink from pan. Yield: 1 loaf.

Mrs. Edward H. Theis, Columbus, Ohio, Ohio State Fair

Orange Slice Bread

¾ c. shortening or margarine
2 c. sugar
1 egg
1 tsp. salt
1 c. cold coffee
1 c. sour milk
1 tsp. soda
4 c. flour, sifted
2 c. dates, cut fine
1 lb. orange slices, cut in small pieces
1 c. nuts
1 tsp. each cinnamon and nutmeg

Cream shortening and sugar together; add beaten egg, salt, coffee and sour milk with soda. Add sifted flour, dates, cut up orange slices, nuts and spices; mix well. Put into 2 well-greased bread pans. Bake at 325 degrees for 1 hour to 1 hour and 30 minutes. Yield: 2 loaves.

Mrs. Elizabeth Stoegbauer, Rhinelander, Wis., Rhinelander County Fair

Pineapple-Blueberry Bread

3 c. unsifted flour
2 tsp. baking powder
1 tsp. soda
½ tsp. salt
⅔ c. shortening
1 ⅓ c. sugar
4 eggs
½ c. milk
1 ½ tsp. lemon juice
1 c. drained, crushed pineapple
2 c. blueberries, rinsed and drained

Sift flour with baking powder, soda and salt. Cream shortening until light and fluffy. Gradually beat in sugar. Stir in eggs, milk, lemon juice, and pineapple. Beat in dry ingredients. Fold in blueberries. Pour into 6 greased and floured 6 x 3¼ x 2¼-inch pans. Bake at 350 degrees for 40 to 45 minutes. Unmold and cool on a rack. Yield: 6 loaves.

Liz Ensign, Bannister, Mich., Gratiot County Fair

Pecan Bread

6 c. sifted flour
6 tsp. baking powder
1 tsp. salt
2 c. sugar
1 c. chopped pecans
1 c. ground pecans
2 eggs, beaten
2 c. milk
1 tbsp. melted shortening, cooled

Sift together flour, baking powder, salt and sugar. Blend in nuts. Combine eggs, milk and shortening; add to dry ingredients, stirring quickly until well blended. Turn into 2 greased 8½ x 4½ x 2½-inch loaf pans. Bake at 350 degrees for 50 minutes to 1 hour. Yield: 2 loaves.

Kathleen A. MacIntosh, Detroit, Mich., Michigan State Fair

 ### Pineapple-Nut Bread

3 c. flour
4 tsp. baking powder
¾ tsp. salt
¾ c. sugar
1 egg
⅓ c. milk
1 c. crushed pineapple
1 c. nuts
⅓ c. salad oil

Sift flour, baking powder, salt and sugar. Break egg in 2-quart mixing bowl; beat slightly with fork. Add milk, pineapple, nuts and salad oil. Stir until combined. Add flour mixture and stir just enough to moisten the dry ingredients; do not beat. Bake in bread tin for 1 hour at 350 degrees.

Mrs. John Tillery, Gary, Ind.

 ### Pumpkin Bread

5 c. flour
4 c. sugar
1 c. oil
3 c. pumpkin
1 c. ground dates
1 c. chopped nuts
1 tsp. salt
1 tsp. cinnamon

(Continued on next page)

1 tsp. cloves
4 tsp. soda

Put all ingredients into large mixing bowl and mix at low speed. Put into 2 or 3 loaf pans; bake at 350 degrees for 70 minutes. Yield: 20 servings.
Mrs. Maurice W. Pickett, Officers' Wives' Club, Wheelus AFB, Tripoli, Libya

 ## Raisin Bread

    1 cake or pkg. yeast
    2 tsp. salt
    ¼ c. warm water
    ½ c. sugar
    1 tbsp. shortening
    1 ¾ c. milk, scalded
    7 to 7½ c. sifted all-purpose flour
    ½ 15-oz. box raisins
    Melted shortening

Dissolve yeast and 1 teaspoon salt in lukewarm water; let stand 10 minutes. Add remaining salt, sugar and shortening to scalded milk; cool to lukewarm. Gradually add yeast mixture and flour, beating thoroughly after each addition. Turn dough out onto lightly floured board; add raisins and knead for about 10 minutes or until light and satiny. Form into ball and place in greased bowl. Brush top lightly with melted butter. Cover and let rise for about 1 hour and 30 minutes or until double in bulk. Divide into 2 portions; knead and shape into 2 loaves. Place in greased loaf pans. Cover and let rise again until double in bulk. Bake at 350 degrees for 35 to 40 minutes. Yield: 2 loaves.

Mrs. Carswell Rahn, Clyo, Ga.

 ## Steamed Brown Bread

    1 c. flour
    1 c. wheat flour
    1 c. cornmeal
    ½ c. sugar
    1 ½ tsp. salt
    1 tsp. baking powder
    ½ c. molasses
    1 ½ c. sour milk
    2 tbsp. salad oil
    1 c. raisins
    ½ c. nuts (opt.)

Combine dry ingredients. Stir in molasses and sour milk. Blend in remaining ingredients. Fill a greased or oiled 2-quart covered brown bread mold or use

(Continued on next page)

large peanut butter jars two-thirds full. Set on a rack in a large kettle. Pour in boiling water to half the depth of mold. Cover tightly and steam 3 hours and 30 minutes on top of stove. Keep water boiling throughout entire period, adding water when needed. Run spatula around mold to loosen bread. Invert on a cake cooler. Yield: 24 slices.

Gertrude F. Conrad, Painesville, Ohio, Lake County Fair

Aunt Etta's Bran Muffins

⅓ c. butter
½ c. sugar
1 lge. egg
1 c. sour cream
½ c. raisins
1 tbsp., heaping, molasses
1 ¼ c. bran
Dash of salt
½ to 1 tsp. nutmeg
1 tsp. baking soda
2 c. flour
½ c. walnuts, chopped

Cream butter; add sugar and egg. Beat well. Add sour cream, raisins, molasses and bran. Sift together salt, nutmeg, soda and flour; mix well. Add nuts; mix again. Fill well-greased muffin tins 2/3 full. Bake 20 minutes at 375 degrees. Serve hot or cool on a rack. Yield: 16 muffins.
Personal Comment: This recipe won the rosette for "Best in Breads" in 1965.

Mrs. William T. Gardner, Waterbury, Conn., North Haven Fair

Carrot Muffins

1 c. Crisco
½ c. brown sugar
1 beaten egg
¼ tsp. each nutmeg and cinnamon
1 ½ c. flour
½ tsp. salt
1 tsp. baking powder
1 ½ c. grated carrots

Cream shortening and sugar thoroughly. Add egg. Dissolve spices in 1 table-spoon hot water. Add to mixture. Sift dry ingredients together. Add carrots, then dry ingredients. Bake in a greased ring about 1 hour at 350 degrees. These may be baked as muffins also. Yield: One ring or 12 muffins.

Claire C. Wiedeman, Lewistown, Mont., Fergus County Fair

Peach Upside-Down Muffins

2 c. cake flour
½ c. white sugar
3 tsp. baking powder
½ tsp. salt
¼ c. melted shortening
2 eggs
1 c. milk
Butter
Brown sugar
Cooked dried peach halves

Sift together flour, white sugar, baking powder and salt 3 times; add the shortening, eggs and milk. Beat until batter is smooth and light. Place 1 teaspoon butter and 1 tablespoon brown sugar in each muffin cup and heat until melted and thoroughly blended. Cut peach halves in 3 sections to resemble petals; place in muffin cups, with cut-side up. Fill cups half full of batter. Bake for 25 minutes at 375 degrees. Serve with vanilla ice cream.

Mrs. Jerry W. Green, McMinnville, Tenn.

 ## Poor Man's Muffins

1 c. granulated sugar
½ c. margarine
1 c. raisins
1 c. water
½ tsp. nutmeg
1 tsp. cinnamon
¼ tsp. allspice
2 c. sifted all-purpose flour
1 tsp. baking soda
1 tsp. baking powder
¼ tsp. salt

Place in saucepan, sugar, margarine, raisins, water and spices; bring to boil. Boil 1 minute; cool. Blend in flour, baking soda, baking powder and salt; put in paper-lined muffin cups. Bake at 375 degrees for 15 to 20 minutes. Yield: 1 dozen muffins.

Mrs. Ronald Singleton, Troy, Mo.

 ## Yummy Nut Muffins

2 c. sifted flour
3 tsp. baking powder
¼ c. sugar
½ tsp. salt

(Continued on next page)

1 egg, beaten
1 c. milk
¼ c. soft or melted fat
½ c. chopped nuts

Heat the oven to 400 degrees. Grease muffin cups. Sift together flour, baking powder, sugar and salt in a large bowl. Make a well in center. In a small mixing bowl, beat egg until foamy. Add milk and melted fat. Add the milk mixture all at once to dry ingredients. Stir in nuts; keep stirring until dry ingredients are moist but mixture is still slightly lumpy. Fill muffin cups ½ to 2/3 full. Bake for 15 to 20 minutes. Yield: 12 servings.

Ann Denise Kirking, Lodi, Wis., Dane County Fair

 ## Blueberry Break-Cakes

1 c. fresh cultivated blueberries
2 tbsp. butter
1 c. sugar
2 eggs
2 c. flour
2 ½ tsp. baking powder
¾ c. milk

Wash blueberries and set aside to drain thoroughly. Cream butter and sugar together. Mix in eggs, flour and baking powder. Add milk and beat dough. This will make a stiff dough. Carefully fold in blueberries. Bake in well-greased muffin tins for 30 minutes at 350°. Yield: 12 muffins.

Photograph for this recipe below.

Wal-D'Apple Muffins

1 ¾ c. all-purpose flour, pre-sifted
2 ½ tsp. baking powder
¾ tsp. salt
Sugar
2 eggs
¾ c. milk
2 tbsp. melted butter
Black walnuts
¾ c. chopped dates
1 c. grated raw apples
2 apples
2 tsp. cinnamon

Combine flour, baking powder, salt and ¼ cup sugar. Beat eggs in a separate bowl; add milk combined with butter. Stir liquid ingredients into flour mixture quickly. Add ¾ cup chopped black walnuts, dates and grated apples. Spoon batter into greased and floured muffin pans, filling each about 2/3 full. Peel and core apples. Slice into thin slices. Dip each apple slice into mixture of cinnamon and 6 teaspoons sugar. Place 1 slice on top of each muffin. Fill hole in center of apple with black walnuts. Bake muffins in a pre-heated 425-degree oven for 25 minutes. Yield: 15 muffins.

Mrs. Foster Starcher, Parkersburg, W. Va., Wood County Fair

Crepes Suzette

2 tbsp. butter
1 c. sifted flour
¼ c. sugar
¼ tsp. salt
3 eggs, beaten
1 c. milk
1 tsp. grated orange or lemon peel
1 tsp. curacao
¼ tsp. vanilla extract

Melt butter in 6-inch skillet. Sift together flour, sugar and salt. Beat together eggs and milk; beat in melted butter, grated peel, curacao and vanilla extract. Combine egg mixture with dry ingredients and beat with rotary beater until smooth. Heat skillet moderately hot; pour in just enough batter to cover bottom. Immediately tilt skillet back and forth to spread batter thinly and evenly. Cook each crepe over medium heat until light brown on bottom and firm to touch on top; loosen edges with spatula. Turn and brown second side. It should be unnecessary to grease skillet for each crepe. Serve with melted butter. Batter may be prepared hours in advance, stored in a cool place and crepes cooked just before serving. Crepes may be cooked in advance and kept warm in oven. Yield: 8 servings.

Sister Rose Marie, OSB, Home Economics Teacher, East Grand Forks, Minn.

Corn Bread Jelly Roll

Corn bread mix
2 tbsp. cooking oil
1 c. berry jam
¾ c. powdered sugar

Prepare favorite corn bread mix according to package directions, adding ¼ cup more liquid than required and 2 tablespoons cooking oil. Mix only until all ingredients are moistened. Bake on griddle as hot cakes. When done, place about 1 tablespoon or more berry jam on top in center. Tightly roll; secure with toothpick. Roll in powdered sugar and serve hot. Yield: 12 servings.

Mrs. Charles S. Carlisle, Pearl Harbor, Hawaii

 ## Cottage Cheese-Fruit Pancakes

3 well-beaten eggs
1 c. cream-style cottage cheese
2 tbsp. salad oil
¼ c. sifted enriched flour
¼ tsp. salt
Frozen-style strawberry or raspberry jam
Confectioners' sugar

Preheat grill. Combine eggs, cheese and salad oil. Sift flour and salt together; add to egg mixture. Beat only until blended. Bake 4-inch cakes on lightly greased griddle. Place about 1 tablespoon jam in center of each cake; bring edges of pancake together and roll under. Sprinkle with confectioners' sugar. Serve at once, while hot. Yield: 8 cakes.

Mrs. Arthur H. Raasch, Lake Oswego, Ore.

Sugar Plum Strawberry Hot Cakes

2 c. packaged layer or pound cake mix
1 egg
½ c. water
⅓ c. flour
⅓ c. chopped nuts

Add egg and water to cake mix; beat until smooth. Stir in flour and nuts. Preheat grill. Drop by tablespoons onto lightly greased surface. Cook about 5 minutes. Serve hot with sweetened strawberries, spooned over cakes shortcake-style, and whipped cream. Yield: 6-8 servings.

Marlene Caszatt, Whitehall, Mich.

Thin Pancakes

    3 eggs, separated
    3 c. milk
    ½ tsp. of salt
    1 tsp. sugar
    3 tbsp. flour
    2 tbsp. butter, melted

Beat egg yolks until very light; add gradually milk, salt, sugar and flour. Beat to a smooth batter and let stand 3 hours. Add butter and fold in stiffly beaten egg whites. Drop small spoonfuls of batter on sizzling hot greased griddle. Serve hot with jelly or sugar. Yield: 6 servings.

Mrs. Esther Darst Minton, Home Economics Teacher, Phoenix, Ariz.

Black Walnut Caramel Rolls

    Butter
    Brown sugar
    Black walnut pieces
    2 tbsp. white sugar
    ½ tsp. salt
    ¼ c. soft shortening
    1 egg
    1 ½ c. plus 2 tbsp. all-purpose flour
    1 pkg. active dry yeast

Prepare muffin cups by mixing 1 teaspoon soft butter, 2 teaspoons brown sugar and ¼ teaspoon water in each. Arrange black walnut pieces on mixture in bottom of each cup. Mix next 4 ingredients and 1 cup flour together. Add yeast dissolved in ⅝ cup warm water. Combine with mixer on low speed. Beat 2 minutes at medium speed, guiding batter into beaters with rubber scraper. Add remaining flour; beat with rubber scraper until smooth. Spoon into muffin cups a scant half full. Let rise in warm place for 30 minutes or until batter reaches top of cups. Bake at 375 degrees for 18 to 20 minutes or until golden brown. Yield: 12 to 15 rolls.

Bessie Ash, Wilbur, W. Va., Tyler County Fair

Butterhorns

1 c. shortening or butter
Sugar
¼ tsp. salt
2 eggs, well beaten
1 yeast cake
¼ c. warm water
2 c. sifted flour
Grated lemon rind
¾ c. chopped nuts
1 tbsp, approx., cream

Cream butter and 1 tablespoon sugar. Add salt to eggs; beat well. Add to butter and sugar mixture. Add yeast dissolved in water and 1 teaspoon sugar. Add flour and a little lemon rind; mix well. Divide dough in 3 equal parts. Roll out like pie crust in circles. Spread with mixture of chopped nuts, ½ cup sugar and enough cream to make a soft paste. Cut each circle into 7 pieces, like pie; roll each piece, beginning at wide end. Place on greased pan; let rise 20 to 30 minutes. Bake 15 to 20 minutes in 350-degree oven. Ice while hot with powdered sugar and milk icing. Yield: 21 servings.

Ruth Rohrbacher, Toledo, Ohio

 ## Buttermilk-Cinnamon Rolls

2 pkg. dry yeast
2 ¼ c. lukewarm water
5 c. flour
2 tsp. salt
1 tsp. soda
6 tbsp. powdered buttermilk
½ c. white sugar
6 tbsp. melted butter
Cream
¼ c. brown sugar
1 tsp. cinnamon
Chopped nuts

Dissolve yeast in lukewarm water. Sift together flour, salt, soda, powdered buttermilk and white sugar. Add half the flour mixture to water and yeast mixture; beat well. Beat in melted butter; add remaining flour mixture. Mix lightly; turn upside down on floured board with bowl on top. Let rise for 10 minutes. Remove bowl and knead until smooth. Put bowl on top of dough again for 20 minutes. Roll out dough; spread with cream. Sprinkle with brown sugar, cinnamon and nuts. Roll up and slice; let rise. Bake at 425 degrees for 7 to 10 minutes. Frost with powdered sugar icing.

Mrs. Dorothy Trimble, Elma, Wash., Mason County Fair

Cocoa-Cinnamon Rolls

¾ c. warm water
1 pkg. yeast
1 tsp. salt
1 egg
¼ c. shortening, softened
⅓ c. cocoa
2 ¼ c. flour
2 tbsp. butter
½ c. sugar
2 tbsp. cinnamon
Powdered sugar frosting

Measure water into mixing bowl; add yeast and stir until dissolved. Stir in salt, egg, shortening, cocoa and flour; mix well. Cover in lightly oiled bowl and let rise once. Roll dough into oblong 15 x 9 inches. Spread with butter and sprinkle with sugar and cinnamon. Roll up like jelly roll; cut into 1-inch slices. Place in lightly greased pan; cover and let rise until double, about 30 to 45 minutes. Bake about 25 to 30 minutes in 375-degree oven. While slightly warm frost with powdered sugar frosting. Yield: 12 rolls.

Nancy Bennett, Sheridan, Wyo.

 Heavenly Rolls

3 c. flour
½ lb. margarine
1 ½ yeast cakes
1 tbsp. sugar
½ c. light cream or top milk
2 egg yolks
1 whole egg
Pinch of salt
1 tsp. vanilla
Raspberry jam

Mix flour and margarine as for pie crust. Dissolve yeast in small amount of water. Add sugar. Add cream, egg yolks and whole egg, salt and vanilla. Add to flour and margarine mixture. Work on floured board until easy to handle, like pie crust. Divide into 3 balls. Roll out into circles; cut 8 wedges from each. On larger part of wedge, place a teaspoon of raspberry jam. Roll into crescent shape roll. Place on greased cookie sheet. Let rise about 2 to 3 hours in a warm place. Bake about 20 to 30 minutes in a 350-degree oven or until brown. When hot, frost with confectioners' sugar icing and sprinkle with chopped nuts, if desired. Yield: 24 rolls.

Mrs. John H. McLeod, New Haven, Conn., North Haven Fair

Danish Nut Horns

¼ c. plus 1 tbsp. sugar
4 c. flour
¼ tsp. salt
1 lb. Spry or Crisco
4 eggs, beaten
1 cake yeast
½ c. evaporated milk
1 c. ground walnuts
2 tbsp. honey

Put 1 tablespoon sugar, flour and salt in large bowl; blend in Spry as for pie crust. Add eggs. Dissolve yeast in ¼ cup milk and add. Blend well. Cover with waxed paper; refrigerate overnight. Divide dough in 4 parts; roll out on board sprinkled with sugar. Cut in triangles. Combine walnuts, honey, remaining milk and remaining sugar; place filling in center of each triangle of dough. Roll up each triangle; place on cookie sheet. Bake at 350 degrees for 20 minutes. If desired, strawberry or apricot preserves or peanut butter may be substituted for filling.

Stella Bartsch, Glendale, W. Va.

Orange Rolls

1 c. milk, scalded
½ c. shortening
½ c. sugar
1 tsp. salt
1 cake or 1 pkg. yeast
3 beaten eggs
4 ½ c. flour
Orange Filling

Combine milk, shortening, sugar and salt; cool to lukewarm. Add yeast and stir well. Add eggs, then flour; mix to smooth soft dough. Place dough in greased bowl; cover and let rise until doubled in bulk. Divide dough in half; roll ¼ inch thick and spread with Orange Filling. Roll as jelly roll. Cut 1-inch slices. Place cut-side down in greased, shallow pan. Cover and let rise until double in bulk. Bake for 20 minutes in 375-degree oven.

ORANGE FILLING:

½ c. sugar
¼ c. butter, melted
1 orange peel grated

Mix ingredients together and spread on dough. Yield: 2 dozen.

Mrs. John Urquhart, Marshalltown, Iowa, Iowa State Fair

Orange Yeast Rolls

½ c. milk
1 ½ c. sugar
1 ½ tsp. salt
¼ c. margarine
2 pkg. dry yeast
½ c. warm water
2 eggs, beaten
4 ½ c. unsifted flour
¼ c. grated orange rind
½ c. raisins
¼ c. margarine, melted

Scald milk; add ½ cup sugar, salt and margarine. Cool. Add yeast dissolved in warm water. Stir eggs and half of flour into lukewarm milk mixture. Beat. Stir in remaining flour. Turn dough out on lightly floured board. Knead until smooth. Punch down; turn out on floured board and shape as desired. When dough is ready, combine remaining sugar, orange rind and raisins. Divide dough in half. Roll each half to 18 x 9 inches. Brush with melted margarine. Sprinkle with sugar mixture. Roll from long side. Cut into 1½-inch slices; place in 2 greased 9-inch pans. Cover; let rise until double in bulk. Bake 25 minutes at 375 degrees. Remove from pans; frost with orange icing. Mixture may be sprinkled with nuts.

ORANGE ICING:

2 c. confectioners' sugar
3 tbsp. orange juice

Mix sugar and juice. Yield: 2 dozen.
Personal Comment: This recipe also won a ribbon at the Burlington County Fair.

Mrs. James Ringenary, Mount Holly, N. J., New Jersey State Fair

 ## Pecan Rolls

1 cake compressed yeast
1 tsp. salt
½ c. sugar
2 eggs
5 tbsp. fat
1 c. warm water
5 c. flour
Cinnamon
1 c. butter or margarine
2 c. brown sugar
¼ c. white corn syrup
Chopped pecans

(Continued on next page)

Crumble yeast in lukewarm water; add salt and sugar. Add eggs, fat and warm water; beat 2 minutes. Add half the flour; beat 3 minutes. Add remaining flour; mix well. Cover with greased waxed paper; wrap in towel. Refrigerate until needed. Roll on floured board; sprinkle with sugar and cinnamon. Roll up and slice. Melt butter; add brown sugar and syrup. Boil 2 minutes; pour into pans. Sprinkle with pecans; add cinnamon rolls. Let rise 1 hour and 30 minutes. Bake at 350 degrees for 30 minutes. Yield: 24 rolls.

Mrs. Lowell Rothbart, Grand Mound, Iowa

Coconut-Butterscotch Rolls

1 pkg. butterscotch pudding mix
1 ½ c. evaporated milk
1 stick oleo
2 unbeaten eggs
1 tsp. salt
2 pkg. yeast
¼ c. warm water
4 ½ c. flour

Combine pudding mix with milk; heat until thickened. Remove from heat; add oleo, eggs and salt. Cool to lukewarm; add yeast dissolved in warm water, and flour. Put in refrigerator; let rise until light. Divide in 3 parts; roll each in circle. Cut in 12 wedges; put 1 teaspoon filling on each wedge. Roll up like crescent rolls.

FILLING:

¼ c. melted oleo
⅔ c. coconut
⅔ c. brown sugar
⅓ c. pecans, chopped
1 tsp. flour

Combine ingredients; spoon onto wedges. Bake about 18 minutes at 350 degrees until lightly browned. Spread frosting on while rolls are warm.

FROSTING:

¼ c. brown sugar
2 tbsp. evaporated milk
2 tbsp. oleo
1 c. powdered sugar
1 tsp. vanilla

Boil first 3 ingredients together 1 minute. Blend in powdered sugar and vanilla. Spread over warm rolls. Yield: 3 dozen.

Mrs. Grace Turnbull, Phillipsburg, Kan., Rooks County Free Fair

Chocolate Waffles

1 ½ c. flour
3 tsp. baking powder
½ tsp. salt
6 tbsp. sugar
1 c. milk, warmed
2 eggs, beaten
2 tbsp. butter
2 squares chocolate

Mix and sift dry ingredients; add slightly warmed milk, beaten eggs, melted butter and chocolate all at once. Stir until mixed. Preheat waffle iron 5 minutes. Cook waffles.

HARD SAUCE:

¼ c. butter
¾ c. powdered sugar
½ tsp. vanilla
1 tbsp. hot water

Cream butter; stir in sugar gradually. Add vanilla. Stir in hot water, a few drops at a time, to prevent separation of sauce. Pile lightly into serving dish. Chill thoroughly. Top chocolate waffles. Yield: 4 servings.

Mrs. Gladys E. Meier, Detroit, Mich.

Raisin-Cream Waffles

1 c. seedless raisins
3 eggs, separated
1 c. light cream
1 c. milk
18 drops liquid sugar substitute
2 ½ c. flour
5 tsp. baking powder
1 tsp. salt
5 tbsp. melted butter or shortening

Boil raisins for 5 minutes in water to cover; drain and cool. Beat egg yolks; combine with cream, milk and sugar or substitute. Sift dry ingredients; add to yolk mixture. Stir in butter and raisins. Beat egg whites until stiff; fold into batter. Bake in hot waffle irons. Yield: 6 servings.

Florence B. Stanfield, Oklahoma City, Okla.

Foreign Desserts

Gugelhupf (Austria)

½ c. milk
1 pkg. dry yeast or 1 cake compressed yeast
¼ c. very warm water
½ c. sugar
½ tsp. salt
2 ¾ c. sifted flour
2 eggs
½ c. plus 1 tbsp. melted margarine or butter
2 tbsp. fine bread crumbs or finely ground almonds
15 or 16 whole blanched almonds
½ c. chopped raisins
1 tsp. grated lemon rind

Scald milk; pour into mixing bowl and cool to lukewarm. Sprinkle or crumble yeast into very warm water in cup; stir until dissolved. Add sugar, salt and 1½ cups flour to milk in bowl; mix well. Add dissolved yeast; beat until smooth. Add eggs; beat thoroughly. Add ½ cup melted and cooled margarine, about 1 tablespoon at a time, mixing well after each addition. Stir in remaining flour; beat about 5 minutes. Cover and let rise in warm place for 1 hour and 30 minutes or until double in bulk. While batter rises, prepare baking pan. Use 1-quart fancy mold, two 1-pint molds or 7-inch angel food cake pan. Rub the inside pan generously with remaining margarine; sprinkle fine bread crumbs into pan. Shake to coat inside of pan with crumbs. Arrange almonds in a design in bottom of pan. When batter has doubled, punch down; mix in raisins and lemon rind. Carefully spoon the batter on top of the almonds; cover and let rise in warm place for 1 hour and 15 minutes or until double in bulk. Bake at 350 degrees for 45 to 50 minutes. Look at the cake after it has baked 15 minutes. If it is turning brown, lay a piece of clean brown wrapping paper over the top for the rest of the baking period. Turn out of pan onto wire cake rack. If desired, dust lightly with confectioners' sugar. To make a design on top of the cake, lay a scalloped lace paper doily on the cake and sift confectioners' sugar over it; lift the doily carefully.

Sharon Gilbert, Flint, Mich.

Sachertorte (Austria)

¾ c. butter
6 ½ oz. semisweet chocolate
¾ c. sugar
8 egg yolks
1 c. flour
10 egg whites, stiffly beaten
2 tbsp. apricot jam or whipped cream

Beat butter until creamy. Melt chocolate. Add sugar and chocolate to butter and stir. Add egg yolks, 1 at a time; add flour. Fold in egg whites. Pour mixture into greased and buttered 8 or 9-inch cake pan. Bake at 275 degrees for 1 hour

(Continued on next page)

or until torte tests done. Remove to rack and cool. Turn upside down; split into 3 layers. Heat apricot jam slightly; spread between layers.

ICING:

> 1 c. sugar
> ⅓ c. water
> 7 oz. semisweet chocolate

Cook sugar and water until mixture spins a thin thread. Melt chocolate in top of double boiler; add sugar mixture to chocolate gradually. Stir constantly until icing coats the spoon. Pour on top of cake. Yield: 12 servings.

Mrs. L. L. Jones, Pierre, S. D.

 ## Koekjes (Belgium)

> 1 c. butter, softened
> ½ c. sugar
> 1 tsp. vanilla
> ¼ tsp. salt
> 2 c. flour, sifted
> Milk
> 1 c. blanched ground almonds
> Powdered sugar

Cream butter and sugar; add vanilla, salt and flour. Mix well to form a ball of dough; chill for 2 hours. Roll out on lightly floured board; cut into strips. Brush with milk; sprinkle with almonds. Pat lightly with spatula; place on un-greased baking sheet. Bake at 325 degrees for 10 to 12 minutes. Place on rack; sprinkle with powdered sugar.

Darlene Heilmann, Home Economics Teacher, McFarland, Cal.

 ## Preserved Kumquats (China)

> 2 qts. firm kumquats
> 5 c. sugar

Remove stems and leaves from kumquats; wash and drain fruit. Prick each kumquat several times with a darning needle; place in a saucepan. Cover with boiling water; simmer for about 20 minutes or until tender. Skim kumquats from the water; stir sugar into water. Boil syrup for 5 minutes; add kumquats. Cook gently for 1 hour or until fruit is transparent. Let kumquats stand in the syrup overnight to plump; reheat to boiling point. Take kumquats from syrup; pack in hot sterile jars. Continue to cook syrup until thick; pour over kumquats. Seal jars. Kumquats may be partially split and stuffed with a maraschino cherry, a blanched almond or a wedge of peach, if desired. Yield: 13 servings.

Mrs. C. Paul Clark, Newark, Ohio

Empanaditas De Crema—Cream Turnovers (Bolivia)

1 c. milk
¼ tsp. salt
¼ c. sugar
1 tbsp. butter
6 tsp. cornstarch
4 tsp. cold water
2 egg yolks, beaten
1 tsp. vanilla

Bring milk, salt, sugar and butter to a boil. Dissolve cornstarch in cold water; add to milk mixture. Allow to thicken; carefully stir in egg yolks and vanilla. Stir until thickened; set aside to cool.

CRUST:

1 c. flour
2 tbsp. butter
1 egg yolk
3 tbsp. milk
Dash of salt

Put flour in bowl; cut in butter. Combine egg yolk, hot milk and salt; pour into flour mixture. Knead well to make a smooth dough. Divide into portions; roll out very thin. Cut into 4-inch rounds. Put a spoonful of filling on dough rounds; moisten edges. Fold over dough to make crescents; pinch edges together tightly. Fry in deep fat at 360 degrees until golden brown on both sides. Yield: 20 servings.

Evelyn Hackney, Iola, Kan.

Bolo De L'Aranja—Orange Cake (Brazil)

5 eggs, separated
8 tbsp. orange juice
2 c. flour
2 c. sugar
1 tsp. baking powder
½ tsp. vanilla
5 beaten egg whites

Combine egg yolks and orange juice. Mix flour, sugar and baking powder together; add slowly to egg yolk mixture. Beat for about 2 minutes. Add vanilla; fold in beaten egg whites. Pour in well-greased pan. Bake at 350 degrees for 25 minutes. May be served with topping of orange juice if desired. Yield: 6 servings.

Louise Figueiredo, Leonville, La.

Buche De Neige (Canada)

2 c. sifted all-purpose flour
3 tsp. baking powder
¼ c. sugar
½ tsp. salt
¼ tsp. mace
1 c. milk
3 tbsp. melted butter
½ c. clean white snow, dry and crisp
½ c. raisins

Sift dry ingredients into a bowl; make a well in the center. Pour in milk and butter; stir slightly. Add snow and raisins; stir only until dry ingredients are moistened. Spoon into buttered muffin pans, filling them two-thirds full. Bake at 400 degrees for 18 minutes. Serve hot with butter and jam or maple syrup. Yield: 12 servings.
Personal Comment: This is an authentic recipe from the far-back days of Canada's pioneer homemakers.

Mrs. Richard Baker, Saint Albans, Vt.

Svestkovy Kolache—Prune Kolache (Czechoslovakia)

½ c. sugar
½ c. lard
1 tsp. salt
2 eggs
2 pkg. dry yeast
¾ c. warm water
4 c. sifted flour

Cream sugar, lard, salt and eggs thoroughly. Dissolve yeast in water; add to creamed mixture and beat well. Let rise until double in bulk. Divide into 24 equal parts; shape into smooth round balls. Place on greased cookie sheet. Cover with cloth; let rise about 1 hour. Make a depression in center of each roll.

FILLING:

1 lb. dried prunes, cooked in 2 c. water
1 c. sugar
1 tsp. cinnamon
1 tbsp. lemon juice

Combine all ingredients. Fill each roll with 2 tablespoons filling. Bake at 375 degrees for 15 to 18 minutes. Yield: 24 rolls.

Mrs. Shirley Hofacker, Home Economics Teacher, Weyerhauser, Wis.

Appelsinfromage—Orange Snow (Denmark)

10 eggs, separated
1 ½ c. sugar
1 envelope unflavored gelatin
¼ c. cold water
Juice of 6 oranges, strained
Whipped cream

Beat egg yolks and sugar until lemon colored. Soak gelatin in cold water; dissolve over hot water. Add gelatin and orange juice to egg yolk mixture; cool until mixture begins to thicken. Beat egg whites until stiff; fold into egg yolk mixture. Refrigerate until set. Serve with whipped cream. Yield: 16-18 servings.

Mrs. Edith Jorgensen, Emery, S. D.

Danish Wedding Cake (Denmark)

3 lb. almond paste
1 ½ lb. granulated sugar
8 egg whites, unbeaten

Mix ingredients well into stiff paste; heat mixture, but do not boil, in top of double boiler over hot water. Roll paste into rings about ½ inch thick. Lay a length of waxed paper over a cookie sheet. Use a compass to draw the circumference of the bottom ring, the largest one, and as many more of the progressively smaller rings as can be fitted on cookie sheet. Continue in this fashion until as many rings as desired are marked out. Butter and dust cookie sheets with flour. Lay rings on sheets after they have been shaped on waxed paper patterns. With fingers, squeeze tops of rings enough to make them slightly pointed in the center to build foundation for smaller rings which will top each. Bake at 250 degrees until edges are browned. Place on rack to cool. Frost between layers.

ALMOND PASTE:

1 ½ lb. shelled almonds, blanched
3 c. sugar
1 ½ c. water
9 tbsp. orange juice
6 drops rose water
Powdered sugar

Put almonds at least 4 times through finest blade of meat grinder to get nuts as oily as possible. Cook sugar and water in pan to soft ball stage or 240 degrees. Add nuts, orange juice and rose water. Stir until well blended and creamy; cover with towel and let rest 10 to 12 hours. Dip hands in powdered sugar to make kneading easier. Place paste on clean hard surface dusted with powdered sugar; knead until smooth. Place in covered jar or tin to ripen for 6 to 8 days.

(Continued on next page)

ROYAL ICING:

> 4 egg whites
> 1 ½ c. powdered sugar

Beat ingredients by hand until stiff. Squeeze through pastry bag to decorate each ring before putting cake together.

Personal Comment: This cake consists of at least 20 rings called kranse, of graduating sizes, placed on top of each other to make a cone. It is decorated with four large candles and as many smaller ones as you wish. Favors, white birds, and candy flowers in gay colors of the bride's choice are stuck on the cake with melted sugar. The traditional miniature bride and groom decorate the top.

Mrs. George Nielsen, Junction City, Ore., Lane County Fair

 Rodgrod—Red Pudding (Denmark)

> 2 pt. raspberries
> 1 pt. red currants
> 1 pt. black currants
> ½ c. cornstarch or potato starch
> Cream

Clean and wash berries and currants; place in saucepan. Add 2 pints water; boil until tender. Strain through a fine sieve; return strained juice to heat. Bring to boiling point; stir in cornstarch which has been dissolved in ½ cup cold water. Cook over low heat until thickened; remove from heat and cool. Serve with cream. Yield: 12 servings.

Mrs. Adrianna H. Mills, Home Economics Teacher, Johnson, Vt.

 Apricot Trifle (England)

> 1 1-lb. pound cake, sliced
> 1 10-oz. jar apricot preserves
> ½ c. chopped pecans
> 2 c. boiled custard
> ½ c. sherry
> Whipped topping
> Cherries

Alternate layers of pound cake, apricot preserves and nuts in silver serving bowl. Pour hot custard over layers; add sherry. Refrigerate overnight. To serve, top with whipped topping; decorate with cherries. Yield: 8-10 servings.

Mrs. Frederick A. Ware, Augusta, Ga.

Banbury Tarts (England)

½ c. raisins, chopped
½ c. sugar
1 ½ tbsp. cracker crumbs
1 egg yolk
½ tsp. soft butter
Dash of salt
1 tbsp. lemon juice
1 tbsp. grated lemon rind
2 tbsp. chopped walnuts
1 recipe pastry for 1-crust pie

Mix all ingredients except pastry. Roll out pastry into 12-inch square; cut into nine 4-inch squares. Spread filling over half of each square; moisten edges. Fold into triangles; press edges together with fork. Prick tops. Bake at 450 degrees for 12 to 15 minutes or until delicately browned. Yield: 9 servings.

Mrs. Judy Tupper, Home Economics Teacher, Winnebago, Minn.

 ### Cherry-Port Mold (England)

1 c. port wine
2 ½ c. canned pitted Bing cherries, drained
1 ¾ c. Bing cherry juice
1 ½ c. cold water
2 pkg. cherry gelatin
Sweetened whipped cream

Pour wine over drained cherries; cover and refrigerate overnight. Drain port from cherries; set aside. Combine cherry juice and ¼ cup water; heat. Add gelatin; stir until completely dissolved. Add port and remaining water; chill until slightly thickened. Fold in cherries; pour into 1½-quart mold. Chill until firm; serve with whipped cream.

Mrs. Vaughn Huckfeldt, Lyons, Colo.

Scones (England)

Sugar
2 ⅓ c. sifted cake flour
2 ½ tsp. baking powder
½ tsp. salt
6 tbsp. shortening
5 tbsp. milk or light cream
2 eggs

Sift 2 teaspoons sugar, flour, baking powder and salt together; cut in shortening with pastry blender. Add milk. Separate 1 egg; reserve 1 tablespoon egg white.

(Continued on next page)

Beat remaining eggs; add to flour mixture. Roll dough ½ inch thick on lightly floured board; cut into 3-inch squares. Cut each square in half diagonally to make 2 triangles; arrange on greased cookie sheet. Brush with slightly beaten reserved egg white; sprinkle with 2 tablespoons sugar. Bake at 450 degrees for 10 to 15 minutes or until done. Yield: 10 servings.

Mrs. Spencer Baltimore, Federalsburg, Md.

 ## Tea Cakes (England)

¼ c. butter
¼ c. shortening
¾ c. sugar
1 egg
3 tbsp. milk
1 ½ tsp. baking powder
1 ¾ c. sifted flour
¼ tsp. salt
½ c. finely chopped citron
½ c. currants or raisins
1 egg white

Mix together butter, shortening, sugar, egg and milk; cream thoroughly. Sift together baking powder, flour and salt; add to creamed mixture. Mix in citron and currants; chill dough. Roll into balls the size of a walnut; dip balls in slightly beaten egg white. Dip in additional sugar; place, sugared-side up, 2 inches apart on ungreased baking sheet. Bake at 400 degrees for 12 to 15 minutes or until delicately browned. Yield: 3 dozen cookies.

Frances Hallett, Southington, Conn.

Mansikkatortu—Strawberry Torte (Finland)

5 eggs, separated
¾ c. sugar
3 c. crushed fresh or frozen strawberries
1 c. cookie or cake crumbs
1 tsp. almond extract
Whipped cream

Beat egg yolks until light; add sugar and beat until mixture is stiff and lemon colored. Add drained strawberries; add crumbs and almond extract. Beat egg whites until stiff but not dry; fold into strawberry mixture. Pour mixture into buttered 8 x 12-inch baking dish. Bake at 350 degrees for 35 minutes. Serve with whipped cream. Yield: 8 servings.

Marquita K. Christensen, Marshall, Minn. Favorite Recipes Food Fair

Marja Puuro—Cranberry Whip (Finland)

2 c. cranberries
3 c. water
1 ½ c. sugar
½ c. farina or cream of wheat
Whipped cream

Boil cranberries with water until tender; drain cranberries, reserving juice. Force cranberries through sieve; add enough reserved juice to make 3 cups liquid. Add sugar; boil briskly. Add farina; boil until thickened. Remove from heat; set into pan of ice cubes. Beat with electric beater until frothy; serve with whipped cream.

Mrs. J. A. Kirklyn, Yankton, S. D.

Crepes Suzette (France)

1 c. milk
½ c. water
1 c. flour
1 egg
½ tsp. salt
½ tbsp. salad oil
Cognac
Butter
Sugar
1 tbsp. confectioners' sugar
Juice of 1 orange
6-8 oz. orange liqueur
1 tbsp. grated orange peel
1 tsp. grated lemon peel

Add milk and water to flour; beat until smooth. Add egg, salt, salad oil and ½ tablespoon cognac; beat until velvety. Refrigerate overnight. Melt just enough butter in small frying pan to cover bottom of pan; pour in 1 serving spoon batter for each crepe. The crepe should be gossamer-thin and honey-colored on both sides. Turn crepe gently with spatula. Sprinkle sugar lightly between pancakes. Melt ½ stick butter in chafing dish over very hot fire. Add confectioners' sugar and orange juice; boil vigorously until sugar is completely dissolved. Add orange liqueur, orange and lemon peels; bring mixture to second boil. Place 1 crepe at a time in chafing dish; turn over and fold twice. Slide over to edge of pan; repeat with remaining crepes. Add 6 to 8 ounces cognac to liquid in dish; bring to boil and ignite. Ladle flaming mixture over crepes; continue to ladle until the flame is gone. Serve on warm plates with a little of the remaining juice. Yield: 6-8 servings.

Mrs. Ward W. Martindale, Officers' Wives' Club, Sault Sainte Marie, Mich.

Baba Au Rhum (France)

> 1 pkg. yeast
> ½ c. lukewarm water
> ¼ c. plus 1 tsp. sugar
> ½ c. butter or margarine
> ½ tsp. salt
> 1 ½ tsp. grated lemon rind
> 3 eggs, beaten
> 1 ½ c. plus 1 tbsp. flour

Sprinkle yeast over lukewarm water in which 1 teaspoon sugar has been dissolved; let stand for 10 minutes. Cream butter, remaining sugar, salt and lemon rind thoroughly; add eggs and mix well. Beat 1/3 cup flour into yeast mixture; beat for 3 minutes. Add to creamed mixture; beat in remaining flour, 1 tablespoon at a time. Beat with wooden spoon for 4 minutes; mixture will be soft. Fill greased muffin pans or ring molds half full; let rise until double in bulk. Bake at 350 degrees for 20 minutes. Turn out and cool; return to pans.

SYRUP:

> 1 c. sugar
> ½ c. water
> ¼ c. rum
> Whipped cream

Cook sugar and water for 10 minutes; add rum. Drizzle hot syrup over cake 1 hour before serving, using as much syrup as cake will absorb. Top with whipped cream. Yield: 12-16 servings.

Mrs. M. Gravil, Springfield, Mass., Favorite Recipes Food Fair

Pots De Creme (France)

> 3 c. heavy cream
> ½ c. sugar
> 1 tbsp. vanilla extract
> 5 egg yolks
> 1 1-oz. square semisweet or unsweetened chocolate
> Sweetened whipped cream

Five hours before serving, preheat oven to 325 degrees. Place eight 5-ounce custard cups or ten 3-ounce pot-de-creme cups in baking pan. Combine cream and sugar in medium saucepan; cook over medium heat, stirring occasionally, until sugar is dissolved and mixture is hot. Remove from heat; stir in vanilla. Beat egg yolks until blended but not frothy; gradually add hot mixture, stirring constantly. Strain, using fine strainer, into 4-cup measure; pour into cups. Set baking pan on oven rack; pour hot water to ½-inch level around cups. Bake 25 to 30 minutes or until mixture begins to set around edges. Immediately remove cups from water; place on wire rack. Cool 30 minutes; refrigerate,

(Continued on next page)

covered, at least 4 hours. For chocolate curls let chocolate stand in paper wrapper in warm place 15 minutes. For large curls draw vegetable scraper across broad flat surface of square. For small curls, draw scraper across side of square; lift curls with wooden pick to avoid breaking. Top each cup with whipped cream and chocolate curls. For variety use 1 tablespoon instant coffee powder and reduce vanilla measurement to 1 teaspoon. Or use 1½ squares unsweetened chocolate, broken; reduce vanilla measurement to 1 teaspoon and use 4 egg yolks. Yield: 8-10 servings.

Mrs. Vernene Boyd, Chico, Cal.

 ### Delicate Nut Roll (Germany)

> 6 *eggs, separated*
> ¾ *c. plus 3 tbsp. sugar*
> 1 *tsp. baking powder*
> 1 *c. wheat germ*
> ½ *c. grated pecans*
> 1 ½ *c. heavy cream*
> ¼ *tsp. vanilla*
> *Confectioners' sugar*

Beat egg whites until stiff. Beat egg yolks with same beater until thick, gradually adding ¾ cup sugar. Combine baking powder, wheat germ and pecans; fold into egg yolk mixture. Fold in egg whites; spread in waxed paper-lined 15 x 10 x 1-inch pan. Bake at 350 degrees for 20 minutes. Remove from oven and cover with damp cloth; chill in refrigerator. Turn cake out on cloth; remove waxed paper. Beat cream until it begins to thicken; gradually add remaining sugar and vanilla. Continue beating until cream holds its shape; spread on cake. Roll cake gently from narrow end; chill in refrigerator. Sprinkle with confectioners' sugar; serve. Yield: 8-10 servings.

Mrs. Chester Jelesnianski, Springfield, Va., Favorite Recipes Food Fair

 ### Kugelhoff Mit Haselnuss—Hazelnut Coffee Cake (Germany)

> ½ *c. milk*
> 1 *pkg. dry yeast*
> 2 ⅔ *c. sifted all-purpose flour*
> 1 *c. seedless raisins*
> ⅔ *c. butter or margarine*
> ½ *c. sugar*

(Continued on next page)

4 eggs
2 tsp. light rum
¾ tsp. salt
2 tsp. grated lemon peel
¼ c. graham cracker crumbs
⅓ c. whole filberts, toasted
1 c. toasted chopped filberts
Confectioners' sugar

Scald milk; cool to lukewarm. Dissolve yeast in ¼ cup warm water; add to milk. Beat in 1 cup flour. Cover bowl with towel; let rise in warm place for 1 hour and 30 minutes. Plump raisins in 1 cup boiling water; drain. Cream butter and sugar until light and fluffy; add eggs, 1 at a time, beating well after each addition. Stir in rum and salt; stir in yeast mixture and remaining flour. Beat until smooth; stir in lemon peel and raisins. Beat batter for 10 to 15 minutes or until shiny and elastic. Generously grease a 2-quart mold; coat with graham cracker crumbs. Arrange whole filberts in bottom of mold; carefully pour in 1/3 the batter. Sprinkle with half the chopped filberts; add another 1/3 the batter. Sprinkle with remaining chopped filberts; add remaining batter. Cover mold and let rise in warm place about 1 hour. Bake at 350 degrees for 55 to 60 minutes or until cake tests done. Let cool in pan 15 minutes. Remove from pan; sprinkle with confectioners' sugar, if desired. Serve warm or cool. Yield: 1 cake.

Photograph for this recipe below.

Lebkuchen (Germany)

    2 c. flour
    1 tsp. cinnamon
    1 tsp. nutmeg
    1 tsp. salt
    ½ tsp. cardamom
    ½ tsp. baking powder
    2 c. brown sugar
    ½ c. chopped citron or chopped mixed candied fruit
    ½ c. chopped walnuts
    2 drops oil of anise
    1 tsp. vanilla
    Powdered sugar icing

Sift together first 6 ingredients; set aside. Mix sugar, citron and walnuts; add dry ingredients, oil of anise and vanilla. Add a little water if needed. Spread thinly in greased 10 x 15 x ¾-inch pan. Bake at 350 degrees for 15 minutes or until brown. Immediately cut in squares and remove from pan. Ice with powdered sugar icing.

Mrs. Leland Kimball, Officers' Wives' Club, San Diego, Cal.

 ## Kaidopita—Nut Cake (Greece)

    6 eggs, separated
    2 ½ c. sugar
    1 c. ground or chopped nuts
    ½ c. toasted bread crumbs
    1 ½ c. water
    ¼ tsp. cinnamon
    Juice of ½ lemon

Beat egg whites until stiff; set aside. Beat egg yolks with 1 cup sugar; fold in egg whites. Add nuts and crumbs; pour batter into lightly greased 8-inch square pan. Bake at 325 degrees for 35 minutes or until golden brown. Cook remaining sugar, water, cinnamon and lemon juice over low heat until cake is done. Cut warm cake into diamond-shaped servings; pour syrup over cake. Yield: 8 servings.

Mrs. Glenna Beckholt, Fredericktown, Ohio

 ## Baklava—Pastry (Greece)

    2 lbs. chopped walnuts
    1 tsp. cinnamon
    ½ tsp. ground cloves

(Continued on next page)

¾ *lb. butter*
1 *lb. pastry sheets phyllo (purchased at Greek stores)*
½ *pt. honey*
¼ *tsp. lemon extract*
1 *lb. sugar*
Juice of ½ lemon

Combine walnuts and spices. Melt butter, removing salt until butter is clear. Brush bottom of 10 x 14-inch pan with melted butter. Place 1 pastry sheet over butter; brush with melted butter. Repeat 3 times; sprinkle fourth pastry layer with nut mixture. Repeat process until nut mixture is all used; end with 4 layers of pastry brushed with butter. Cut into diamond shapes. Bake at 300 degrees until golden brown. Boil remaining ingredients to make syrup. Cool. Using a spoon, pour syrup very slowly over baked Baklava. Yield: 20-25 servings.

Niki Sitaras, Warren, Mich., Favorite Recipes Food Fair

Hagelslag (Holland)

1 *c. margarine or butter*
1 *c. sugar*
1 *egg, separated*
2 *c. flour*
½ *tsp. salt*
1 ½ to 2 *tsp. cinnamon*
1 *tbsp. water*
1 *c. chopped nuts*

Cream margarine and sugar; add egg yolk. Mix well. Sift flour, salt and cinnamon; add gradually to creamed mixture. Pat dough evenly into thin layer in foil-lined 17 x 12-inch jelly roll pan. Blend water with egg white; stir until syrupy, but not foamy. Pour over cookie dough. Tilt the pan in all directions until dough is well coated. Sprinkle nuts over top. Bake at 300 degrees for 30 minutes. Turn off heat; leave in oven for 15 minutes. Cut into fingers or squares while warm. Yield: 48 cookies.

Ruth C. Peabody, Sunnyside, Wash.

Dobas Torta (Hungary)

¾ *c. sugar*
12 *eggs, separated*
7 *tbsp. flour*
½ *tsp. baking powder*

Beat sugar and egg yolks well; add flour. Mix; add baking powder. Beat egg whites very stiff; fold slowly into egg yolk mixture. Pour a thin layer of batter into 6 well-greased 8-inch cake pans. Bake at 350 degrees for 5 minutes.

(Continued on next page)

ICING:

> ½ lb. butter
> 1 egg yolk
> ½ tsp. coffee
> 1 square chocolate or ¼ c. cocoa
> 1 lb. powdered sugar
> 1 tsp. vanilla

Combine all ingredients well. Frost between layers and top of torte. Yield: 10 servings.

Mrs. Marilyn Frederick, Wampum, Pa., Favorite Recipes Food Fair

 ## Ponnukokur—Pancakes (Iceland)

> 3 eggs
> 2 c. milk
> 1 c. flour
> ½ tsp. salt
> ½ tsp. vanilla
> 1 tbsp. sugar
> 4 tbsp. (about) butter or margarine

Combine all ingredients in electric blender; blend for few seconds. Heat 6 or 8-inch teflon saute pan. Butter slightly. Pour in 2 tablespoon batter; tilt pan to cover bottom. Fry until lightly browned; turn. Keep warm in folded towel in warm oven. Serve for dessert with whipped cream and fresh fruit. Yield: 6-7 servings.

Melba E. Heide, Mt. Home, Idaho

 ## Soda Bread (Ireland)

> 3 c. sifted flour
> ⅔ c. sugar
> 3 tsp. baking powder
> 1 tsp. soda
> 1 tsp. salt
> 1 ½ c. currants or raisins
> 2 eggs, beaten
> 1 ¾ to 2 c. buttermilk
> 2 tbsp. melted shortening

Sift first 5 ingredients together; stir in currants. Combine eggs, buttermilk and shortening; add to dry ingredients. Mix just until flour is moistened; turn batter into greased loaf pan. Bake at 350 degrees for approximately 1 hour. Remove bread from pan immediately.

Mrs. Patrick Hillery, Chicago, Ill.

Haman Taschen (Israel)

½ lb. golden raisins
½ lb. dried apricots
1 lb. prunes, pitted
¼ lb. coconut
¼ c. strawberry jam
1 c. butter
1 c. sugar
4 eggs
2 tsp. vanilla
4 c. flour
4 tsp. baking powder

Grind raisins, apricots and prunes; mix thoroughly with coconut and jam. Set aside. Cream butter, sugar and eggs together; beat in vanilla. Sift flour and baking powder; add to creamed mixture, working in thoroughly. Roll out; cut into squares. Place a scant tablespoon filling on each square; fold to make triangles. Place on greased cookie sheet. Bake at 375 degrees for 30 minutes. Yield: 50 turnovers.

Personal Comment: These are served at the Feast of Purim, commemorating Queen Esther's saving the Jewish people from destruction at the hands of the wicked Haman.

Myrtle Mack, Ilwaco, Wash.

 ## Cannoli—Cream Rolls (Italy)

3 c. flour
¼ c. sugar
1 tsp. cinnamon
¼ tsp. salt
3 tbsp. shortening
2 eggs, well beaten
2 tbsp. white vinegar
2 tbsp. cold water
1 egg white, slightly beaten
½ c. pistachio nuts, chopped
Sifted confectioners' sugar

Sift first 4 ingredients into a bowl; cut in shortening until size of peas. Stir in eggs; blend in vinegar and water, 1 tablespoon at a time. Turn dough onto lightly floured surface and knead; wrap in waxed paper and chill for 30 minutes. Roll chilled dough ⅛ inch thick on floured surface; cut into oval shapes. Wrap dough loosely around tubes just lapping over opposite edges. Seal edges by brushing with egg white. Fry in 360-degree deep fat for 8 minutes or until golden brown, turning occasionally. Drain over fat before removing to absorbent paper. Cool slightly; remove tubes. Cool completely; fill with ricotta filling. Sprinkle ends of Cannoli with chopped nuts; dust shells with confectioners' sugar.

(Continued on next page)

RICOTTA FILLING:

    3 c. ricotta cheese
    1 ¼ c. sugar
    2 tsp. vanilla extract
    ½ c. finely chopped candied citron
    ¼ c. semisweet chocolate pieces

Mix all ingredients thoroughly; chill. Yield: 16-18 servings.

                        Mrs. John Gudeman, Stanford, Ill.

Zabaglione—Wine Custard (Italy)

    6 egg yolks
    Marsala wine
    3 tbsp. sugar

Beat egg yolks in top of double boiler, gradually adding 4 half eggshells of marsala wine and sugar; cook over hot water, beating vigorously, until very thick. Serve hot. Yield: 4 servings.

                        Rosalie Race, New City, N. Y.

Quesillo (Mexico)

    ¾ qt. frozen pineapple juice
    3 c. sugar
    12 eggs
    ½ c. raisins

Boil pineapple juice and sugar together until about a pint of syrup remains. Reserve 1 cup syrup. Beat eggs until light and fluffy; add remaining syrup. Add raisins; pour into 2-quart mold. Place mold in pan of water. Bake at 350 degrees for 1 hour or until done. Cool. Place on a platter; pour reserved syrup over custard. Garnish with pineapple, if desired.

                        Mrs. Mildred Christofeno, Elkhart, Ind.

Lefse (Norway)

    3 c. mashed potatoes, cooled
    ½ c. lard or shortening
    1 tbsp. sugar
    1 tsp. salt
    ½ tsp. baking powder
    1 ½ c. flour

(Continued on next page)

Place mashed potatoes in bowl; cut in lard. Sift together remaining ingredients; add to potato mixture. Knead; shape into pieces the size of a walnut. Roll thin as paper with a lined rolling pin on a floured board. Bake on lefse baker or griddle until lightly browned, turning only once. If desired, spread with butter and sprinkle with additional sugar and cinnamon. Fold, cut and serve. Yield: 8-10 servings.

Janice Olson, Mobridge, S. D.

 ## Brandy Krumkake (Norway)

    4 eggs
    1 c. sugar
    ½ c. water
    1 c. flour
    1 tsp. ground cardamom
    1 tsp. almond extract
    1 tbsp. brandy
    ½ c. melted butter

Beat eggs; add remaining ingredients. Beat until well mixed; drop 2 teaspoons mixture onto hot Krumkake iron. Bake. Remove from iron and roll on peg immediately. Yield: 12 dozen krumkakes.

Mrs. Patricia S. Irrthum, Wanamingo, Minn.

 ## Malasadas—Doughnuts (Portugal)

    1 cake yeast
    ⅓ c. plus 1 tsp. sugar
    2 lb. flour
    1 tsp. salt
    1 ⅓ c. cream
    ⅓ c. butter, melted
    8 eggs, slightly beaten

Dissolve yeast in 1/3 cup warm water with 1 teaspoon sugar. Place flour, remaining sugar and salt in large bowl. Mix cream and 1 1/3 cups warm water together; add to dry ingredients. Add butter and eggs; add dissolved yeast. Mix well to form a soft dough; cover and let stand in warm place for 1 hour and 30 minutes or until doubled. Drop by spoonfuls into deep hot oil; fry until light brown. Drain on absorbent paper. Yield: 5 dozen doughnuts.
Personal Comment: This is served on Shrove Tuesday before Lent.

Avis E. Colgrove, Fort Lupton, Colo.

Blinchiki—Pancakes (Russia)

 2 tbsp. (heaping) flour
 1 tbsp. sugar
 ½ tsp. baking powder
 2 eggs
 Milk
 ¼ tsp. butter

Mix dry ingredients. Add eggs and mix to a paste. Dribble in enough milk to make batter consistency of sweet cream. Heat 8-inch skillet with butter. Drop just enough batter in skillet to thinly cover bottom. Quickly drain off excess batter. Fry on one side until pancake bubbles; cool.

FILLING:

 1 carton creamed cottage cheese, drained
 ¾ c. sugar
 1 tsp. nutmeg
 1 tsp. vanilla

Combine all ingredients, mixing well. Place 1 heaping tablespoon cheese filling in center of brown side of pancake. Fold like envelope and roll. May be frozen at this stage. When ready to serve, brown in sizzling sweet butter. Serve with sour cream and jam or fresh fruit. Yield: 4 servings.

Mrs. Paul A. Adams, Officers' Wives' Club, US Nav. Supp. Act., Villefranche,
France

Mazourka—Walnut Cake (Russia)

 9 eggs, separated
 2 c. sugar
 3 c. flour
 1 lb. walnuts, ground
 ½ lb. candied fruit peel, ground
 2 tbsp. lemon juice

Beat egg yolks in bowl; add sugar and beat well. Beat egg whites in a separate bowl until stiff, but not dry and fold into yolk mixture carefully. Add flour, walnuts, candied fruit and lemon juice, mixing lightly. Preheat oven to 325 degrees. Butter a flat pan, about 8 x 12-inches and dust lightly with flour. Pour mixture into pan. Bake at 325 degrees for 30 minutes or until a cake tester comes out clean. Dust with powdered sugar. The resulting cake will be about 1-inch high and should be served in long, thin slices. Yield: Twenty-four 2-inch squares.

Mrs. Sandi Hartmann, Home Economics Teacher, Riverside, Cal.

Oatmeal Scones (Scotland)

> 3 c. rolled oats
> 3 c. all-purpose flour
> 2 c. shortening
> 1 tbsp. salt
> 1 c. brown sugar
> ¼ c. cold water

Preheat oven to 400 degrees. Mix all ingredients together in order given until consistency to roll. Roll to about ¼-inch thickness on lightly floured board. Cut in squares or desired shapes; place 1 inch apart on ungreased cookie sheet. Bake 20 minutes or until golden brown. Yield: 3-4 dozen scones.

Anne Thurbide, Reno, Nev.

 ### Shortbread (Scotland)

> ½ c. sugar
> Pinch of salt
> ½ lb. butter
> 2 c. flour

Cream together sugar, salt and butter; add flour, a little at a time. Dough should come into a stiff ball. Using fingers, roll into small balls; place on cookie sheet and prick each cookie 3 times with a fork. Bake in a 300-degree oven for 1 hour until very light in color. Do not preheat oven. Yield: 36 cookies.

Mrs. James Stultz, Mundelein, Ill.

Flan—Caramel Custard (Spain)

> 1 ½ c. sugar
> 8 eggs
> 4 c. milk
> 1 stick cinnamon
> 1 tsp. vanilla
> ⅓ tsp. salt

Caramelize ½ cup sugar by cooking in a pan or skillet until melted and a golden brown, stirring constantly. While still hot, spread evenly over bottom of a shallow 2-quart casserole or in individual dishes. Cool. Beat eggs until foamy; gradually add remaining sugar, beating well after each addition. Scald milk with the cinnamon stick. Gradually add hot milk to egg mixture, stirring constantly until sugar is dissolved. Add vanilla and salt. Pour into casserole. Place in hot water. Bake at 375 degrees for 1 hour and 10 minutes. Cool. Yield: 8-10 servings.

Mrs. Henry Mills, Jr., Del Rio, Tex., Favorite Recipes Food Fair

 Merengues De Cafe—Coffee Meringue (Spain)

> *4 egg whites, at room temperature*
> *¼ tsp. cream of tartar*
> *¼ tsp. salt*
> *1 c. sugar*
> *1 tbsp. powdered instant coffee*

Preheat oven to 275°. Combine egg whites, cream of tartar and salt. With electric mixer or rotary beater, beat egg whites until soft, moist peaks form. Gradually add sugar, 1 tablespoon at a time, beating well after each addition. Add coffee with last sugar and continue beating until very stiff, glossy peaks form. Spread half of the meringue on bottom of well-buttered 10-inch pie plate. Using a spatula or pastry tube, swirl or pipe remaining meringue around sides and rim of plate, making a decorative edge. Bake 1 hour or until crisp to the touch. Cool before filling. Yield: 8 servings.

Photograph for this recipe on page 331.

Holiday Custard (Sweden)

> *2 eggs*
> *¼ c. flour*
> *½ c. sugar*
> *1 12-oz. carton small curd cottage cheese*
> *1 c. whipping cream*
> *1 c. milk*
> *1 tsp. almond extract*
> *1 c. lingonberries*

Beat eggs slightly. Add flour, sugar, cottage cheese, ½ cup cream, milk and extract. Pour into a 1-quart casserole dish. Bake at 375 degrees for 45 minutes or until set. Serve warm or chilled with remaining whipped cream topped with lingonberries. Yield: 6 servings.

Mrs. Barbara Klish, Home Economics Teacher, Plainville, Kan.

Fruit Soup (Sweden)

1 c. prunes
1 c. dried peaches
1 c. dried pears
1 c. dried apricots
½ c. raisins
1 apple
3 qt. water
1 c. fruit juice
Pinch salt
1 stick cinnamon
½ c. red sage
2 c. sugar
2 tsp. potato flour or cornstarch

Soak prunes, peaches, pears and apricots before using. Cook all ingredients together for about 1 hour, thickening with potato flour. Other fruits may be added, if desired. Yield: 8 servings.

Mrs. Alice Hansberger, Home Economics Teacher, Canton, Ill.

 ### Saffron Bread (Sweden)

½ tsp. saffron
1 c. lukewarm cream or milk
2 pkg. active dry yeast or compressed yeast
⅓ c. sugar
½ tsp. salt
1 egg, beaten
½ c. butter or margarine, melted
½ c. raisins
4 c. sifted all-purpose flour

Dry saffron a few minutes in low oven to keep its color. Crush with mortar and pestle or with a spoon in a bowl until powdery. Spoon 1 tablespoon warm cream over saffron and let stand for a few minutes. Dissolve yeast in remaining cream; add sugar, salt, egg, butter, raisins, dissolved saffron and half of the flour. Beat with wooden spoon until well blended. Gradually add more flour until dough is smooth and not too firm. Turn dough out onto floured surface and knead for 10 minutes. Place dough in a buttered bowl, turning dough so that it will be greased on all sides. Cover with towel and let rise in a warm place until double in bulk, about 1 hour and 30 minutes. Punch down dough. Knead dough lightly. Four hands and shape buns. Pinch off small pieces of dough and roll out on floured surface into 7-inch long strips. Pinch 2 strips together in center; curl in each end. Stick a raisin in each curl. Place buns on buttered cookie sheet. Cover; let rise for about 45 minutes or until impression remains, when finger is gently pressed into dough. Brush buns with beaten egg. Bake in 400-degree oven for 10 to 15 minutes. If desired, roll dough out in

(Continued on next page)

thinner strips and place 3 together to have 6 curls. Or you can just have one thick strip and roll ends into an S-shaped bun. Yield: 20 buns.

Personal Comment: Saffron Bread is traditional Christmas sweet bread served on the thirteenth of December, the day of St. Lucia, with early morning coffee.

Mrs. George J. Lippert, Kent, Wash., Favorite Recipes Food Fair

Meyva Kompostosu-Fruit Compote (Turkey)

1 ½ tbsp. gelatin
¼ c. cold water
1 ½ c. hot unsweetened grape juice
¾ c. sugar
⅛ tsp. salt
1 tsp. lemon juice
1 tsp. grated lemon rind
⅓ c. Cointreau
1 c. strawberries
1 c. seedless green grapes
1 c. pitted black cherries
1 c. fresh peach halves
Whipped cream

Soften gelatin in cold water; stir in hot grape juice, sugar and salt. Stir until sugar and gelatin are completely dissolved; cool. Stir in lemon juice and rind; chill until beginning to set. Add Cointreau and whisk well. Add fruits; pour into an oiled mold. Chill until set. Unmold and serve with whipped cream flavored with Cointreau. Yield: 8-10 servings.

Mrs. Paul M. Dickens, Moody, Ga.

Plum Dumplings (Yugoslavia)

3 med. potatoes
2 heaping tbsp. Crisco
2 small eggs
Flour
12 blue plums, pitted
4 tbsp. sugar
Buttered crumbs

Boil potatoes in jackets, peel and mash. Add Crisco, eggs and enough flour to make a soft dough. Divide dough into 12 sections. Pat each section into a 4-inch circle. Place a plum and 1 teaspoon sugar into each circle. Bring the edges together and smooth out; twist top. Drop into boiling salted water and cook for 20 minutes after boiling point has been reached. Drain and roll in buttered crumbs. Yield: 1 dozen.

Rose Shular, Home Economics Teacher, Ottawa, Kan.

Special Occasion Desserts

Confetti Pie

    6 *eggs, separated*
    3 *c. sugar*
    3 *lb. ricotta cheese*
    ¼ *lb. candied pineapple*
    ¼ *lb. candied red cherries*
    1 *tsp. vanilla*
    ¼ *c. toasted almonds*
    ¼ *c. pinnulla nuts*
    1 *6-oz. pkg. semisweet chocolate chips*
    2 *partially cooked pie crusts*

Cream egg yolks and sugar together. Add remaining ingredients, except egg whites and pie crusts. Mix thoroughly. Beat egg whites and fold into mixture. Pour into partially-cooked pie crusts. Bake at 350 degrees until top browns. Yield: 16-24 servings.

Fran Wray, Clark, N. J.

New Year Daiquiri Mold

    2 *envelopes unflavored gelatin*
    2 *c. sugar*
    ⅛ *tsp. salt*
    6 *eggs, separated*
    ½ *c. water*
    1 *c. fresh lime or lemon juice*
    ⅔ *c. white rum*
    2 *c. heavy cream, whipped*

Heat and stir gelatin, 1½ cups sugar and salt together in saucepan. Beat egg yolks, water and lime juice together until combined; gradually stir into gelatin until mixture thickens slightly and gelatin dissolves, 6 to 12 minutes. Do not boil. Stir in rum; chill, stirring occasionally, until mixture mounds slightly when dropped from a spoon. In a large bowl, beat egg whites until they hold stiff straight peaks; gradually beat in remaining sugar. Continue to beat until very stiff; fold gelatin mixture into egg whites. Fold cream into mixture; turn

(Continued on next page)

into a 10-cup shallow mold. Chill until firm; unmold. Decorate with angelica to form the face of a clock.

Mrs. Catherine D. Myers, Las Cruces, N. M.

 ## Valentine Cake

 2 ½ c. sifted cake flour
 1 ½ c. sugar
 3 ½ tsp. baking powder
 1 tsp. salt
 ½ c. shortening
 ¾ c. milk
 ¼ c. maraschino cherry juice
 1 tsp. vanilla extract
 1 tsp. almond extract
 4 egg whites
 18 maraschino cherries, well drained and finely chopped
 ½ c. walnuts, finely chopped

Sift dry ingredients into mixing bowl and add shortening. Combine milk and cherry juice. Add ¾ cup liquid to dry ingredients. Add flavoring extracts. Beat 2 minutes by hand or low speed of mixer. Add remaining liquid and egg whites and beat 2 minutes. Blend in cherries and nuts. Pour into 2 aluminum heart pans which have been lined with waxed paper. Frost with Seven-Minute frosting. Garnish with additional cherries, if desired.

Lotus Wingfield, Wray, Colo.

Meringue Hearts With Strawberry Ice Cream

 3 egg whites
 Dash of salt
 ½ tsp. vinegar
 ¼ tsp. vanilla
 1 c. sugar
 ½ gal. strawberry ice cream

Place egg whites in small deep bowl of electric mixer. Add salt, vinegar, vanilla to whites. Beat on high speed until peaks form. Gradually add sugar until whites are very stiff. Make 6 mounds of egg white on a cookie sheet covered with brown paper. With the back of a teaspoon, form each mound into a heart shell. Bake in 300-degree oven for 45 minutes. Remove from paper immediately. Cool. Fill meringue hearts with scoop of ice cream.

Darlene Hicks, Atlanta, Tex.

Cherry Bavarian Valentine

  2 *envelopes unflavored gelatin*
  1 *tsp. ginger*
  ¼ *tsp. salt*
     Syrup from maraschino cherries, plus water to equal ¾ c.
  6 *eggs, separated*
  1 ¼ *c. milk*
  1 *jar maraschino cherries, chopped*
     Red food coloring, optional
  ½ *c. sugar*
  2 *c. heavy cream, whipped*

In top of double boiler, mix together gelatin, ginger, salt and maraschino cherry syrup. Stir in egg yolks and milk; blend thoroughly. Cook over boiling water, stirring constantly, until gelatin dissolves and mixture thickens slightly. Remove from heat and chill until mixture mounds from spoon; stir in chopped maraschino cherries and a few drops red coloring. Beat egg whites until soft peaks form; gradually add sugar and beat very stiff. Fold in cherry mixture. Reserve ¾ cup whipped cream. Fold remaining whipped cream into cherry mixture. Turn into 10-cup heart-shaped mold; chill 4 hours or overnight. Unmold onto serving plate and outline heart shape with additional cherries. Force reserved whipped cream through star tube in cake decorator to make lace fluting around cherry heart. Yield: 10-12 servings.

Photograph for this recipe below.

Hot Cross Buns

1 ½ c. scalded milk
1 c. lukewarm mashed potatoes
1 c. soft margarine or butter
⅔ c. white sugar
1 ½ tsp. salt
2 cakes compressed yeast
½ c. warm water
2 eggs, slightly beaten
5 to 6 c. all-purpose flour
1 tsp. cinnamon
¼ tsp. nutmeg
1 c. raisins
½ c. citron
Confectioners' sugar icing

Combine milk, potatoes, margarine, sugar and salt in large mixing bowl. Let stand until lukewarm. Add yeast softened in water. Add eggs and 1½ cups flour; beat well. Cover; let stand in warm place 1 hour or until full of bubbles. Stir in 3½ to 4½ cups flour to make a stiff dough. Knead 10 minutes on floured board. Return to greased bowl; let rise until double in bulk. Divide dough into thirds. Combine cinnamon, nutmeg, raisins and citron. Add filling to each third. Roll out dough to ¼ to ½-inch thickness; cut with 2 to 3-inch cookie cutter. With a sharp knife cut a cross on top of each. Let rise until double in bulk. Bake at 425 degrees 15 minutes. Decorate cross on top with confectioners' sugar icing with decorator tube. Yield: 3-4 dozen.

Mrs. Billy Jefferson, Greenville, Miss.

Easter Delight French Savarin Cake

2 pkg. yeast
¼ c. lukewarm water
½ c. milk
⅓ c. sugar
1 tsp. salt
⅔ c. melted butter
4 c. sifted flour
1 ½ tsp. vanilla extract
4 eggs, beaten
Confectioners' sugar icing
Chopped blanched almonds
Candied fruit pieces

(Continued on next page)

Soften yeast in water; scald milk. Add sugar, salt and butter; cool to luke-warm. Add enough flour to make a thick batter; mix well. Add softened yeast, vanilla extract and eggs; beat well. Add more flour to make a stiff batter. Beat thoroughly until smooth. Cover and let rise in warm place until bubbly. Stir down. Turn batter into well-greased 10-inch tube pan. Let rise until doubled in bulk. Bake at 350 degrees for 35 minutes. Remove from pan and cool. Drizzle with confectioners' sugar icing and decorate with almonds and fruit. Yield: 12-15 servings.

Mrs. D. T. Hamilton, Home Economics Teacher, Michie, Tenn.

 ## Easter Lily Cookies

>   *1 c. egg yolks*
>   *1 c. sugar*
>   *½ tsp. vanilla*
>   *Pinch of salt*
>   *1 c. flour*

Beat egg yolks until light; add sugar gradually, beating constantly. Add vanilla and salt. Stir in flour with spoon. Drop batter onto greased baking tin and spread out, making a flat circle 2½ to 3 inches in diameter. Make 3 or 4 circles. Bake at 375 degrees until tinged with brown, 10 to 13 minutes. Remove pan from oven and place on oven door; quickly shape cookies into lillies. Serve filled with whipped cream and garnish with cherries.

Mrs. Robert Rowland, Hopkins, Minn.

 ## Butter-Cream Easter Eggs

>   *½ lb. plus 1 tbsp. butter*
>   *1 8-oz. pkg. of cream cheese*
>   *3 boxes confectioners' sugar*
>   *8 oz. bitter or semisweet chocolate*
>   *1 2-in. square wax*
>   *¼ tsp. vanilla*

Cream ½ pound butter and cream cheese; gradually blend in sugar. Shape into small eggs. Cool for about 1 hour. Melt chocolate, remaining butter, wax and vanilla over hot water. Dip eggs in mixture and allow to cool. Yield: 90-100 eggs.

Mary H. Llewellyn, Home Economics Teacher, Lansford, Pa.

Caramel Easter Eggs

2 c. white sugar
1 c. brown sugar
½ c. water
1 c. evaporated milk
3 tbsp. dark corn syrup
⅛ tsp. salt
¼ lb. butter
2 c. finely chopped nuts
2 pkg. of dipping chocolate

Cook together in a 4-quart pan at medium heat white sugar, brown sugar, water, milk, syrup and salt until candy thermometer reaches 240 degrees or soft ball when dropped in water. Break butter in small pieces in bowl; add nuts. Pour in sugar mixture; let cool to touch. Beat until mixture becomes too stiff for mixer; turn onto marble slab or buttered surface. Knead with heel of hand until mixture is very velvety; shape into 4 eggs. Place on cake rack; put into refrigerator for 24 hours to set. Melt chocolate in top of double boiler; do not allow to boil or bubble. Dip eggs into chocolate; return to cake rack to drip. Return to refrigerator for 1 week to allow eggs to age. Can be decorated with cake icings. Yield: 4 eggs.

Mrs. Floyd R. Grimes, New Cumberland, W. Va.

Lamb Cake

½ c. shortening
1 ½ c. sugar
3 eggs, separated
2 ½ c. flour
½ tsp. salt
4 tsp. baking powder
1 tsp. vanilla
1 c. milk

Cream shortening; add sugar gradually, cream well. Add well beaten egg yolks and cream again. Sift flour, salt, baking powder together. Add vanilla to milk. Add dry ingredients to sugar mixture alternately with milk. Fold in stiffly beaten egg whites. Bake at 350 degrees in well greased lamb mold for 25 minutes on face of mold and 20 minutes on back. Before closing mold, place a tooth pick in each ear on top of batter, and place 1 skewer in neck for reinforcement. Cool. Cover with boiled icing. Add 2 raisins for eyes; add ribbon around neck. If desired, coconut may be tinted green with food coloring and placed around lamb cake on plate. Yield: 8 servings.

Mrs. Roy W. Liebau, Pittsburgh, Pa., Favorite Recipes Food Fair

Grasshopper Cream Cornucopias

¼ c. butter
½ c. blended maple syrup
½ c. flour
1 c. heavy cream
2 tbsp. creme de menthe
1 tbsp. clear creme de cacao

Heat butter and syrup over high heat until blended; boil hard about 30 seconds. Remove from heat; add flour, beating until smooth. Grease and warm a baking sheet; drop mixture by level tablespoonfuls about 2 inches apart onto sheet. Bake at 300 degrees 9 to 12 minutes. When slightly cool, remove each wafer and quickly lap over two edges to form cornucopia shape. Place on wire rack to cool. If wafers harden before they all are rolled, return to oven for a few seconds. Beat together heavy cream, creme de menthe and creme de cacao until stiff. Do not overbeat. Lightly spoon mixture into cornucopias without packing; wrap individually for freezing. Place in freezer at once. Serve without defrosting as finger food. Cornucopias may be stored in tightly covered container and filled with grasshopper cream at serving time. Yield: 12 servings.

Mrs. Edwin H. Moore, Roanoke, Va.

Mincemeat Cake

2 ½ c. flour
1 ½ tsp. baking powder
½ tsp. soda
½ tsp. salt
1 1-lb. jar mincemeat
1 c. white raisins
1 c. chopped nuts
1 c. sugar
½ c. melted butter
1 tsp. rum
2 eggs

Sift dry ingredients. Mix mincemeat with raisins, nuts, sugar, butter and rum. Add to dry ingredients. Add eggs, 1 at a time, beating well after each addition. Put into lightly greased and lined tube pan. Bake at 300 degrees for 1 hour and 30 minutes. Yield: 12 servings.

Mrs. Robert May, Birmingham, Ala.

 ### Candy Cane Cookies

½ c. soft shortening
½ c. sifted powdered sugar

(Continued on next page)

2 tbsp. slightly-beaten egg
1 ¼ c. sifted flour
½ tsp. salt
½ tsp. almond flavoring
½ tsp. vanilla
¼ tsp. red food coloring

Thoroughly blend shortening, sugar and egg. Mix in flour, salt and flavorings. Divide dough in half. Tint half of dough with red food coloring. Leave other part plain. Roll small piece of plain dough between palms to 6-inch length. Roll small piece of red dough in same manner to same length. Twist together and shape to resemble a cane. Bake at 375 degrees for 8 to 10 minutes. Yield: 2½ doz. cookies.

Mrs. J. F. Smith, Corpus Christi, Tex.

 ## Christmas Cheer Candy

3 c. sugar
1 c. white Karo syrup
1 ½ c. light cream
1 tsp. vanilla
½ lb. English black walnuts
½ lb. almonds
½ lb. pecans
½ lb. candied pineapple
½ lb. candied cherries

Place sugar, syrup and cream in a heavy aluminum boiler. Let come to a boil; boil for 8 minutes or until mixture forms a soft ball in water. Stir constantly while boiling. Remove from heat; add vanilla. Beat until mixture begins to thicken and is very light in color. Add nuts and fruit. Pour in a 10 x 15-inch buttered pan. Let cool and cut. Candy mellows with age and is much better after 2 or 3 weeks. May be frozen.

Mrs. John C. Martin, Clayton, Ala.

 ## Christmas Coconut Wreath

1 tbsp. unflavored gelatin
1 c. plus 2 tbsp. milk
1 c. sugar
2 c. heavy cream, whipped
2 c. finely grated fresh coconut
Red candied cherries
Green candied pineapple slices

Soften gelatin in 2 tablespoons of milk. Heat remaining milk. Add sugar. Stir in softened gelatin; cook until mixture thickens slightly. Remove from heat;

(Continued on next page)

beat until light and fluffy. Fold in whipped cream. Add coconut. Pour into wet ring mold. Chill until firm. Unmold onto flat platter, tray or plate; garnish with cherries and pineapple to resemble clusters of holly.

SAUCE:

> 1 c. brown sugar
> 1 c. sugar
> 2 tbsp. (level) flour
> ¼ lb. butter
> ⅔ c. light cream

Combine all ingredients; cook until thick. Serve with dessert. Yield: 12 servings.

Mrs. O. M. Harper, Clendenin, W. Va.

 Christmas Star Cookies

> 1 c. shortening
> 1 c. plus 2 tbsp. sugar
> 3 eggs
> 1 ½ tsp. each lemon and vanilla extract
> 3 c. sifted flour
> ⅛ tsp. salt
> 1 tsp. cream of tartar
> 1 tsp. soda

Cream shortening; gradually add sugar, beating until smooth and creamy. Add eggs and flavorings; beat thoroughly. Sift dry ingredients together. Add to creamed mixture. Set oven at 400 degrees. Roll dough ⅛-inch thick on well-floured board. Cut into star shape with cookie cutter. Place on ungreased cookie sheet. Bake 6 to 8 minutes. Yield: 4 dozen cookies.

Mrs. Ross Gutierrez, Hurst, Tex.

 Eggnog Cake

> 1 c. butter
> 2 c. sifted sugar
> 5 egg yolks
> ¼ c. brandy
> 1 c. slivered toasted almonds
> 1 angel food cake
> ½ pt. heavy cream, whipped

Cream butter and sugar; mix in egg yolks one at a time, blending well. Stir in brandy and ¾ cup nuts. Slice cake in thirds; fill with mixture. Chill 24 hours. Just before serving, frost with whipped cream. Sprinkle with remaining ¼ cup nuts. Yield: 16 servings.

Mrs. L. D. Haldeman, Hawthorne, Nev.

Festive Ice Cream Brick

1 c. whipping cream
¼ c. sugar
½ gal. brick cherry-vanilla ice cream
1 ¼ c. moist toasted coconut
9 maraschino cherries
6 sm. strips green citron

Combine whipping cream and sugar in bowl. Beat until cream will hold soft peaks. Peel carton from brick of ice cream; invert ice cream onto a well-chilled platter. Quickly spread whipped cream over top and sides; sprinkle with coconut. Arrange cherries on top in three clusters; add citron strips to resemble leaves. Freeze until ready to serve. Yield: 10-12 servings.

Mary L. Vaughn, Dallas, Tex.

Fruit Cookies

½ lb. white raisins
1 lb. candied cherries
1 lb. green and red pineapple
1 lb. pecans, cut up
Flour
2 c. sugar
1 lb. butter or oleo
3 eggs
½ tsp. cinnamon
1 tsp. soda
1 tsp. baking powder
1 tsp. vanilla

Dredge fruit and nuts with ½ cup flour. Beat well sugar, shortening and eggs. Sift 4 cups flour and dry ingredients together and add gradually to first mixture. Add vanilla. Add fruit and nuts. Mix with hands and form into rolls. Store in freezer. When ready to bake, slice ¼-inch thick and bake at 370 degrees for 10 minutes or until lightly browned. May be stored in freezer for a long time. Yield: 18-20 dozen cookies.

Mrs. Helen Coffman, Clyde, Ohio

Fruit-Nut Wreaths

> 1 c. soft butter or margarine
> ½ c. (firmly packed) brown sugar
> 1 egg
> 2 c. sifted flour
> ½ tsp. baking powder
> 1 c. rolled oats
> ¼ c. finely chopped pecans
> ¼ c. finely chopped red candied cherries
> Thin confectioners' sugar frosting
> Flaked or shredded coconut

Beat butter until creamy; add sugar gradually, beating until fluffy. Beat in egg. Sift flour and baking powder together; stir into butter mixture. Stir in oats, nuts and candied cherries. Shape into wreaths. Bake on ungreased cookie sheets in preheated 350-degree oven for 12 to 15 minutes. When cool, frost with thin white confectioners' sugar frosting. Sprinkle with coconut and decorate with additional small pieces of red candied cherries. Yield: 3½ dozen cookies.

Mrs. Evangeline Heasley, Corpus Christi, Tex.

Fruit Wreath Cake

> 1 box yellow cake mix
> 1 box white cake mix
> ½ box chocolate cake mix
> 1 tsp. orange flavoring
> ¼ tsp. grated orange rind
> 3 drops yellow food coloring
> ½ tsp. cinnamon
> ½ tsp. allspice
> ½ tsp. nutmeg
> 1 tsp. almond flavoring
> 5 drops red food coloring
> 1 tsp. lemon flavoring
> ¼ tsp. grated lemon rind

Prepare each cake mix batter separately, according to directions on box. Divide yellow mix batter in half. Add orange flavoring, orange rind and yellow food coloring to one half; add spices to other half. Pour each batter into a 9-inch layer pan and bake. Divide white batter in half. Blend almond flavoring and red food coloring into one half; blend lemon flavoring and lemon rind into other half. Pour each half into layer pans and bake. Bake chocolate batter in a 9-inch layer pan. Cool cakes. Put cake together with favorite filling, alternating golden, chocolate, rose, white and spice layers. Frost with a fluffy white frosting. Garnish with candied fruits to make a wreath. Yield: 12-16 servings.

Mrs. C. Schneider, Onamia, Minn.

Holiday Cranberry Cake

    1 c. sugar
    3 tbsp. butter
    2 c. flour
    3 tsp. baking powder
    ½ tsp. salt
    1 c. milk
    2 c. whole raw cranberries

Mix all ingredients thoroughly; pour into a 9 x 9-inch square pan. Bake at 350 degrees for 30 minutes. Serve hot.

BUTTER SAUCE:

    1 c. sugar
    ½ c. butter, melted
    ¾ c. cream

Combine all ingredients; heat to boiling point. Serve hot over cake. Yield: 9 servings.

Mrs. James D. Hereford, Mechanicsburg, Pa., Favorite Recipes Food Fair

Holiday Jewels

    ⅓ c. butter
    ½ c. sugar
    2 eggs, beaten
    1 ½ c. flour
    1 ½ tsp. soda
    ½ tsp. salt
    1 ½ tbsp. milk
    4 oz. bourbon
    1 lb. chopped dates
    ½ lb. choped candied pineapple
    1 lb. chopped green and red candied cherries
    4 c. chopped pecans

Cream butter and sugar. Mix in eggs and half the flour. Add soda and salt. Add milk and bourbon; beat well. Mix remaining flour with fruit-nut mixture. Blend all ingredients. Drop from teaspoon onto greased cookie sheet. Bake 15-25 minutes in 300-degree oven. Yield: 160 bite-size cookies.

Mrs. C. W. Wahl, Key West, Fla.

Holiday Pie

PIE SHELL:

    1 ¼ c. Brazil nuts
    3 tbsp. granulated sugar

(Continued on next page)

Put nuts through meat grinder, using fine knife. Add sugar and blend; press mixture to bottom and sides of 9-inch pie plate up to rim. Bake at 400 degrees for 8 minutes or until lightly browned.

FILLING:

>1 envelope unflavored gelatin
>¼ c. water
>3 eggs, separated
>½ c. sugar
>⅛ tsp. salt
>1 ½ c. milk, scalded
>½ c. thinly sliced glazed cherries
>2 tbsp. light rum

Soak gelatin in water. Beat egg yolks; add ¼ cup sugar and salt. Gradually stir in scalded milk. Cook in double boiler over very hot water until mixture coats metal spoon. Remove from heat; stir in gelatin. Chill until custard mounds when some is dropped from spoon. Whip until smooth. Add cherries and rum. Whip egg whites until they peak; add ¼ cup sugar gradually. Whip until stiff; fold into custard mixture. Pour into cooled pie shell. Chill overnight.

TOPPING:

>¼ c. Brazil nuts
>¾ c. heavy cream
>Sugar to taste

Soak Brazil nuts in boiling water 30 minutes. Whip cream; sweeten to taste. Spoon around edge of pie. Drain nuts; with sharp knife, shave over pie. Refrigerate until serving time. Yield: 6-8 servings.

Mrs. R. E. Sink, Naval Officers' Wives' Club, San Diego, Cal.

 ## Kris Kringle Animal Cookies

>½ c. butter
>½ c. shortening
>2 c. sugar
>3 eggs
>5 c. flour
>1 ½ tsp. cream of tartar
>1 ½ tsp. soda
>1 tsp. salt
>2 tbsp. milk
>2 tsp. vanilla
>2 tsp. almond extract
>Grated orange rind

Cream butter, shortening and sugar; add eggs and beat well. Add sifted dry ingredients alternately with liquid ingredients. Add orange rind. Chill. Roll on lightly floured surface. Cut any desired shape. Bake on greased cookie

(Continued on next page)

sheets at 400 degrees for 12-15 minutes. Cookies may be decorated when cool. A small amount of orange juice may be added to batter. However, batter should be stiff. Yield: 6 doz. cookies.

Mrs. William O. Antozzi, Fort Lee, Va.

 ## Marshmallow Christmas Wreaths

30 marshmallows
½ c. butter or oleo
½ tsp. vanilla
¼ tsp. green coloring
3 ½ c. cornflakes
Red hots and silver decorations

Melt marshmallows and oleo in double boiler; add vanilla and coloring. Stir in whole cornflakes while warm, drop on foil and shape into wreaths. Trim with red hots and silver decorations; keep cool or refrigerate. Yield: 1½ dozen cookies.

Sue A. Arnholt, Denver, Colo.

Oregon Christmas Tart

1 c. butter or margarine
1 c. white sugar
3 egg yolks
1 c. toasted finely chopped filberts
1 ¼ c. unsifted all-purpose flour
½ tsp. salt
3 c. fresh cranberries
½ c. (firmly packed) light brown sugar
3 to 4 tsp. grated orange peel
⅓ c. orange juice
Whole filberts

Cream butter and white sugar until light and fluffy. Stir in egg yolks, chopped filberts, flour and ¼ teaspoon salt. Mix well. Chill dough about 1 hour and 30 minutes or until firm enough to handle. Combine cranberries, brown sugar, orange peel, orange juice and remaining salt in medium saucepan. Bring to a boil. Simmer, uncovered, 10 to 15 minutes or until mixture is thick as jam. Cool. Set aside about ½ cup of dough. Press remaining dough against bottom and sides of 9½-inch tart or cake pan. Spread cranberry mixture over dough in pan. Roll out reserved dough to ¼-inch thickness on floured surface. Cut into strips. Arrange in a lattice pattern on top of cranberry mixture. Place a filbert in each square. Bake at 375 degrees for 40 minutes or until brown. Serve with sour cream, ice cream or whipped cream.

Mrs. Paul Bressner, Boise, Idaho

Snowballs

¾ c. soft butter
1 tsp. vanilla extract
1 tbsp. water
⅛ tsp. salt
⅓ c. sugar
2 c. sifted flour
1 c. chocolate pieces
1 c. finely chopped pecans
Powdered sugar

Combine first 5 ingredients; blend well. Stir in flour and chocolate pieces. Form into 1-inch balls; roll in chopped pecans. Place on ungreased cookie sheet. Bake at 300 degrees for 30 minutes. Roll in powdered sugar while warm or for that extra holiday decoration, use red or green tinted sugar. Yield: 5 doz. cookies.

Mrs. A. L. Cummings, Del Rio, Tex.

 ## Springerle Christmas Cookies

4 eggs
1 lb. confectioners' sugar
3 ½ c. cake flour
Grated rind of 1 lemon
1 tbsp. melted butter
8 drops anise oil
½ tsp. anise seed
1 tsp. baking powder

Beat eggs and sugar for 1 hour. Add 1 cup cake flour, grated lemon rind and butter. Add remaining flour, anise oil and seed. Mix in baking powder. Chill dough. Roll out to ¼-inch thickness. Press with springerle rolling pin and cut in squares. Keep cool overnight. Separate and place on a greased cookie sheet. Bake at 325 degrees for 20 minutes. Store in tight container for 3 to 4 weeks.

Mrs. Walter L. Clarke, Jr., Lemoore, Cal.

Steamed Fig Pudding

⅓ c. shortening
⅔ c. sugar
2 eggs, beaten
¼ c. finely chopped citron
⅓ c. diced candied orange peel
1 c. chopped dried figs
½ c. chopped nuts

(Continued on next page)

½ tsp. salt
2 tsp. baking powder
4 c. graham cracker crumbs
1 c. milk

Cream shortening and sugar. Add beaten eggs; mix well. Stir in figs, orange peel, citron and nuts. Combine salt, baking powder and cracker crumbs; add alternately with milk to fruit mixture. Place in greased 6-cup mold; cover. Steam for 3 hours. Unmold; serve with hard sauce. Yield: 10-12 servings.

 ## Birthday Cake A La Creme

3 sq. unsweetened chocolate
2 ½ c. sifted cake flour
1 tsp. salt
1 tsp. baking soda
¾ c. shortening
1 ½ c. granulated sugar
4 eggs
1 tbsp. grated lemon rind
1 c. milk

Preheat oven to 350 degrees. Lightly grease two 9-inch layer cake pans 1½ inches deep. Melt unsweetened chocolate in double boiler over warm water. Cool slightly. Sift flour with salt and baking soda. Cream shortening with sugar at high speed. Beat in eggs, 1 at a time, until light and fluffy. Beat in lemon rind. Add flour mixture alternately with milk in small amounts, beating well after each addition. Stir in unsweetened chocolate until well blended. Pour into 2 lightly-greased 9-inch layer pans. Bake 30-40 minutes at 350 degrees. Cool in pans on wire racks for 10 minutes; remove from pans and cool.

COCOA-BUTTER FILLING:

2 sq. semisweet chocolate
1 c. butter or margarine
¾ c. confectioners' sugar
½ c. cocoa
1 tsp. vanilla extract
2 c. heavy cream, whipped

With vegetable parer, shred warm semisweet chocolate into curls; refrigerate. Cream butter; gradually beat in sugar, cocoa and vanilla until fluffy. Spread between layers. Mound whipped cream on top of cake around edge in large circle. Sprinkle with chocolate curls. Refrigerate until needed. Yield: 12 servings.

*Mrs. W. S. Palmer, Pres. Officers' Wives' Club, Roosevelt Rds., Naval Sta.,
Puerto Rico*

Miami Beach Birthday Cake

1 c. semisweet chocolate morsels
½ c. graham cracker crumbs
⅓ c. melted butter
½ c. chopped walnuts
2 c. sifted flour
1 tsp. soda
1 tsp. salt
½ c. soft butter
1 ½ c. plus 2 tbsp. sugar
2 eggs
1 tsp. vanilla
1 ¼ c. buttermilk or sour milk
1 c. heavy cream

Heat oven to 375 degrees. Melt 1/3 cup chocolate morsels. Grease and flour bottom of two 9-inch layer pans. Combine graham cracker crumbs and melted butter. Stir in walnuts and 2/3 cup morsels; set aside. Combine flour with soda and salt. Cream soft butter. Gradually add 1½ cups sugar; cream well. Add eggs, 1 at a time; beat well. Blend in melted morsels and vanilla. At low speed, add dry ingredients alternately with buttermilk, beginning and ending with dry ingredients. Turn into pans. Sprinkle with crumb mixture. Bake for 30 to 40 minutes. Cool. Beat cream with 2 tablespoons sugar until stiff. Fill and frost sides, keeping layers top side up. Refrigerate.

Mrs. Audrey Henderson, Home Economics Teacher, Jefferson, S. D.

Butterfly Cake

2 ¼ c. flour
1 ½ c. sugar
3 ¼ tsp. baking powder
1 tsp. salt
½ c. vegetable shortening
1 c. milk
4 egg whites
1 tsp. vanilla

Sift flour, sugar, baking powder and salt in bowl. Add shortening and milk. Beat until moist. Beat 1 minute and 30 seconds at low speed. Add eggs and vanilla. Beat 1 minute and 30 seconds. Pour batter into 13 x 9 x 2-inch greased and floured pan. Bake in 350-degree oven for 25 to 30 minutes until cake is golden on top and springs back when touched lightly in center. Remove from oven and cool in pan 5 minutes. Put on large platter. Cut cake to form a 4 x 9-inch piece. Cut remaining cake diagonally into 4 wedge-shaped pieces. Put oblong piece in center for body. Arrange other pieces for wings. Decorate with favorite frosting and candies. Use licorice for antennas. Yield: 6-8 servings.

Mrs. Jean Hoag, Ririe, Idaho, Jefferson County Fair

Sweet Sixteen Cake

1 pkg. angel food cake mix
½ c. chopped Maraschino cherries
Powdered sugar, sifted

Prepare cake batter as directed on package. Pour half the batter into a 10-inch tube pan. Mix 1 cup of remaining batter with cherries; spoon mixture in a ring on top of batter in pan. Pour remaining batter over. Zig-zag through batter with a knife to distribute cherries. Bake at 325 degrees for 1 hour, or until top springs back when pressed. Cool. Remove from pan; sprinkle with powdered sugar. Stand decorative candles in center hole; circle cake with roses. Yield: 8 servings.

Mrs. James Babuscio, Pittsburgh, Pa.

 ### Chocolate Ice Cream Waffle

½ c. shortening
1 c. sugar
2 eggs, unbeaten
2 oz. melted chocolate
1 ½ c. flour
½ tsp. salt
1 tsp. baking powder
½ c. milk
1 tsp. vanilla extract
Peppermint ice cream
Chocolate sauce
½ c. pecans (opt.)

Cream shortening and sugar; add eggs. Beat mixture until light. Add chocolate; add sifted dry ingredients alternately with milk and extract. Spread on medium hot waffle iron. Serve ball of peppermint ice cream on top of square of hot waffle; spoon chocolate sauce over ice cream. Sprinkle broken pecan meats over chocolate sauce.

Mrs. Arthur Feallock, St. Petersburg, Fla.

 ### Ice Cream Balls

Ice cream
Flaked coconut
Finely chopped nuts

Have ice cream just soft enough to roll in hands. Roll in balls about size of small orange. Roll each in flaked coconut; press down firmly enough that coconut is pushed into ice cream. Roll in finely chopped nuts. Place individually in plastic bags; put into freezer. To serve, remove from freezer; serve plain or with hot fudge sauce.

Mrs. E. A. Syriac, Houston, Tex.

Lollipops

2 c. sugar
⅔ c. light corn syrup
1 c. water
½ tsp. oil of peppermint
5 drops red food coloring

Combine sugar, syrup and water. Place over heat; stir until sugar dissolves. Cook, without stirring, to hard-crack stage. Add oil of peppermint and coloring. Cool slightly. Lay 24 lollipop sticks 4 inches apart on greased cookie sheet. Drop syrup from tip of teaspoon over sticks to form 2-inch discs.

Mrs. L. R. Maddox, McAlester, Okla.

 ### Pansy Cake

2 c. sugar
1 c. butter
1 c. milk
3 ¾ c. flour
3 tsp. baking powder
3 eggs, separated
Lemon flavoring
Vanilla flavoring
Melted chocolate

Cream 1 cup sugar and ½ cup butter; add ½ cup milk. Sift together 1¾ cups plus 2 tablespoons flour and 1½ teaspoons baking powder; add to butter. Fold in beaten egg whites; add lemon flavoring. Divide batter; color half pink. Repeat for a second batter, using remaining ingredients except chocolate and flavor with vanilla. Divide batter; color half with melted chocolate. Bake in 4 layer pans using 4 different colored batters in each pan. Start a ring of dough around outside of pan, using all 4 colors; each time begin with different color. Bake at 350 degrees until cake tests done. Ice with caramel icing.

Mrs. Monique Mason, Winston-Salem, N. C., Favorite Recipes Food Fair

Bridal Veil Dessert

2 c. fine graham cracker crumbs
1 c. currant jelly
1 c. chopped nuts
1 c. whipped cream

Mix crumbs, jelly and nuts; mold in a round 1-quart bowl. Chill. Unmold onto plate. Ice with whipped cream. Serve in wedges. Yield: 8 servings.

Mrs. Wallace Walton, Kennebec, S. D.

Calla Lilies

 1 c. sugar
 1 c. flour
 1 tsp. baking powder
 ½ tsp. salt
 3 eggs, slightly beaten
 2 tbsp. cold water

Sift together dry ingredients; add eggs with water. Beat for 3 minutes. Drop rounded tablespoon of mixture on greased and floured cookie sheet, leaving plenty of room for spreading. Bake at 350 degrees for 5-8 minutes or until lightly browned. Roll hot cookies into shape of lilies and pinch to hold shape; cool. Fill with whipped cream or vanilla ice cream. If desired, top with a little yellow-tinted powdered sugar icing to form stamen. Do not bake more than 6 cookies on each cookie sheet. Yield: 18 servings.

Mrs. Lloyd Humphreys, Dover, Del., Favorite Recipes Food Fair

Orange Blossom Cakes

 1 ⅓ c. sugar
 2 eggs, beaten
 1 ½ c. flour
 ½ tsp. salt
 1 ½ tsp. baking powder
 ½ c. water
 1 tsp. vanilla flavoring

Gradually add sugar to eggs. Sift flour with salt and baking powder. Add water alternately with flour to egg mixture. Add vanilla. Pour into greased cupcakes tins. Bake at 350 degrees for 12 to 15 minutes or until tests done. Remove from tins.

ORANGE DIP:

 1 ¼ lb. confectioners' sugar
 Juice and grated rind of 2 oranges
 Juice and grated rind of 2 lemons

Sift sugar. Add juice and rind to sugar. Cream until smooth. Dip hot cupcakes into sugar mixture. Place on waxed paper and allow to dry.

Mrs. B. William Wyskoczka, Oxford, N. C.

Petits Fours

 ¼ c. butter
 ¼ c. shortening
 1 c. sugar

(Continued on next page)

½ *tsp. vanilla extract*
¼ *tsp. almond extract*
2 *c. cake flour*
¼ *tsp. salt*
3 *tsp. baking powder*
¾ *c. milk*
¾ *c. egg white, beaten*
¼ *c. sugar*

Cream shortening and 1 cup sugar, add extracts, sifted dry ingredients alternately with milk. Beat until smooth. Beat egg whites to stiff froth. Add remaining ¼ cup sugar. Beat until mixture forms peaks. Fold into batter. Bake in wax paper lined 9 x 12 pan in moderate oven 350°F. for 40 minutes. Cut in squares, ovals, and triangles. Use confectioners' frosting. Yield: 25 servings.

Charlsie Biggs, Home Economics Teacher, McCalla, Ala.

 ## Wedding Cakes

½ *c. oleo*
¼ *c. sugar*
1 *egg yolk*
1 *c. sifted flour*
¼ *tsp. salt*
1 *tsp. vanilla*
1 *egg white*
1 *c. chopped nuts*
Powdered sugar frosting

Mix all ingredients except egg white, nuts and frosting. Form into 1-inch balls. Roll balls in unbeaten egg white and then dip in nutmeats. Place on ungreased cookie sheet. Bake 5 minutes in a preheated 375-degree oven. Remove from oven and press thumb in center of cookie. Return to oven and bake for 8 minutes longer. Cool and fill centers with powdered sugar frosting.

Charlotte Chally, Coralville, Iowa

 ## Wedding Ring Cookie

1 *c. plain flour*
3 *tbsp. powdered sugar*
1 *stick butter*
1 *tsp. vanilla*
1 *c. nuts*

Sift flour and sugar. Cream butter; add flour and sugar. Add vanilla and nuts. Chill dough 1 hour and roll about the size of little finger and bring ends together like ring. Bake on ungreased cookie sheet at 300 degrees for 12 to 15 minutes but not until brown. When done roll in additional confectioners' sugar.

Mrs. W. H. Smarr, Forsyth, Ga.

INDEX

ACKNOWLEDGMENTS

We wish to express our appreciation for the use of photographs supplied us by the following: Cover—The California Strawberry Advisory Board and Frontispiece—Best Foods, Division of Corn Products Company.

Color photographs were supplied by The California Strawberry Advisory Board; Best Foods, Division of Corn Products Company; and Cherry Growers and Industries.

Title page and half page photographs were supplied by the following: National Dairy Council; Nestle Company; The Borden Company; Standard Brands, Royal Desserts; Dudley-Anderson-Yutsey; American Dairy Council; The R. T. French Company; Ocean Spray Cranberries; J. Walter Thompson; Franklin Dry Toasted Mixed Nuts; Ruth Lundgren Company; Best Foods, Division of Corn Products Company; Crisco; Keith Thomas Company; American Molasses Company; Florida Citrus Commission; Theodore Sills; The California Strawberry Advisory Board; National Peanut Council; National Cherry Growers, Inc.; and The Filbert-Hazelnut Institute.